HAMBLIN

HAMBLIN

A MODERN LOOK AT THE FRONTIER
LIFE AND LEGEND OF JACOB HAMBLIN

Hartt Wixom

ISBN: 1-55517-273-3

Published and Distributed by:

925 North Main, Springville, UT 84663 • 801/489-4084

CFI   Publishing and
       Distribution Since 1986

Cedar Fort, Incorporated
CFI Distribution • CFI Books • Inside Cougar Report

Cover Design by Lyle Mortimer
Printed in the United States of America

Acknowledgments

With a project covering years in the research and writing, the author has many people to thank. In addition to those listed in the interviewing section of Chapter 17 and sources cited, I would like to personally thank my wife, Judene, for her help in focus and direction for this book; for daughter Peggy in mechanical preparation, and her husband, Robert Proffit in researching End Notes dealing with the Mountain Meadows Massacre. Thanks go also to James Kimball, LDS Church Historian's Library and the Archives Office, Salt Lake City, in locating sources; also the Special Collections Library computer researchers at Brigham Young University, Provo, Utah.

Mark Hamblin, Kanab, Utah and Dr. Thales Smith, Provo, Utah were especially helpful in providing primary manuscripts and information about their great, great grandfathers and families. Many Hamblin relatives also provided helpful (secondary source) information vital to this book. Others dedicated to historical research assisted in obtaining maps and documents, including Jim Schreiner, U.S. Forest Service, Fredonia, Arizona. In addition, Stephen Clark and Dr. Rafael Del Vecchio helped in the effort to retrace Hamblin's steps.

The author would also like to thank Jacob Hamblin. He proved to be an extraordinary person—worth the time and effort in undertaking such a formidable task.

Table of Contents

Historical Highlights

Jacob Hamblin: a modern look at the life and legend

1812   Born Ashtabula County, Ohio.

1839   Married Lucinda Taylor.

1842   Baptized a member of the Church of Jesus Christ of Latter-day Saints.

1849   Married Rachel Judd.

1853   Had "spiritual experience" in Tooele area which changed his life

1857   Married Sarah Priscilla Leavitt

1857   Named president of the Southwest Indian Mission.

1858   Began missionary journeys to visit the Hopi Indians.

1858   First whiteman to cross Colorado River at Ute Ford since Escalante-Dominguez expedition.

1869   First whiteman to cross Colorado at Lee's Ferry.

1862-63   First whiteman to travel completely around Grand Canyon.

1865   Married Louisa Bonelli.

1869   Moved to Kanab.

1870   Assisted Major John W. Powell to visit Arizona Strip Indians.

1870   Helped forge peace treaty with Navajos at Ft. Defiance.

1874   Imprisoned, "tried" and released by Navajos; brought peace to the frontier.

1877   Testified at second trial, Mountain Meadows Massacre, of John D. Lee.

1878   Moved to northern Arizona; helped colonize upper Little Colorado.

1882   Moved to Pleasanton, New Mexico

1886   Died at Pleasanton.

Prologue

We had just looked at the magnificent Tuacahn ampitheatre against a background of crimson and orange cliffs west of St. George when my son, Wade, said: "Won't people ask—who is Jacob Hamblin?"

A good question. Promotions for the "Cowboy and Indian Musical," scheduled to run under the title *UTAH*, June through October each year, say its premiere hero will be Jacob Hamblin. It is a name heard by many coming and going throughout the West. But who was Jacob Hamblin, really?

Much has been written about the man in years past. But there is much to know about this unusual individual who spent more time with warring frontier Indians than perhaps even Daniel Boone or Kit Carson. Some of his accomplishments are enumerated here. Jacob Hamblin:

- Developed a unique philosophy about the value of the redman as a child of God and defended him against an encroaching white civilization.

- Believed he could not be killed by the most hostile of Indians so long as he refused to shed their blood. Time and again he eluded injury.

- Was ordered by superiors to kill captive Indians but thrust himself in front of them and said: "You'll have to kill me first."

- At the peril of his own life went against a conspiracy of white settlers, many of them neighbors, who wanted to place all blame on Indians for the ambush massacre of 120 emigrants.

- Was the first whiteman to encircle the Grand Canyon and crossed the Colorado River dozens of time when no other would go there for fear of Navajos, Apaches and other warring Indian tribes.

•Refused to give up Indian members of his own party to angry Navajo warriors when told he must do so or die.

•Calmly told Navajos preparing to burn him over hot coals that he felt no fear. "Why should I be afraid while among my friends?"

About the Author

Hartt Wixom, age 63, is the author of seven other non-fiction books, several hundred magazine articles and a lifetime of newspaper stories. He was trained as a journalistic reporter, writing some 25 years for the *Deseret News* and *Provo Daily Herald*, and later, editing for a national magazine. He has spent most of his life writing and teaching writing. Wixom has a B.S. and Master's degree from Brigham Young University where he now teaches. He also did post-graduate work at the University of Utah, receiving instruction from veteran historians Charles Peterson, Davis Bitton, and David Miller. Wixom is a member of the Mormon History Association.

Over the years, Wixom has received several awards in his chosen profession, including national recognition for "unbiased writing and reporting." A colleague, Dr. Jack Nelson, BYU Communications Dept., says, "He is known for tenaciously tackling difficult challenges head-on and not quitting until he finds answers, wherever the chips may fall."

The author served an LDS mission in the mid-West where he lived on an Indian reservation and helped write a Lamanite teaching plan "more in their own language and understanding." It was then, in 1955, that he first became interested in researching the life of Jacob Hamblin.

He now lives in Provo, Utah with his wife, Judene. They are the parents of seven children, and have been foster parents to two Navajo boys who now live on the reservation in Utah and Arizona. Hartt Wixom has also spent considerable time in the region of which he writes, the rugged Grand Canyon and arid Arizona Strip country, which figured so prominently in the life of Jacob Hamblin.

Chapter One

Introduction and Overview

Fortunately for our era, Jacob Hamblin kept many journals and diaries. Historian James A. Little also sat down with the frontier explorer-missionary in 1881 and persuaded Hamblin to record his extraordinary adventures in an (edited) autobiography. Hamblin did so while his many expeditions into southern Utah and northern Arizona's hostile Indian country were still vividly in mind. Early LDS historian James G. Bleak also recorded Hamblin's official Church activities almost daily up to 1877 in his Annals of Southern Utah Mission A and B.

But it is in Hamblin's own journals that one can discover the most valuable treasures in the history of this remarkable man. (The author has in his possession a copy of Jacob's lengthy journal discovered in one of Hamblin's saddlebags. It was received from Jacob's great-great-grandson, Mark Hamblin of Kanab.) Since this journal and other Hamblin writings have never been published, the next chapter will examine them more fully.

The purpose of both Bleak and Little in chronicling Hamblin's life was mostly ecclesiastical. Little said, "Whoever reads this precious document will not only awaken a deep human interest in Indians and men, but strengthen his own appreciation for the restored work of the Lord." Hamblin was often termed a "Buckskin Apostle" of the "restored" Church of Jesus Christ of Latter-day Saints (Mormons).

In Little's edition, Hamblin's concluding words are: "I desire this narrative to be a testimony to all who may read it, that the Lord is not slack concerning any of His promises to His children. My whole life, since I embraced the gospel, proves this fact. If this little book shall leave a testimony of this to the coming generation, I shall be satisfied."

Since many of the stories by Little and Bleak about Hamblin have been told and retold in Mormon circles, it would appear that both accomplished their purposes. LDS historians such as

Milton R. Hunter said this of Hamblin in *Brigham Young the Colonizer*: "No better choice than Jacob Hamblin could have been made for the director of the Lamanite Mission. He was without doubt the most influential and successful Mormon missionary to the Indians while Brigham Young was at the helm. So great was his power with the natives, so highly was he esteemed, that he has aptly been called the 'Apostle to the Lamanites.' Hamblin was a tall, thin, angular man, with a voice so low that to hear him one had to get very close to him and listen with great attention."

Hunter then quotes LDS historian John H. Evans: "Although Jacob Hamblin generally carried a gun of some sort, his dependable weapon was prayer and the most absolute trust in God...he knew more perhaps than any other American ever knew of the native, and exerted more influence among them."

Unfortunately, however, Jacob Hamblin is little known outside his own Church and immediate region. One wonders why Hamblin's name appears in so few general histories or encyclopedias—even those focusing on Southwest Indian history. By contrast, one cannot escape seeing the name of say, Kit Carson, in any mention of Navajos or their neighboring Indian tribes. And incredibly, although Hamblin easily had far more to do with the colonization of northern Arizona than any whiteman who ever lived, he is not even mentioned in dozens of extensive histories of that state!

As a frontier explorer, not even the venerable Daniel Boone had more daily contact with the American aborigine than Jacob Hamblin. The latter entered warring Navajo and Hopi country so many times—against explicit warnings of friends and family—that not even LDS historians numbered beyond the 10th or eleventh expedition; perhaps they decided the precise number didn't matter anymore. And perhaps it didn't.

As for Hamblin's "close escapes" at the hands of the Indians, they can scarcely be equalled by even James Fenimore Cooper's fictitious Natty Bumppo, or "Leatherstocking," as Cooper called him. In fact, non-Mormon F.S. Dellenbaugh, accompanying Major J. W. Powell in his exploration of the Grand Canyon in 1869

(*Romance of the Colorado*, p. 93) used that same comparison: "Jacob Hamblin, whom I knew very well, was the 'Leatherstocking' of Utah—a man who knew the Amerinds (Indians) of Utah and northern Arizona better than anyone who ever lived."

Although there was no Guiness Book of World Records kept at the time, it is entirely unlikely anyone journeyed as many miles in the saddle during any 30-year span in world history than did Jacob Hamblin between 1856 and his death in 1886. He has been credited with being the first whiteman to encircle the Grand Canyon and the first to cross the Colorado River at Lee's Ferry where millions of tourists now travel U.S. 89A. Monuments there honor others. None honor Hamblin.

But let us compare Hamblin's dealings with hostile Navajos more closely to Kit Carson's tenure among them. The champion of western justice in myriad dime novels, Carson lived among the Navajos for a time, then joined the U.S. Army's war of extermination against this people. His purpose was to subjugate the Navajo Nation, not gain insight into their ways and customs in order to make peace with them, as did Hamblin. Carson invaded the Navajo's sacred inner sanctum, Canyon De Chelly, destroying their beloved peach orchards, and forcing them into submission. These were largely get-in-and-out forays intended to make the enemy surrender without direct face-to-face confrontations. Carson did not risk his life repeatedly in so doing as did Hamblin sitting down with angry Navajos to attempt harmonious reason–sometimes while held hostage at gun and knife point. Nor was Hamblin's intent merely provincial "Mormon business;" he intended to bring peace to all who might have reason to enter Navajo country, Latter-day Saint or otherwise.

Historian Dee Brown's monumental *Bury my Heart at Wounded Knee* has a long chapter on Carson and the Navajos; Brown never once mentions Jacob Hamblin. In addition, at the time of this writing, no major government map, while labeling many trails throughout the Southwest, names a single route after the man who pioneered so many of them. Prominently mentioned on nearly all government maps of the Southwest is the Dominguez-Escalante trail of 1776, and even the Honeymoon

Trail (just to prove no anti-Mormon bias) traveled by LDS couples in Arizona seeking in the late 1800s to spiritually solemnize marital vows in the St. George, Utah Temple. Kaibab Forest Service maps do show "Jacob's Canyon," a route Hamblin took when crossing the Kaibab Plateau via Pipe Springs from his home in Santa Clara. But there is no trail named after him on any of the dozens of large maps of southern Utah-northern Arizona put out by the U.S. Bureau of Land Management, Forest Service, or U.S. Geological Survey. It is true that some publications coming out in the early 1900s did term the route from Kanab to Lee's Ferry and on up the Little Colorado River as "Hamblin's Road." But for some reason, the designation never found its way onto modern government maps.

Perhaps one reason for the seemingly diffident treatment is that Hamblin has long been perceived as benefitting only localized members and contacts of his own Church. Yet, Father Escalante attempted the same for his own religion and is well remembered for one single trek across the trackless wilderness. Hamblin made dozens of such trips.

If the omission is due to Hamblin's supposedly "narrow interest" missionary efforts, consider the pages in any history text book devoted to say, Father Pierre Jean DeSmet in Wyoming. Or Marcus Whitman, who garners a major story in the World Book Encyclopedia for establishing a Presbyterian mission in Oregon. Whitman was killed by the Indians he served. Hamblin was never in his lifetime actually harmed by any Indian, although one narrowly missed at close range with three arrows. The mystery may be resolved by concluding that martyrs (those who actually die rather than nearly so) are better remembered than those who live to tell about it. Irony creeps into this fact of historicity.

Consider, too, how much has been written about Dr. David Livingstone, devoted missionary among the natives of frontier Africa. Who can forget the line made immortal by the media in quoting the explorer H.M. Stanley: "Dr. Livingstone, I presume?"

One must also ask if Hamblin's lack of national recognition dealt with possible prejudice against The Church of Jesus Christ of Latter-day Saints (Mormon) during the 1800s—a time when bias clearly prevented Utah from being recognized for statehood. If so, it is time to strip away such shallow thinking of the past, and examine objectively in these modern times the man's now well-documented accomplishments.

The world also scarcely realizes how much Hamblin had to do with protecting the lives of non-Mormon emigrants as well as members of his own Church in Utah, Arizona and particularly southern Nevada. Wagon train travelers faced many painted savages in the "Muddy" region in 1858-60. Extensive records show that some Californians today may well owe their very existence—when ancestors were spared death at the hands of hostile Indians—to the express intervention of Hamblin and those he directed.

After the Mountain Meadows Massacre (see Chapter 5), some non-Mormons included Hamblin in their blame for the tragedy because he lived among the perpetrators. After all, it was well known that Hamblin encouraged the Fancher party to camp on his land and it was there they were massacred. That was the message which made its rounds in the nation's media.

A claim was made in a 1995 account of the massacre that Hamblin was present. This, in effect, calls Hamblin a liar, for he wrote repeatedly that he was away in Salt Lake City during the bloodletting. If he had been present, he certainly would not have remained silent. The incident nearly destroyed all that he stood for, his missionary work among the local Lamanites, for years to come.

For those taking time to learn the truth, Jacob spent many hours, as did several missionaries under his charge, in dissuading Moapites, Mohaves, and other plunder-bent tribes from attacking California-bound travelers. Once Jacob found the Indians about to torture a man to death who said he was not a Mormon. Jacob assured him that made no difference, halted the process and told the Indians to return his clothing, which they did.

Hamblin not only forged the first semblance of peace between warring natives and white settlers in the Southwest but risked what seemed imminent demise in 1874 by meeting with

Navajos targeting the prominent Mormon for death. His repeated efforts finally prevented all-out Navajo raids along a vast frontier, including attempts to homestead the upper Little Colorado River region. Hamblin assuaged Mormon and non-Mormon anger with his peace-making tactics, saving the lives of many on both sides.

While Hamblin easily spent more energy and time in establishing peace between whitemen and Utah-Arizona Indians than any man who ever lived, Grand Canyon adventurer-scientist Major John W. Powell alone brought it to national attention. But Hamblin was for the most part lost in the Major's primary focus, being first to explore the Grand Canyon. One modern era publication chronicling Powell's accomplishments did mention Hamblin twice. They misspelled his name both times as "Hamlin."

Through all he encountered, Jacob seemed to sense only the one word, duty. He seemed willing to suffer any deprivation, thirst, hunger, cold, loneliness, ill health, jeers of neighbors, and even death if necessary, to carry out what he perceived as duty. Danger came with the job. Two miners who accompanied Hamblin on one "suicide" expedition into the heart of Navajo country declared Jacob "the bravest man who ever lived." There were, to be sure, many close calls. But Jacob's daily crusade in the Southwest helped soften hardened traditions of the fierce and proud Navajos, fed and taught the primitive Piutes-Shivwits, and forged lasting trust with many wary Hopis.

Hamblin obviously gained great influence among the Hopis in that several of their number traveled with him to meet the "Big Chief," Brigham Young, in Salt Lake City. This in spite of the fact they had long held to a tradition never to cross the Colorado River. A major reason they accompanied Hamblin might be that Hamblin left Mormon missionaries with the Hopis. (Mormons first called them Moquis or Moquitch until learning it was a word used derisively by their enemies, the Navajos, meaning "sissy," "the dead ones.") If the Hopis in Jacob's care met an ill fate, missionaries like Thales Haskell and Marion Shelton most certainly would have also. They became in effect, hostages, their fate resting with Jacob Hamblin. Only one person in Hamblin's party, 15-year old George A. Smith, Jr., ever died at the hands of the Indians. Because of that one incident, Jacob suffered considerable mental anguish, and since he was expedition leader, some public umbrage as well.

In his intrepid excursions, some say Jacob survived because of incredible luck and courage more so than his own explanation, i.e. divine benevolence. Either argument would be difficult to prove with certainty. But a purely humanistic analysis may stretch credulity further than Jacob's own accounting: that he felt inspired to say if he did not spill the blood of a Lamanite (term for Indian from The Book of Mormon), they would not spill his. It was an impression derived from his experience with Goshute Indians in the Tooele area after finding that guns of he and comrades would not fire. Hamblin thus concluded that the Lord "must have a use for the Indians."

Being hard-pressed to explain how he extricated himself from death so many times, a skeptic might claim Hamblin's "cool" sprang from a blind belief in the divine nature of his mission. Whatever it was, Jacob seemed so calm in the face of repeated adversity that Indians themselves said he was guarded over by "strong medicine." Even that traditional bastion of Indian culture, the tribal medicine man, gave way to Hambln's influence, albeit with some jealousy. This was especially true among the Piutes watching their sick wane and die until Hamblin brought healing based on his religious beliefs. Whatever one's convictions, one might well ask: "Would I put forth the supreme effort for what I believe in as did the man Jacob Hamblin?"

Was his "good fortune" primarily connected to the Mormons' feed-them-rather-than-fight-them philosophy advocated by LDS Church President Brigham Young? Somewhat, perhaps. But that did not spare dozens of Latter-day Saints killed by Indians on the frontier. Historian David Lavender says in his "Pipe Spring and the Arizona Strip" that some 70 LDS lives were lost to Ute Chief Blackhawk's warring parties in 1865-68. LDS convert James Whitmore and brother-in-law Robert McIntyre were murdered by Navajos near Pipe Springs, a frequent waystop for Hamblin, in 1866. The Navajos who killed them hailed from across the Colorado where Hamblin frequently visited. Even the so-called "docile" Pahvant Indians were capable of mass murder, as government surveyor Capt. John Gunnison found when he and seven of his men were ambushed and brutally killed on the Sevier River in 1853. The Berry brothers, Joseph and Robert, and Robert's wife, Isabel, were murdered by Indians (believed to be Piutes) along a route Hamblin frequently trod enroute to Pipe Springs. Monuments to murders by Indians can be found in several places along U.S. 89 and other central or southern Utah highways. Several Catholic priests were also "hurled over cliffs" by Arizona Hopis prior to Hamblin's arrival.

How did Jacob come and go without harm among these same "savages" for so many years?

Jacob's religious motives have not always been understood by those outside his Church, and perhaps not by some inside. Author P.T. Reilly in his "Roads Across Buckskin Mountain" gives Jacob's purpose in crossing the Colorado to find a route to Mexico that Mormons "might escape the wrath of Gen. Sydney Johnston's federal troops." Jacob announced a simpler purpose, i.e., to learn Indian customs and language so as to gain greater influence among them and teach them the Mormon version of Christianity. If we fail to comprehend Hamblin's total confidence in The Book of Mormon as a religious history of the aborigines he dealt with–and the need he felt to bring that message to them–then we simply don't understand the dynamic force behind Jacob Hamblin. He firmly believed those teachings would sway the hearts of the Indians from contention to peace. His motives in dealing with the Navajos were thus precisely opposite to those of Carson. Any attempt at retaliation or reprisal against Indian depredations disgusted him and he managed to wrangle out of several such attempts, including rebellion against one of his own Church leaders (whom Jacob considered misguided), who ordered him to physically destroy Indian "raiders." Jacob stepped out in front of one and said, "Shoot me first."

Hamblin sought his peace by gaining insight into Indian character. He danced, ate food that whitemen found disgusting, smoked the peace pipe, and observed Indian campfire ceremonies; he spent many hours in quiet conversation with their leading chiefs and/or malcontent followers. He once berated an acquaintance for maligning a Piute who suggested torturing an aged and invalid whiteman in order to dilute Navajo anger. Jacob said that the Piute was just trying to help protect a white settlement in the only way his limited background allowed him.

Western novelist Louis L'Amour might be skewered verbally for his unrealistically "noble" portrayals of the redman, but he also basically understood their militant upbringing. He wrote truthfully many stories of Indians taking scalps because this sort of coup was the peer-accepted method of proving manly prowess in battle. Another inbred cultural custom was the need for exact racial justice. If one Navajo was killed by a Hopi (or whiteman), then the Great Spirit demanded one Hopi or whiteman be killed in atonement by the Navajos.

Hamblin did not totally succeed in purging this eye-for-eye, tooth- for-tooth philosophy which once guided Moses and the Children of Israel. Jacob was nearly killed at times in the trying. But he did soften native savagery, particularly among the Piutes he worked with, on a daily basis. The bottom line was this: while others attempted to destroy the redmen, Hamblin sought to understand them and gain a greater influence for their own betterment as well as his own white peers.

Using the works of Little and Bleak as a springboard, several historians such as Paul Bailey and Pearson Corbett expounded two lengthy books on the missionary-explorer. Much of Bailey's *Jacob Hamblin, Buckskin Apostle* is easy reading; but one must keep salt handy to separate speculated conversations from historical fact, especially alleged discussions between Hamblin and Major Powell. It might have happened that way; maybe not. If the latter, one cannot call it history.

Corbett indulged in occasional unlabeled speculation, but his widely-researched book *Jacob Hamblin, the Peacemaker*, (copyright, 1952) is a genealogical classic that calls on many Hamblin relatives for details theretofore unknown about the early life of this pioneer. Author Juanita Brooks exhaustively researched much of the frontier Southwest where Hamblin lived. Indeed, her *Mountain Meadows Massacre* has long been the most completely documented book about the tragedy. Her in-depth probe caused a deep stir in southern Utah circles felt even today. Yet, her focus fell primarily upon John D. Lee and others, not Jacob Hamblin.

Some of her interpretations about causative factors in the massacre are, in this modern era, also subject to re-examination. Her first edition of *Massacre* was first published in 1950. Since then, including her biography of John Doyle Lee of that era, much research and thought has gone into the why of the massacre. Modern researcher Kenneth W. Godfrey, presenting a paper in 1992 to the Mormon History Association, does not agree with some of Brooks' claims or conclusions. Nor does this author. Those claims and conclusions will be examined herein.

As for Brooks' *Jacob Hamblin, Mormon Apostle to the Indians*, printed in 1980, it focused on Hamblin's sterling character. But the 136 pages did not seem intended by Brooks in any way to comprise a thorough documentary of Hamblin's lifetime work.

Since the publications of these biographies, much more has become known about Hamblin's multiple accomplishments. Several historians, including the prolific Charles Petersen, suggest strongly that Hamblin was not particularly successful in his missionary efforts among the Navajos and Hopis; Hamblin said the same during his own lifetime. Yet, the book *Me and Mine* by Hopi Indian Mary Sekaquaptewa (latest edition published in 1977, but not receiving wide circulation until more recently) sheds new light on Hamblin's influence among her people. She portrays them as divided about many things, including Hamblin's *Book of Mormon* message concerning their forefathers. Among the traditionalists and a younger generation, the Hopis were also deeply divided about whether to allow American government to force their children into white schools. The conflict raged between holding true to imbued tradition, or yielding to the new program, as has become the practice to a certain degree today. This book probes the influence Hamblin might have had on the Hopi's viewpoint in many matters today.

A master's thesis by David K. Flake also records modern efforts among north-central Arizona Latter-day Saints to follow up on Hamblin's many visits to the Hopis and Navajos. While the missions were closed down for a time, Flake indicates prose-lyting success among those tribes picked up considerably when building specifically on the earlier mission work of Hamblin.

Some of the early histories (for example, Charles Kelly's *Outlaw Trail*, 1959) mention that three Navajos were killed in 1874 by whites in Grass Valley, east of present-day Richfield. Kelly linked this killing to outlaw friends of Robert Leroy Parker (more commonly known today as Butch Cassidy). The episode nearly precipitated a monumental Navajo war against all Southwest settlers. However, adverse effects on Hamblin and Utah-Arizona settlers were outside the scope of Kelly's book which never explained the shockwave impact of the incident on Southwest settlers. It is time to take a closer look at this challenge to frontier peace which nearly cost so many lives, including that of Jacob Hamblin.

While many attempted to turn back nomadic and marauding Indians with armed force, Hamblin preferred to use his Christian beliefs to forge a lasting peace. It was, indeed, a wild land and the people who inhabited it were often even wilder. But Hamblin put his Church and his beliefs ahead of his own personal comfort and safety in order to tame both land and people.

Too often historians recognize military enforcers like Alexander the Great (he "united" the world) or William the Conqueror, yet give little credit to those who subdue without bloodshed. One might look at Colonel Patrick Conner, U.S. Army officer, Ft. Douglas, Utah, who garnered national publicity (and was immediately promoted to general) for ambushing and killing some 400 peaceful Shoshone Indians at the Battle of Bear River near Preston, Idaho. Most of the dead were women and children; there was also serious question at the time whether any of the braves were guilty as charged of petty pilfering from local settlers. To applaud such a compassionless act is highly questionable at best, and seemingly indefensible at worst, in the annals of U.S. history. Compared to Hamblin's many victories in bringing peace to the frontier, Conner's oft-heralded solution appears strained, indeed.

It isn't that Hamblin saw the savage as the "mistreated red-man" depicted by so many novelists. He simply took a different route to resolving what pioneer settlers, even among some of his own people, referred to as an "Indian problem." Given results, who can say that Hamblin's approach was not only ethically correct but by far the most pragmatic?

One of the greatest tributes to Hamblin in this regard was by Raymond Carlson, editor of "Mormon People in Arizona," Arizona Highways, April 1943, p. 33: "As a missionary to the Indians, this good man, so fervently a believer in the teachings of his religion, made friends with the redmen of this region and did more with kindness and patience and truth to pacify them than six companies of U.S. cavalry could do with bullets."

A reader attempting to explore Hamblin's many accomplishments would have to read a number of books to obtain even a modest portrait of this man's successful efforts among native Americans. It is the purpose of this publication to gather them under one cover and to assess how they affect us as students of history today.

To be true, Jacob also had his detractors. At the trial for his role in the Mountain Meadows Massacre, John D. Lee termed Hamblin a "fiend from hell." Due to his reputation for absolute honesty, Hamblin's testimony weighed heavily in sealing Lee's execution in 1877.

In addition, several "True West" type magazine articles, generally little known outside shadowed archives, came forth after the Corbett and Baily biographies to brand Hamblin's storied fetes as "over-rated" and label him a "coward." As recently as 1993, it was also suggested by a southern Utah history professor and further publicized by an Associated Press reporter, that Jacob lied when he told Major Powell that Shivwits Indians had killed three defectors from his Grand Canyon expedition in 1869. This book will examine those charges, which occurred since Corbett and Baily completed their Hamblin biographies. Indeed, it is the purpose of this book to examine such data about Jacob

Hamblin to the present time, and attempt to totally separate the legend from the legacy.

Some said Jacob neglected his family and placed too much of a domestic burden on them; that he should have spent more time helping loved ones building a home on the frontier. An example given was when Hamblin returned from one of his many expeditions to find his portion among the Kanab fields in the "poorest soil" of all. Perhaps neighbors, noting his frequent absences, decided he wouldn't be around anyway to take care of planting and harvesting.

It is true that Jacob didn't seem to relish routine domestic chores. He wasn't much at all for mundane yard work. On one occasion, he felt "ill" while attempting to weed his garden, and felt "much better" when heading out to personally oversee an Indian matter others perhaps might have resolved. Hamblin also trusted, perhaps too heavily, that those promising to do work for his family would follow through. And as history records, he remained home a full year bent on being a business-man...and failed. It has been suggested he was too charitable with "accounts receivable." Some charges of "domestic neglect" bid scrutiny. They will be examined as objectively, it is hoped, as those which built the man's reputation for daring and duty.

Any complete treatise on this man must also recognize his seeming idiosyncracies. He was described by a member of the U.S. Geological Survey in Kanab as sometimes "going off by himself to build his own fire" and that he "acted like an Indian" more than a whiteman. Then, too, Jacob was not your awe-struck tourist. He rarely mentions aesthetic features among his lengthy travels other than to say what obstacles they presented. Most are mentioned as a footnote to survival, i.e., distance to the next known water. Scenery or scenic views are almost never mentioned, although the trails he trod took him to the Grand Canyon and the Havasupai Indians' secret paradise of tropic-like waterfalls. He never attempted to affix a name to them, as did Major John Wesley Powell. The latter was a modern publici-ty director's dream, labeling nearly every natural wonder encountered and most of those names, like Flaming Gorge and the Grand Canyon, stuck in the public mind.

Another thing Hamblin seldom wrote about was his family. Wives and children are scarcely mentioned unless part of his mission journey. He wrote nothing according to the Little account, about marrying Rachel Judd. This information is included only in personal notes. Hamblin's focus was on the task ahead and how it was met. His personal life was obviously not to interfere with duty, either in action or word.

Whether in good health or poor, Jacob without hesitation responded to every call from LDS Church headquarters; yet he also made some journeys with no such call. One particularly dangerous and certainly loathsome assignment from his president was to return as quickly as possible for the physical remains of George A. Smith Jr., murdered by Navajos on an expedition with Hamblin. Jacob himself had been fortunate to return alive from the ordeal, yet was asked to risk his life once again. Without question or complaint, Hamblin immediately responded. Finding no one in Kanab willing to go with him, Hamblin rode to Parowan, some 140 miles round trip, to ask for assistance. (Those living farther away may not have known as well as those in Kanab how dangerous this return mission was.)

It must have also been more than a little galling to wives and children, rejoicing on their husband and father's safe return from his last "duty," to watch him turn around and go again. A daughter once asked if he was "home to stay" this time. He was not. There are indications, however, that Jacob's unquestioning devotion to duty may have precipitated more assignments from Church headquarters than if he had mentioned important domestic chores needing his help at home. He never did.

After returning from one long journey, Jacob found that his foster Indian son, Albert, had died in his absence. On another, his beloved wife, Rachel. She had been dead and buried for weeks. But as history records, he departed soon for another mission.

Even casual scrutiny indicates that Jacob's wives, Rachel, Priscilla, Louisa and their offspring, working behind the scenes, deserve a lion's share of credit for whatever their husband and father accomplished. Making his families' lot even more difficult was a zealous U.S. government bent on pursuing and imprisoning polygamous husbands. While little attempt was ever made to arrest wives and children, the effect was often as dire upon them in that the latter were deprived of their provider. This was particularly impactive upon Jacob's families because he returned from "Indian business" infrequently. Jacob's writings indicate that "feds" harassed him more than all the Southwest's so-called "barbaric savages" put together. Those same "feds" more than anyone forced a hounded Hamblin to flee into New Mexico where he died without ceremony. It is ironic today that due to changing attitudes and mores, many known Southwest polygamists are virtually ignored by federal authorities.

We must also examine more closely Hamblin's leadership role in the conquest of the rugged and formidable Southwest. Like a coach or principal, whatever happens within his watch is laid at the leader's feet. One of Jacob's most loyal followers was Thales Haskell (who wrote an extensive diary provided the author by a great-great-grandson, Thales Smith, to be examined herein); Jacob's story from 1859 through the 1860s cannot be told without Haskell. Nor should Hamblin's first guide, the Piute Naraguts, be forgotten, nor the resolute Enos, who guided Hamblin away from angry Navajo warriors. Why the Piutes (or others) have not erected a monument to these guides as was done for the Shoshone Sacajawea who led the Lewis-Clark expedition is not known. Spaneshank and Hastele, friendly Navajo chieftains, also courageously aided Hamblin against Indian enemies seeking his life. Hastele's resolute honesty and courage stands out in particular as an example for people of all races to follow.

Hamblin and his missionary companions were rarely reimbursed for their missionary activities, even though often leaving home during critical periods of planting, cultivating and harvesting crops.

Clearly, with greater knowledge now gained about Jacob Hamblin, it is time to re-evaluate and interpret his full role and impact, not only within the Church he championed, but beyond. It is time he take his place among the world's notable missionaries, frontiersmen, explorers, and trailblazers.

– Chapter Two –

Jacob's Unpublished Story

Several biographies of Jacob Hamblin have mentioned what seem Herculean accomplishments for one man in one lifetime. His own diaries and journals show him to be simply dedicated to a cause he considered of greater importance than himself. This seems an inescapable conclusion in all of Hamblin's personal journals and diaries. Whatever level of success attained, there is no record of him ever crediting other than a higher principle or power.

But to rely on these primary sources written by Jacob himself, one must be something of a language sleuth to decipher their full meaning. Hamblin wrote in the "modified Middle English" style of his time in an elite penmanship, which has at times baffled even some of the translation experts in modern times. Yet, it is well worth the effort to examine Hamblin's life story in his own words for one major reason: no one else knew it better, nor could tell it in richer, more powerful prose. His personal writings make a valuable contribution to historical literature in the winning of the West. However, his story is not one of bullets and hatchets so much as one of understanding and insight.

Jacob had a unique writing style which reflected the tendency of those in his era to speak in an oblique manner. Rather than say he found food and ate it, Hamblin says that the starving missionaries stumbled across a vegetable garden grown by some Indian(s) and "appropriated it for our use."[1] In describing how he nearly died from eating roasted cactus leaves when desperately hungry, he told it this way: "I soon became satisfied that I had been poisoned."

Close scrutiny of Hamblin's personal writings also offer interesting comparisons to other works about him. Jacob's "hard history" sometimes differs slightly from that of his biographers, even James Little who edited Hamblin's autobiography. The latter starts out this way: "I was born in Salem, Ashtabula County, Ohio, on the 6th of April, 1819." On the first page of his own journal, Hamblin gives his birth date as April 2, 1819. The latter being acknowledged as the correct date (so stated on his tombstone in Alpine, Ariz.), it is speculated that Little must have misread this portion of Jacob's handwritten manuscript. Or it may simply be that Hamblin forgot when writing the autobiography what date he was actually born; but that is hardly likely.

Since all such fine points can be lost in translation, it is wise to closely examine Jacob's personal writings for our own understanding—at the same time being careful to correctly interpret all we read.

But perhaps the most significant reason for relying on Hamblin rather than secondary sources only is that Jacob places greater emphasis on certain experiences he deems important that are omitted by biographers, including Little. There is, for example, the "money dream" in the cold of northern Arizona's Buckskin Mountain. Penned with slight variations in two journals, Jacob worries about the welfare of his family. One journal says that wet and cold, he dreamed about his family needing money; his wife told him she "needed a Dollar very mutch." He discovered a gold coin in his pocket. Upon awakening, he says, "I know this to be of the Lord. It means good." In the second journal account, he gives us an added interpretation of what the dream means to him: "I a woak and it was a dream I was cold and wet   I hav written this bcaws I know it has meaning   it comforted my hart."[2]

The main thing we gain from the dream episode is that it had special value to Jacob. It comforted his heart. It was typical of his adult life after conversion to The Church of Jesus Christ of Latter-day Saints (Mormons) that he viewed *Homo sapiens'* time on earth as a test of faith. If one took care of the Lord's work, the Lord would take care of the individual and loved ones in this life and hereafter. Jacob's life indicated that he placed implicit trust in that concept.

As for deciphering his journals today, it should be remembered that in Hamblin's era there were fewer rigid standards of

English, especially in spelling. Periods were often omitted. Shakespeare and his contemporaries wrote words in various "creative" ways, and for that time, no one would accuse the Bard of being unlearned. The *World Book Encyclopedia* says simply: "There were no English grammars or dictionaries, no accepted standards of spelling." Things had changed by the mid l800s but not as much as today. While Hamblin admits to little formal schooling, it was typical of his time for a contemporary in Ohio to write: "They had got within 4 miles of home after a very fat-ueging journey, greatly antissipating seeing their familys."[3]

Hamblin's faith provided a powerful force in his missionary calling which carried him far from home on many occasions— allowing him (as he explains it) to do so with a unique peace of mind. Perhaps it is one reason why Jacob so seldom mentions his family in all his writings. He seems confident his family will be taken care of in his absence. His personal writings are filled with such statements as "returned to find all well."[4]

True, several members of his immediate family died in his absence, including wife Rachel and two sons. In this Jacob seemed to take the attitude they were in the Lord's hands; he would be with them in the next life; "all would be well."

Let us also take a closer look in this chapter at successfully comprehending Hamblin's written communications from unpublished primary sources. Like others of his period, Hamblin was prone to capitalize certain letters for no apparent reason. For example, Hamblin's letter "S" was invariably written in upper case, despite its place in word or sentence. Yet, he rarely capital-ized the first word of a new sentence, or proper nouns. Since there are occasional commas, but never any periods, the end of one sentence and beginning of another requires more than casual scrutiny in translating his journals.

A typical paragraph from his writings goes like this: "I was the oldest Son of the family my parents were poor whose names were Isaiah and daphne Hamblin my father was the Son of Barnabus Hamblin who according to the best of my information Came over from england at the Setling of the Colony at plimoth Mass."[5]

Note that "plimoth" is lower-cased. But it was often written this way, according to *Our Mayflower Ancestors and their Descendants*, p. VIII.

Then there was a serious problem with weathering, i.e., natural paper-ink deterioration over the years. Where modern editors or curators cannot determine the correct translation, they have placed a question mark. This is seen in copies of Hamblin's original diaries and journals in Brigham Young University's Lee Library, Provo, Utah. One entry in typescript reads: "Tells of a conference conducted by Brigham Young on April 2, 1870 in Kanab...[Author: Jacob Hamblin (?)]" Another entry says the author "appears to be Jacob Hamblin."[6] In other writings, things mentioned in first person are known to be Jacob's work. It is remarkable, really, considering how Jacob's tiny books were tucked away, perhaps in a saddlebag during a blizzard, that so much is comprehended today at all.

A careful study of Hamblin's personal writings sometimes directly refutes later biographies. Corbett wrote the most complete and well-documented history of Jacob Hamblin, yet he makes this remark: "Jacob never in all his journeys says anything of the remarkable country he explored."[7] Actually, Jacob's journal does include one rather singular outburst of praise for nature's handiwork during exploration east of present day Hanksville, Utah. In 1871 he was attempting to locate the mouth of the Dirty Devil River (lower Fremont River today) to drop off future supplies for Major John Wesley Powell's second expedition down the Colorado River. Jacob writes: "Seenery in this canian is grand and Sublime."[8]

So far as can be determined, this ejaculation of emotion regarding physical surroundings is unique in his many travels across the Colorado River Plateau and around the Grand Canyon, including the picturesque Havasupai waterfalls which today grace so many western calendars. It is ironic that the precise location which draws this single rave notice is not known today. The entire region, of course, draws many "oohs and ahs" from modern tourists traveling the Golden Circle of national parks and scenic wonderlands. Perhaps he was just too busy or too focused on missionary endeavors to write about what he regarded as trivial pleasantries enroute.[9]

The explorations for Powell did seem to allow a more relaxed Hamblin than his dozens of goal-oriented and highly focused missionary forays. The trips taken for Major Powell also brought in money for Jacob's family, whereas he normally refused money or reimbursement from Salt Lake City Church headquarters on all mission expeditions. One might surmise that he wouldn't face the many dangers he did merely for money.

Of course, even today it is traditional for Mormon missionaries to pay their own way for up to three years of labor. Hamblin declined reimbursement from LDS Church President Brigham Young for decades of full-time proselyting service. He seemed satisfied with such an arrangement. If he had any complaints about his ecclesiastical call, none are ever voiced in his voluminous writings.

Hamblin's journal gives sensitive and valuable insight into one period of his life that was noticeably unhappy and somewhat misunderstood: that with first wife Lucinda. We find out more about it from Hamblin's personal writings than from any secondary source. Historian Corbett includes a harsh rebuke from Lucinda to Jacob when parting company from her husband in Iowa: "Take your Mormon brats and get out." Following that is Corbett's comment: "They had been extremely happy, except for having to move so often, thus upsetting their plans for a personal home."[10]

This would seem an unexplainable, sudden rift. Not so, according to a Hamblin journal. He says that he regarded his marriage to Lucinda as a mistake almost before the ink dried on the wedding certificate. "The third of oct 1839 I Mared Mrs. Lucinda Taylor young and little experience as was my Self this was contrary to the feelings of my parence when the marriage ceremony was over I felt condmed for what I had don I would have given all I possessed if I could of ben freed thus I was pead for my disobediance in that I had no joy in the wife I had taken."[11] (One key to deciphering Hamblin's journals is to read them phonetically).

These words place little or no blame on his new bride but it is clear that Hamblin clearly felt he had erred. Perhaps he began to covet the full freedom to go and do as he pleased from his bachelorhood days. Yet, it appears much deeper than that. His new religion was his joy for living and he soon learned that his wife did not share his feelings. He says, after returning home from a trip: "I antisipate a great comfort and Satisfaccion of again being with the Church but my Wife proved to be a treacherous mischievous woman which proved to me a great annoyance to my life as she took evry advantage She could to oppose me in every thing that was good."[12]

Specifically, Jacob said that Lucinda began to teach the children their father was a "bad man." If Hamblin had patience in other matters, he had little in having his children told he did not set a good example. From his writings it appears nothing on earth was more important to him than that.

Finally it came to this: "I would not bend one inch from the order of God to liv with hur." She cursed, as Jacob relates it, and said she would not yield, and so "thus ended the conference."[13]

This incident was typical of Jacob's later life. He would not yield an iota on matters of spiritual conviction. He would yield to God, not man. Perhaps it explains his difficult years later with a southern Utah ecclesiastical leader who Jacob believed at times to be uninspired. Again, Jacob would not yield. He was likewise stubborn when meeting with hostile Indians who would bend him to their will. He would be a good listener and sympathetic to their most illogical superstitions; but he would not be manipulated to go against what he perceived as right. While often longsuffering, he wrote in p. 38 , "Journals and Letters of Jacob Hamblin," that he ejected one Piute Indian from his home "by pulling him out by the hair." If someone did not agree with his spiritual standards, "thus ended the conference."

It could be one reason Jacob was so successful in dealing with the often doubting native. Those less certain of themselves (as were many of the poorer, destitute Indians Hamblin encountered) showed a propensity to follow someone with a more resolute assurance.

When Jacob married a second time, he wrote in his simple style these poignant words: "I then went to see Mrs. Rachel henderson...I found this woman was of a mild, jentle disposition...I have had pease at home or in my family ever since I have lived with this kind, effction companion. I hav tasted the bitter. I know well how to appreciate the Sweet."[14]

Harmony was of particular importance to Jacob wherever he went, white or Indian. He often noted, "There is a good spirit prevailing," etc.

Hamblin does not mention any time for courtship when he married Mormon convert Rachel Judd Henderson. With Jacob's own four children and Rachel's two, it began as what can only be termed a mutually satisfactory business arrangement for motherless children. But his comment above indicates the marriage developed into much more than a matter of convenience in finding a stepmother.

Not all of Hamblin's journal pages are as significant as the above reference in finding a loving companion. It appears that like many of us, he also wrote down whatever mundane thing came to mind at the moment: things to buy, prices of things sold, horses lost and captured, people visited, just about everything, including a remedy for tape worm and "malerial poison in the blood." At least such writings were found among his papers. No name appears with the remedies.

Hamblin was, of course, encouraged to keep a journal about official Church business because it was a tenet of his religion to maintain records of blessings, baptisms, etc., he participated in. Most of those entries were turned over to Church historian Bleak. The latter's two large volumes following the history of missionary activies in southern Utah include many references to Jacob Hamblin receiving various local Church and civic assignments rarely mentioned in Jacob's own diaries and journals.[15] It appears that he sometimes simply verbally reported Church activities to Bleak who then recorded them. Jacob almost never mentions baptizing dozens of Lamanite converts in and around Santa Clara, although such ordinances are included in Bleak's two volumes.

Some minor mistakes can occasionally be found in Jacob's writings. The first sentence in his own journal (after giving the birth date) reads: "…of of (sic) our Lord 1819." It would appear he wrote this particular journal quickly, without re-reading it, quickly storing it away.

There was a writing lapse of over a year after arriving in Utah, a dearth almost certainly caused by laboring day and night to establish a new home in the new wilderness-paradise.

Hamblin mixed up his dates at least once. He wrote that he departed Kanab for a mission across the Colorado on Nov. 15 when he couldn't logistically have done so. Ecclesiastical records show he had been "set apart" (an important ordinance then and now in the LDS Church) hundreds of miles away in Salt Lake City to be president of the Indian Mission South and Southeast of the Rio Virgen (sic) two days after the Nov. 15 date.[16]

At other times Jacob seems to have written in haste. He says "kneeding" in one sentence while a few words away he renders the same word as "needing." He spells Santa Clara by at least three different modes. This could be a product of the times, since the town was first named Tonaquint Station (named for the black soil, caused by volcanic action) by the local Piede Indians. When the name of Santa Clara was left behind by those traveling the old Spanish Trail winding through southwestern Utah (a place of "good weather") there must have been some guesswork for a time by Mormon settlers how the name should be spelled.

But once correctly understood, let us not miss what is surely the most important overall contribution of Jacob's hitherto unpublished manuscripts: his introspection about what motivates him. His business-like autobiography says on page two: "I have nothing very esential to write Consering my past life…my education was very limited, altho I was taught to respect my pearents and reverence the god of heaven."

These two sentences (missing in the Little autobiography) speak volumes about Hamblin. He tells us more about himself and his unassuming, humble approach to life here, perhaps, than in anything ever published about him. "My education was very limited," but "I was taught to respect my parents and reverence the god of heaven." Another revealing statement about Jacob was that he was taught "to learn all the good that I could."[17] It was a rather clear-cut, black-white philosophy to live by, but also a seemingly common sense approach which he adhered to with more than casual dedication throughout his life.

After stating that he visited several religious services, his mind casting about which faith to embrace, Hamblin wrote: "I Could see no beauty nor comeliness in thear religon no promises of the gifts and blessings of the gospel...I remember one evening while reading and reflecting on these things a thought Came to me that if I would pray for understanding I would get it." But Hamblin says he "Could not get Confidence enough to belive" that his prayer would be answered. Later, "I Could not refrain from sheading tears for I felt Condemed to think I had not prayd."[18]

This is an important admission in his early life, for as Hamblin explains it, after joining the Mormon faith "I prayd often." He later felt "inspired" to do a number of things attributed to saving his life and that of his comrades when in danger. Perhaps this renewed confidence in his life's mission explains why he would be so willing to make the sacrifices he did. His confidence in the teachings of the LDS Church, particularly The Book of Mormon as it recounted a divine destiny for the Lamanites (and thus his own divine destiny), replaced earlier doubts and satisfied the inner yearnings which found so little outlet in his youth.

Hamblin often prophesies about eluding hostile Indians by taking a certain course and learning afterward that the opposite would have ended in disaster. He says he once prayed for rain when the Indians desperately needed it and many present "watched a small distant cloud bring rain directly to us." Thereafter, Hamblin went on to gain greater influence among the Hopis. This occurred often enough, according to Hamblin's journals (usually after Jacob had persuaded his Indian friends to put in crops) that some of the Piutes began to think Hamblin had power even over the clouds.[19] It might have been mere good fortune but it apparently happened more than once or twice. In a zeal to promote his gospel cause, did he exaggerate or make such things up? It is not known today, but his claims were never refuted by any of his peers.

Some historians, in fact, have not known what to do with the "cloud" statement, perhaps backing off because he appeared to them a mystery or an enigma. Jacob's own brother Oscar once called Hamblin a "visionary" but by following directions, the brother found horses and needed assistance where Jacob said it would be.[20] As for prayer, or spiritual faith for that matter, many have little known over the years what to do with it. This in spite of the fact that many publications mention scientists believing in faith healings today, and that some 90 percent of Americans believe in God.[21] But even if one does choose to argue with Hamblin's accounts, it is difficult to argue with his accomplishments. Some 120 years later, all one can do is tell it the way now that Jacob said it then. Setting any sort of agenda to omit Hamblin's subjective (religious) feelings is doomed from the beginning, for it cannot tell the inner (objective) story of just who Jacob Hamblin is. The man seemed to accept inner whisperings in meeting formidable hurdles much as did Joan of Arc in waging so many successful battles against the enemies of France.[22] Joan of Arc was sainted by the Catholic Church. Since all members of the Mormon Church are considered "saints" merely by being members, Hamblin cannot be so canonized. Thus, his official "state of veneration" in modern times must be left to others who make such decisions. But one might ask concerning heroes, why elevate Hollywood protagonists to that status, as opposed to quiet and unassuming pioneers like Jacob Hamblin? As for Jacob's place in today's public mind, one might wonder why there have been no films made about his life from any source, ecclesiastical or otherwise. This is an especially appropriate question considering the wealth of information Hamblin provided to the literature of westward expansion from his own diaries and journals.

In any event, Jacob's unpublished writings reflect the thinking which propelled him to his extraordinary accomplishments. His feelings about his own personal role in a divine plan develop very early in his journal and seem to provide a foundation for all he did. One cannot escape the conclusion from those writings that while he often indulged in exploration and adventure as a side curiosity, the driving force of his life sprang from a missionary zeal. The same would appear to be one of the world's greatest motivators as witnessed by the proselyting journeys of the Apostle Paul and in later years, crusaders like Dr. Livingstone in Africa and Mother Teresa in India.

Hamblin does not state how many years of formal schooling he received. They appear meager. More important to him was the schooling he received at home. His mother died on the journey westward and he revered her; but Jacob most often mentions the ideals of honesty and industry fostered by his father, serving as valuable guideposts for Jacob the remainder of his 67 years. Jacob was sorely vexed when his father turned him out of the house for "following priestcraft," but Isaiah Hamblin later determined his son to "have found truth." It is typical of Jacob (and seems to show his parent's upbringing) that his first rule of conduct given to "manage" the Indians was, "Never talk anything but truth to them."[23]

On many occasions Hamblin writes that he or his family were so ill that many despaired of their lives. Some of these events are documented by the various biographers. Still, a few are worth examining in Jacob's own hand. He says that his wife, Rachel, was taken with the cholera, a dread disease killing many pioneers. But Hamblin "prayd for hur and anointed hur in the name of the Lord Coled on Brs. Pectal and Hill to administer. She was relievd immediately."[24]

Later, Jacob was given up for dead but testified he was healed through devout prayer. It was almost routine the way Jacob explained it. In fact, after saying Rachel was healed instantly, he adds in the same sentence: "met the mail from Salt Lake Valley."

While enroute west, Hamblin says his son Duane appeared dying after a wagon wheel passed over his head. Blood gushed from his mouth. "I gave him up for lost my father administered to him he was immediately heeled"[25]

It may possibly be that those who Jacob deemed near death were not so near dying. He was not trained in medicine, nor were many in his day. Hamblin never once mentions a physician being present. But faith healings are frequently mentioned. While an agnostic might turn away from such testimony, it would appear Jacob was one peers wanted to have around in any medical emergency. LDS literature is filled with stories of faith healing, but few recorded more of them than Jacob Hamblin.

Many recipients of such healings, as attested by associates of Hamblin like Thales Haskell, were Piede (Piute) Indians. One native woman was given up for dead, the medicine man adorning his head with eagle feathers, sticking arrows in the ground around her lodge, making "hideous noises," as Hamblin explained it, and placing his mouth against the woman's, chanting for her all through the night. Jacob said he and his companions "laid our hands upon hur" and she was "instantly heeled." She suddenly sat up "and asked for Some thing to eat." Members of her family said she had not eaten anything for three days.[26]

Jacob seemed to have an uncanny ability to find his way in totally unfamiliar terrain. At no time in all his travels does he mention being confused for long about where to go next, except for his first trip into the Santa Clara country when he tried to proceed after dark to avoid desert heat. This was true even though journeys were hundreds of miles long into new country and seldom included a guide. One insight into this ability to find his way is recorded as follows: "Bro. Peter Shurts left us...Said he had ben wandering in the Mts long enough he was going to Fish Lake Bro. Lewis put it upon me to leed the company to fish Lake...I took the leed and in one hour ware in sight of of the lake Bro Shurts came in the next day"[27]

In contrast, Mormon explorer Henry Bigler lamented that he carried no maps (nor did Hamblin for that matter) and became hopelessly lost somewhere in the Southwest. He wrote: "To tell the truth, we do not know where we are, only that we are somewhere in the mountains."[28]

Gaining a reputation among his peers for fair and wise judgment, Jacob was often called on to settle disputes, a task he did not relish. After stating that one of his colleagues became "out of humor" with another, they left settlement of the quarrel to Jacob. "I hated to Say what they Should do as Bro Curtis was mutch older in the Church than my Self they insisted on my speeking my mind I then Spoke my mind freely the dificilty was Setled a good feeling prevailed 3rd Soad Some wheet."[29] The matter thus resolved, no mention is made of any further dispute between the two men.

From Hamblin's various journals, we learn the major events of his early life, which took an abrupt turn at the age of 23. It was February of 1842 when Hamblin heard the preaching of Mormon missionary Elder Lyman Stoddard. The latter claimed his new religion included latter-day scripture. He held up as evidence *The Book of Mormon*, an account of the forefathers of today's American Indian and how Christ had not forgotten them, appearing to them in the New World after being crucified in Jerusalem. The Indian, or Lamanite, was more than a primitive infidel; he was a child of the same God as Abraham, Isaac and Jacob. The book taught that in the passing of time the redman turned his back on those teachings. But Jacob reasoned that the Golden Rule, the better life promulgated by Jesus, could be taught again, as it was in the Meridian of Time. And why should not the emissary to teach them about their God-centered heritage be one who now embraced it, namely he, Jacob Hamblin?

The teachings of the book so intrigued Hamblin that he sought baptism where he once had said that he could be persuaded to join none of the various churches. One of the first things he did after being baptized at Spring Prairie, Wisc., and attending an LDS Church conference, was to go on a short mission for his new faith. Interestingly, this mission was to the Lamanites. "I was sent to Preach to the Sochbridge and Brothertown Indians living about 80 miles north of Winebago Co. this journey was prformed with mutch hardship and fategue as the snow was very deep..."[30] This account from Jacob's diaries, before the death of Joseph Smith, does not appear in most accounts, including the autobiography edited by Little. But since the Indians had gone hunting and couldn't be located, Hamblin's first known attempt to teach Christianity to the natives failed.

Back home, Jacob found his wife Lucinda in much pain from an infected tooth. He administered to her and he said the pain left her instantly. But Lucinda was not as impressed, apparently, with such seeming miracles as was Jacob. According to the Hamblin journal, however, Lucinda said that her deceased father (who had much persecuted Jacob for his religious beliefs) appeared to his daughter in a dream to tell her he had been wrong about his son-in-law. This is, indeed, a phenomenal admission on Lucinda's part, for she had opposed Jacob vehemently in his new religion. Still, when she did not want to accompany her husband in joining the saints, nothing could persuade her to accept Mormonism. She was happy with the status quo and did not want a new lifestyle.

Jacob was nevertheless so impressed with his new Church and its "restoration of all things that had been in Christ's earlier ministry"[31] that he made a pilgrimage to Nauvoo, Illinois. Here the saints resided peacefully for a time after being driven from Missouri for their peculiar beliefs. Jacob met Joseph Smith personally and although some made disparaging remarks about the Mormon Prophet, Jacob records that he took a quick liking to the man. He was also much enamored by the feeling of harmony and cooperation displayed by those gathering to Zion from England, Europe and various parts of the world. They were as one energetic force in draining the malaria-infested swamps and building comfortable homes. They also spent much time building a temple overlooking the new city. This temple was no small project, costing tens of thousands of hours of the saints' labor and an estimated $1 million. History records that the Mormons were later forced to leave this sacred edifice behind very soon after completion. Mormons then headed west "willingly because we had to."[32]

Jacob soon accepted a longer mission call to Maryland-Pennsylvania. Again he said he suffered much for his beliefs,

but he was beginning to take on a greater feeling of responsibility in his new religious duties. He wrote, "We ware mutch perse-
cutted for the gospell sake." There was no lamenting his lot
despite finding few listening ears.

It was in the East when he learned of the death of Joseph
Smith; there is nothing in all his writings to indicate a more
lowly and sorrowful feeling than that expressed at this time in
his journals. "I could not refrain from weeping…for a moment
all was lost."[33]

A sensitive man like Jacob undoubtedly failed to comprehend why anyone would want to murder a person who had
given such hope and meaning to the lives of others as had the
Mormon prophet. It was a time of severe anguish, yet also of
resolve for Jacob to do his part in helping build up the fledg-
ling Church.

Returning to Nauvoo, he found Church members in turmoil.
Those who had murdered Joseph and his brother Hyrum, as they
awaited trial in the Carthage Jail, thought it the charisma of the
two brothers which had sustained Mormonism. But there was no
question among Church faithful that one would soon rise to lead
the "Restoration." Jacob wrote that Sidney Rigdon, a counselor of
Joseph's, sought to become a "guardian" of the Church. Hamblin
joined others in renouncing Ridgon's shallow claim to leadership. "I listened a few minits and Said in my hart that it was not
the vois of the trew sepherd [shepherd]."[34] Hamblin concluded
along with the body of the saints that the prophet's mantle
should be cloaked upon the wide shoulders of Brigham Young.

Young had said that, upon death of the prophet, leadership
reins would be placed in the hands of the Quorum of Twelve
Apostles. Young was now president. Jacob soon placed his trust
in Brigham, who then led the Church across the Mississippi
River into Iowa, with plans to settle in the Great Basin. From
that point, Jacob's writings indicate he might go against *local*
Church counsel—but if the orders came from Church headquar-
ters, it was as good as carried out. (Advice not to go into hostile
Indian territory was uniformly ignored. Throughout his life,
Jacob would refuse to place personal safety over Church duty.)[35]

Missionaries were once advised to "look behind every rock before proceeding," a thing not practical, for one couldn't look behind tens of thousands of badland rocks. But the spirit of reminder was there, that the expeditions into unknown Indian country demanded caution. And yet, if one became too cautious, one wouldn't venture beyond the known bounds of civilization at all, a thing Jacob apparently felt compelled to do.

While residing in Iowa, Hamblin did not join his fellow Church members in immediately traveling to their "Promised Valley." There was, for one thing, the problem of getting Lucinda to follow. Later, Jacob's parents and family, noting his zeal for the new religion, studied for themselves, attended LDS Church conferences and were baptized. Only then did the Hamblin entourage eagerly face the setting sun.

In journeying west, the pioneers were not molested by Indians, except financially. Jacob says that "we were visited by the Chiefs of the Oto with thare interpreter they demanded ten cents a wagon for the privilige of pasing through thare teritory." There were some 100 wagons in the train.[36]

Hamblin also has this entry for June, 1850: "13th travailed 17 miles butiful preitie Country."[37] It is not known whether the next-to-last word here should be translated "pretty" or "prairie," but if the former, it constitutes one of the few times Jacob used any (let alone two) adjectives to describe physical surroundings. Always aware of geographical location and potential danger, Hamblin says for the 14th: "Campt in Pawnee teritory... Stood gard."[38]

Hamblin's journal depicts an awful scene of carnage on more than one occasion, not from Indian ambush but from cholera: "15th Brothr John Shipley died with the colery... Johnson and some two or three others this was truly a mournful Scene to See women mourning for thare Husbands and Childrin for their Fathers but we ware obliege to leav them on the plaines burying them as desent as we could 16th travailed Some eight or ten mile."

Owing to ill health and inconvenience after arriving in Utah, Jacob makes no journal entries from July, 1850 to April 10, 1851. Following the long trek from Iowa, Jacob settled in Tooele, 40 miles west of Great Salt Lake City, on the edge of the arid Great Basin. Jacob soon learned that the settlers' greatest problem was not crickets or drought, but marauding Indians. Always on the search for food, the natives repeatedly raided the pioneers' cattle and sheep herds. When pursued into the mountains by relentless posses, the raiders escaped and returned to steal from the settlement again and again.

On one occasion, Hamblin "read until about 12 O' clock, then watched for fires in the mountain." Locating one, he alerted his company and they subsequently surrounded an Indian village. But when Jacob saw the fleeing women and children and heard their screams, "I could not bare the thought of killing them." An additional episode of this nature was soon to forever confirm in Hamblin's mind that settlers ought not to kill a single Indian whatever his depredations.[39]

Several pestiferous natives were soon captured and placed in a stockade. As some escaped, a settler was killed. Community leaders were furious. Jacob was sent along to help find and kill the perpetators. He was nearly killed himself. An Indian named "Old Bigfoot" hid behind a tree to kill Hamblin; when times later became more friendly, Bigfoot explained that if Jacob had taken three steps closer he would have "sunk an arrow in him to the shaft."[40] Hamblin describes in his journal how three arrows nearly hit him. One struck the guard of his rifle.[41] In Little (p. 24) Jacob says that a second arrow "passed through my hat...a third "barely missed my head."

Feeling it was his duty to destroy the Indian who had tried to kill him, Jacob "burnt two more caps...but the gun would not go."[42] He then discovered that the weapons of the other settlers would not fire. He took it as a divine signal that the Lamanites should not be killed...that God had a "youse for them."[43] Jacob's "Lamanite policy" was now established. He was impressed that if he should "never spill the blood" of an Indian, they would "never spill his."[44]

Jacob's Olive Branch of Peace was not shared by all of the local homesteaders. On one occasion, Hamblin took prisoners, perhaps with the idea of civilizing them. Settlers demanded the

Indians be shot. Jacob stepped in front of one and said, "Shoot me first." In time, as Jacob writes in his "Journal and Letters," "We gave them blankets and treated them kindly. In a bout a month from that time a portion of the Same band came again to Steel cattle and was discoverd by one of the Indians we brought in." The thieves were apprehended by one of their own. It would appear that Hamblin's conciliatory policy, toward some Indians at least, had begun to pay off.

In time, "the hole tribe came in and wanted to live with us...promising to Steel no more."[45] Jacob had, indeed, set himself apart from the norm. Indians were more than a mere obstacle in the way of pioneer livelihood.

Particularly revealing about Jacob's feelings was this statement of his autobiography [p. 29] relating to what an Indian chief told him: "'If you shoot, I will; if you do not, I will not.' I was not familiar with their language, but I knew what he said. Such an influence came over me that I would not have killed one of them for all the cattle in Tooele Valley."

On another foray into the mountains, Hamblin came across an Indian squaw with a young boy. Hamblin's autobiography says that the Spirit told him, "Take that young boy with you; that is part of your mission here." The boy had dreamed a whiteman would come, and that he should go with him. The mother apparently could not provide for the boy, and determined Jacob would treat him kindly. The lad, named Albert, embraced the gospel taught him by the Hamblins and remained faithful in it to the end of his days.

After some three years in Tooele, Jacob was called along with others in April conference, 1854, to serve on a mission to the Indians of southern Utah. He took with him the make-peace philosophy adopted in the Tooele years. But some of the settlers in Jacob's new home thought of the Lamanites differently than Hamblin, just as many had in Tooele. True, Jacob could point out from The Book of Mormon that the native Americans were "redeemable," i.e., had once been a chosen people in the Lord's work, and were in fact, of the House of Israel as were the Jews. But from a practical standpoint, many saw only savage ways prevailing within the natives and thought Jacob's "Lamanite program" naive and unworkable.

Upon arrival in his southern Utah home, Hamblin's family totalled ten. Meeting their needs alone would seem a formidable task. But anyone who thought that would occupy all of his energies in the new frontier challenge didn't know the inner strivings of this man known as Jacob Hamblin.

36

End Notes, Chapter Two

(All references at first occurance are spelled out.
See "Sources Cited" for key to abbreviations)

1. *Little Autobiography of Jacob Hamblin*, p. 64; See also
   "Journal Contents of Jacob Hamblin," p. 10: "[received]
   word that Hyrum Judd and I mite manage the frontier
   to sutt ourselves." "Journal and Letters of Jacob
   Hamblin:" "I felt Satisfide we could not work our way
   through for the exploring party…"
2. J-C, p. 7; Also, J & L, p. 18. The two versions are
   slightly different.
3. *Women's Voices*, p. 64. Also see *World Book Encyclopedia*,
   S, p. 270. "Well educated men spelled the same word
   in different ways."
4. J & L, p. 23;
5. J & L, p. 1.
6. Preface to J-C.
7. "He [Hamblin] makes no mention of the waterfalls that
   have brought fame and sightseers to the Land of the
   Sky Blue Waters…As a matter of fact, in all of his
   reports of his extensive journeys, Hamblin never once
   comments on the scenic beauty of the regions he traversed…" *Jacob Hamblin, The Peacemaker*, Pearson
   Corbett, p. 513, f.
8. J & L, p. 54.
9. There were other minor references to physical surroundings of aesthetic quality, but nothing evoked as
   many adjectives as the one cited.
10. Corbett, Prelude, p. 6.
11. J & L, p. 4.
12. Ibid, p. 4.
13. Ibid, p. 11
14. Ibid, p. 13
15. A glance at almost any page in Bleak's two volumes of
    LDS history indicate his thoroughness in recording
    daily Church business. Quite possibly, no blessing or
    baptism, etc. went unrecorded. Many of Jacob's civic
    callings are also mentioned, such as appointment to the
    local school board. It would appear such callings rec-
    ognized Hamblin's reputation for sound and fair judg-
    ment. One entry included, at Jacob's suggestion, a
    brother being set apart as bishop in his (Hamblin's)
    stead because he was away from home so much.
16. Corbett, p. 520f. Corbett also says in this footnote that
    Jacob "was ordained an apostle (special emissary)" in
    the LDS Church. However, in said Church, such a term

is normally used to mean a member of the Council of the Twelve Apostles. Hamblin was at times referred to as a "Buckskin Apostle," but that was never an official title. Perhaps Corbett is saying that Hamblin deserved the title "apostle." But use of the term as written here could be confusing to members of the LDS Church.

17. J & L, p. 1.
18. Ibid, p. 3.
19. J & L, p. 16.
20. Little, p. 58.
21. Believers in faith healings need no further explanation. But an article appearing in the Salt Lake City *Deseret News*, Oct. 1, 1994, B-1, is of interest. It quotes a Dr. Mark Rosen as saying that he considers himself "a man of science" but has "trouble explaining what happened to one patient without using the words 'prayer', 'God' and 'miracle.'" He describes a patient that modern medical technology could nothing for. He says, "The only thing I can say is prayer healed her." A poll cited in *Basic Media Writing,* Melvin Mencher, 1993, p. 273, say: "90 percent of Americans believe that God exists" and "80 per cent believe God works miracles." An article in the newspaper magazine supplement, *USA Weekend*, Dec. 23, 1994, says that "90 per cent of Americans believe in prayer."
22. *World Book Encyclopedia*, J, p. 107.
23. J & L, pp. 5-6. Rules for managing Indians: see Ch. 17.
24. J & L, p. 14.
25. Ibid., p. 15.
26. J & L, pp. 21-22; Jacob mentions a Brother Henifer who said, "…the woman was near dead and he did not think it much use [for us] to go."
27. J & L, p. 26.
28. Henry Bigler, who had been a member of the Mormon Battalion and explored more than a little of the Southwest, wrote: "…we had no good map for the one we brought from Los Angeles…did not have the rivers marked in it…and to tell the truth, we do not know where we are, only that we are somewhere in the mountains."*Utah Historical Quarterly*," Vol. 5, No. 4, Oct., 1932. Hamblin's peers, including Thales Haskell, also wrote at times of being lost. The only such mention by Jacob is an occasional adjusting of direction. If he ever was lost, other than the one time traveling by night to avoid desert heat in the Santa Clara region, he chose not to mention it.
29. J & L, p. 37. No explanation or reason is given here by Hamblin for the dispute. Corbett suggests, without reference, that the argument was over goods received (United Order system of disbursal) from the tithing house.

30. J & L, p. 4. "Thare was no chance to preach, so we returned holm."
31. The phrase "restoration of all things" is frequently mentioned in LDS Church histories. The Church claims to be a continuation of Christ's early Church. For further information on this term in LDS literature, see *Mormon Doctrine* by Bruce L. McConkie, p. 633; Doctrine and Covenants, 101: 23-31 and LDS Tenth Article of Faith.
32. After the Mormons were forced out of Nauvoo and trekked some 1,000 miles to Great Salt Lake City, it became a standing saying among Church members that "We came west willingly because we had to."
33. J & L, p. 8.
34. Ibid, p. 8.
35. Hamblin wrote (Little edition) that he could not see fit to heed the advice from Bishop Levi Stewart of Kanab inasmuch as he had received instructions "from the highest authority of God on earth" (referring to Brigham Young) to cross the Colorado and convince the Navajo chieftains that Mormons had not killed the three young Navajos. Church leaders often cautioned those in hostile Indian country to be careful but "to do what they thought best." For Jacob, that was usually getting the job done. One possible reason in wanting to visit the Navajos personally was that Jacob had promised safety to Navajos trading with Mormon settlements; he was adamantly opposed to the idea any Lamanite might suppose he had lied to them.

  It would also appear that in promising safety to Navajos crossing the Colorado, Hamblin did not foresee the possibility of them having social intercourse with non-Mormons. In actuality, there were very few non-Mormons in the region at the time.
36. J & L, p 13.
37. Ibid
38. Ibid. Date was June 14, 1850; the Pawnees had a reputation at the time of being fierce and war-like. However, there is no indication Jacob knew much about this tribe; he was probably assigned his duty from a supervisor, along with others expected to take nightly watches.
39. Little, p. 24.
40. The Indian "Old Bigfoot" is not mentioned in Hamblin's personal writings. See Little, pp. 23, 25-26.
41. J & L, p. 17
42. Ibid
43. Ibid
44. This statement is not made in Jacob's journals. See Little, p. 25.
45. J & L, p. 17.

– Chapter Three –

Saint Against Savage

Jacob and twenty-one others departed for the recently set-tled area of Harmony some 250 miles south of Great Salt Lake City on April 8, 1854. Rufous C. Allen, who had served a mission to Chile the year before, was appointed by Apostles Parley P. Pratt and Orson Hyde as Southern Utah Indian Mission President. The missionaries were sent forth with an admonition to "help civilize the Lamanites and teach them the Gospel."[1] (It is interesting that this account, written years later in *Brigham Young, the Colonizer*, refers to Jacob Hamblin as "noted Mormon scout and Indian interpreter." But, of course, he didn't have that reputation in 1854. He would not have earned the title for sever-al more years.)

These men were not the first Mormons to see the country. In 1850, Pratt and some fifty men had formed the "Southern Exploring Company" and set out to take a first-hand look at the region on the outskirts of civilization. Their travels took them to the area now known as Parowan[2] where they recommended the first community in southern Utah be built. They also found good locations for settlements in what were to be Fillmore, Beaver and Cedar City. Along the way, where Hamblin would later labor, they found Piute sub-tribes eating lizards and grasshoppers, living in conditions so primitive that they were barely able to eke out a living. Apostle George A. Smith explored more of the region in 1851 (soon dubbed "Utah's Dixie" because it lay to the south) and returned with additional reports of areas which could be cultivated and settled. Smith would also be called to coordinate southern Utah missionary work with Church headquarters in Salt Lake City.

Ever eager to expand and colonize, and with more converts pouring into Salt Lake Valley monthly, Brigham Young had sent Isaac C. Haight and John Doyle Lee to scout out the corridors of southern Utah and southern Nevada for arable land. Las Vegas

Springs and environs were settled by Mormon colonizers who also later founded San Bernadino in southern California.

It was a year after Smith's exploration when John D. Lee and approximately a dozen other LDS families began tilling soil at the place called Harmony.[3] Water could be obtained from Ash Creek on the northeast slope of Pine Valley Mountain, southwest of present day Cedar City. Lee did not seem particularly excited about the responsibility of being among the first whitemen to break ground here, but he carried out his duty faithfully as he had in other trying circumstances as a Church member.[4]

When President Allen and his contingent arrived, Lee likely greeted them eagerly, happy to have company in a difficult, new land. The brethren there were proud to show President Allen their ecclesiastical accomplishments: some ten Indian children were already attending Sunday School.[5]

Utah's "Dixie" was also deemed valuable for more than agriculture. Large deposits of iron ore were discovered north of Harmony and smelters set up, typical of Mormon ingenuity and energy dating back to origins near Palmyra, New York. It was found, too, that cotton, now unattainable because of growing hostilities between northern and southern states, could be grown in the warm, lower elevation climate south of Harmony. Church leaders saw it as a way to become more self-sufficient, rather than being dependent upon government or gentiles (non-Mormons). The Latter-day Saints had long felt that self-reliance should play an ever increasing role in their religion. This philosophy loomed ever more important after being driven from Missouri and Illinois by local mobs, some with overt state government ties.

Missouri Governor Lilburn Boggs, declaring that the Mormons "must be exterminated from the state,"[6] left the Mormons with a distaste for being at the mercy of "gentile" government. When the Church was later driven from Illinois, and Governor Ford seemed to condone the action, or did nothing to halt it,[7] the feeling of vulnerability was further aggravated. But while being driven about by those in power caused a deep wound bordering on resentment among these Latter-day Saints, it also cultivated in them an intensely self-sufficient spirit which men like Hamblin took with them to the western frontier.

They hadn't been at Harmony long when Hamblin found himself in philosphical opposition to his new mission president. Jacob was not exactly a greenhorn in Indian affairs and had concluded that while some labeled the Lamanites "ignorant barbarians," they were children of the same loving God as other races.[8] "God had a youse for them," if they could but learn His way. Wasn't that why the missionaries were being sent?

President Allen took the view that the first thing to be accomplished in the new frontier (termed a sea of "chaotic matter" by the camp historian in the Pratt expedition, *Brigham Young the Colonizer*, p. 44) ought to be taming the arid landscape. It would require the settlers' utmost, united energies before anyone could be comfortable here. Fields and orchards must be planted, ditches and canals dug to bring water, building of homes secured against desert dust, and scorpion. The natives, too, must do their part in the whiteman's dream for Zion.

Jacob seemed to have his head elsewhere. Perhaps it was clouded in the spiraling desert heat, for he talked about the missionaries' initial priority being to teach and convert the childlike natives to the ways of their Christ-taught ancestors who gilded so many pages in The Book of Mormon. Catching his attention was the translation page of that book which declared: "Written to the Lamanites who are a remnant of the House of Israel."[9] Also verses saying the Lamanites (before the time of Christ) were "a wild and ferocious and a bloodthirsty people..."[10] Later the book says "...the Lamanites did observe strictly to keeping the commandments of God, according to the Law of Moses."[11]

By the time America was discovered by Europeans, the people named by Columbus as "Indians" (those who built the civilization of the Mayas and Incas) had slipped from a Christ-like, industrious lifestyle and reverted once again to indolent and heathen ways. Hamblin also took special note of a particular verse in the *Doctrine and Covenants*, another latter-day scripture revered by the Latter-day Saints: "And this testimony [gospel of Jesus Christ] shall come to the knowledge of the Lamanites—who dwindled in unbelief because of the iniquity of

their fathers…and for that very purpose are these plates preserved [The Book of Mormon] that the prophesies of the Lord
might be fulfilled which he made to his people; and that the
Lamanites might come to the knowledge of their fathers and
that they might know the promises of the Lord and that they
might believe the gospel and rely upon the merits of Jesus
Christ, and be glorified through faith in his name, and that
through their repentance they might be saved."[12]

All this had a profound effect upon Jacob Hamblin. Others
might read the same latter-day scriptures and suppose the work
could be done by someone else. But who, if not he and his missionary peers sent to teach the Lamanite here and now? And
certainly if heathen traditions could be replaced with scriptural
beatitudes, it would also do much to terminate frontier bloodshed at the hands of those The Book of Mormon called
Lamanites.

Hamblin also believed that his peers must follow the scriptural injunction just as much as these primitive Indians. He
sometimes found himself unpopular by chastising his own
white neighbors for not diverting as much water from the limited flow of Santa Clara Creek to the Indian crops as to their
own.[13] At one point, Hamblin said he moved away from some
of his brethren in Pine Valley to Pinto because they "wanted his
room more than they wanted his company."[14]

It was true the settlers didn't always agree on the best way to
meet a harsh new environment. Yet, they needed a united front to
combat the elements, as well as a show of strength to the Indians
pressing in on them from all sides. Brigham's counselor in the First
Presidency, Heber C. Kimball, cautioned them that "…if the
brethren were united, they would be prospered and blessed. But if
they permitted the spirit of strife and contention to come into their
midst, the place would come to an end in a scene of bloodshed."[15]

While his neighbors often regarded the aborigines as a
potential enemy at best, Hamblin reminded them that the redmen were remnants of the same House of Israel as the whites.
All were equal in spiritual potential. The Lamanites appeared to
need some special help in bringing this potential out. Hamblin

worded it this way in his journal: "As for the Brotherin (sic) that had come here as missionaries they were not sent to build themselves up nor anyone else but Lamanites."[16]

Taking a pragmatic viewpoint, Allen appeared to interpret the latter directive to mean helping the Lamanites convert to a more civilized lifestyle, i.e., build houses and put in crops and make the natives more useful to the overall plan of colonizing southern Utah. Making long mission expeditions away from Harmony to outlying Indian tribes did little to help the pioneers become better established against the local elements.

Was it hopeless to attempt converting these primitives to the ways of civilization and Christianity? It would seem so. Escalante, nearly a century before, had labeled the local Piutes, "timourous and deceitful," living in "wretched conditions." They were "slow spirited." While the new white settlers may not have had access to Escalante's journal, they could have reached these conclusions on their own. But for Jacob, these primitives were like "broken wings,"[17] which ought to receive splints that they might mend, however slowly.

From the start, Jacob sought permission to make proselyting journeys to the various Indian tribes. But it required time to seek and receive permission for travel. In today's vernacular Jacob's philosophy is often described as "thinking it easier to seek forgiveness than permission." Hamblin took his message to outlying tribes but found he was rarely forgiven upon return. He wrote that he felt deeply vexed.[18]

How could he make much of a dent in the many Southwest Indians tribes' backward thinking if he forever remained comfortably inside the shadows of the pioneer settlements? True, the stubborn frontier soil needed planting, cultivating, fertilizing and watering, but so did the suffering souls of many thousands of local Indians.

It was not long before Hamblin was making unauthorized proselyting visits to the Muddy region of southern Nevada and into the far corners of southwestern Utah's Beaverdam Wash. He also took trips toward the border of present-day Arizona.

What would be Jacob's reward for visiting these primitive

tribes in an effort to mend "broken wings"? Possibly nothing more than to know he had helped the Lord find a "youse" for a seemingly forgotten people.

Dellenbaugh had said Hamblin was a "poor man who did his work for the people with little compensation." He was "content if he had straw for a pillow."[19] As Little said in the preface of *Hamblin's Autobiography*, "He is such a modest man that he would be content to ever remain in obscurity."

But to President Allen, Hamblin might have appeared an upstart ambitious for control. Without listing any sources, Historian Corbett states on p. 79 of his *Jacob Hamblin, The Peacemaker,* that Allen inspected the progress of Hamblin's and other missionaries' work at Tonaquint Station (Santa Clara) "and said little in praise of the work accomplished there. His feeling toward Jacob was none too friendly."[20] Hamblin said both in his personal writings and in the autobiography edited by Little that Allen reproved him "very roughly for some little thing that did not suit him."[21] Between "upstart" and supervisor, disharmony clearly reigned for the moment in the little community of Harmony.

Either because Allen wanted to put some distance between himself and the super-zealous Hamblin, or else he genuinely recognized the potential in Elder Hamblin, he placed him in charge of the Indians at Tonaquint (Santa Clara). To no one's surprise, Jacob soon had the local Indians tilling land, helping to build dam and ditches to serve the parched plantings, and building a log house. The Indians were often invited into his own home as part of the family, at least those he found he could trust. Whether the wives and family preferred it that way or not, they knew it was Jacob's way. Soon the Piutes were learning about the Mormon version of Christianity in the Hamblin home.[22]

Yet, in a few short years, due apparently to his obvious energy in proselyting Indians near and away, it was Hamblin who found himself president of the Church's Southern Utah Indian Mission. He was called to the leadership by Brigham Young himself on Aug. 4, 1857, with the following words: "Elder Jacob Hamblin, You are hereby appointed to succeed Elder R.C.

Allen as president of the Santa Clara Indian Mission...unite the hearts of the brethren.... Continue the conciliatory policy toward the Indians and seek by works of rightousness to obtain their love and confidence.... Omit promises where you are not sure you can fulfill them."[23]

It is not likely Hamblin would have done otherwise, of course, but it must have been especially satisfying to know (l) that the Church's top official felt the same conciliatory philosophy toward the Indians Jacob had long espoused (if there was a note of "rebellion" in his procedure as missionary, it was now officially expunged) and (2) that he now had the freedom to further inculcate those philosophies and policies throughout the entire Southwest from southern Utah to the California and Mexican borders. He could now, as official leader, release his full energies to teach and influence the Lamanites over a wide area. The assignment spelled sky-wide opportunity to some day reach out into the Unknown of northern Arizona and eventually, to the mighty Colorado River of which he had only heard rumors. The responsibility must certainly have also incurred some apprehension in thinking about how to meet the challenge of so many primitive Indian tribes, some docile, and some like the Navajos and Apaches known to kill whitemen on sight.

Hamblin's appointment letter also carried this admonition: "Do not permit the brethren to part with their guns and ammunition, but save them against the hour of need."[24] Jacob may have thought that the warning was directed entirely against the potential hostilities of local Piedes and Santa Claras. In actuality, the Mormon chief knew something Hamblin didn't, that a U.S. Army was marching against the Mormons. U.S. soldiers were sent directly by President James Buchanan to "quell a refusal" by the Mormons to replace Brigham Young as governor of Utah Territory.

While the door had suddenly flung open for Jacob to share his beliefs with the aborigines across the Colorado, he was to now focus his efforts on the surrounding tribes known loosely as the Piutes, which included the Shivwits and Kaibabs as well as the Piedes and Santa Claras. Hamblin attempted first to ascertain their survival needs, preaching less than offering food, drink and friendship. He says he spent many hours sitting around their campfires "where I learned their simple and child-like ways and heard them talk over their wrongs. I fully made up my mind to do all I could to alleviate their conditions."[25] Hamblin made "it a specialty to go among them, regardless of their numbers or anger. Through the blessings of the Lord, I have never failed in accomplishing my object, where no other persons have interfered in a matter they did not understand."[26]

One character trait Jacob always cultivated with the Lamanite was to speak the truth. No Indian during Hamblin's lifetime could accuse him of speaking with a "forked tongue." LDS Church historian Andrew Jensen said simply "The Indians said Jacob never lied." Prof. H. A. Thompson of the U.S. Geological Survey said of the man: "I would trust my money, my life and my honor in the keeping of Jacob Hamblin, knowing all would be safe."[27]

Hamblin tells of trying to mediate Indian quarrels which typically ended in one dead Indian, then revenge for the first. One squaw from a rival sub-tribe was tied to a tree and burned to death before Jacob could intervene. He seemed helpless to put a stop to the senseless blood-letting. One Piute told Hamblin that he must not think ill of them for it was their way and they "were as good as they knew how to be."[28]

As the Indians became more materially dependent upon the Mormon settlers, Jacob gained more of the Indians' ear. It wasn't necessarily, at least to begin with, that the missionaries convert-ed them to their "old religion" of The Book of Mormon. Even Jacob was never sure how fully from day to day the natives had purged themselves of heathen customs and could be trusted. The propensity to raid and steal, as Jacob put it, remained. The missionaries didn't dare leave their women and families alone for long even among the most familiar of the local Santa Claras. It seemed the local Indian way to just take what you needed, although after being chided by the settlers, the Indians learned to avoid detection. Jacob said he didn't hold this against them. It was just Lamanites being Lamanites.[29] One must not become a

should write good [about you] to the Great Mormon Chief?"
Hamblin said the chief answered him "Oh yes." Jacob then said, "When I write, I write truth and when I talk, I talk truth." He and the principal men counseled on it that night. The next morning he came to me and said he did not want me to say anything about what had been done. They were ashamed of themselves...they would stop such fights that night."[34]

Hamblin seemed to consider the most detestable of all Indian practices that of stealing children to be sold as slaves. The Utes in particular seemed inclined to raid the weaker Piutes to take whatever children they could to sell in Mexico or to other tribes. Hamblin spent some time with frightened Piute parents who were told by Indian runners the Ute chief Walkara was on his way to southern Utah. Walkara, who spent much of his time in Sanpete Valley, often took lengthy forays to steal both horses and children, breaking his baptism promise to Brigham Young that he would live by Mormon rules. He did so for a time, but soon reverted back to the old Indian ways, raiding anew. Walkara seemed pleased when the Mormon chief sent Church members to help the Utes grow crops. The old chief often differentiated between the "Mormonees" (Mormons) and "Mericats" (Americans), saying if battle came, he would side with the former. But when he returned to raiding, he did so on a grandiose scale, stealing both horses and children as far away as California.[35] When Walkara died, it was deemed proper that two of his wives, two Piede children and 20 horses must die with him that he not be lonely in his journey to a post-Earth life. One could expect no less at the death of such a powerful Ute chief.[36]

This barbaric act did little to endear the Utes to their white missionary neighbors, many with genteel English and European backgrounds who had known no aborigine customs in the Old Countries. It is no wonder some of these settlers, called upon to teach Christianity to so-called savages, preferred almost any other duty. It is easy to imagine that having someone like Hamblin around goading them into further missionary activity among the Lamanites did not always set well among his peers.[37]

One particularly galling experience Hamblin relates is that

judge over their child-like ways.

The local natives possessed a primitive code of ethic
er, which Jacob one day unwittingly violated. At first h
to become involved in the Indian practice of fighting fo
often into the night until only one brave remained stanc
says Jacob, "They taunted me with being a coward, cal
squaw etc. I soon took in the situation and saw that it w
be well to lose caste among them. I had little anxiety a
result, for they were not adept in the art of self-defense."[30]

He accepted on the condition that they not hold him
he hurt anyone. They agreed. But when wrestling a brav
out a squaw who didn't want him ("she refused to sleep
brave") Jacob knocked his opponent down and kicked hi
fell to the ground. For the latter, he was chided and told
acted unfairly. Having watched several tribesmen drag
maidens and rival bucks by the hair, seemingly doing ai
to win over an opponent, it must have left Jacob somewh
fused. Even the women waged war by dumping hot coa
the fire over the men they did not want to win. "One won
on the ground with her mouth filled with blood and dirt."[3]
sometimes fought for several days to determine a love
But Jacob allowed that by participating with them, h
"becoming useful in gathering Israel."[32]

Finding himself in such Piute squabbles, Hambli
more than once that he wished he could work with a
advanced people "...they are in a low disgraced cond
indeed loathsome and filthy beyond description. I have w
many times for the moment that my lot was cast among a
cleanly people."[33] Yet, he continued to be patient in lea
their ways, befriending both the gladiators and bystan
while trying to persuade them to settle disputes more amiab

When Hamblin made it clear that he disapproved o
way the Piutes matched husband to wife, the chief answ
thusly, "It is the way we get our women." Hamblin said, "I
them there was a better way...as he was chief, if a man want
wife, he could find a woman that wanted him [and] he shc
marry them and they should love their women...you wa

while helping prevent the Utes from stealing Indian children, the visitors struck bargains for the Piute youngsters. When asking the Piutes why they allowed this, several parents said they "had no food for the young ones. Better that they should be taken away and fed than remain and starve."[38] Some parents and children wept openly at this arrangement, but for a time, Hamblin watched many Piute children led away. While it may have torn his heart out to witness the same, Jacob did not physically attempt to intervene. What had been done for centuries could not be undone overnight. Hamblin himself often lacked food to share with the Piutes, although on several occasions he purchased children and left them with frontier families who could care for them. Such a policy led Ute chief Sanpitch to suggest Hamblin and the other missionaries go away and leave Indian matters to Indians.[39] Jacob continued to prevail upon the Piutes to let their children go no longer. He may well have been reasonably successful, for after a time, the child-selling practices were no longer mentioned. Either Jacob grew weary of writing about them, or they were resolved.

In some cases when Jacob couldn't change the Piutes, he joined them. If an Indian transgressed, such as in a petty theft, a peer put the whip to him. Hamblin decreed the number of lashes to be meted out.[40]

In truth, it is not known if changes in the traditional lives of these Indians indicated purely altruistic resolve. The palefaces had almost "magical" knowledge of firearms for procuring game and many tools for growing and harvesting crops. If everyone cooperated, it appeared the palefaces could upgrade the standard of living for everyone. This was dramatically demonstrated when Hamblin found the primitive Santa Claras cutting their wheat by using sticks to loosen the stalks, then pulling them from the ground by the roots. "I loaned them a knife which greatly assisted them in their labors."[41]

The local Indians' willingness to change also seemed to indicate that they wanted to be thought well of by Jacob and his faraway Mormon Chief. So enamored became the Piedes and Shivwits of the Mormon missionaries' teachings in some instances that they demanded baptism. Jacob says on p. 21 of his "Journals and Letters" that "We tried to persuade them to wait until they understood more about it...but they insisted on baptism so we baptized them."

There were also rebellious sub-chiefs like Agarapoots who threatened Jacob to his face after the chief's boy died; Jacob failed to save him. But Jacob took on himself to visit the angry chief. So fearful of Agarapoots were other settlers that none would accompany him to call upon Agarapoots who had removed himself hermit-like to the mountains. His white peers, except for Thales Haskell, said they would "rather go into a den of grizzly bears." All of Agarapoots friends went with Hamblin and Haskell back to the settlements but the old chief did not follow. Soon the cantankerous old chief grew mysteriously ill, "unable even to take a drink of water by himself." The Piute told Hamblin that Agarapoots died a few months later. Another unnamed chief opposed Jacob and died suddenly.[42]

With the missionaries also healing the sick, some Indians waited to first see what the medicine man could do, then called in Hamblin and his companions to work their "poogie."[43] The accounts of Hamblin and his peers, white and Indian, document the awe with which the Piute sub-tribes began to view the settlers generally and Jacob in particular. Essentially, the word got out that if you crossed Jacob, it was "bad medicine."[44] By 1860, few local Piedes or Santa Claras dared. They shared their superstitions when visiting Moapites, Mohave, Muddy and other tribes of southern Nevada. It didn't really matter whether Hamblin had some special power or not as long as the Indians believed he did; the effect was the same. It may also be true that Jacob exploited their superstitious nature to further his missionary goals, but he never claimed any success with them unless giving credit to a higher power.

How much may have been, in fact, due to divine intervention is not known. But it is important that Jacob himself thought his work to be watched over.[45] He never failed in all his writings to credit a higher power for his success. In the 1860-70s, he attributes his good fortune with the local Indians (and later the

Hopis) to prayers for much-needed rain in behalf of that people. The supplications proved, according to Hamblin's diaries and those of peers such as Thales Haskell, to be more effective than the traditional Indian rain dances. On one occasion, Hamblin listened to a Piute chief ask why he had promised them a bounteous harvest and now the creek had dried up and there was no snow in the mountains and "what will I do for food next winter?" Hamblin said he went off by himself and prayed for rain. "It was a clear cloudless morning while still on my knees, rain began to fall...I think more corn and squash were grown that year by us than I ever saw before or since...The Indians gathered and stored up a large amount of corn, beans and dried squash."[46]

"From that time," said Hamblin, "they began to look upon us as having great influence with the clouds. They also believed we could cause sickeness to come upon any of them if we wished. We labored to have them understand these things in their true light, but this was difficult on account of their ignorance and superstitions."[47]

This growing influence with the Indians was one reason Hamblin was able to venture forth with confidence into the vast Muddy country of 1858-60 where hostile tribes waited to prey on unsuspecting travelers. Hostilities seemed to ease almost with Jacob's mere presence. When Hamblin associates like Dudley Leavitt or Ira Hatch appeared on the scene, they were also effective if declaring they represented Jacob and followed his policies.[48]

Many of the tribes in southern Nevada had not laid eyes on Jacob Hamblin personally; yet, news of Hamblin had gotten around. Those which did not feel a close friendship with the man nevertheless seemed to respect and fear him. On one expedition to the Muddy, Hamblin said that to prevent bloodshed, he supped with the Indians and kept an eye on their activities. So long as he was near, the Indians felt restrained and behaved themselves. The key seemed to be that the Indians did not want Jacob to know they were causing mischief. If he didn't, or couldn't know, they seemed more disposed to do as they wished.[49]

Hamblin and the missionaries often invited the Indians into their homes for holidays such as Christmas. The natives were then given gifts of food and clothing. There were no doubt many attempts at teaching charitable Christianity during the Christmas holidays.

But while trying to impart kindness to the redman, at no time did Hamblin allow any Indian in his presence to get away with threats. Jacob once led an unruly Piute out the door "by the hair of his head and took my foot from his seat of honor which gave him to think I meant what I said. (J & L, p. 38)." One angry Piede told Hamblin that Ute Chief Walker would come to southern Utah and kill him and the other Mormons. While the surly Piede was at it, he also asked Jacob for bread. On pp. 30-31, J & L, Hamblin answers thusly: "I told him he lied. Walker would not come here to fight. The Piedes were fools to shoot their friends. If the Piedes had killed one of the Mormons they would all be shot. He said he did not want me to say more for it would make him cry." After making it clear he could not be bluffed in that manner, Jacob added: "I thought it was not best to throw the Piedes away that lived about Harmony, so gave him some matches and told him that I had no bread to spare, to go and talk good to all the Piedes he found where he went. He said he would. So we shook hands and parted with better feelings than when we met."[50]

Note that Jacob did not try to belittle or put down the Indian. Hamblin kept belligerents in their place but attempted to put friendship above personal ego or pride. He let them know he would not be bullied. Yet, at the same time he would not let them be his enemy.

It would later be said of Hamblin that "he knew the Indian better than any other frontiersman."[51] That was saying a lot considering Daniel Boone and the many other legends of history. But first, Jacob had to pay the price; he spent many hours with the Lamanites before he learned their ways, and could earn the title given him.

In working side by side with the Indians, Jacob sought always to help them gain a feeling of greater self-worth. This was the way one helped a child-like people to grow, gain confidence and accept responsibility for their own actions. He wrote in his journals that the settlers and Indians finally began to overcome their wariness of one another and reach out in trust.

The Piutes began to express great love for Jacob and the missionaries.[52] On one occasion when Jacob was attacked by a violent fever, the Piutes "crowded around, mourning and crying," greatly afraid the man they had grown to love so would die. The chiefs "cried until midnight for me."[53]

In recovering, Hamblin marveled at the Piutes' compassion. There was reason to believe his work of bringing the Lamanites to the rich promises of The Book of Mormon were, for the most part, now beginning to succeed.

The period from 1854 to early 1856 had been challenging. But Jacob had witnessed much progress in bringing the gospel message to the Piutes and their allies, in working side by side with them and helping them gain a feeling of greater self-worth. Jacob's writings indicate that the settlers and Indians had begun overcoming their wariness of one another and felt the other could be trusted. Jacob would have reason to feel that his work of bringing the Lamanites to the rich promises of The Book of Mormon had, for the most part, succeeded. But as Jacob would soon learn, many difficult challenges lay immediately ahead.

End Notes, Chapter Three

1   Milton R. Hunter, *Brigham Young the Colonizer* , p. 301; Hunter emphasizes, "Hamblin was one of the important members of the company."

2. Parowan, first known as Center Creek, would be the epicenter of southern Utah settlement for some 10 years. Parowan came from the local Piutes, meaning "marsh water" or "marsh people," according to John W. Van Cott, *Utah Place Names*.

3. The town was first called Harmony, then with fortification against Indians, Fort Harmony. Today the community shows on the map as New Harmony about 10 miles west of I-80 in Iron County. It was moved north due to water problems involving both drought and flood. Interestingly, Brigham Young made a recommendation to move the town north shortly after John D. Lee and companions established the "old" town of Harmony.

4. There are numerous references to Lee's expressing personal dislike for a Church assignment, yet fulfilling it in order to be considered fully obedient. In *Brigham Young the Colonizer*, p. 50, Hunter has this comment: "Although the project [exploring for an area to settle south of Parowan], was at first distasteful to Lee..." John D. is then quoted as saying personal experience had taught him "to hearken."

5. Hunter, p. 301

6. Joseph Smith, Jr. *Documentary History of the Church*, Vol. 3, p. 175. Governor Boggs seemed to be interested in more than just expelling the Mormons. One sentence in his extermination order reads: "...proceed to the same point for the purpose of *intercepting* the retreat of the Mormons to the north."

7. DHC, Vol. 6, pp. 585-631

8. Author's conclusion from Hamblin's J & L. See p. 17

9. From the title page in The Book of Mormon. In the Old Testament, of course, God first gave his commandments to his covenant people, the House of Israel. The Book of Mormon declares that the Lamanites are descended from Manassah, son of Joseph (who was a son of Isaac), making the Indians as much a covenant people as the descendants of Judah, or the Jews.

10. *Book of Mormon*, Mosiah 10:12.

11. *Book of Mormon*, Helaman 13:1.

12. *Doctrine and Covenants* 3:18-21.

13. J & L, p. 44; "I come out against them [white peers] which offended them very much."

14. Ibid. Dated Aug. 9, 1856.

15. Little autobiograpy, p. 33

16. "Journal and Letters," p. 19

17. L. H. Creer, "Jacob Hamblin in the Region of the Colorado, no. 33, p. 32," May, 158 (from anthropological papers), University of Utah Press, Salt Lake City, Utah. Creer states that a friend of Jacob's father said Hamblin had a compassion for anyone with a "broken wing."

18. J & L, p. 46, "...felt as though it was not my fault."

19. Creer, "Jacob Hamblin-Colorado," no. 33, p. 32. "Hamblin lived a lived a simple life and "recognized greatness in simple things."

20. Based on J & L, p. 42. Corbett says: "Probably Jacob and the others wondered how long Brother Allen would remain as mission president in view of the apparent lack of harmony existing among them."

21. J & L, p. 46

22. J & L, p. 38

23. Little, p. 44. See Appendix B for the complete letter of appointment sent from Brigham Young to Jacob Hamblin, dated Aug. 4, 1857.

24. Young knew for a certainty by Aug. 4 that a federal army was marching toward the Mormon's Zion in the mountains, having been notified by Orrin Porter Rockwell on July 24 at Brighton, Big Cottonwood Canyon southeast of Salt Lake City. Yet, he writes in his letter to Hamblin, "All is peace here..."

25. Little, p. 35

26. Ibid

27. Andrew Jensen, *LDS Biographical Encyclopedia*, Vol. 3, p. 100. Reference to Thompson is also a quote from p. 101. Thompson, of course, spent much time on Powell's second expedition visiting Kanab and relying on Jacob for supplies and friendly relations with the local Indians. Jensen adds: "The Indians placed great confidence in Jacob."

28. "We cannot be good; we must be Piutes." J & L, p. 39

29. Little, p. 44. Jacob concludes here that punishment of the Indian, ignorant or otherwise, should be left to God. But Hamblin emphasizes on this page that the Indians would be left without excuse after being preached the gospel of their fathers.

30. Little, p. 36. This is a strange statement by Hamblin. Why would a people who placed so much emphasis upon physical prowess for survival be weak in the art of self-defense? Perhaps these Indians were small or undernourished; or it may be that Jacob's life on the frontier coupled with better food and living conditions had made him a physically stronger man.

31. J & L, p. 38.
32. Ibid, p. 34
33. Ibid, p. 38
34. Ibid, p. 34
35. Gustive O. Larson, *Outline History of Utah and the Mormons*, p. 94. The raids were frequent in Utah during what was known as the Walker War.
36. Ibid, p. 95
37. Creer, "Jacob Hamblin...Colorado," p. 4: "Hamblin's characteristic policy of leniency and patience with the Indians made him increasingly unpopular with the settlers, but his reputation as a peacemaker and Indian diplomat was enhanced with Church authorities."

    In conversations with residents of Kanab, Utah, (1995) stories were passed down to the author from ancestors which indicate some impatience with Jacob, i.e., he was "too zealous" in time spent attempting to convert the Indians when rigors of settling a new frontier were more on the minds of peers.
38. J & L, p. 28
39. Ibid.
40. Little, p. 43. "The Indians did the whipping while I generally dictated the number and severity of the lashes." This position was, in effect, that of a judge and indicates the tremendous sphere of influence Jacob had by this time over many local natives.
41. J & L, p. 22. Little, p. 34. Bleak, p. 16. This reference was in helping the Santa Claras in their harvest near the present town of Washington. It gave Hamblin an early look at the primitive ways of these natives.
42. Little, pp. 33-34
43. Ibid, p. 34
44. Corbett, pp. 99-101; this chapter is labeled "Jacob has strong medicine." Also, Little, p. 45. "They [the local Indians] soon learned to regard our word as law." In Little, pp. 50-51 is contained an indication of Hamblin's ever-growing influence with the local Indians as he saves the life of a man being tortured to death by natives. The man stated he was not a Mormon. Hamblin records he told him it that made no difference whether or not he was a Mormon; he then proceeded to save the man's life.
45. In all his endeavors, Jacob is not known to personally take credit for any accomplishments. He acknowledges Deity in all instances. Nowhere is this more evident than in pages 23-45 J & L and Little p. 39-40.
46. Little, p. 40
47. Ibid.

48. Little pp. 46-47. Hamblin explains how the missionaries (under Jacob's direction) saved the lives of California-bound travelers. On one occasion, Jacob simply told Ira Hatch to pursue some Cedar Indians to a certain spring, and they would relinquish their stolen horses. "Brother Hatch found matters as I had predicted." Little, p. 46.

49. This idea appears several times in Hamblin's journals. See also his report in the *Deseret News* of May 20, 1958, "...I spent the night with the largest collection of them, so that they could not make any general move without my knowledge."

50. J & L, pp. 30-31. This is a lengthy example of diplomacy at work among the Piutes. The latter attempted to threaten Jacob and the Mormons but Hamblin was not intimidated; he simply reminded the native that if he harmed any Mormons, he would be shot immediately. Then he shook hands and made friends with the Piute who had been his enemy.

51. F.S. Dellenbaugh, *A Canyon Voyage*, Yale University, New Haven, Conn., 1908, pp. 166-68, 174-5. Dellenbaugh, a non-Mormon, thought highly of Hamblin and the Latter-day Saints. On Powell's (second) 1871 expedition, he visited Kanab several times and traveled the length of Utah, often relying on Mormon settlers for help and directions. "As pioneers, the Mormons were superior to any class I ever came in contact with." He credits Hamblin's "wise management of the natives" in the Kanab-Arizona Strip area with their not being dangerous or hostile. Dellenbaugh also writes: "He [Jacob] was a poor man for he did his work for the people with very slight compensation."

52. J & L, p. 35

53. Ibid.

– Chapter Four –

Calm Before the Storm

When Hamblin arrived in southern Utah, he was sensitive to the fact that whites had moved in on Indian lands. The pioneers, no matter how frugal and honest, were in fact, squatters on terrain hunted and resided on for centuries by the natives.

True, the latter's meager efforts to raise corn and squash hadn't amounted to much. The natives had no technology to till the land. There was no irrigation in place; no bounteous yield. Still, what right did the settlers have infringing upon vested terra firma of the Lamanite?

This entry in Little, p. 30, indicates Jacob's concern: "While with them [Indians], I spared no labor in learning their language, and getting an insight into their character…the whitemen have settled on their lands, and his cattle have destroyed much of their scanty living."

In this statement, Jacob, a shrewd observer of both nature and the Indian, realized what many other settlers apparently did not. While the local Piutes ran no cattle and had few horses, they did rely heavily on natural browse and weed seeds for food, supplementing that with rabbits and grasshoppers. Directly, or indirectly, this was impacted by the incoming whiteman's livestock feeding upon the vegetation. Thus, it seemed to Hamblin, the whites could justify intrusion only if atoning for the loss.

The Indians Hamblin referred to were mostly the Piutes which included Santa Claras (Tonaquints), Piedes (Pedes), Shivwits (She bits), and local Indians sometimes called by geographical names like "Pinto" (corrupted from Pintiats).[1] Minor tribes in the region are referred to as Deserets (a name undoubtedly bestowed by Mormons), or the locally labelled Matooshals and Pahcupits. Farther north were the Pahvants (or Pauvants) in the mountains between Beaver and Fillmore. They lived on the edge of Piute territory, and were often called Piutes but considered themselves Utes. The latter were numerous in the rich

hunting grounds of what is now Sanpete (named after Chief
Sanpitch) Valley. Utes farther north occasionally raided "Dixie"
but were not native there. Southern Nevada tribes included the
Iyats, Mohaves, Moapites, and the "Muddy" Indians[2] north of
present Las Vegas. On the edge of the Great Basin farther north
were the Goshutes. Along the Utah-Arizona border lived the
Kaibab (Kibab) Indians after which today's Kaibab Plateau and
Kaibab National Forest are named. The Navajos seldom ventured west of the mighty Colorado River from their vast empire
in northeastern Arizona. If they did, it was in early winter and
autumn when the Colorado was low enough to ford safely. The
Moqui (Hopi) lived among the Navajos but rarely left their
pueblos to be seen in Utah. Farther east in New Mexico resided
a branch of pueblo-building Indians known as Zuni. Apaches
were known to move up from southern Arizona on occasion to
make raids. Hamblin talked with a few Apaches, but there is no
record of him proselyting among them. The spectre of
Geronimo, a rebel Apache who defied all whitemen to capture
him until 1886, was always present. But Hamblin and the crafty
Geronimo never met.

Jacob's daily encounters were with some 800 Piedes and
Santa Claras, mostly men, since many women and children had
been removed by the slave trade. Hamblin recorded in his journal, p. 19-41, that there were once many more Piedes; many not
stolen away had died of malnutrition and starvation.

Hamblin wrote that the two tribes were extremely timid of
whitemen. At first, only the males, naked except for loin cloth,
would come out to talk. Women and children, if present,
appeared from "dens and caves and holes" when all appeared
safe. The Indian braves explained that they thought these
strangers, like so many others, had come to take away their
squaws and children. When they were satisfied that Hamblin and
his companions came in peace, the Piedes not only greeted the
missionaries warmly but in their child-like enthusiasm, "hugged
each one of us" as Jacob wrote on p. 20 of his "Journals and
Letters." These Indians knew almost certainly that the white settlers would attempt changes in their simple lifestyle. The natives

had relied almost entirely on tradition and habit, changing little over the centuries. Yet, they'd suffered so much at the hands of militant tribes that the newcomers did, indeed, seem to promise improvement. This Jacob seemed determined to bring about.

Some Indians, however, questioned whether Jacob and the other missionaries would remain among them. Some hinted that the palefaces were trespassing. Hamblin explained to them, in a style they could understand, that the settlers had been sent here by their Big Chief in Salt Lake City. They would remain here unless Brigham sent new instructions.

At the same time, Jacob realized the whiteman's concept of land ownership could precipitate conflict. The Piutes, like most aborigines, had no need in a basically nomadic lifestyle to own property. Springwater, timbered lands, grassy meadows, et al., belonged to everyone. The Piutes could show no written document to these latecomers proving exclusive rights to any geographical feature. No one owned the sky. Why should anyone be allowed to own the earth or water beneath it?

Then the Anglo-Saxons came with their strange concept of property ownership, filing for usage permits to run livestock—as did Hamblin at Mountain Meadows—or fill out papers in some land office claiming possession of springs, watering holes and other real estate. No Indian could compete with the complicated new laws. How was it the intruders could claim exclusive rights to what had been commonly owned by all merely by displaying a piece of paper? As Hamblin saw it, how could the Indians be expected to honor something on which they had never placed any value? Or suddenly be expected to understand Anglo-Saxon ways?

Whatever their altruistic motives, the Mormons were no different from other whitemen regarding the traditional concept of ownership. These traditions came from from England, from which many of the Latter-day Saints emigrated. Across the entire West, pioneers bound for Oregon and California, or stopping enroute anywhere west of Missouri, declared that by their "Manifest Destiny" the lands utilized by nomadic tribe for centuries were now theirs. In western Oklahoma, the palefaces merely lined up and fired a gun and whoever got there "soonest" could claim it as their own. So what if it had been the hunting grounds of Kiowa and Osage? The tribes of southern Utah were no different.

Among the Indians, various clans or families may have fought, of course, at times over who had the right to be at a waterhole or lushest grass some period of the year; but none claimed to own it outright. Indians who found themselves in the whiteman's Dixie didn't resist as much militarily as they did Mormon efforts to change them socially. After all, they had been living for centuries as is. The attitude of some of Jacob's kinsmen, as he wrote it, was that they wanted the native to do more than stay out of the way. They expected the native to help them take over.

Hamblin adopted the attitude that this process was morally ethical if the life of the native was bettered. But assimilation into the whiteman's ways couldn't be hurried. Was it not right to treat the original occupants, original stewards, with a full measure of respect? True, the Mormon settlers eventually had the weapons and technology to take over any time. But Hamblin abhorred that approach, and wrote that instead of applying harsh punishment to the natives for horse theft or other activities long considered acceptable by the local Indians that they take the time to educate them to Christian principles. He learned the native mind: if one could steal livestock and get away with it, that was simply part of the game. Survival was competitive.

But Hamblin was also a pragmatist and knew he must draw a line between acceptable and unacceptable behavior. He declared in his journal on one occasion that if the Indians began shooting whites, they would be quickly annihilated. The settlers here could well have done what Hernando Cortes and the Spanish conquistadores did in Mexico: by force of arms overpower the aborigines and take whatever they coveted.[3] Hamblin sat around many Indian campfires to remind them of this.

But were these Piedes and Santa Claras, despite their lowly station, not remnants of the same people visited by Jesus Christ in times past? Why should the Savior care about the ancient Lamanites and not their offspring? Were the latter not as redeemable as their ancestors? Did the fact they had lost the vision of their rich spiritual heritage make them any less worthy today of conversion to Christian principles?

There were precedents in American history for treating the native with respect, even for altruistic as well as self-serving (survival) reasons. After the Quaker religionists were very badly treated in England, William Penn established a colony in America setting up harmonious Indian/white relationships. Penn made treaties with the Indians in Pennsylvania and respected their rights. His dealings with the Indians "were so just that they never attacked the colony."[4]

Hamblin may have never read about Penn's policies, but it appeared he had the same concept, perhaps going one better. He wanted not only harmonious relationships between Indian and white, but between the native tribes themselves. He wanted them to reach full spiritual potential for their own individual worth, not merely to embellish the whiteman's dream of conquest.

Jacob may have thought more of such an energetic crusade after receiving a blessing from the hands of his father, Isaiah. The latter laid his hands on Jacob's head at Santa Clara and declared: "Jacob, I…bless you with the blessings of Abraham, Isaac and Jacob and you shall reach forth and obtain all the blessings laid up in store for the faithful because thou loved the gospel and obeyed it in thy youth and hast had integrity in thy heart. Thou shalt be blessed with all that thou desirest, even wisdom, knowledge and understanding. Thou shalt understand all mysteries as fast as thou desirest. The Lord will have his eye over you on your present mission and will bring you safe through all difficulties. Hundreds and thousands of the scattered remnants of the House of Israel shall be brought into the fold of good through your preaching. Generations yet unborn shall rise up and call you blessed. You shall preach the gospel in distant lands. The time will come when you will command the winds and they shall cease. You shall speak to the waves and they shall be smooth. The bowels of the Earth shall open up treasures unto you. You shall overcome all your imperfections, for your name is written in the Lambs Book of Life, never to be erased. Thou art one of the hundred and forty four thousand that shall come on Mt. Zion to redeem the earth. This is thy blessing wherewith. I bless you and I seal them upon your head in the name of Jesus Christ, Amen."[5]

Jacob says in his "Journal and Letters" that "After my father had blest me, I then blest my wife and children. The Lord poured out his Spirit upon me. I felt to rejoice in the Lord and give thanks to His Holy name."

Any attempt to totally fathom the joy here in Jacob's family within the bosom of the gospel net can scarcely be touched upon. The bottom line is that the hardships and struggles must have been worth it, for Jacob continued teaching the aborigine with patience and vision. Rachel does not express herself here on this subject but must have shared her husband's feelings. It appears that the Hamblin family was quite content with Jacob's way of treating the natives, or at least there is never any comment from Hamblin's journals otherwise.

But human design does not always equal human demonstration. From the first contact, even some of the missionaries might have observed askance what appeared to be dirty, unkempt and quarreling Shivwits, Piedes and Santa Claras. They were, perhaps better left outside the settlers' homes and likewise, their trust. For when it came to intense proselyting, and sharing spiritual blessings with the Lamanites, only Thales Haskell seemed somewhat equal to Hamblin's zeal. In this, one should not think the settlers adverse to helping the Lamanites. Many, including Ira Hatch, Dudley Leavitt and Samuel Knight, risked their lives to bring about more harmonious relationships between white and red. But many did not see the vision of the Lamanite as these few men saw it.

The admonition to teach the Lamanites how to farm and become civilized and live gospel standards was promoted by no less than the first Mormon leader Joseph Smith, Jr. Followers had examples. Yet, these destitute Piutes could tax one's patience. The spiritual injunction that the Lamanite should some day "blossom as the rose," just didn't seem to be happening soon enough for some of the settlers.

Jacob himself said in his "Journal and Letters" that the tribes in Dixie were the "most destitute people I ever saw." Brother Brigham had suggested going hunting with the natives and proving to them that they could, indeed, trust the settlers and missionaries. But Brigham had also said that the Mormons should be careful not to become too familiar with the Indians and risk losing respect. He added: "It will be better for our settlements not to be so familiar with the Indians; it makes them bold, impudent and saucy and will become a source of trouble and expense to you. Keep them at a respectful distance, all the time, and they will respect you the more for it."[6] Young also emphasized that the colonists "could not be too cautious nor too much prepared for defense, for they might be deceived by the apparent overkindness of the Indians and at unguarded moment suffer loss."

Hamblin seemed well aware of the dangers outlined, yet seemed to proceed, nevertheless, on the basis that familiarity –properly done–could dissipate differences. Whatever problems existed could be overcome by getting to know how the natives thought, and starting from there, uplift them from their barbaric ways. One might not precipitate changes overnight; but one must become more than arms-length friends with them.

In order to treat his Lamanite brothers fairly, Hamblin more than once took the Indians' side in differences with peers. If Jacob felt the latter did not allow a fair share of irrigation water to the Indian, or failed to grant equal harvest, he quickly intervened. He said once when the natives were not treated properly that his personal "feelings were hurt."[7]

Some "housekeeping" directives from Salt Lake City were also exasperating for Jacob at times. He had been instructed by Church headquarters that the missionaries should teach the natives to wash and clean themselves before assisting them with health problems.[8] When Jacob developed a reputation for healing natives by the laying on of hands, Chief Agarapoots appealed to Hamblin that he do the same for his ailing son. But before administering to the boy, Jacob attempted to comply with mission rules, i. e., apply soap and water first. The chief refused this breach of custom; the boy died; Jacob was blamed.[9]

While Jacob never directly complained about such domestic directives, one gets the idea from his journal that he wouldn't have initiated the policy on his own. Jacob never mentions complying with the wash-first admonition again. There were some things he knew more about on the scene than could anyone making up housekeeping rules hundreds of miles away.

Yet, it would be wrong to suppose that Jacob gave in to Lamanite mores and customs. They would not get away with stealing and lying. At one time, Jacob wrote he was tempted "to thrash the ground" with a thieving and lying Piute, but "thought better of it" and restrained himself. Still, the Indian must learn to exhibit honesty and work for the food and shelter received, as per guidelines Brigham himself put down. The dole was not part of Brigham's or Jacob's program. Attaining the fine line between assistance and outright welfare would be a long and arduous challenge, requiring much fortitude and earnest friendship.

Things could have been worse. At the Elk Mountain Mission, begun in 1855 in Utah's eastern Grand County near the Colorado border, the Utes had at first seemed to accept the whitemens' teachings. But after a year or so, some Utes felt incursion against their primitive customs and traditions, lashing out and killing several Mormon missionaries. The remainder barely escaped; the mission was closed.[10] One valiant Ute with his family did attempt to protect the newcomers who had helped his people so much. Yet, it required but one or two crafty Utes to make trouble and close the mission. Indians also rose up to smite their white brethren in the Salmon River country of Idaho, closing the mission there. Jacob took care that a similar firestorm of trouble did not ignite in Dixie.

In general, President Young's pronouncement that it was "cheaper to feed the natives than to fight them" proved sound. The Mormons seemed to have fewer fatal clashes with the red-men than occurred in many areas, such as in the Dakotas and Northwest. But for some natives, freedom to do exactly as they pleased was more important than a full belly at the whiteman's table. The palefaces must not try to replace cherished traditions and primitive instincts with meaningless new restrictions.

Indeed, at any time, Jacob did not know if he might return from an irrigation turn to find Rachel and the children safe, including Albert, the undernourished Indian boy brought with him as his own from the Oquirrh Mountains near Tooele.[11] Any family member could be stolen or wasted by outside raiders, or worse, Indians inside his family circle yielding to primitive voices.

As in the Elk Mountain Mission, one did not always know the aborigine mind. Rachel had often found it necessary to lock out snooping Indians from the fort at Santa Clara more than once after the men left to work in the fields.[12] One just could not always know what a deviate Piute might be up to. Like Elk Mountain, it would only require one or two rebels to destroy what the settlers held most precious, their wives and children, and of course, the mission concept itself.

The natives could also cause problems in other ways. Take for example, the Indian boy in the home of Hamblin's good friend Thales. One day, the boy, snooping about, took a rifle from the Haskell mantle and clicked the trigger. The shot hit Thale's wife, Maria, in the abdomen. It was not clear whether the lad had merely misfired the gun, or intended criminal mischief. Thales explains it this way, p. 16 of his autobiography: "[The boy] claimed he was cleaning his gun when it accidentally went off, but others of the Indians said no, and wanted to hang him on the nearest tree. The bullet pierced my wife's body as she was getting the noonday meal, mortally wounding her and killed our unborn child. My wife lived but a few days."[13]

With steady nerves, Jacob took a knife and cut deeply enough to remove the slug without causing deep bleeding; but she died anyway from infection, that bugaboo of the times which the pioneers so little understood. It was a time of deep mourning in the remote settlement.

As for the boy, he was never heard from again. Haskell strongly suggests the boy was hung out of sight from white-men's eyes.[14] No further questions were asked. Life on the frontier was difficult. Such was Piute justice.

Some Piutes also attempted to bluff or bully Jacob and the missionairies into getting what they wanted. On page 45 of his

"Journals and Letters," Jacob says that one stubborn chief refuted him openly, although somewhat fearfully. "When I was talking to him he trembled like a leaf…but still persisted in his ways… sneered at our instructions…heard the Mormons could not pray him to death." Another chief, Titsegavets, told Hamblin that the stubborn chief had always been a bad man and "would be as long as he lived. It would be right for him to die."

Jacob would not harm the man but says he (Little, p. 39) prayed–"if it would be for the glory of His name," that the chief "might not have the strength to shed the blood of any of us." In a few days the chief grew sick. "He lingered until spring and died."

Hamblin also says on p. 45: "One Lamanite…said he was not afraid to steal from the first Mormon that came along. He stole a cow and killed it, and partly skinned it…when he was taken sick and died. This fully established our influence among them."

For many weeks thereafter, Jacob was called on to return stolen squaws to their husbands and pilfered children to their rightful parents. In some cases the best way was to barter with a quantity of bright beads or colorful clothing to buy an Indian child to save its life. In an effort to combat Indian child stealing, Brigham influenced the Utah legislature to pass laws allowing for adoption of Lamanite children. The settlers bought young ones and raised them or found someone who could. Jacob says in his journal he found homes among the settlers for such children.

Some Piutes expounded deeply-felt superstitions to Jacob, who listened patiently, pondering their veracity. One Lamanite told of a tall man, l0 feet high, who performed many wonders. Hamblin explains in his journal how he listened patiently to such talk, but used these occasions to gently counter with the Christian concepts he was sent to teach. Once he preached from a rooftop to a large audience of curious Lamanite brothers.

Jacob believed that many of the Piutes had good hearts and simply needed guidance and instruction. They seemed to note his care and beneficient love for them. It was a "tough love," of course, one where he made it clear the missionaries held expectations for them. Jacob found this love reciprocated several times when he became ill. Once, when many feared he was dying, Hamblin found the Indians hovering around him, expressing deep concern. "I was attacked by a violent fever. The Piedes crowded in around me. They were afraid I would die. The chiefs got together and cried and made a mournful noise all the fore part of the night."[15]

He tried to climb on a horse to ride to Harmony where it was believed he could receive greater care, but could barely do so. During the night, Jacob was in sore need of water and a Brother Atwood was able to carry some cool water in a holster from a nearby creek. After that Jacob attempted to get some sleep. He could hear water gurgling nearby but was not well enough to reach it. He wrote in his journal that it "was hell to want a thing and not be able to get it...to lay in hearing of a crystal stream of water and my mouth parched with a burning fever and not be able to get one drop of it."[16]

Hamblin said he was sick all night: "I was so weak I could scarcely sit on my horse." But he was nursed to health and eventually recovered. Jacob does not say why he could not have received this same assistance at home, but perhaps he and Rachel were afraid one of the children would catch his fever. It may also be that more medicine calculated to help the illness could be found in Harmony.

In time, Jacob recovered, attributing it to the prayers of himself, peers and his Lamanite friends. It was one of many times when Jacob lay near death and somehow recovered, always after diligent prayer.

There are some items in his journal which today are not fully understood. He said at one time the Indians dined with the settlers but had not much *yunt* for meals. This must have been in the spring, for Jacob said the Piutes sat in awe as he and others plowed up the sagebrush for planting. The Indians called this *throwing the chort*, apparently the Piede expression for breaking up the soil.

Throughout the period from 1854-57, Jacob and the missionaries took several exploratory proselyting journeys. Hamblin had noticed fairly sophisticated pottery scattered around in the hills and inquired whose work it was. He wrote in his "Journal and Letters:" "The Piedes told us the Moketes [Moqui or later called Hopi] Indians made it…that they lived on that land. Long ago the Piedes fought them and drove them over the Colorado."

Jacob determined that some day he would visit this industrious class of Indians. At one point, he did take a short journey into the unknown canyon country southeast of Santa Clara toward the Moqui Nation with several Ute Indian guides. But Jacob cut it short. The reason for this is not entirely clear, except that Jacob "felt impressed to go home." Shortly after doing so, he reported to mission president Allen "late at night" what he had done. Jacob said Allen was "much dissatisfied with me for presuming to start to the Moquiches without being sent."[17] This could explain in part why Jacob turned back; he apparently wanted very much to go but after thinking it over, realized he had no ecclesiastical authority to do so.

It appears he overcame for the time being a restless spirit to proselyte among distant tribes and settled down to the more immediate tasks at hand: clearing the land, cutting logs at Pine Valley, hauling in stones from the desert southward, and building up Fort Clara, as it was then called. In time storage houses were added for grain. Ever more land was cleared, planted and irrigated. The harvest was ample, even bountiful in those early years when water was plentiful. The pioneers grew more comfortable in their wilderness home.

Not all was work. There were times of relaxation, especially celebrating the Fourth and Twenty-fourth of July (anywhere in Mormondom, more work went into the latter in commemorating pioneer entry into Salt Lake Valley.) But there is no evidence anywhere that Jacob took up any particular hobby or pasttime as did others. Dudley Leavitt loved to keep time to a fiddler's tune, and was "light on his feet."[18] Hamblin did say he went fishing once at Fish Lake, a well known destination in those days to gather both fish and eggs, considered a pioneer delicacy. Jacob does not say if he caught any fish. He mentioned big game hunting a few times, but always his intent seemed to be to visit with the natives more than to find game.

There is nothing to indicate he did anything recreationally. It was a well-developed habit of his to never write anything down but that which pertained to his Church responsibilities.

When Jacob was present, local Church leaders from Parowan to Santa Clara asked him to speak at the Mormon sacrament meetings. Jacob preached integrity and patience in dealing with the Lamanites and often said afterward there "was a good flow of the spirit." He told of his proselyting efforts among the local natives, how some said that they had heard of a God and personal savior, although these "testimonies" were often "tainted" with beliefs in a sun or moon-god, etc. One Piute told Hamblin, "The Eutahs (Utah or Ute Indians) know about the Lord." Was this a reference to the "Great Spirit" which encompassed the mystery of nature and the seasons, or did it refer to the God Jacob believed in? The latter would not be the Protestant or Catholic god of the Trinity (three gods in one) but a glorified human being in whose likeness and image man is, as taught in the early chapters of Genesis.

There was much to learn about this fascinating and primitive people. Would there be enough time in one life to replace their many superstitions with wisdom from the scriptures? But did the Indian possess word-of-mouth truths, passed down over the centuries, from which the whiteman might benefit? The idea always seemed to intrigue Hamblin, and had much to do with guiding his steps later toward more "disciplined" and spiritually ritualistic tribes like the Hopi.

By late 1856, the Hamblin household consisted of Jacob and Rachel, the four children from Hamblin's former marriage to Lucinda (Duane, 15, Martha, 13, Maryette, 11, Lyman Stoddard, 8) and two children were born in Tooele, Lois and Joseph. There was also Albert (about the same age as Duane), the adopted Piute lad that Jacob had taken as his own in the mountains east of Tooele when his mother feared she could not afford to feed him. At various times up to three Indian girls also resided with the Hamblins, the idea being to assist Rachel in homemaking chores. Thus, there were about ten in all in the immediate family, plus Jacob's father Isaiah, reluctant for a time about departing Tooele but eventually moving south to be with his oldest son. As for Jacob's younger brothers, William, Oscar and Frederick, Hamblin never mentions them unless they figure in directly with some mission or Church duty. One must suppose they drew strength from one another's company, although Jacob never says so directly.

Little is known about the two children Rachel bore by a former marriage and which she and Jacob brought west. Corbett says (p. 503, no. 5 endnote) that the two were taken away by an uncle while they lived at Tooele. Their ages and names are not listed. Why they did not remain with Rachel and Jacob remains a mystery, for Rachel raised Jacob's four offspring as her own and seemed to love children. Perhaps the two were old enough to decide they preferred city to rural life, or someone else decided they should be raised in another faith. If so, it would seem strange that these two parents so dedicated to their own religion would let them be raised outside it. Jacob makes no mention of them at all in his voluminous writings.

One thing Jacob did say when marrying Rachel was that she told him she could have no children. Jacob prophesied otherwise. He told her: "I'm Jacob, you're Rachel," referring to the Old Testament, "and we will have two sons named Joseph and Benjamin."[19] That's the way it happened. Benjamin was born at Santa Clara.

Toward the end of 1856, Jacob's aging father, Isaiah, grew more ill. In his journal, p. 44-45 Hamblin wrote the following poignant words: "I got word that my father was very sick. I started on horse back, arrived there the next day. When I came to the door of the house where he was I heard him say I am afraid Jacob will be too late getting here. I want to see him before I go. He caught me by the hand and said Jacob, I…am not afraid to die. I never wronged a man in my life. I once dreaded the grave. I now hail it as a pleasure…what is the use of my suffering in this old tabernacle any longer. I comprehend Mormonism. I know the worth of the Gospel of Jesus Christ. I now appoint you to act as Patriarch over my family. You are older than your brothers. Council them in in all important matters. Do as I tell you and it will be worth to you all the gold of California."

Jacob says, "I laid my hands on his and prayed for him, asked the Lord that he might be freed from pain and depart in peace. After giving us much instruction…he died."

Hamblin had watched many of his friends and their loved ones suffer death while crossing the plains. Thales' wife, Maria, was also gone. But Isaiah was the first of Jacob's immediate family to die since coming west. This struck much closer to home for Hamblin. His father had left a rich legacy for family members to remember and live up to. But no longer could Jacob talk directly with his father about sensitive matters that troubled him, nor feel his presence on a daily basis.

There were many instances when natives posed threats and problems, sometimes far from Santa Clara. On one occasion, Hamblin was heading toward Great Salt Lake City when he and other brethren were cautioned to stop near Payson. Indians in the area south of Utah Lake were, for some reason, upset and angry. It wasn't safe to pass through, Hamblin was told. But Jacob felt they couldn't allow themselves to be pinned down forever. There was work to be done in Salt Lake.

Jacob hired a Ute to check the terrain ahead. Fires were seen on the mountain, which scared some of the brethren. But after conferring with the Ute, Jacob said he was impressed it was safe to move through what is now Utah Valley. He did so; the party encountered no problems the remainder of the journey. Jacob saw to it that the Ute was paid with a blanket.[20]

Hamblin followed the same Indian policy wherever he went. He sought advice from the local natives whenever possible and tried to keep their trust. Why should any of them wish him harm? There were occasions when Jacob learned a particular Piute sought to kill him. But a mystique had grown around Hamblin. He seemed to have an aura about him which made would-be enemies shirk from harming him. One major reason for it was peer pressure. Jacob had often prevented angry comrades from taking up arms against the Piutes. The word spread. On one occasion, Hamblin said after other settlers angrily armed themselves with weapons: "I felt impressed that a peaceful policy would be the best, and for that reason, I requested them to let me manage the matter." He did so without anyone getting hurt.[21]

Many an Indian who had huddled around a few campfires with Hamblin long into the night testified to others that Jacob had a good heart. He was their advocate with the whiteman and in many instances, with the Great Spirit. The admiration the natives had for Hamblin's good heart clearly shows that the Indians themselves, many of them more like children than the "savages" some made them out to be, recognized and appreciated a man of integrity. This, Jacob proved to be.

There is no intention here to enshrine the concept of "noble redmen," i.e., as depicted in the Hollywood movie *Dancing with Wolves*. This would be unrealistic. It was just that the Indians knew Jacob as a valued friend, someone they could count on as an advocate and one who could speak with courage and devotion in their behalf. In their child-like ways, somewhat awestruck by the power and knowledge of the whiteman, they needed someone like Jacob Hamblin to instruct and look out for them.

In time, he managed to forge valuable friendships beyond the local tribes to the more war-like Iyets and other southern Nevada Indians. Many of these Lamanites, being nomadic in nature, talked of Jacob wherever they went. Some were seemingly transformed from savage to saint. A number of Shivwits Indians in particular were baptized into the Latter-day Saint[3] faith during and after the time Jacob lived with them in Santa Clara.

In August, 1857 came the letter from President Young naming Hamblin new president of the Southern Utah Indian Mission.[22] He could now proselyte among the Indians as he wished. He could speed up missionary work among the Piutes and in time, the Moquis and all of the other Southwest tribes. Indeed, things could scarcely look more promising.

But the autumn of 1857 would quickly change all that.

End Notes, Chapter Four

1. Origin of the name Pinto is not known for certain, but in *Utah Place Names,* John W. Van Cott, p. 296, suggests it was named after local Indians, the Pintiats. (The word seemed to be corrupted from that name.)

2. While it is generally assumed the "Muddy" Indians were named after the creek of that name in the Moapa, Nev. area, Corbett says (p.506) referring to an interview with an occupant of that country that the name came from the Indian word for mesquite bean which they called "moudy."

   The Mormon town of Bunkerville was often referred to as the "Muddy Mission;" see *Deseret News,* Jan. 30, l992, p. C-l. But the Muddy referred to here would be some 60 miles northwest.

3. The *World Book Encyclopedia,* Ci-Cz, p. 854.

4. Ibid, P, p. 2l7

5. J & L, p. 24

6. *Journal History of Church,* May l9, l849; May 28, l849.

7. J & L, p. 29

8. Little, p. 37. This appeared to be aimed specifically at the Mormon practice of administering to the sick by the laying on of hands.

9. Ibid. A more detailed account is given in previous chapter about Chief Agarapoots.

10. BY-C, pp. 3l7-320.

11 Little, pp. 26-27.

12. Corbett, pp. 94, 505

13. "Autobiography of Thales Haskell," p. l6. "The bullet pierced my wife's body as she was getting the noonday meal, mortally wounding her, and killed our unborn child. My wife lived but a few days."

    Haskell wrote a 22-page autobiograpy focusing on the southern Utah experience. A 98-page journal by him was also edited and assembled by Albert E. Smith. A master's thesis by David K. Flake, "A history of Mormon missionary work with the Hopi, Navaho, and Zuni Indians" sheds light.

    Also see Brooks' *Jacob Hamblin,* pp. 53-60 for a dramatization of Maria's death.

14. In his "Thales Hasting Haskell" (edited by A. E. Smith), p. 23, Haskell says he judged the shooting to be "an accident." But later when the Piutes were asked where the boy was, they answered he would not be back ...they knew where the bones were."

15. J & L, p. 35

16. Ibid, pp. 36-37
17. Ibid, p. 42
18. *Dudley Leavitt*, p. 40
19. Corbett, p. 32, 502f.
20. Corbett, p. 60
21. Little, p. 37.
22. J & L, p. 46; Hamblin prophesied that a new mission president would be named and that it would be among those assembled.

– Chapter Five –

The Massacre and Jacob Hamblin

Along Utah 18 in Washington County between the communities of Central and Enterprise is a handsome granite memorial more than a dozen feet long. Placed there in September, 1990, it reads: "In the valley below between September 7 and 11 in 1857, a company of more than 120 Arkansas emigrants led by Capt. John T. Baker and Alexander Fancher[1] was attacked while enroute to California. This event is known in history as the Mountain Meadows Massacre." Known names of those who died in the ambush-massacre are listed. The memorial was erected by the "State of Utah, and the families and friends of those involved and those who died."

Those "involved" included Piute Indians supported materially and physically by local Mormon leaders. Indians attacked the train and then were assisted by whites in the killing of some one hundred and twenty adult emigrants from Arkansas. For years the idea persisted that the one Mormon executed for this tragedy, John D. Lee, was the lone non-Indian responsible. But the chilling facts as documented by historian Juanita Brooks in her deeply investigative book, *Mountain Meadows Massacre*, 1950,[2] exposed others as more guilty than Lee. Time has also uncovered additional pertinent information, along with differing viewpoints.

What happened so profoundly impacted the life and work of Jacob Hamblin–indeed, the entire Church to which he devoted his life–that we must more closely examine the event. These impacts on Hamblin and his work have never been fully scrutinized and/or compiled under one cover. We shall draw from primary sources wherever possible, particularly the transcript of J.D.Lee's murder trials in 1876 (on microfilm, hereafter referred to as Lee Transcript)[3] and from other sources wherever helpful in providing information, explanation or interpretation.

As an overview, historians agree (for reasons to be explored later) that both Indians and settlers became incensed with

behavior of the Fancher train as it made its way through the
hamlets of southern Utah. In the beginning, whites from
Parowan and Cedar City persuaded Indians to plunder or at the
very least, harass the train. On Monday, Sept. 7, after stalking
their prey, Indians began firing on the emigrants. By
Wednesday, the battle escalated and at least one brave was
killed and another injured, by the defending Fancher sharp-
shooters.

This apparently surprised the Indians, who had supposed
that those who enticed them into the attack (local Mormons)
possessed "special powers with the gods."[4] According to one
account, they, the Piutes, were to be the "Battleax of the Lord" (a
term Brooks attributes to Brigham Young; see page xiii of her
MMM) in destroying perceived "gentile" enemies. But now,
with one of their number dead, the Indians were angry. Those
who had talked against the train must help finish the dirty
work. If they didn't, the settlers themselves might find their
lives and loved ones in peril.[5]

Testimony later given before federal authorities agreed that
by Friday, Sept. 11, whitemen took on a major role in helping
Indians with the killing. Indeed, the awful feat could not have
been consummated without assistance provided by local whites.
While primary motive for the Piutes seems to have been a
promise of loot and livestock, vengeance for alleged wrongs
against their Indian brothers was also involved.[6] Motives for the
whitemen–coming from as high a level as local stake presi-
dent/miltia leaders William Dame and Isaac Haight—are still
not entirely clear some 150 years later. Some imply it was for
material gain against a wagon train thought to be more affluent
than most. It is well-documented that clothing and goods of the
Fancher party were worn and used by those who participated in
the massacre, including the family of John D. Lee. But statements given by Lee for years after the massacre (if indeed, he is
to be fully believed) indicate a deeper reason, i.e., settlers feared
for their lives in an atmosphere of mass hysteria, claiming the
Fancher train would, if not stopped, encourage U.S. military
attack from California[7] to join with Johnston's Army coming

from the east. The latter had been dispatched by President James Buchanan for an alleged "rebellion" against federal authorities sent earlier to govern Utah Territory. Deeper analysis also indicates a possible motive of revenge for wrongs suffered by the Mormons in Missouri in the 1830s.

MMM prepretators sent a message to Brigham asking what they should do with the Fanchers. But they did not wait for an answer. The president's message called for prudence, not panic; the emigrants must be allowed to pass through peacefully. Two lines read, "You must not interfere with them...you must not meddle with them." Courier James Haslam also says he was told verbally, "Go in haste and do not spare horseflesh. The emigrants must be protected if it takes all the men in southern Utah to do it."[8]

President Young's letter was dated Sept. 10. Riding speedily back to Cedar City with that message, Haslam nevertheless arrived two days after the massacre.[9] "Too late! Too late!" exclaimed stake president Isaac Haight. Not first waiting for this message from President Young, it became clear the local Mormons acted upon emotions uniquely their own. One must ask if they acted as they did before they could be told not to proceed.

There is no intent here to reopen old wounds. No one who had any part in the tragedy, or who are related to any who did, have ever stepped forward to claim pride in the deed. Almost the second it was over, that group of people which participated was each "ashamed of his part and certain of public condemnation."[10] Historian Kenneth W. Godfrey then asks this question: "Why could Brigham Young see clearly what Isaac Haight, [William] Dame and [John D.] Lee could not?"

In addition, local residents did not show support for what took place, leaving conspirators to talk among themselves in whispers and take a vow of secrecy regarding the nefarious deed. LDS Historian B. H. Roberts says concerning the Mountain Meadows Massacre, "Church people...have been naturally slow to admit all the facts that history may insist upon as inevitable."[11] Some histories have been simplistically naive, refusing to face the fact that high-ranking southern Utah Mormon officials could be involved in ordering such an attack. One report states, "William Dame was able to prove that he was not near the Mountain Meadows at the time of the massacre; nor was Isaac Haight, president of the Parowan Stake (sic)."[12] These men, prominent in the ecclesiastical affairs of southern Utah, were named by Lee (after being sentenced to die) as those giving him orders to destroy the wagon train. Lee said his orders were: "None who are old enough to talk must be spared."[13]

The only important search here must be for truth, shocking as it may be to comprehend. It seems typical of much history and many historians that hard facts are more often uniformly agreed upon than the interpretations and implications which follow. It must also be admitted that not all students of MMM history will ever agree on all conclusions, let alone any attempt to explain perspective and implication. In pursuit of any truth it is assumed devoted historians applaud further evidence, whatever it may be, which adds to their own inquiry. Meaningful research is cumulative, with one researcher building upon another until the summit of greater understanding is achieved. Thus, the search for facts in the MMM incident, or any facet of history, is never-ending.

One problem in ferreting out truth in the Mountain Meadows Massacre has always been that perpetrators entered into a most solemn pact of secrecy. For decades, the MMM was discussed only in hushed whispers in southern Utah. Research among descendants via word of mouth "testimony" nearly a century later could possibly be colored, perhaps partially forgotten. Yet, any incident involving one hundred and twenty dead was also of such massive proportions that participants attempting to keep the matter incognita might as well have tried to halt the relentless desert wind.

Lee always insisted that the aforementioned vow among participants meant death to anyone who let it slip out that the massacre was not solely the work of Indians.[14] There were rumors in the national media for years that Mormon "Danites" under orders from Brigham Young kept the whole ugly incident under cover, that no Mormon dared speak of it; thus, prosecution of the guilty was seriously thwarted, or at the very least, delayed.

If so, none of the above muzzled Jacob Hamblin. He went immediately to authorities, civil and ecclesiastical, including President Young, with what he knew. Recording in his journals that he was not present at the massacre, he learned much about it from speaking with the Indians who were directly involved, as well as white participants, including Lee himself. Hamblin was one, apparently, who dared speak up, and did so, seeking full and immediate punishment for the guilty.[15] If there was a pact to prevent anyone from discussing the tragedy, pact-makers failed to frighten or restrain a deeply-incensed Jacob Hamblin. He mentions no attempt in his "Journal and Letters" or autobiography of anyone trying to prevent him from pursuing prosecution of the guilty, even his misguided peers caught up in zealously "defending" Zion. No one threatened Jacob's foster Piute son, Albert, 16, who watched the terrible drama unfold before him (with another Indian boy named John) while tending Hamblin livestock from a hill overlooking the Meadows, according to the Lee Transcript. Jacob later testified that Albert led him to the bodies of some of the slain.

Hamblin said that he met Lee riding toward Salt Lake City to report the massacre, as inevitably the Church leader must be told. Jacob says Lee blurted out to him in an emotional catharsis that he and other whitemen had taken part. Hamblin says Lee admitted to him at that time of killing at least one girl.[16] This was later vehemently denied by Lee; Brooks says in her *Mountain Meadows Massacre* that "Lee denied ever having discussed the massacre with Hamblin."[17] If Hamblin is correct, Lee would have had to vacate his vow of total secrecy when talking with Jacob. But Lee might also have wanted Hamblin to know about it; the latter might even offer some sort of solace, by now a commodity Lee could use.

Hamblin records in Little, p. 46, that Lee disclosed to him the terrible truth of the massacre to this extent: "We met John D. Lee in Fillmore. He told us that the Indians attacked the company and that he and some other whitemen joined them in the perpetration of the deed. This deplorable affair caused a great sensation of horror and deep regret throughout the entire community, by whom it was unqualifiedly condemned."

If Lee or any of the perpetrators sought sympathy or understanding from Hamblin, they got none. Hamblin further records in Little, pp. 59-60, that under directions of Brigham Young, he accompanied Church leader George A. Smith to visit the new Governor Cumming, urging upon him the "propriety of an investigation of this horrid affair, that if there were any whitemen engaged in it, they might be justly punished for their crimes. Governor Cumming replied that President Buchanan had issued a proclamation of amnesty and pardon to the Mormon people and he did not wish to go behind it to search out crime."[18]

Hamblin also wrote: "If the business had not been taken out of our hands by a change of officers in the Territory, the Mountain Meadows affair is one of the first things we should have attended to in...southern Utah. We would see whether or not whitemen were concerned in the affair, with the Indians."[19]

For some reason, this statement by Hamblin has been largely ignored. There is probably no excuse for the MMM investigation taking so long, not coming to first trial for more than a decade and a half, but part of that blame would seem to lie on the federal government itself. Cumming seemed to be a milquetoast who didn't want to make any waves, quite possibly with the Mormons themselves, now that he had finally been installed as governor.

U.S. Indian Agent Jacob Forney said in 1858, "Mr. Hamblin and others of Santa Clara expressed much anxiety to bring the guilty to justice."[20] For reasons to be explored later, Hamblin and others were not in fact successful for many years in doing so. When Lee did go to (second) trial, it was Hamblin who gave the most damning testimony resulting in Lee's conviction.

But someone is not telling the truth about Lee's role in the MMM. Jacob said Lee admitted complicity at Mountain Meadows; Lee denied it. Hamblin's statement is corroborated by

Thales Haskell, who was with Hamblin when the latter met Lee at Fillmore. Haskell's edited journal says that "they met a horseman [saying] that the Indians and *some whitemen* [author's italics] had massacred a company of immigrants at Mountain Meadows."[21] Haskell's personal journal makes it precise that John D. Lee was one of the participants. "We were met by a horseman coming poste haste to deliver a message to Pres. Young that the Indians, *led by* John D. Lee, [author's italics] had massacred a company of emigrants at the Mountain Meadows."[22]

Haskell does not say here that the "horseman coming poste haste" was Lee himself but there is the phrase "led by John D. Lee."[23] If Lee did not admit to Haskell that he led the conspirators, it might have been Thales' interpretation. Either way, Lee's later denial that he spoke with Hamblin (while accompanied by Haskell) about the massacre rings hollow. Either John D. forgot what he told Hamblin many years later, or else he knowingly lied.

Hamblin explains in the Lee Transcript that he spoke with Indians involved and they told him Lee was very much in on the tragedy, including the killing of one girl, the same story his foster son, Albert, gave.[24]

One point of examination regarding Lee's veracity is the message Lee took to Brigham Young shortly after the massacre. As recorded in the *Journal of Wilford Woodruff* shortly after the massacre, Lee does not implicate any white peers or himself. Clearly, if Woodruff tells the truth, Lee lies. As Woodruff records Lee's message, "the Indians fought them [Fancher party] five days until they killed all their men...when Brother Lee found it out, he took some men with him to the place and buried their bodies."[25] Later another large company of emigrants came through, and "Brother Lee had to send interpreters with them to the Indians to try to save their lives." This not only absolves Lee from any blame but makes him out to be a hero of sorts.

In a later letter written to Young of MMM details, Lee mentions no Mormon involvement because as Lee always insisted, it "was implicitly understood" between himself and President

Young that only Indians were to be blamed in Brigham's official report to federal authorities.

Lee's statement to Church leaders Young and Woodruff directly contradicted what Jacob said Lee told him. Indeed, it was contrary to what Albert and local Indians told Hamblin afterward. But if Lee evaded the truth here, was he doing the same in claiming he only followed orders from ecclesiastical and military superiors Dame and Haight?

We must digress here to examine a charge, and a rather serious one at that, claiming that Jacob Hamblin was present during the massacre. According to *Mountain Meadows Massacre, the Life and Times of Bishop Philip Klingensmith*, by Anna Jean Backus, 1995, a descendent of Klingensmith, Backus says on p. 162: "Many documented stories claim that Jacob Hamblin was not at the massacre. The belief could be argued that perhaps he was there. Rebecca Dunlap, the oldest girl to survive the massacre, saw and heard things she remembered all her life. Rebecca lived with the Hamblins for at least a year after the massacre and remembers begging him to save her life while on the Meadows. She even remembers the color of Jacob's suit."

While some advance publicity for Backus' book declares Hamblin was, indeed, present at the massacre, the author wisely says *perhaps* he was there. Rebecca is described by those who knew her as an intelligent girl, but she was seven years old and told her story many years later as follows according to granddaughter, Isabel Kratz:

"She could see only one man who was not painted up like an Indian. It was Jacob Hamblin. He was wearing a suit of green material. She took her sisters, Louisa, five years old, and little Sarah, about one year old, and ran to Jacob Hamblin. He told them he would not let the attackers kill the girls. That indicated that he had an element of control over the attackers."

Rebecca reported the above to John Lynch, U.S. Army, who carried it in his official report on the massacre. Backus also says that J. H. Carleton, U.S. Army, was told by Rebecca that Jacob's foster Indian boy Albert participated in the slayings by taking Louisa and Sarah off to the side and killing them. This report here is confusing as to whether Jacob saved the two or whether Albert killed them. The book continues: "Two of the children are said to have pointed him [Albert] out to Dr. Forney [investigating for the U.S. government] as an Indian whom they saw kill their two sisters."

The account then goes into much detail as to the children being taken to the Hamblin home a few miles from Mountain Meadows and being cared for there. It is based solely on the memory of a seven-year old girl, telling the story years later. The girl credits Hamblin with saving her life, making no accusations against him of any sort. Yet, by naming him as being present, the implications are clear: if Jacob was there, he was a full accomplice. He was as guilty as any who took part, including Lee and Klingensmith. Hamblin would also be a liar and a hypocrite, for he made it very clear in all he wrote that he was not there and held guilty all who were.

But why would he save only Rebecca? Would Jacob have allowed the massacre at all given the fact he had great influence over the local Indians, and his sole reason for being in southern Utah was to persuade them to quit killing and lying and thieving and become converted as were their more noble forefathers in The Book of Mormon? Certainly, he would not be party to persuade them into committing such a heinous and treacherous act as murdering some one hundred and twenty helpless civilians. In addition, Hamblin carried no animosity toward the Fanchers, nor they him. In fact, as we shall see, he actually befriended them.

If Jacob was present at the massacre site, it is remarkable none of the participants or any other witnesses ever saw him. For nearly twenty years before the two trials of John D. Lee, none of the co-conspirators ever claimed Hamblin to be present, and at the trials themselves, all participants and witnesses agreed under oath that Hamblin was not present. In fact, Jacob's testimony bore greater weight because he was not present, had no part in the massacre and "had no ax to grind."

Was Rebecca Dunlap simply trying to say something nice about Jacob for taking care of her in what had to be a time of

terrible chaos and confusion? Those who can testify that
Hamblin was not present at the massacre include Thales
Haskell, Thales' new bride, Margaret, and Jacob's bride, Priscilla
Leavitt, returning from Salt Lake City. Others saw Hamblin in
Salt Lake City and Tooele in September during the terrible
events at Mountain Meadows. Haskell's testimony that he was
with Hamblin near Fillmore (far from Mountain Meadows),
when both first heard about the massacre, will be given later.

There were many conflicting reports about the massacre.
Lee is rumored in some accounts to have raped one of the
girls.[26] This is most unlikely. Lee's last vestige of credibility
would have been utterly shattered if he had been involved in
anything of the kind. Murder might have been ordered in some
greatly perverted spiritual zeal, but sexual perversion coming
down through the existing chain of command would be another
matter. No proof of the same was ever offered, nor did it show
up in either of Lee's two trials.

It should be realized in Lee's defense that he was a zealot to
duty, as was Hamblin. However, the two carried out duty in substantially different ways. Lee followed all orders from superiors
without question. Jacob followed an inner guide that often led
him to question orders from peers. The bottom line is, Lee most
certainly did not take part in the slayings, as Brooks maintained
in her *Mountain Meadows Massacre*, on his own volition. He
appeared psychologically incapable of doing so.

Jacob said he took the awful account given him by Lee without delay to Brigham Young, Apostle George A. Smith, the new
territorial governor, Alfred Cummings, other federal officials, and
anyone who would listen. Some nineteen years elapsed, including
one mistrial, before Lee was found "guilty of murder in the first
degree" and later executed. Brooks has conflicting statements
about the relationship of Lee and Hamblin. In one place she said
the two "had prior to this time [about 1874]...been very friendly";
in another place she says they had "never from the time they first
arrived been on cordial, or too friendly terms."[27]

One thing is certain. Lee complained bitterly before his trials
that Jacob indiscreetly betrayed him in "a matter of delicate

character."[28] No details were given, but it was almost certainly that Hamblin chose to put "outsiders," i.e., the "gentile" federal government, above that of a brother in Zion. Lee said that "a man in his [Jacob's] position should be ashamed." Lee added that they agreed to drop [the dispute], "but was only one of his [Hamblin's] old tricks to Evade the Truth. I, however, treated him with the same kind respects as I did before."[29]

The conflict between Jacob and John obviously carried deep roots before the Lee trials but accelerated greatly during and after trial number two. Brooks adds in her *Mountain Meadows Massacre*, "They also had a serious difference with regard to the way the Indian affairs were being managed." No details are given. The two eventually warned their children against having anything to do with each other. (There were, however, later intermarriages. If any grudges persisted, they were apparently never made public.)[30]

As for "managing the Indians," the evidence seems to indicate that the primary differences between Lee and Hamblin were this: for Lee, the Indians should be used to further the Church. For Hamblin, the Church should be used to further the Indians. Jacob would not, however, cave into the barbaric whims of ignorant Indians, for that would be an act of irresponsibility. If done out of fear, it could only be labeled cowardice. The Indians were to be guided out of temptation, not into it. The settlers were there to elevate the redman's spiritual destiny, not his baser instincts. To be their friends meant lifting them from moral impoverishment to their full potential as children of God.

If Lee expected Jacob to commit perjury to save a "brother," such was not in Hamblin's nature. The latter did not appear necessarily personal or vindictive against Lee; yet there could have been some cathartic effect in seeing Lee punished, considering Jacob's earlier statement that all of southern Utah "unqualifiedly condemned" the attack in which Lee had admitted complicity. It is interesting that Hamblin felt people in the area condemned the massacre, while Lee seemed to wonder why he and his peers were ostracized for simply "doing their duty." Particularly galling to Hamblin must have been Lee's earlier statement that the Indians "got out of hand."[31] To Jacob, it was Mormon responsibility to not let them "get out of hand."

After testimony from Hamblin helped convict him, Lee referred to Jacob in a letter to Emma, as "Dirty Finger Jake." Lee elaborates as follows on page 259 of *Confessions*: "The evidence of Jacob Hamblin is false en toto. Hamblin lied in every particular so far as his evidence related to me. The fiend from Hell, testified under oath that I cut her [the slain girl's throat]. Such a thing I never heard of before...The old hypocrite [Jacob Hamblin] thought that now was his chance to reek his vengeance on me by swearing away my life."[32] Lee also insisted that others lied about him *(Confessions,* pp. 217-18) in saying he talked about the massacre. It would appear that Lee didn't want to admit talking, or forgot who he told.

Hamblin enjoyed greater credibility in his testimony, of course, because he did not take any part in the MMM, and had no ax to grind other than upon the the wheel of truth. But did he act under orders from Brigham Young, i.e., in a conspiracy against Lee to "make him a sacrificial lamb" in order to get higher-ranking Mormons off the hook? This question will be more fully addressed in the next chapter with details of Lee's second trial.

In addition, blind loyalty or obedience were never as important to Hamblin as individual conscience. If blindly obedient to superiors, Hamblin would not have acted against the orders of President Rufous Allen; befriended the unwashed Piedes looked down upon by peers or stood in front of the Goshutes that at least one Church leader sought to execute at Tooele.

While Jacob could certainly be termed a Mormon patriot, he placed principle above peers. He was not what is often called today "one of the boys." That is, Indian or non-Mormon received as much favor from him as someone he sat by in Church. He was much like non-Mormon Major Gen. A. W. Doniphan who in November, 1838 directly disobeyed orders from a military superior when ordered to execute Joseph Smith. Smith was allowed to go to Liberty Jail where he later escaped into Illinios. In *Missouri Colossus*, p. 426, A. P. Ducheateau said that Doniphan never again mentioned the Smith incident, thus "he can hardly have thought of it as important." Yet, that was the essence of it. No matter who Smith was, Mormon prophet, or fellow human being, he deserved to be treated fairly. Doniphan risked court martial in the process and it is interesting that in championing a cause, i.e., going against Missouri peers of the time, Doniphan was remembered with a 25-foot memorial on his grave, as a "Christian" who "lived life without reproach." A memorial drawn together on paper said he was a man "of duty and right," with character "pure and incorruptible." The state of Missouri later erected a monument to him at the Ray County Courthouse, Richmond.[33] Duchateau said that in spite of all this, the modest Doniphan did not receive the recognition he deserved. Indeed, there are many parallels between (non-Mormon) Alexander Doniphan and (Mormon) Jacob Hamblin. Both placed principle above peers.

But what about unquestioning military obedience? It has been controversial since the first cavemen drilled for combat. Is it morally justified to carry out military orders against one's sense of right? Certainly chaos would occur on the battlefield if every order was questioned. Yet, the Nuremburg trials following World War II held dozens of subordinate Nazi military leaders responsible for their actions.[34] The same dilemma happened in the My Lai incident of Viet Nam in which Lieutenant James Calley was ordered by a higher command to "wipe out" an entire "enemy" village which, while it may have contained a few vocal recalcitrants, proved to be mostly inhabited by non-combatant civilians.[35] Did Lee merely act as did Calley a century or so later?

It has been suggested that Hamblin did Brigham's bidding in never implicating anyone but Lee. Yet, there was never any indication that anyone other than Lee confessed to Hamblin of taking part. Jacob could tell only what he knew. He had also long expressed trust in a "higher tribunal" meting out justice to those who escaped it on earth.[36] If justice wasn't served in this life, it would be in the next. Jacob seemed to have implicit faith in this philosophy.

When it was determined that Lee was a guilty participant at Mountain Meadows, and that he had lied in saying no Mormons assisted in it, Lee was excommunicated from the Mormon Church. Afterward, Lee's wife, Emma, complained that Jacob told her it was not right or good for her to remain married to a man excommunicated. John took it to be a stab at his character, further widening the gap between him and Jacob. Yet, Hamblin may have only been attempting to spare Emma later grief. As it was, some of Lee's wives began "treating him coldly" upon learning he had been cut off from the Church.[37] A short time after speaking with Emma, Jacob also helped get another family to assist Emma in her sometimes dangerous duties at the Lonely Dell ferry.[38]

Historians seem to agree that in the early days of New Harmony that Lee turned no friend from his door. There can be little doubt that Jacob dined at Lee's table more than once. New missionaries lived at the home of the Lees when first arriving in the south. The "wilderness saints" were spiritually bonded against the many challenges of the frontier: drought, flood, Indians, gentiles. But for Hamblin, the MMM was totally indefensible, as barbaric as any perpetrated by Walkara or the other savages, and as senseless. MMM returned the Lamanites to heathen ways as diabolic as any atrocities recorded in The Book of Mormon. In returning the natives to war paint and bloodletting, the perpetrators defiled the very purpose for the whiteman's coming among the primitives. For Jacob, it was also a second tragedy: the carnage had been spurred on by the very people sent to civilize and Christianize the natives. What hurt most of all was that the massacre's perpetrators, peers in the gospel with Jacob, had for him lost their spiritual focus and perspective. The purpose for being there was not to turn the natives to hate or vengeance but to build them from their fallen state to the spiritual plateau like that attained by Samuel the Lamanite.[39] He had been a mighty man among his people, prophesying of the Christ to come.

If Hamblin had agreed with perpetrators of the massacre, perhaps matters would have been simpler for him. But ecclesiastical order was now in disarray, utter chaos and confusion; for could any local Church member again place trust in the higher officials who had ordered participation in the massacre? Jacob and the other Santa Clara missionaries could not pretend it hadn't happened; they undoubtedly wished most earnestly it had not. But all the wishing they might do wouldn't change the facts.[40]

All of this, of course, is heavy argument against Hamblin being present for the massacre. It was not his nature to be near and make no effort to stop an act which would all but totally destroy his devoted missionary efforts. In fact, with all that is known about Hamblin's influence with the natives of southern Utah, he most certainly could have prevented the massacre had he been present, or even known about it. Likewise, the character of Albert, and the way Jacob had brought the lad up, suggest that the story remembered by Rebecca Dunlap is not accurate. Her account simply goes against all else that was known about Hamblin and the influence he had on the Indian population, including on his own foster son, Albert.

In a letter to Brigham Young, Apostle George A. Smith wrote about Jacob's missionary dilemma following the massacre. He said rumors had circulated that efforts were made by some conspirators to "buy the Indians off" in order to save the wagon train. "I have been told that since this transaction [attempting to buy the Piutes off] many of the Indians who had previously learned to labor have evinced a determination not to work, and that the moral influence of the event upon the civilization of the Indians has been very prejudicial."[41]

Adds historian B.H. Roberts: "For they had seen that their white neighbors, instructors in industry, had been capable of an act of treachery and savagery equal to their own, even if not more treacherous and murderous...Surely there could be no more whiteman's moral and spiritual influence over the redmen after what the latter had witnessed at Mountain Meadows."[42]

In a master's thesis reffering to the MMM, David K. Flake wrote: "Three years of missionary work were suddenly set to naught by Mormon participation alongside the Indians in an act of destruction the likes of which the missionaries had time and again told the Indians was bad."[43]

It was a difficult time, indeed, for missionary work in Dixie. Hamblin had exhorted the Piedes, Santa Claras, Moapites, Mohaves and other Southwest tribes to neither steal, lie nor murder. Now, whitemen had done it all on a grand scale. All were hypocrites, including Jacob, to expect them to change from their traditional ways to take on the whiteman's.[44] There might be future moral and spiritual influence over the redmen but no one could foresee when that time might come. If ever there was a time to give up on further missionary work and simply focus on wresting a better living from the arid land, Hamblin must have felt it was now.

In time, a few of the principle participants like Philip Klingensmith, feeling ostracized in Cedar City and Parowan for what was clearly spiritual fanaticism run amok, left for other parts even before federal marshals began snooping about. The tragedy had, indeed, divided the communities. There were those claiming to have "done our duty," and those who wondered if they could ever again obey the will of their local Church leaders. How could ecclesiastical authorities in the centerplace of Zion have chosen such people to be spiritual examples and leaders? Or were these simply once good men who had become unbalanced in the brooding of perceived abuses…until the latter at last eroded common sense and Christian decency?

Jacob was, as history records, doing two things while the massacre took place. First, he was taking ten Indian chieftains to meet the Great Mormon captain, Brigham Young, in Salt Lake City. Brooks said it was for the purpose of enlisting the chiefs to help physically battle Mormon enemies;[45] yet the use of physical force was never condoned by Hamblin and was completely against his nature following his experiences in Tooele in which he vowed to never shed Lamanite blood. More likely for his visit to Salt Lake City is the reason Jacob gives in his "Journal and Letters" (p. 46): the chiefs "were taken to shops, gardens, orchards and other places to show them the advantage of industry and encourage or induce them to labor for a living."

But if either Jacob or Brigham wanted the chiefs to participate in an attack against the Fancher train, it would be rather late to discuss the matter now. Returning to Dixie would require a little over a week, and the emigrants were already on the verge of departing Utah Mormondom at Mountain Meadows.

Jacob's second reason for the trip was to marry Sarah Priscilla Leavitt, the younger sister of his good friend, Dudley. In so doing, Hamblin unwittingly introduced his bride into what can hardly be called a happy first impression of her new home, let alone a happy honeymoon. An attempt to prevent Priscilla from seeing bodies of the dead Fancher group failed; she witnessed the carnage with Thales Haskell's new bride, Margaret. In her unpublished diary, Margaret says on p. 2 that some two weeks after the massacre she and her husband, along with newlyweds Jacob and Priscilla, had to pass on the road directly through Mountain Meadows in order to reach home. "I saw several of the bodies," she said. Thales elaborates. "We were horrified when we saw the dead bodies, we hurried back to the wagons and drove away as soon as possible. This was a terrible experience to have while journeying to our homes so far away from civilization, and for the rest of our lives we thought in horror of the experience of that day."[46]

Hamblin's records his first look at the murder site as follows in his diary: "Oh! Horrible! indeed was the sight…language fails to picture the scene of blood and carnage…my feelings at this time I will not attempt to describe…This was one of the gloomiest times I ever passed through."[47]

Hamblin and Haskell saw the carnage as work of a fanatical faction. But that faction included their leaders, men they were expected to follow in Church business other than direct mission proselyting. It was a time to possess one's own personal testimony. A borrowed one would not do.

Until the guilty were punished, the missionaries must also sort out among the Piutes and, indeed, among all of their Church peers, who could be trusted in the Lord's work and who could not.

As a second wife in the Mormon practice of polygamy, Priscilla spent the first few weeks in her new home, along with first wife Rachel, in caring for the seventeen (some accounts say eighteen) young children spared in the massacre. Some were wounded badly; by the time Jacob arrived home, Rachel was already in trauma, attempting to save one girl; her arm had been badly shattered by a lead ball.

The chore of caring for these children apparently fell to Hamblin and his family because his Pinto home on the eastern edge of Pine Valley Mountain was approximately three miles from the crime scene. Another reason was that the hospitable (and non-participatory) Hamblins would take good care of the young orphans without drawing major ire or attention. But it is ironic that one who took no part in the deed had to shoulder such a heavy brunt of the load in ministering to the sick and wounded. The Hamblin's saw to it that the frightened young children, spared because of their age, were well cared for by other families. For those orphans directly cared for, the federal government later reimbursed hosting families until relatives or suitable homes could be located.[48]

As a side note, Hamblin took a trip across the Colorado River at government expense to look for a child rumored taken there by Indians. Brooks says Jacob would have gone on his own anyway to do missionary work and may have used the pretext of finding a child to perform his missionary duties at U.S. government expense.[49] He did not find any missing child across the Colorado. In this, Hamblin probably engaged in his only missionary journey for which he did not personally foot the expense.

As for the Indian chiefs, Tutsegavit (Yamnawant tribe), Canosh (spelled Kanosh by Corbett) with the Pauvants, and eight others accompanied Hamblin and Haskell to Salt Lake City. Hamblin says they were all treated very cordially by Brigham Young and other Mormon leaders. Nothing is recorded about any impressions expressed by the Indians regarding their look at Mormon civilization. Jacob then went to Tooele to see Priscilla; the matter of wooing and winning could not be hurried, even for a practical man like Jacob Hamblin. Meanwhile, the chiefs went home. Did they return in time to participate in the massacre? Brooks infers in *John Doyle Lee* that they did: "They would be back in the south to overtake the Fancher train at Parowan."[50] Yet, Brooks carries this on page xiii in her *Mountain Meadows*

Massacre: "Whether or not Kanosh and his band were at Mountain Meadows we do not know."[51] To be sure, there is no actual documentation that any of the chiefs who accompanied Hamblin to Salt Lake City returned to participate in the massacre.

If they did, Jacob's mission of preaching peace and brotherly love to the Lamanites had utterly failed. The chiefs were, of course, paramount in any endeavor to reach the hearts of their tribal members.[52]

At a later time, Jacob faced a formidable task. Much of the burial of the one hundred and twenty dead had to be done a second time. The work detail called out from Cedar City for that unpleasant duty had not been forewarned of its task and didn't seem to have much stomach for the assignment. Hamblin says he found that wolves and animals had been at work. To he and Albert fell the unpleasant task, after the ground thawed in the spring, of giving the dead a proper burial.[53]

Some non-Mormons complained that the saints did not honor the slain in a decent burial. At least two did in the persons of Jacob and Albert Hamblin.[54] There were probably others as well who remain unnamed.

What were the motives of the MMM aggressors? Numerous accounts say it was for revenge. Brooks reports that many of these emigrants were from western Missouri (frequently repeated) where Mormon relatives of the settlers were murdered and/or injured at places like Haun's Mill.[55] However, additional research since Brook's treatise on the massacre indicate no known inhabitants of Missouri during the Mormon expulsion period were present at Mountain Meadows. A recent census study by Ricks College professor Lawrence Coates concludes that only three families among the Fancher party that had ever lived in Missouri and that "they lived there after the Mormons were expelled."[56] Nor were any in the Fancher party from Illiniois, where the Mormons built their city of Nauvoo. There was some talk of "Missouri Wildcats" in the Fancher group; it was said they riled both Indians and whites as they traveled the length of Utah. If locals wouldn't sell them food they wanted,

Brooks says there were reports[57] of emigrants "popping off the
heads of chickens in the streets" and whipping oxen named
"Brigham"and "Heber."[58] Yet, there is no indication they were
from Jackson, Clay, Ray, Daviess or any of the other counties
where a long line of thefts and murders and sexual abuses perpetrated upon the Mormon people are detailed in a number of histories. LDS historian Robert Mullen says that the emigrants
became increasingly obnoxious as they worked their way south
through the Mormon hamlets. "They called the Mormon women
'whores,' they poisoned water holes used by the Indians, and
they threatened to join federal forces in subjugating the
Mormons."[59]

But while some of the Fancher party reportedly boasted of
murdering Latter-day Saint leaders, and of raping Mormon
women, there is no known direct evidence whatsoever linking
any member of the Fancher party with any actual, physical
depredation upon any Latter-day Saint. The closest link between
any Fancher member and any act of violence would be that LDS
missionary Parley P. Pratt was murdered in Arkansas on May
13, 1857. Mullen says that the Arkansas travelers "boasted to the
Mormons that they had been in the party that murdered Joseph
Smith" and claimed to know something about the fatal shooting
of Parley P. Pratt." Mullen adds, "There is no reason now [1966]
to believe there was validity in either story. The 'mob' that killed
Joseph Smith had been carefully identified." Pratt had been
killed by one Hector H. McLean, who insisted that his wife left
him "at Pratt's instigation." The bottom line is that while the
Fanchers may have made claims far from prudent, later research
proved their boastings invalid. Yet, as Mullen sums up succinctly: "The Mormons of Iron County had no way to evaluate these
stories" at the time.[60]

In a paper prepared for the Utah Historical Society, Kenneth
W. Godfrey quotes a letter to the *Daily Alta California* from P.M.
Warn (who says he followed the Fancher train through central
and southern Utah): "They [the emigrants] were very free
speaking of the Mormons, their conduct was said to be reckless
and they would commit little acts of annoyance for the purpose

of provoking the saints. Feeling perfectly safe in their arms and numbers, they seemed to set at defiance all the powers that could be brought against them." Godfrey points out that Warn was not LDS, "and seems to have no reason to write a report favorable to the Latter-day Saints."[61] The letter was printed six weeks following the massacre.

Apostle Smith also said he had heard of the Fancher party "threatening the destruction" of Fillmore.[62] Smith told of reports the Fanchers poisoned cattle which resulted in the death of the Pahvant Indians. This story, which originated with the Pahvants,, may have become exaggerated in the retelling. The number of dead Indians varies with each report and it is difficult to ascertain years later precisely what did happen. Brooks suggests the story of poisoned water or beef is apocryphal.[63] However, Indian reports of Fanchers poisoning beef seem to have been widespread.

Hamblin says news reached him that the Fanchers threatened to rob Mormon settlers of more than petty goods. "They threatened, when the army came into the north end of the Territory, to get a good outfit from the weaker settlements in the south."[64] This reference to stealing horses and wagons would be more than casually offensive anywhere in the West in the 1850s. Horse thieves were reportedly hung in many parts of the West during that era. Whether the concept of the Fanchers stealing "outfits" originated with some source other than Lee's claims given in the Lee Transcript is not known. It is not mentioned anywhere but in the above reference by Hamblin, who may well have first heard it from Lee.

Jacob's record shows that he met the Fancher party in early September, 1857 at Corn Creek (a clearwater spring near present day Kanosh) on their way to southern Utah. He was with George A. Smith at the time. "[The Fancher party] inquired of me about the road and wrote down the information I gave them. They expressed a wish to lay by at some suitable place to recruit their teams before crossing the desert. I recommended to them for this purpose, the south end of Mountain Meadows, three miles from where my family resided."[65]

If Hamblin knew at that time about any threats made by the Fanchers, he did not so state in any of his writings. And why should it be that the Fanchers breathed fire against the Mormons all the way into southern Utah, then suddenly held their tongues within Hamblin's hearing? Perhaps it was because of his friendly offer for them to stop at the Meadows (legally leased in Jacob's name only) with its lush grass and water. Or perhaps it was an intimidating presence of ten Indian chiefs. In any event, it is singular that Hamblin met the Fanchers and had no quarrel with them in the early fall of 1857. Jacob was known as a peacemaker among both acrimonious Indians and white settlers. Did he exhibit some of those peacemaking traits here among "gentiles" as well?

Hamblin's personal "Journal and Letters" (p. 46) says Apostle G. A. Smith mentioned perceived trouble with the Fanchers: "There was a strange atmosphere surrounding [the Fancher party]. George A. spoke of it. Said he believed some evil would befall them before they got through." This statement may have been discussed and recorded by Hamblin following the massacre. Thus, it is not known if Smith's "prophecy" came more from Heaven or from hindsight.

On Aug. 7, 1858, Smith wrote to Young that he had tried to fully investigate the affair, hearing reports Lee was at the Meadows "during [the] combat but for what purpose, or how they conducted themselves, or whether, indeed, they were there at all, I have not learned."[66] But Jacob would have certainly given Smith more than a vague "report" when they went together to see Governor Cummings. There is no mention of Smith reporting what Hamblin must surely have told both him and Brigham. The reason for this is not known other than that Smith may have been intent on downplaying ill will in Mormon ranks about the massacre until more facts were known. It does seem true, for whatever reason, that Smith was slow in gathering and reporting those facts.

Brigham writes that John D. repeated such lurid tales of bloodletting by Indians "that I told him to stop, as from what I had already heard by rumor, I did not wish my feelings harrowed up with a recital of details."[67] Clearly, if he knew about Mormon involvement, the "Lion of the Lord" was in a difficult position. All about him were reports of a U.S. Army coming to annihilate the people he was entrusted to nourish and protect. Then, his devoted servants in the south over-reacted and thought they were doing their duty as loyal Church members, serving he, Brigham, in destroying Zion's enemies. How many brethren were involved here? Had they acted sincerely in declaring it a military obligation to participate? Must he cut all from the Church who had served with such loving and coura- geous dedication for these many years...these same souls who stood loyally and courageously for unpopular beliefs against a horde of bitter enemies in Missouri and Illinois? How would it be determined who should be cut off—ostracized from promise of celestial salvation and for now, become bereft of any local social standing? The value of the latter in isolated and provincial Utah of the middle 1800s cannot be overstated. Trust of neigh- bors would surely be shattered, loss of wife or wives imminent. Here were those who had rallied with the children of God to enter an unknown land no one wanted! Here were those who had carried out the Lord's will against all odds and enemies. If pressed to find the guilty, would each man be set against his neighbor—the work of converting the Indians and building an extended Zion totally thwarted? How could it be decided who was more than guilty than another? And what had he or other Church leaders said which could be so misconstrued as to justi- fy the death of one hundred and twenty souls about to pass from the area? Were the leaders partly to blame in that they had spoken of the Indians helping to fight Zion's enemies with the coming of Johnston's Armies?

It must, indeed, have been a time of deep mourning, and of deep supplication for the wisdom of Heaven. Here were Brigham Young's loyal subjects sent to the remote corners of Zion seeking approval for what they apparently felt was service to a spiritual cause shared by all Church members.

Strangely for one who chronicled so much of LDS Church activity in southern Utah during the 1850s, Bleak says almost nothing of the massacre in his official history of the LDS Church. The meticulous Church historian may have simply wished it was not linked to Church business. But how could one say that when it involved the ecclesiastical elite of southern Utah? There are also a number of histories, including *Under Dixie Sun* (with a chapter by Brooks) which scarcely mention the MMM before, during or after.[68] The reason may well be that the book was meant to be a pleasant history of southern Utah progress; Brooks apparently agreed to keep it that way.

Corbett says without any footnotes or references that some emigrant trains "took potshots" at Indians they would see along the way "as if they were dogs."[69] Corbett seems to infer that the Fanchers did so. It might be a reference to Brigham Young con- jecturing why the Indians could have attacked the Fanchers. But it would appear at this time that Young was under the impres- sion from Lee's report that the tragedy was solely the work of redmen. Yet the truth had to be known with Hamblin's report of what Lee himself told Jacob. It was just hard to swallow.

In any event, as the Fancher train rolled deeper past the vil- lages of southern Utah, depredations and boasting did not set well with local inhabitants. From all credible accounts, the Piute Indians did become infuriated with the Fancher train at some point near Corn Creek, insisting that the emigrants poisoned a cow there and that several Indians died as a result of eating strychnine-laced beef.[70] Why anyone with any common sense would so rile up local savages at whose mercy they were is any- one's guess; but such reports of the Fanchers seem to have been widely circulated by the time the wagon train reached Beaver. Stories of Fancher indignities reached a crescendo by the time the train neared Parowan, 35 miles to the south, and many in Cedar City were angered before the train ever reached that point.

The Piutes of southern Utah were known to be a rather backward tribe. They would not of themselves have sufficient firearms with which to attack a company of one hundred and twenty armed emigrants. Yet, they had them when attacking the train. This would be enough to indict local whitemen who must surely have supplied the weapons of war even if they hadn't actively participate in the massacre. Whoever did so, whether Lee or others, would have gone against the thinking of Southern Utah Indian Mission President Hamblin, much more inclined to supply Indians with scriptures than the desire and weapons for spilling blood.

But to better understand the environment prevailing during the fall of 1857, one must know more about Johnston's Army and its march on Utah. History records that during this fateful autumn, a U.S. militia, openly boasting and cursing what they would do upon penetrating Utah, sent panic through many corners of the Mormon empire. Officially, the soldiers came to quell a "Mormon rebellion." Reports had reached Washington D.C. that Mormon leader Brigham Young refused to seat an appointed territorial governor and had destroyed important civil records. Without recalling the extensive patriotic services by the Mormon Battallion in 1847, or taking time to determine truth of the sedition charges, President James Buchanan sent out an army to "put down the Mormon rebellion."[71]

In the meantime, Young sent out guerrillas like Lot Smith and Orrin Porter Rockwell to burn wagons, drive off stock and generally stall the advancing army until the truth could be known. Through non-Mormon emissaries, U.S. President Buchanan finally became convinced the costly military maneuver was a colossal mistake (some called it "Buchanan's Blunder")[72] and the army reversed its earlier intentions, camping peacefully outside Salt Lake Valley near today's Fairfield until called into the Civil War.

But the threat of the federal government coming to annihilate them resurrected old wounds among the Mormons. They had been driven out of the United States, at least once with the help of such government directives as Missouri Governor Lilburn Boggs' infamous Mormon extermination order.[73] Redress attempts in Washington also brought President Martin Van Buren's famous (and seemingly empty) words which yet reverberate in every sympathetic history: "Your cause is just but I can do nothing for you; if I take up your fight, I should lose the entire vote of the state of Missouri."[74] Finally finding solace in their western mountain sanctuary, the saints determined to be driven no further. It was time to take a stand!

Into this tense mood came the Fancher party. Brooks says she feels that speeches made by George A. Smith, Mormon apostle to southern Utah, encouraging Indians and whites to "stand together" against the "gentile" enemy, fired up the saints to battle.[75] Brooks says Lee was present for at least some of Smith's "lecture tour" and seemed enflamed by the speeches. Brooks depicts Lee as one who still smoldered from past depredations upon him and felt justified in "getting even" with the gentile enemy. As she puts it, "[Lee] made it clear that he had no love for the Christians who drove us from their midst; at one time he publicly rebuked a brother who preached kindness to their enemies, saying that he himself would not hesitate to steal from the Gentiles who had so often robbed the Saints."[76]

If so, it would have been a philosophy opposite to the attitude of Hamblin. There is nothing in his writings hinting of revenge against anyone, although history certainly records he was often placed in jeapordy while following religious duty.[77]

There were some who remained hostile to passing emigrants even after the MMM.[78] Who might have been behind this is explored more fully in the chapter "The Trial of John D. Lee." Particularly unsettling to Hamblin was the idea of local Mormons gaining further plunder against travelers via local missionaries who were supposed to be acting under his supervision. It was, in effect, a verbal civil war among Dixie Church leaders. Some spoke of "secret orders" to waylay emigrants, while Hamblin was in the very act of seeing they were protected! In addition to concern for passing trains was Jacob's worry about what this lingering conspiracy would do to the Lamanites. He and his associates were sent to southern Utah to build up the Lord's kingdom among the Lamanites. Someone among his peers had missed the vision.

It was also reported that Jacob's close ally in so many difficulties, Ira Hatch, had accompanied Indians in pursuing and killing at least one escapee who might "tell tales."[79] With his interpretive skills in Indian dialects, Hatch was later valuable to Hamblin in visiting Indian tribes across the Colorado. Jacob makes no mention of Hatch's previous activities in the MMM. Quite likely, both men sought to forget what had happened, and hoped to get their minds on more pleasant and constructive endeavors.

If Lee felt vengeance for what had happened to him in Missouri, he was not alone in much of Mormondom. The idea that Missouri should be punished for multiple nefarious offenses prevailed strongly in the LDS culture as late as 1880,[80] long after the Civil War had cruelly levelled Jackson and other counties near slave-free Kansas caught in the border war between North and South. These were counties, of course, which had driven out saints in mid-winter. (If the saints had remained they would most certainly have been pummeled by both sides, as were all citizens of western Missouri during the mid 1860s.) Citing news from May 2, 1880, a Franklin County, Idaho (predominately LDS) newsletter carrying information about local Church and school activities interprets it this way: "Telegraphic news was read...showing the terrible judgments that had been poured out in the state of Missouri resulting in great destruction of life and property."[81] No explanation was given by the newsletter editor for inclusion of this singular item of vengeance against Missouri. Apparently none was necessary for a predominately LDS readership.

Nearly a century and a half later, under cool reasoning of Christian logic, one must ask why massacre participants did not wait for an answer from ecclesiastical superiors. Were they more intent on self-defense against a perceived enemy, or more intent on punishing one which might slip from their grasp? For while the Fanchers may have talked unwisely, they made no known overt physical act to force any settler into a position of direct self-defense. Mountain Meadows, on the Old Spanish Trail,[82] was a day or more west (California side) of Cedar City and at least half a day from Santa Clara or New Harmony. If the emigrants wanted to steal an outfit, they could have gotten one from Jacob Hamblin's home some three miles away. Nothing of the kind happened. The emigrants would soon head into what is now Nevada, onto the lower Virgin River, then out into the barren desert. That would have led the wagon train directly away from the territory of Utah and Mormondom. They offered no further threat at Mountain Meadows, real or imagined.

Hamblin saw no compromise in the matter. While he could perceive and even understand some feelings of fear on the part of his associates, he could see no excuse at the time for what happened at Mountain Meadows. Neither have any surfaced since.

End Notes, Chapter Five

1 The 1990 memorial replaces a small stone base plaque which was displayed on a small, winding dirt road half a mile west of Utah 18. The latter stood for decades as the only marker to this tragedy.

   Several historians make it *Charles* Fancher but he will be referred to here by his first name given on the monument. Also, while the monument lists Capt. John Baker as a co-leader, the emigrant train has emerged in history as the "Fancher party." That name will be used herein.

2. The book has gone through a number of printings, including paperback, 1991. Theme in all printings is that John D. Lee acted upon orders of ecclesiastical and military superiors.

3. The Transcript of John D. Lee's trials, referred to here as the Lee Transcript (copy of U.S. court records, 1875-76) is on microfilm at the LDS Church Historians Office, 50 N. Temple, Salt Lake City, Utah, Archives Search Room. Also see *The Trials of John D. Lee*, (excerpts), with commentary, Fay E. Reber, J. Reuben Clark Law Library, BYU, Provo, Utah. A complete book transcript of the first trial (*The Lee Trial*) can be found in the BYU Special Collections Room, BYU Lee Library.

4. Juanita Brooks, *John Doyle Lee*, p. 210.

5. This is a constant theme of JDL. See *MMM*, p. 72.

6. Letter from G.A. Smith to Brigham Young dated Aug. 17, 1858, says 10 Indians died from poisoned beef at Corn Creek. The number varied with telling, but all accounts seemed to agree one or more Indians died from eating beef poisoned by emigrants. *History of Brigham Young*, 1857, pp. 481f. See also "Autobiography of Thales H. Smith," p. 16. Brooks suggests that the Indian cattle ate a poisoned weed, JDL, p. 205.

7. Lee Transcript, Hamblin testimony. Lee, *Confessions*, p. 233. See also MMM, p. 72. Little, p. 54.

8. Lee Transcript, Haslam testimony. Also Little, p. 45. Hamblin's statement is incomplete here. For complete letter, see Roberts, *Comprehensive History of Church*, Vol. 4, pp. 149-50, f. Also Haslam affidavit, Supplement to Charles Penrose's *Mountain Meadows Massacre*, pp. 94-95.

9. Ibid, p. 151.

10. "The Mountain Meadows Massacre and its Historians: Separating Myth from Reality," Kenneth W. Godfrey, paper presented before the Mormon History Assn., pp. 20-21.

11. Roberts calls it the "most lamentable episode in...the history of the Church." *Comprehensive History of the Church*, p. 139. Certainly nothing in LDS history brought more condemnation upon the Mormon Church for a longer period of time than the MMM.

12. Endnotes, *Desert Saints*, Anderson, p. 305, no. 21. Haight is incorrectly listed here as president of the Parowan Stake. He was president at Cedar City.

13. *Confessions*, p. 232.

14. Ibid, p. 245. Lee always insisted that he explained to President Young what happened and was told to say nothing about Mormon involvement. Lee also maintained in *Confessions* that Brigham said, "what you did was right " etc. The latter statement is not corroborated by anyone else. Also, see Roberts (CH-Y, p. 152) who says that in his judgment, "Lee...can never be accepted as a reliable witness." Paul Bailey, *Buckskin Apostle*, pp. 164-174, says the same. But before Brooks' MMM and JDL, the world knew little other than the name John D. Lee in placing blame for what happened.

15. Little, pp. 59-60

16. Lee Transcript, Hamblin testimony. For presence of other Indian boy, John, see MMM, p. 107.

17. MMM, p. 107. This seems a conclusion reached by Brooks and is not specifically footnoted.

18. Little, pp. 59-60.

19. Ibid. Hamblin's zeal to prosecute the perpetrators of the massacre seems most apparent here.

20. Forney letter to Judge Elias Smith, *Deseret News*, May 11, 1859.

21. "Thales Hastings Haskell" ("assembled" by A. E. Smith), p. 24.

22. "Autobiography of Thales H. Haskell," p. 16.

23. Little, p. 46. Hamblin says, "We met John D. Lee at Fillmore" which would seem to indicate the presence of Thales Haskell. But in Jacob's testimony of Lee's second trial, he seems to be saying that he, J. Hamblin was the only one actually within Lee's hearing as Lee related the story of the massacre.

24. Albert also recounted the incident but did not name Lee as a participant in killing anyone. A written response to this effect was given to Brevet Major J. H. Carleton, May 1859. See 57 Congress, 1 session, House Document 605, p. 6.

25. M. F. Cowley, *Journal of Wilford Woodruff*, 1909, Salt Lake City, Utah, p. 388. Cowley refers to Lee's initial statement to Young (no mention of any white participation) as "truthful"; apparently it was wholly believed by

Woodruff and Young at the time. Cowley adds: "If President Young neglected at this time to give the report as much attention as it perhaps should have received, and if an investigation was not immediately instituted, there is ample excuse…the army [Johnston's Army] was pressing upon the people and uttering dire threats as to what would take place when it reached the Valleys."

26. MMM, pp. 105-6.
27. Compare Brooks' *John D. Lee*, p. 332 with her MMM, p. 107.
28. JDL, p. 332.
29. Ibid.
30. Ibid. "The net result was …a great many intermarriages with mixed loyalties to the fourth generation."
31. A notebook kept by John Higbee (17 pages) carries the theme that whiteman's help was "necessary to appease the Indians." Typescript in Utah Historical Society, Salt Lake City. In JDL, p. 212, Brooks says this account is signed "Bull Valley Snort," but there is no question that Higbee is the author. See also MMM, p. 167 and letter from G. A. Smith to Brigham Young, History of Brigham Young, ms. entry for Aug. 17, 1858, pp. 929-937.
32. JDL, p. 365. Lee also said Hamblin had "pretended sympathy" for MMM victims and "stole cattle" belonging to emigrants. *Confessions*, p. 270.
33. See also the *Richmond Conservator* (Missouri) for Aug. 11, 1887.
34. *World Book Encyclopedia*, N-O, p. 455.
35. The My Lai Massacre in Vietnam involved a Lieutenant William Laws Calley who was court-martialed in March of 1968 for what he claims was "merely following orders," while destroying more than 100 innocent civilians in a raid ordered by higher ranking U.S. Army officers. Arthur Everet et al, *My Lai Massacre*, Dell Publishing Co., New York, N.Y., 1971.
36. Little, pp. 40-41; The idea is also summed up by Baily, p. 174.
37. Emma's complaint about Hamblin, JDL, p. 325. Wives treated John D. more coldly, Ibid, p. 295.
38. Hamblin explained to authorities the potential danger that Emma was in and procured help in her behalf. Ibid, p. 342.
39. *Book of Mormon*, Hel. chapters 13-15; date given as 6 B.C. Promises made to Lamanites, Alma 9: 16-18, 24.
40. Some of this is the author's conclusion based on reading of Jacob's J & L, pp. 16-36.
41. "A compromise to…buy the Indians off." Interestingly, Smith concludes, "For the citizens to have attacked and killed the Indians in defense of the emigrants would have been little less than suicide." "History of Brigham Young," ms. entry Aug. 17, 1858, pp. 929-937.

42. CH-C, pp 165-6.

43. "A history of Mormon missionary work with the Hopi, Navaho and Zuni Indians," p. 15.

44. Little, p. 43. The Piedes and Santa Claras had often told Hamblin they could not be expected to change their traditional ways. Jacob laments that the redmen can't be persuaded to change their ways if the teachers (whitemen) won't change theirs. The MMM seemed to give the Indian an express excuse to resist further change.

45. Brooks seems eager here to involve Hamblin in military plans for the Indians. She says, "Jacob Hamblin, faced with his new responsibility for the Indians and concerned about making them understand their part in the approaching war...," etc. MMM, pp. 40-41. But after his Tooele experiences, Jacob shunned violence. Why would he now teach violence to the Lamanites in his charge? Why not accept the reason Hamblin himself gave for going?

Interestingly, Corbett says: "It is quite probable that the Mountain Meadows Massacre would not have taken place had the senior Indian chiefs, [who were in Salt Lake City] been present to curb the young hotheads of the tribes." Corbett, pp. 124-25.

Regarding the number of chiefs present at Salt Lake City, see *Journal History of the Church*, Sept. 1, 1857, which says that 12 chiefs were present.

46. "Autobiography-THH," p. 16.

47. Hamblin Diary, 1854-57, (microfilm, Church Historian's Office, LDS Office Bldg.), reel 1, folder 3, second item, pp. 41-42.

48. JDL, p. 216. Brooks includes many details about Rachel's loving care for orphans of the massacre. Some complained that Hamblin benefitted financially (government money for care of the wounded) from the massacre. JDL, p. 251.

49. MMM, pp. 101-103. Forney letter to Kirk Anderson, May 15, 1859, published in (weekly) *The Valley Tan* (Salt Lake City newspaper) May 10, 1859. Corbett, pp. 148-49, explanation. Source: letter from William H. Roberts, Feb. 29, 1869, published in *The Valley Tan*, V. 2, No. 16. Roberts describes *The Valley Tan* (pp. 521-2) as a "bitter anti-Mormon sheet circulating primarily at Camp Floyd." It lasted 18 months.

50. *John D. Lee*, p. 203. MMM, p. 42

51. MMM, p. XlII

52. It should not be supposed here that a Piute chief necessarily commanded large numbers of braves. Status of chiefs grew and waned in popularity; a sub-chief

might take over among small bands. Nevertheless, most chiefs were general centers of influence for others of their tribe.

53. Several parties attended to burial at various times. A work detail was sent out immediately after the massacre, but many of the bodies placed in shallow graves were dug up by animals. Hamblin took up the task one more time in the spring. Lee Transcript, Hamblin testimony.

54. One James Lynch complained in a court affidavit (Lee Transcript court records) that the Mormons, including Hamblin, and government Indian agent Jacob Forney, did not see to it that the dead received a decent burial. Lynch makes many accusations contrary to Forney's findings. He also makes many obvious mistakes (Lee is a Mormon "president," Hamblin is a Mormon "bishop," "Cedar County," etc.).

54. Lee Transcript, Hamblin testimony.

55. Seventeen Mormons were brutally murdered by Missouri mobsters at Haun's Mill in western Missouri; others were seriously injured. All attempts at redress were denied by state officials and legislators. DHC, Vol. 4, pp. 183-6.

56. Godfrey, p. 28, f. 72.

57. JDL, p. 203.

58. This is the theme of most LDS histories. The theme of *Confessions* and other anti-Mormon histories generally agree, but place more blame on the Mormons.

59. Mullen, LDS: *The Mormons Yesterday and Today*, p. 154.

60. Ibid

61. Godfrey, p. 11.

62. Bancroft, *History of Utah*, p. 549; *Confessions,* pp. 218-219. Repeated, explained by Roberts, CH-C, p. 142.

63. JDL, p. 205.

64. Little, p. 45.

65. Ibid.

66. "History of Brigham Young," manuscript entry for Aug. 17, 1858, pp. 929-937.

67. Lee Transcript, Young deposition.

68. Chapter titled "History of Washington County, 1850-1950. P. 32 does contain this statement after citing the MMM: "Now the natives wished to live by plunder."

69. Corbett, p. 116.

70. Brooks quotes T.W. Cropper, 15 years old at the time, as being present when the Fancher emigrants camped on Corn Creek and "poisoned it," seeing dead cattle etc. "People believed the latter, and it gave them one more offense to add to the mounting list," JDL, p. 205. An

Indian chief also testified in the first trial of Lee that he
and his braves attacked for promise of material gain.
"There was no poison or provocation involved." "The
Lee Trial," p. 53, Daily Tribune Printing Co., Salt Lake
City, Utah, 1875, BYU Special Collections Library, Provo,
Utah.

71. JWW, pp. 384-393. This account of an approaching
Johnston's Army from the journal of Wilford Woodruff
provides perhaps the most grim and forbidding por-
trayal of this event in LDS history.
72. *N.Y. Tribune*, June 12, 1858; *N. Y. Times*, June 14, 1858.
BY-C, p. 181.
73. *Documentary History of the Church*, Vol. 3, p. 175.
74. *Documentary History of the Church*, Vol. 4, p. 80. See also
p. 89
75. MMM, pp. 35, 36, 60; Also see text of speech in Appendix.
76. Thomas Brown, "Journal of the Southern Utah Indian
Mission," March 18, 1855.
77. Hamblin was placed in several extremely dangerous
situations in following Brigham Young's orders. One
reason Jacob might not have complained about the
same was his assurance he would never have his blood
spilled by the redman if he did not thirst for theirs.
This assurance, says Hamblin (Little, p. 25), came to
him during the Tooele period. With that trust, Hamblin
did not waver at "dangerous" missions assigned him.
78. "For some reason a plan had been laid and matured in
their mind to kill off this company and take the
spoil...they had "secret instructions." Hamblin Diary
1854-57; (on microfilm, Church Historian's Office.)
Hamblin informed them he had instructions from
Brigham Young to see the company through safe and
"I would stand by them to the last."
79. MMM, p. 100. Three men who escaped the initial massacre were tracked from Mountain Meadows and killed
by Indians. This account says Ira Hatch was present.
Furthermore, C. P. Lyford says he learned that "an honest old Mormon (most likely Jacob Hamblin "owner of
the ground then and now,") was given a letter from an
Indian chief, Jackson, written by the Fanchers seeking
help. Jackson gave it to Hamblin who said he showed it
to John D. Lee "who destroyed it," Lyford, *The Mormon
Problem*, pp. 296-99. See also MMM, pp. 98-99. See John
H. Beadle, *Western Wilds and the Men Who Redeem Them*,
pp. 500-01. This is never mentioned by Hamblin. As
sub-Indian agent, Hamblin was also asked to have
Indians help him capture Lee, but refused. Hamblin
told U.S. Judge John Cradlebaugh, "It was contrary to

my instructions [from Forney] to encourage the Indians in any way to interfere with whites." *History of Brigham Young*, 1859, pp. 471f.

80. This is not to say comments were not written or stated at a later date complaining of Missouri atrocities against Mormons.

81. "Cache Valley Newsletter," Editor Newell Hart, June, 1979, Preston, Idaho, gathered from local data written in 1880 in Frankin County.

82. The "Spanish Trail," looping into central Utah, had been used off and on since the early 1800s to get from Sante Fe to southern California. The distance of some 1,200 miles could have been shortened considerably by going straight east-west, but lacked sufficient water sources across the vast Arizona-California desert to make it practical. After wending north as far as Castle Dale, Utah to the edge of Manti Mountain, the route swung southwest past Beaver to Mountain Meadows through present-day Gunlock, to the Las Vegas area and Los Angeles much as does today's I-15 (U.S. 91-466 on older maps). See story by Jason Swensen, *Deseret News*, B-2, Jan. 7, 1995, for attempts to locate the precise trail in some areas.

Chapter Six

Reverberations

As soon as news about Mountain Meadows reached the nation's press, the howling of anti-Mormon wolves seeking Brigham Young's jugular echoed across the land. He had masterminded the massacre; or at the very least, it was his teachings which had caused the murders. If not that, his vengeful Church henchmen should have been held on a tighter leash.[1]

As time went on, a clamor arose for the guilty to be apprehended. No less could be expected. It was well known that the Indians alone could not have slain the one hundred and twenty. Whitemen helped out and only Mormons were present. Therefore, a Mormon or Mormons must pay for the crime

The press was especially hostile after Lee's first trial ended in a hung jury. Even though convicted in the second, the stain of MMM could not be erased, it seemed, nor could leaders of the Mormon Church be forgiven.

Yet, never at any time did Lee in his most vehement bitterness ever claim the MMM was ordered out of Salt Lake City. Lee's claim is that he told Brigham everything and the latter tried to cover up what happened. Lee even went so far as to say at times that Young condoned the tragedy; Lee was the only participant publicly making that claim.

Jacob Hamblin said Brigham told him "to say nothing more of the massacre until it could be put before the proper authorities."[2] Those authorities waited for some 18 years to hold their first trial.[3] Of course, little could be done without willing witnesses. Most of those were participants who had sworn not to implicate one another. U.S. Judge John Cradlebaugh went south with U.S. army protection determined to serve many arrest warrants in 1859; but he could not find those named in the indictments.[4]

No Mormon would testify at Lee's first trial (including Hamblin) in 1875, quite possibly because the Church seemed to be a defendent along with Lee. Openly anti-Mormon U.S. District Attorny R.N. Baskin repeatedly berated Latter-day Saints present, including the jury and what few witnesses could be mustered, for "parting with their manhood" and individuality in taking "secret oaths" in the Endowment House.[5] Not so surprisingly, the jury of eight Mormons (and one "gentile" who happened to be the jury foreman) voted for acquittal; three non-members voted for conviction. Considerable wrangling must have occurred, for court records show the jury to be out three days. When a newly appointed U.S. District Attorney, Sumner Howard, made it plain in the second trial that the excommunicated Lee, not the Church, was on trial, witnesses suddenly showed up and began to recall what happened. All twelve jurors voting for conviction were Latter-day Saints.[6]

Brooks says Brigham "ordered" witnesses to testify at the second trial;[7] whatever Young told them, this time they were there, including Jacob Hamblin. But the trial itself will be covered in the next chapter. Let us take a closer look at events leading up to the two trials.

According to William H. Rogers, government agent who accompanied Hamblin in locating the surviving MMM children (figures vary from sixteen to eighteen, depending on the scource),[8] Jacob told Rogers he knew some who had been involved. It is highly unlikely that he knew all of those involved, but it is significant that he knew some of them, including Lee, a thing he later testified to under oath. But Rogers says Hamblin would not name anyone at that particular time, that he would reveal names later to Governor Cummings. Rogers said Cummings told him that Hamblin did not do so.[9] This statement makes Jacob Hamblin appear to be an accomplice after the fact.

But it should be remembered that shortly after the massacre, Hamblin went to the governor with G.A. Smith to find and punish the guilty. He was put off by the new Governor Cummings. Rogers did not likely know this when making his statement. Rogers did seem satisfied that Hamblin was not in any way connected with the tragedy.

How much did Brigham know of Mormon involvement in the MMM before talking with Hamblin? Most probably nothing, according to Wilford Woodruff's journal. In the latter's presence, Lee told a story bereft of any white involvement. Woodruff wrote that Lee arrived from Harmony "with...an awful tale of blood." The Indians did it via their own volition/action. Thus, Brigham, if believing Jacob's report, would know that Lee initially lied.

Why did Brigham then wait so long to excommunicate Lee? Was it just an unpleasant task long procrastinated? Roberts (p. 178) says that Young early appointed Erastus Snow and W. L. Roundy to investigate Lee's participation, but Lee did not make any report on Lee's involvement until the year 1870. Lee was soon thereafter excommunicated.

Why did it take some thirteen years to search out the facts? It may be that Church leaders were not willing to face the truth that their own brethren could have participated in such brutal murders, putting off the sordid details of such a reprehensible act. Neither Brooks nor Backus pull any punches in telling of the treacherous manner in which the emigrants were lured from their wagon fortress and slain without mercy. Nor shall we here. Yet, none of this author's investigation finds any link between participants and Church leaders in Salt Lake City. The facts show that if the former had waited for the latter's guidance, there would have been no Mormon involvement in the massacre. That is a hard fact for enemies of the LDS Church then or now to swallow, but that is what the hard data shows.

Lee's excommunication was announced to him without a formal hearing of any kind. The latter did not fit well with Church critics. As Brigham explained it, he had heard Lee's side of it and the graphic tales of bloodletting by the Indians several times. In time, he appeared tired of it all. In addition, Young showed he had no more confidence in Lee, stating that "under no circumstances should Lee ever again be admitted as a member of the Church."[10] Of course, Brooks' later documentation indicating that Lee followed higher orders was undoubtedly a major reason why the LDS Church reinstated Lee to full membership in 1961. Brooks insisted she was besieged by Church authorities not to publicize that fact in the next edition of her *Mountain Meadows Massacre.* It was as if Church officials were not sure the reinstatement would meet with approval in some vital quarter, perhaps in Heaven. In any event, Brooks went ahead with the announcement. Lee's family rejoiced.[11]

Lee quotes Young as saying, upon learning of Mormon involvement in the massacre, "This is the most unfortunate affair that ever befell the Church."[12] Brigham may not have wanted to accept what happened, but he quickly grasped the enormity of the terrible mistake in the world and the condemnation it was certain to bring. Young also stated, according to Lee, that he was concerned with the effect this would have on the brethren involved. If Lee is correct in this, does it mean that Brigham didn't want the brethren who were involved arguing among themselves and blaming and/or harming one another? Upon receiving Young's message (delivered by Haslam) to let the emigrants pass through safely, it had to be immediately obvious to the conspirators that they could blame no one else. If Brigham "went after them" would they then be at one another's throats with no way to determine the truth—until in a court of law under oath?

But to better understand the turmoil of southern Utah in 1857 and the impact it had on Hamblin's psyche, as well as his beloved missionary work, we must better try to understand the thinking which led to the Mountain Meadows Massacre. To understand that, we must analyze the claims made by John D. Lee. He maintained that if the settlers refused to help the Indians, the latter might cause future depredations upon Mormon settlements. There is an anomoly here. Lee says he and peers stepped in to prevent Indians from taking any more loot than already stolen. He says the bulk of that plunder, including much livestock, was transported to the nearest LDS tithing office for distribution to the "poor." But after killing one hundred and twenty innocent souls, what kind of misguided virtue is this? And didn't the act of restraining the Piutes itself risk incurring their wrath upon the Mormon settlements? Did the perpetrators keep little for themselves so they couldn't be accused of murdering for material gain? Are panic and/or revenge better motives? An enigma of massive proportions arises the more one attempts to apply any logical thinking here.

John D. is, himself, an enigmatic figure. In *John Doyle Lee* (pp. 17-44), Brooks pictures the man as an unwanted child trying to find his place in the world. He might be naive about the faults of others, and perhaps too eager to please higher-ups, but he could never be accused of being disrespectful to those in authority. After marriage and the death of two children, he studied LDS literature, and joined the Mormon movement at the age of twenty-five. He and his wife Aggatha were baptized June 17, 1838 at the height of persecution in Missouri. Both Lees caught first hand the wrath of enemies against their new religion and its adherents. Nevertheless, both seemed determined to be valiant in their new faith.

Many details of his life are presented in *Mormonism Unveiled, Life and Confessions of John Doyle Lee*,[13] written after his death sentence. Lee explains his role in the MMM as a military operation (pp. 231-248 unless otherwise noted). After riding out to the Meadows to see what the emigrants were up to, he and the others prayed to know what they should do. But there was no time to meditate the answer. Major John M. Higbee arrived and presented written orders from Colonel William Dame, commander in-chief of all military operations in Iron County. The orders: the wagon train "must be done away with."

A major in rank, Lee says in *Confessions* that when he read the orders, he dropped them to the ground and and said, "I cannot do this." Lee said Higbee told him that the orders came from Lieutenant Colonel Haight who said he got his orders from Colonel Dame. Haight was stake president in Cedar City (including Harmony) and Dame stake president in Parowan. Thus, with their twin titles, Dame and Haight possessed both ecclesiastical and military control for all of southern Utah south of Beaver. There was no other authority one might be expected to answer to, save Brigham Young–and he was a week's travel away, another world.

If local Church officials had thought it out more carefully, at least a courtesy call should have been made on Hamblin, for he was president of the Southern Utah Mission to the Lamanites. If they were to be involved, Hamblin should have been consulted.

But if Lee or any person in the local milita were to be disobedient, it would be insubordination militarily if not spiritually. With Johnston's Army approaching, a recalcitrant would likely face indefensible court martial with serious consequences. Lee's grief about what to do must have seemed to him isolated and terrible. What could he do but comply? The others seemed to be doing the same. What argument might he offer for any aberrent behavior?

Especially troubling to Lee, he said, were the spiritual aspects. He was not in on the original planning meeting discussing this matter. He had been given no say in it. His superiors decided what he must do. He had been advised from a young age that if he erred while following spiritual leaders, the sin be upon those above him. He could not err while following orders of the LDS priesthood heirarchy. He must not fail; if he did, there was no promise for him, no highly coveted salvation in the Celestial Kingdom.[14]

Lee says he was counseled that the wagon train before him was a segment of Johnston's Army, or at least in sympathy with it, and that to let the emigrants go through would mean them stirring an attack of militia from California to come from the rear and "wipe out all the [southern] settlements." Hamblin himself says in his (Little, p. 54) autobiography that, "Elders coming in from the European mission, by way of California, thought the government would send a force into southern Utah by that route." Still, Hamblin did not seem particularly disturbed by the news. What would Brigham think of it? He would ask when in Salt Lake.

Stirred into preparation as minute men to combat a coming enemy, alert to the point of hysteria, says Lee, participants were certain the entire company, carried "not a drop of innocent blood."[15] The perpetrators were in divine favor. The enemy was "delivered into our hands." All must act as soldiers, do their part...or perish. It was a time to stand unified.

However, testimony at Lee's first trial by a Mrs. Ann Eliza Hoge stated John D. called a meeting before the massacre and advocated on his own "putting the emigrants out of the way." Others testified that Lee seemed to have his own mind made up to go ahead with the killing; testimony was given that Lee was also seen doing so. Joel White said at the second trial that he was sent by superiors to save lives of the emigrants and Lee told him, "I have something to say in that matter and will see to it."

Written orders commanding Lee and his cohorts to attack the wagon train cannot be found today. History does not record such a note ever being submitted by Lee as evidence at his trial, or to anyone else other than his wife, Emma. She said the note was kept by her but taken by someone and destroyed.[16] If such a note did actually exist, it would most likely have found Haight and/or Dame more guilty in the massacre than their subordinate, John D. Lee.

Lee admits in *Confessions* that he deceitfully led members of the Fancher party to their deaths by pretending to honor a white flag of truce. Lee said he managed to effect the surrender of all weapons before promising to guide Fancher members safely back to Cedar City. Instead, whites and Indians ambushed the helpless emigrants. This makes the act all the more reprehensible. But in doing so, Lee says he was specifically ordered to decoy the emigrants from their wagons and weapons, that in the truce and betrayal he was only following military orders.

Was the entire Church at fault through innuendo? True, there were scriptures proclaiming, "Vengeance is mine, sayeth the Lord." Brooks points out the militant words of "Up, awake ye defenders of Zion." "Remember the wrongs of Missouri."[17] Yet, other songs of the saints trumpet forgiveness.[18] Which would the Church assembly heed?

Only John D. Lee was excommunicated in aftermath of the MMM. Haight was cut off briefly "for not restraining Lee," but reinstated shortly thereafter. LDS historian B. H. Roberts says there were some mitigating circumstances in Haight's case which allowed him to return to full membership. Was this, in hindsight, an error? Haight clearly gave orders to Higbee who relayed them to Lee; but was he merely following orders of Dame, the chief military commander?

No Church action was ever taken against Dame; all the other participants, including Higbee and Klingensmith,[19] were allowed to retain their membership, although the latter moved to Pioche, Nev. The latter seemed greatly troubled by his role in the MMM and eventually apostatized, according to some records.

Lee defends his actions on page 36 of *Confessions* thusly: "By the world at large, I am called a vile criminal, and have been sentenced to be shot for deeds committed by myself and others, nearly twenty years ago. I never willingly committed a crime...I have acted as I was commanded to do by my superiors." He ends his book in the same vein: "I declare my innocence...I freely would have given worlds, were they at my command, to have averted that evil...I wept and mourned over them before and after, but words will not help them, now it is done. I have been treacherously betrayed and sacrificed in the most cowardly manner by those who should have been my friends."[20]

Apparently, Lee includes Hamblin as one who has cowardly betrayed him. Statements in his diary kept while in prison indicate he included President Young as another.[21]

At Lee's trial, Brigham offered the following reasoning for not taking action sooner to find the guilty at MMM. He had already been accused of not fully turning over the political leadership of Utah to appointees from Washington. Now they were here to take charge. He, Brigham, must not attempt any interruption in matters of political jurisdiction. Taking the reins, top-ranking territorial official Governor Alfred Cummings announced he would do nothing for the time being.

Many historians have drawn heavily from the book *Confessions of John D. Lee*, including Juanita Brooks, to show Lee's feelings about the massacre. However, published in 1877, the book emerged well after Lee's death; there is no way of knowing what might have been altered by editors before being initially offered as *Mormonism Unveiled*. Is it likely that lifetime Church member Lee, however bitter against Church leaders, would select *Mormonism Unveiled* as the title of his book? Lee never renounced Mormonism per se. Even after being excommunicated, Lee told F.S. Dellenbaugh on the Colorado River at Lonely Dell that he was still a practicing Mormon and believed in its tenets.[22]

In addition, one account says a Beaver newspaper editor (non-Mormon) saw Lee's book manuscripts before publisher W. W. Bishop took the same to Pioche, Nevada to prepare for publication. (Bishop had served as Lee's defense counsel in the second trial.) The Beaver editor said, "Lee declared that Brigham Young and other Church leaders had nothing to do with the massacre. Lee told nothing because there was nothing to tell."[23]

Lee refused at least twice to "name names" when it might have commuted his death sentence. He said he would let himself "be eaten up by the bedbugs" in prison "before I will dishonor myself by bearing fals (sic) witness against any man, much less an innocent man."[24] Who was meant by the phrase "innocent man"? Was it a generic statement...or did he mean Brigham Young?

How much bias did publishers of Lee's book, the Bryan Brand Co. of St. Louis, Mo., have concerning the Mormons?[25] As a minor note, the publishers make many charges in their preface and opening pages, i.e., that Young is the "greatest criminal of the Nineteenth Century." In the second printing, they included a biography of Young, as one who controlled what Lee did.

Located in Missouri, the publishers would have likely heard little good about the Mormons when they published *Confessions*. Indeed, the publishers make some rather broad statements about Mormonism in general, claiming in their preface that LDS "Danites" attempted to kill editor W. W. Bishop in Pioche, Nevada rather than allow Lee's journals to be published." The publishers claim: "When they [the papers] were ready to go, the Wells Fargo and Co. Express refused to receive them until they were furnished with an armed guard until they were beyond reach of the Mormons." But if Brigham wanted the papers, could he not have sent out hundreds of Mormons and twice as many Indians to do his will just as the publishers suggest he did at Mountain Meadows?

Since all Utah palled under a cloud of MMM suspicion, Young shouldered heavy blame in many sectors of the country even before *Confessions* was published. U.S. Indian agent Jacob Forney sought a more open-minded approach. He wrote a letter to the administrator of Indian Affairs in Washington as follows: "I fear, and I regret to say, that with certain parties there is a greater anxiety to connect Brigham Young and other Church dignitaries with every criminal offense than diligent endeavor to punish the actual perpetrators of the crime."[26]

Bishop added this in his preface: "Lee was a fanatic and as such, believed in the Mormon Church...I believe it is my duty to publish this work, and to show mankind the fruits resulting from obedience to Mormon leaders."[27] Duty or not, this rather sweeping statement as given would include all products of Mormonism. It included men like Jacob Hamblin who abhorred all that transpired at Mountain Meadows and all it represented– and would have done anything within his power to prevent it. This is mentioned to show the cloud that Hamblin worked under for years to come because of something done because of poor judgment of peers.

Was the MMM officially ordered from Church headquarters? Indeed, this is the entire crux of the charge made by enemies of the LDS Church. An acquaintance of the author who does not side with the LDS Church in many matters nevertheless has this to say: "I may not like what I read about the Knights of Columbus, but unless I can lay their talk or actions at the feet of the Vatican pope, it does not represent the official Catholic Church. To infer so not only lacks credibility but seriously taints the claimant."

But it does appear Lee's immediate ecclesiastical leaders made plenty of mistakes, even if one were to conclude they hadn't ordered the MMM. Dame and Haight sent courier James Haslam to ask President Young, their spiritual and military superior, what should be done concerning the Fanchers, then failed to wait for the answer. If Young was the general in this military organization, as seems logical, with Haight and Dame of lesser rank, then failure to wait for orders would certainly result in censure in any other militia. Yet, the two never faced any type of courts-martial whatsoever.

But if Dame and Haight had thought out future consequences, need they seek direction from anyone at all? If the federal government supposed it had cause to punish the Mormons
for possible improprieties, what about the actuality of one hundred and twenty non-combatant civilians being murdered in the
heart of Mormon country? It would appear Dame and/or
Haight, even if bent on some sort of justifiable revenge, did not
act in their own best behalf. In the eyes of the eastern media and
Washington officials, even if the massacre was solely the work of
Indians, the nearby Mormons with their considerable influence
among the Piutes surely could have done something to prevent
it. Did the settlers do anything to appease the natives?

Those who had heard of Hamblin had to also wonder how
such a nefarious deed could happen within his backyard. But of
course, they could not know in times of such slow communication that Hamblin was not present at the massacre site. The
problem this might pose with people like Major John W. Powell
who would come to the Colorado River country will be
answered in a future chapter.

If the perpretators had thought it out, they would also realize
that the story of Indians killing all but the children was totally
illogical. The latter might be considered a compassionate touch
for whitemen; but anyone who knew Indians knew that if they
did not kill the children, they would take them, as was Indian
custom for years, for slavery and barter. And if any children
were to be saved, the older children, capable of doing more
work, would have brought far more remuneration than the
younger ones.

All this had to cross Hamblin's mind when first hearing Lee's
account of the massacre. It is doubtful if at any time Jacob was
fooled by any of the conspirators' reports that the Indians acted
alone.

Lee also alleges that Dame and Haight, after arriving at
Mountain Meadows and viewing the carnage, profaned
(Haight swearing "By G--") mightily against one another,
arguing how to handle the report which must inevitably be
made to President Young. Dame told Haight he "would not
take responsibility for it."[28]

Lee says Haight was "furious with rage." Lee qoutes Haight as saying: "You know that you issued the orders to wipe out this company and you cannot deny it! You had better not try to deny it! If you think you can shift the blame for this onto me, you're fooled. You'll stand up to your orders like a man." Lee said he stood by the scene of carnage listening to his superiors haggle over who would take the blame.

Following the deed, Lee says in *Confessions,* he had no trouble getting to sleep that night. He was considered a hero among the Piutes as they celebrated victory. He joined in the festivities, "humoring" his red brothers, as he said the Church often counseled the settlers to do. He later filled out a phony, itemized bill for $2,220.00, seeking reimbursement (to the U.S. Indian Office) for services rendered to the local Piutes. "I did it to show off," says Lee. He then claimed that Brigham did the same thing, turning in vouchers "without having spent a dime on the Indians, except during times of war."[29] Yet, there were few times in the history of Utah Territory, 1847- 1857, when it could not be said Utah was at war with Indians somewhere within its borders.

Lee later admitted he did not tell the truth in his Indian report. Thus, can he be trusted to correctly chronicle the exchange of words between Haight and Dame–some nineteen years later? Brooks says Lee kept many diaries all his life which could have been written with events fresh in his memory but that those detailing events before the trials were destroyed by someone when Lee was sent to prison.[30] Or did the editor/publisher put posthumous words into Lee's mouth in *Confessions?*

But let us examine Dame's words more closely following the massacre. Lee quotes Dame thusly: "I didn't think there were so many of them [Fancher immigrants]." Is there anything in Christian and/or Mormon scripture condoning the shedding of innocent blood, be it one person or 10,000?[31] One way or the other, Dame is on swampy moral ground here if quoted accurately. The LDS *Doctrine and Covenants* does not condone killing. In Sec. 42: 18, 19 it states: "…thou shalt not kill. He who does so is not forgiven…"

Bishop explains Lee's failure to testify at his trial this way: "Why he [Lee] refused to confess at an earlier day, and save his own life by placing the guilt where it of right belonged, is [that] he was still a slave to... Danite oaths."[32]

There was never any evidence of so-called Danite activity to punish Mormon enemies in Utah, although the same was alleged by anti-Mormon writers such as Charles Kelly.[33] Lee did admit to being a member of the Missouri "Danite" group seeking to punish Mormon enemies that state refused to prosecute or restrain.

Joseph Smith (*Documentary History of the Church*, Vol. 3, pp. 178-180) said he dissavowed all Danite activities. Smith declared Danite organizer, apostate Sampson Avard, to be an enemy of the Church. Smith said that Avard sought to gain sufficient power to overtake the Church. While there is no mention of Lee being involved in Utah as a "Danite," John D. does use the term "destroying angel" in warning what would happen to MMM participants if they told on one other.[34] But attempts to link this statement of Lee's with Danite activity continuous from the Missouri period appear futile.

If there were reprisals promised upon the head of anyone "telling" about Mormons participating in the Meadows massacre, Hamblin never mentioned being threatened. And evidence abounds he told Brigham all he knew about the involvement of Lee and other Mormons in it.

But let us examine what might possibly be a mitigating circumstance with Dame. Brooks says Dame claimed to have sent an order to Lee: "I trust that you will have influence enough to restrain the Indians and save the company. If not possible, save the women and children at all hazards."[35] There is no proof of such a letter today. Later, Dame did issue written orders (preserved in the Parowan Ward history, LDS Church archives) seeking to prevent further Indian depredations against emigrants.[36]

If all this sounds confusing, let it be admitted the truth does seem to point in differing directions. If it was an Iron County military operation, the blame must be Dame's. But on Aug. 12, 1858, at a four-day Church court "hearing," Haight signed, along with twenty-two others, a certificate exonerating Dame from all blame![37] If Dame is out of the picture, Haight is left as the highest-ranking figure involved. If *Confessions* (p. 251) can be believed, Haight is the one giving orders to Higbee. "I sent an order to Higbee to save the emigrants after I had sent the orders for killing them all." Haight refused to write a report to Young; Lee is flattered into doing so: "You know Brigham better than I." Haight then orders Lee "not to expose the brethren...to take as much on yourself that you can." Haight promises a "Celestial reward" for doing so. Lee reports back to Haight he has faithfully done this.[38]

Yet, Haight is never punished, other than brief excommunication, for his role in the massacre.

Brooks opines that Charles Penrose's militant song, "Up, Awake ye Defenders of Zion" was "an expression of the emotional climate" inciting Utah's south into militant behavior. But Godfrey's research shows that Penrose wrote the song while in England on a mission on Oct. 2, well after the incident.[39] It would not have been in the hands of Utah saints at any time preceding the massacre.

Did Church leaders incite the action by militant talk? Brigham Young's official advice to Church members in Salt Lake City was to avoid any direct confrontation with advancing U.S. soldiers of Johnston's Army. Church members were counseled to retreat into the mountains if necessary, with a few remaining to torch homes so soldiers would have to start all over from scratch.[40] That was a sobering thought for militiamen who had already marched some two thousand weary miles. But the idea hardly sounds confrontational. Young's announced policy here was (1) to discourage the enemy, while (2) avoiding bloodshed wherever possible. Even Lot Smith and Orrin Porter Rockwell were instructed to harm no one in their guerilla warfare in halting Johnston's advancing army, and there is no historical evidence that they ever did. Why would Brigham Young suddenly declare a different defense, if required, to deal with combatants in southern Utah?

One might argue that George A. Smith was making the same point as Brigham in advising settlers in his "inflammatory" speeches to be alert for the hour of attack—to "set the torch to every building where the safety of the people is jeapardized."[41] The precise wording here appears to be a defensive measure rather than inflammation to go on the offensive. Smith might have stirred up militant action in some other way, but not here.

Some press for indictment against Young in that he said regarding the coming of Johnston's Army, "I can no longer hold the Indian by the wrist...they shall go ahead and do as they please."[42] But this statement was given two days before the attack, some two hundred miles away, at least four days by horseback. Thus, it could have had no direct bearing on the Mountain Meadows Massacre.

However, it is also true that in Young's appointment of Hamblin as southern Utah Lamanite mission president the preceding August can be found the phrase, "Continue the conciliatory policy toward the Indians...seek by works of righteousness to obtain their love and confidence, for they must learn that they have either got to help us or the United States will kill us both." This phrase is missing from the letter of appointment quoted by Hamblin in Little, p. 44; whether deleted by Jacob himself or by editor Little is not known. It is also missing in Bleak's account. Whoever attempted to thus alter history, the deletion must be condemned in all quarters. Either Hamblin, or Little made a serious mistake, and one bound to be discovered later when the Little-Bleak versions were compared with the original. (A copy of the appointment letter with full phrasing can be found today in the LDS Historical Dept. Archives Search Room.)[43]

As an aside, one wonders if Hamblin did not weary of the strife that now clouded Dixie. Did he wish to expunge from his thinking the above facts as they emerged, hoping to return once again to the simple teachings of Christ to love your neighbor as yourself? That might be one reason why the "Indians must help us or the United States will kill us both" phraseology was omitted. Such thinking cannot justify the omission, but it might help us today to put ourselves in the place of dedicated Lamanite missionary Jacob Hamblin and try to comprehend the ordeal placed on him and the other innocent saints of southern Utah now being condemned wholesale as hate-mongers and murderers.

As to Brigham's reference of gaining militant help from the Indians, historian B. H. Roberts offers the viewpoint that in actuality, Brigham never advocated use of Indians to fight Mormon battles. If he did, Young missed a great chance to "toss them" against Johnston's Army as they approached the Utah border, Roberts asserts. He says, "On the part of the Latter-day Saints, strict neutrality for Indians in these Federal-Utah difficulties was the policy determined upon." He quotes the *Deseret News* of April 14, 1858: "When has one of Colonel Johnston's [marching against Utah in 1857] command been killed or their animals run off by Indians incited thereto by the citizens of this territory... Never, for Governor Young and the Mormons have ever counseled the Indians to remain strictly neutral, as all truth-telling red and whitemen, cognizant of the facts, will substantiate."44

Brigham also stated rather benignly (*Journal History*, Aug. 30, 1857) that Johnston's Army "knows no more about you and me than...interior China. Brethren and sisters, do not be angry with them. Instead of feeling a spirit to punish them, or anything like wrath, live your religion."

But the saints were also determined that this time they would not be driven from their Zion. They must defend it at all costs. Concerned about possible attack from California, Hamblin journeyed in 1857 to check out a rumored military expedition up the lower Colorado River. Jacob was much concerned about the purpose of any such military activity. But Brooks concludes in Dudley Leavitt: "Its mission probably had little to do with the difficulties in Utah."45

Hunter concluded differently. He quotes the *Los Angeles Star*, Dec. 5, 1857, as follows: "In the fall of 1857 the United States Dept. of War sent Lieutenant J.C. Ives to explore the Colorado River for the purpose...of learning whether it could be used to advantage in the transportation of soldiers and munitions of war on the way to the valley of Salt Lake."46

Nevertheless, Corbett isn't certain whether the Ives Expedition heralded military harm against the Mormons or not.

He says that both Hamblin and Haskell visited the Colorado (near present day Hoover Dam) to see if Ives brought an exploratory forerunner for a military expedition against the Mormons. Corbett pointed out that it could trap the saints from north and south in a pincer movement, with full escape difficult into the mountains or the desert. He says Haskell and Hamblin saw soldiers on their scouting assignment; it was unclear whether they were attached to the steamer and if they had any designs against the Mormons.[47] However, Haskell says he talked with Ives and others on the boat when it ran aground on its upstream journey and and reported hearing promise of reward to any Indian who would find and kill Mormons.[48]

In spite of it, nothing was ever heard again about the Ives expedition. It could well be that harm was, indeed, intended; but after Buchanan's embarrassing "pardon" to the Mormon people, all miliary motives against the saints were quashed and forgotten. Corbett suggests that Ives might have offered money to the local Iyats to kill Mormons because he suspected who Hamblin and Haskell really were and wanted to frighten them away to prevent any interference with his expedition.[49]

In any event, history records that the Nevada Iyats did no harm to Hamblin and Haskell, even knowing full well they were Mormons. These two men had spent considerable time in the Muddy region among the Indians, trying to protect wagon trains headed into Nevada. It would seem to indicate once again that Jacob's close friendships with the southwest Indian tribes proved to be a most worthwhile investment.

Ives, of course, came along shortly after the massacre; but it indicates that rumors carried by returning LDS missionaries from California about a possible invasion from that direction bore truth. This is borne out by Haskell who wrote in his diary, p. 32, that he built a home in the mountain foothills near Pinto Creek (prior to the massacre) which seemed to be "a safe place just at the time and one which could be more easily defended in case an army were sent in by way of California or the Colorado River."

Added to everything else, it is easy to conclude that rumors of the Ives expedition and its real purpose near the borders of

Utah Territory sent a shiver through the spine of southern Utah. It might also have caused some of the fear felt by massacre participants before the attack.

While Lee and others claimed the MMM was done in behalf of the Church they belonged to, LDS historian Joseph Fielding Smith, later LDS Church president, labeled Lee's deed "treacherous and damnable in the extreme," and "diabolical" (by definition, "of the devil"). Vastly oversimplifying the entire matter, historian H. H. Bancroft called Lee's act the "crime of an individual." Smith did not agree with Bancroft: "Others who were implicated fled from the territory and died fugitives."[50]

Many did flee or hide in the hills for a time. Haight was relieved of his Church position and died in Arizona under a different name. However, Dame remained in the Parowan area for many years and died in apparent good standing within the Church.[51]

But this much was certain: the massacre represented a monumental problem for how the Mormon Church would be perceived outside Utah. For that matter, the perception could greatly impact missionary work by people like Jacob Hamblin.

Members of the eastern media were already maligning polygamy and other seemingly unorthodox LDS doctrines; this surely provided more fodder for sensational feature stories about the people in the Territory of Utah. They were more than "peculiar;" they were "rebellious and seditious." Such sentiment could only delay the Mormons' much sought-after statehood. Only with statehood could Utahns be governed by locally-elected officials, and in 1858, that would certainly be Mormons. The fact that Utah did not receive statehood until Jan. 4, 1896, even though settled for very near half a century, would indicate strongly adverse national sentiment. Nor was the state allowed the name Mormons gave themselves, Deseret, a name from The Book of Mormon meaning "honey bee" and symbolizing cooperative industry.[52]

U.S. court records indicate that in 1892 at least some Americans considered the Mountain Meadows Massacre to be the work of Mormons alone. When a petition was filed by a relative of the deceased William Cameron for redress from MMM losses, it included the phrase "Mormons alone." The affadavit was then rewritten to read: "that said allegation has been proven a mistake by historical evidence; and that the depredation was *committed by Mormons and Indians*" [author's italics].[53]

Still, after statehood, well into the 20th century, the Mormons continued to suffer from a hostile press which likely had some root in the MMM. Popular novel writers like Zane Grey, although known to be generally hostile to all organized religion, feasted on the Mormons' "blood atonement." Millions of Americans read Grey's *Riders of the Purple Sage*, in which he described Mormon life in southern Utah as controlled by evil, conspiring, self-serving Mormon men who manipulated their women and disposed of anyone they didn't like minus any fear of justice.

Eventually, Lee was counseled (and likely saw the wisdom of) moving into remote northern Arizona, a place he had seen before, and spoke of in glowing terms. Emma called it "Lonely Dell," the only label by which it was known during John's lifetime. Known today as Lee's Ferry, some of the original Lee dwellings remain not far from the Colorado River.

Whether this move was an attempt to hide Lee or provide a measure of freedom by Brigham for his "adopted son" (as Lee was known)[54] before the law closed in is up to conjecture. Lee, of course, appeared to be quick in seeing advantages in the new assignment, physically dangerous as it was, away from the mainstream of civilization.

History records that Lee and his wife, Emma, served dutifully and well at "Lonely Dell." Much courage was required in the task inasmuch as the unpredictable Navajo Nation lived not too many miles across the Colorado. An old Navajo chief later told Jacob that his braves camped near Mrs. Lee one night at Lonely Dell after John was arrested and taken away; but she would not be cowed by their presence. She brought her brood out among the Indians and told the chief she trusted him to keep his braves under surveillance. She was done no harm.[55]

The shroud of shame permeating from the Mountain Meadows Massacre deeply biased Californians in particular against Hamblin's reputation for honesty and Christian charity. Adding things up, the calamity occurred on Jacob's summer pasturage and it was well known by all that he had actually invited the Fancher group to "rest up" on his land for a week or so to fatten their cattle before the long trek across the barren Muddy of southern Nevada into California. Would the train have been attacked if Jacob hadn't persuaded them to tarry? Why would a Mormon befriend a gentile train anyway except for some ulterior motive?

Godfrey suggests it would have been better for Mormon public relations if Hamblin had never admitted his invitation to the Fancher party.[56] Yet, it was typical of Hamblin's commitment to total honesty that he did. The invitation might also have been given because Jacob felt the Fancher party should have been treated with more Christian forgiveness and wanted it clear how he felt.

Nevertheless, a government agent who was part of a U.S. Geological survey in Kanab in 1870-72 under the leadership of C. S. Dutton (known only to posterity as "Brind") says this about Hamblin and the MMM: "In those days...the character of Jacob Hamblin was most unfavorably construed...I refer to the Mountain Meadows Massacre, committed on the Hamblin homesite." Brind laments that he was expected to work with a man of unsavory reputation. "I was advised that he [Jacob Hamblin] was the prime factor (or one of them) which culminated in that disaster...comitted on his property."

"Brind" later found Hamblin to be a "good, kindly" person, "a man of mark among his fellows."[57] The suspicion must have lifted by 1871 when Major J.W. Powell asked Jacob to assist him in various geographical surveys. Whatever Powell might have heard about Hamblin, he placed full faith in the man to guide him among hostile Southwest Indians. If he harbored any distrust, it was never mentioned. Nevertheless, there were many non-Mormons throughout the country at that time who thought any gentile stranger in their midst was in danger of his life.

That this was silly superstition, at least for those who came in peace, was proven when national explorer John C. Fremont and his men evaded certain death in February, 1854 on Mormon soil. After being desperately stranded in winter snows in the mountains between Panguitch and Parowan, Fremont's men, out of their last food rations and in danger of freezing, finally located an old wagon track and followed it. Stumbling upon sight of Parowan in the night, Fremont made his way to town and obtained immediate assistance. Fremont later said to the world, "The Mormons treated us very kindly...[they] saved me and mine from starvation." Concluded historian Allan Nevins, "The kindness of these Mormons completely altered the explorer's view of the sect."[58] This befriending of an "outsider" in 1854, only three years before the MMM, indicates that southern Utah Mormons were capable of great generosity if their fears did not exceed their capacity for charity.

Another "outsider," government surveyor John Gunnison spent considerable time among the Utah Mormons prior to 1854 and reported he was treated well by them. Killed by Piute Indians, the gentile surveyor had the posthumous honor of having a Sevier County town named after him.

Jacob Hamblin would obviously be galled by even a hint of personal dishonesty attached to himself or fellow missionaries when visiting the Indians. Fortunately, the Hopis and others he visited across the Colorado after 1857 had heard little of the massacre. Their isolation prevented the sort of bias then being expressed by the whiteman's world.

Could Jacob have prevented the massacre if he had been present? The evidence seems overwhelming. While many others bowed to local authority in the persons of Haight and Dame, Hamblin would have, as usual, followed his own conscience to do all possible in saving the train, and specifically prevented native participation even if he couldn't stop his white peers. His authority as president of the Southern Utah Indian Mission would bring a measure of peer support. Surely most of the missionaries present would have followed his orders over anyone else. Thales Haskell would have backed him immediately, as almost certainly would have Ira Hatch and Dudley Leavitt. It is inconceivable that Hamblin would have tarried idly by, as in fact Brooks said Leavitt did (in Hamblin's absence) while learning about plans for a massacre.[59] It would fly in the face of all Jacob taught the local natives. It would go against all he believed in and for him, all that the Church he belonged to believed in.[60]

But could he have prevented it once the attack began? The answer again appears to be "yes." Lee described a feeling of helplessness when told the Indians would turn against the settlers if the latter didn't help. It was a precarious position; Lee frankly admitted he didn't know what to do.[61]

By contrast, Hamblin wouldn't have promised the Indians any ill-gained booty in the first place. If promised by others, as it apparently was, Hamblin's influence with the Indians could have altered their course. Most believed in the truth of what he taught, even though not all were willing to be baptized into the Church he espoused. After prayers brought rain and healed sick Piutes, he had more influence over many of them than even their own medicine men. They wanted to retain his respect. Certainly, he could have persuaded them to halt atrocities, even if some did so begrudgingly.[62]

As an example of the man's influence with the natives, history records that Indians planned to attack the next wagon train through the Muddy region following the massacre. Promise of booty was high, as with the Fancher train. But this time Hamblin got word of the impending attack. After an all-night ride , reaching Cedar City without sleep, he sent missionaries Dudley Leavitt and Samuel Knight to stave off an attack near the Muddy: "they found a large body of excited Indians preparing to attack and destroy the train."[63] The pair managed to persuade the Indians to take the stock but save the emigrants. Later, Jacob managed to convince the Indians to hand over even the animals. He wrote, "They agreed that the stock not killed should be given up. I wrote to the owners in California and they sent their agent, Mr. Lane, with whom I went to the Muddy and the stock was delivered to him as the Indians had agreed."[64]

Thus, Hamblin persuaded the Iyets to give up almost all they had gained from the raid. This feat shows the immense influence Hamblin had with people who could have used the material plunder. It is ironic that this party, whose lives Jacob saved, threatened to kill him if Jacob ever reached San

Bernadino.[65] Some in the earlier party felt Hamblin and his Mormon cohorts must have been in cahoots with the Indians when not all animals returned.[66] Instead, it was just one more example of how Hamblin's savvy with the Indians saved emigrant lives—many of them non-Mormons.

In addition, Leavitt later stated (*Dudley Leavitt*, Juanita Brooks) that Dudley took his life in his hands to ask the Muddy Indians, painted and dressed for war, not to harm the wagon train. "If anyone but the servants of God had asked me to go, I would have refused, but I was promised... I should return in safety...that not one hair of my head should be injured." He returned safely as promised. Making the promise was Jacob Hamblin.[67]

In summary, fate decreed that Hamblin not be present when the massacre happened. He likely did not know the full details of what occurred. Even today with many documents on hand (which Hamblin could not have seen) precisely what did happen is not entirely clear. Yet, this much can be reasonably concluded: while the tragedy saddened many throughout the world, including a good many members of The Church of Jesus Christ of Latter-day Saints, probably none were impacted more than Jacob Hamblin. The docile Piedes he had worked so hard to teach correct principles had tasted of unmitigated savagery. They had, in religious parlance, not only become backsliders but barbarians. The Indians would now present threat to both settlers and emigrants. Only the bonds of deep and abiding friendship between white and redman, plus respect and to some degree, fear, could keep the Indians at bay. It would be a challenge for a patient and determined individual. Even someone like Jacob Hamblin.

There were rumors of other large-scale massacres, such as one (passed along by oral history, with a large monument today marking the spot) near present Almo, Idaho. A total of three hundred emigrants were said to have died; whether entirely the work of Indians is not known.[68] But it seems to be the Mountain Meadows Massacre, involving Mormons, which enraged the nation during the mid to late 1800s. The perpetrators, indeed, "got even" and more, for there is nothing in the annals of history to indicate that as many as one hundred and twenty Mormons ever died at the hands of Missouri mobocrats.

If there is a lesson to be learned from the MMM, it is that all persons, even in following so-called superiors, must ask themselves if they possess courage of heart to take responsibility for their individual actions. In this case, vengeance overwhelmed forgiveness. A prime example of this was exhibited by Jesus Christ when insulted and flogged before Pontius Pilate. Careful inner thought preceded outer physical action. Had it been so in 1957 there would have been no Mountain Meadows Massacre.

End Notes, Chapter Six

1. A long list of media criticism against Brigham Young can be found in "The Lee Trial, [first trial] an expose of the Mountain Meadows Massacre," published by the *Salt Lake Daily Tribune Reporter*. BYU Lee Library, Special Collections, Provo, Utah.
2. "As soon as we can get a court of justice, we will ferret this thing out." Lee Transcript, Hamblin testimony.
3. Reber, *The Trials of John D. Lee*, p. 12 attributes much of this delay to gaps in territorial legal law, rectified in 1874 with passage of the Poland Bill. Covering both criminal and civil cases, the bill "established federal supremacy over the Utah Territory."

   Undoubtedly, another reason for delay was that a newly-elected Abraham Lincoln had enough trouble with the Civil War in the East, 1860-65, that he couldn't focus much on matters in the West.
4. CH-C, Vol. 4, pp. 173-4.
5. "The Lee Trial," Baskin statement.
6. Ibid. Also, Reber, conclusion.
7. Juanita Brooks, *Mountain Meadows Massacre*, p. 197. Brooks said Hamblin's family (no specific name given) received a letter from Brigham Young, as did other witnesses, to testify. None of these letters suggesting testimony be given are available today.
8. The correct number was eighteen, according to Hamblin's reckoning. (He searched for the eighteenth.) MMM, p. 102. The official number was seventeen, according to National Archives and Record Service, Wash. D. C., Aug. 30, 1966. See Lee Manuscript microfilm records, LDS Church Historian's Office. The discrepancy could be due to one who was not returned and "raised LDS." MMM, pp. 104-5.
9. *Valley Tan*, Vol.2, No. 16, Feb. 29, 1860 . Also see MMM, p. 278.
10. CH-C, p. 178; Affadavit of Erastus Snow, Feb. 21, 1882, *Mountain Meadows Massacre*, Penrose, pp. 67, 68.
11. In his *Juanita Brooks* (p. 274), the most complete biography written about her, author Levi Peterson claims, "By reinstating Lee, the Church had tacitly admitted that Juanita's accusations against Brigham Young [accomplice after the fact] were correct. [The] Church was reluctant to grant recognition of all too-human conduct of the great colonizer before the world at large."

This is, of course, arguable. Reinstating Lee would only seem to admit Lee didn't act on his own volition at Mountain Meadows.

Peterson also says, p. 246: "Juanita held a lifelong grudge against Brigham Young for having sent her ancestors into an impoverished exile on the ragged edge of the Mormon Empire. A recurrent theme in her historical writing, early and late, was Brigham Young's callous treatment of his obedient followers." A friend of Brooks is quoted as saying: "She inherited the feeling that the Church was at fault for sending all those people into those incredible places. They felt that they had been abandoned...She carried in her a paranoia rooted in that situation that colored so many things she did and said."

Brooks is quoted on p. 180 as saying about Fawn Brodie, who had tried to expose the LDS Church as less than divinely inspired, "For those of us to whom God is a reality, there is no common ground in all her study. We cannot accept her major premise."

12. For the full report by Lee to Brigham, see *Confessions*, p. 252

13. After his death sentence, Lee busied himself writing almost daily about prison life, feelings about massacre, Church etc. MMM, p. 194, 206.

14. *Confessions*, p. 251-53.

15. *Confessions*, p. 252.

16. "His wife, Emma, repeatedly told that the original orders were pinned into the diary which was later taken from her home in Lonely Dell soon after his [John D. Lee's] arrest." JDL, p. 212; no footnote.

17. "Vengeance is mine," Romans 12:19. "Up, awake, ye defenders of Zion," and other "vengeance" hymns, MMM, pp. 29-30.

18. "School thy Feelings," ("Condemnation never pass on friend or foe...keep thy rising anger down...let wisdom's voice control"), LDS Hymnbook, p. 336.

19. Haight, see CH-C, p. 178f. Affadavit of Erastus Snow, Feb. 21, 1882, *Mountain Meadows Massacre*, Penrose, pp. 67, 68. Dame, Klingonsmith, Higbee, see MMM, pp. 211-212.

20. *Confessions*, pp. 254, 265.

21. Ibid, p. 245.

22. Dellenbaugh diaries, pp. 149-54, New York Public Library; also letter to *Buffalo Express*, July 11, 1872, Dellenbaugh's diary, pp. 227-9.

23. Reber, p. 34; Whitney, p. 825.

24. JDL, p. 346.

25. The Moffat Co. is also listed by Reber, p. XIV, as publisher for *Confessions*. Barclay Co. is listed as a publisher in the card catalogue, BYU Special Collections Library. (The card reads as originally printed: "Helpless women and children butchered in cold blood by merciless Mormon assassins.") Reber refers here to contents of book as first published.

26. Senate Documents, 36th Congress, first session, ii, 2, p. 86. Cited in CH-C, p. l75. Cited by Roberts, p. l75; Bancroft, p. 56l.

27. *Confessions*, author's preface

28. Ibid, p. 246.

29. Ibid, p. 245.

30. Ibid, p. 259.

3l. Some historians hold up Laban as an example in *The Book of Mormon*, First Nephi, Ch. 4, that Mormons condone murder, but the situation is somewhat different here. Laban had tried to kill Nephi when Nephi attempted to purchase Laban's plates. There was nothing to indicate Laban would not try to kill Nephi again at the first opportunity.

32. *Confessions,* Publisher's and Authors' Prefaces, pp. l5-35 (Introductory), pp. 381-390 (Execution).

33. "Eph Hanks, a [Mormon] pioneer of l847 and member of the religious outlaws known as 'Danites,' or 'Destroying Angels' Kelly, *Outlaw Trail*, (history of outlaw activity in Mountain West), p. l45

34. JDL, p. 221.

35. MMM, pp. ll2-3.

36. Parowan Ward files, LDS Church Historians Office

37. JDL, pp. 243-44, 249

38. It should be noted that as editor of *Confessions*, Bishop could have had Lee say what he wanted. Yet it seems the entry about Haight is credible. If out to blame higher Church authorities, the author/publisher would likely have implicated Dame, since he had broader authority from Brigham than Haight. However, Haight could have acted militarily without Dame, for the Meadows were in Haight's direct locale of responsibility. Haight's actions after the massacre are circumstantially suspect. He fled his home and changed his name even before pressure to put him in court; on the contrary, Dame seemed to have nothing to hide and remained in place.

One must also ask why Higbee was not put on trial as it is generally conceded he gave the orders to Lee which launched the massacre. See also CH-C, Vol. 4, pp. l39-l80; Birney, pp. l34-2l8.

39. Brooks' opinon, MMM, p. 69. Godfrey, p. 19; "Penrose Diary," Oct. 2, 1857, original in the Utah State Historical Society, SLC, Utah.
40. "Torch homes," Mullen, pp. 150-51. MMM, p. 139. "Shed no blood," Cowley, *Wilford Woodruff Journal*, p. 385-87. See also *History of Brigham Young*, Oct. 30, 1857; *Deseret News*, Sept. 23, 1857. Note words "set fire to our property and hide in the mountains," given as defensive measures.
41. *Deseret News*, Sept. 23, 1857. Included is a report from Smith to Brigham Young: "There was only one thing that I dreaded...a spirit in the breasts of some [for] vengeance." A man who had taken lead at the Haun's Mill Massacre in Missouri "wants to pay it back with usury and prayed God would send them [Missourians] along, for he wanted a chance at them."
42. Statement to Capt. James Van Vliet, U.S. Army. History of Brigham Young, ms. entry, Sept. 9, 1857. Van Vliet said after visiting Church leaders "The Mormons have been lied about more than any people I know." See also Cowley, Woodruff Journal, p. 386.
43. Church History Office, Archives Search Room, Brigham Young Collection, Box 4, FD-4-6, access 141869-ARCH-88.
44. Roberts, p. 370.
45. Dudley Leavitt, p. 37.
46. *L. A. Star* Dec. 5, 1857 and *Alta Californian*, May 20, 1858.
47. Corbett, pp. 134-39.
48. THH, pp. 28-29.
49. Corbett, pp. 138-39.
50. *Essentials in Church History*, p. 422; compare to Bancroft, *History of Utah*, p. 544.
51. MMM, pp. 211-13. Brooks says Haight died "away from his family" at Thatcher, Ariz. "after assuming his mother's maiden name of Horton."
52. *Book of Mormon*, Ether 2:3.
53. Preface, TLT; Record Group 60, Dept. of Interior. Government records shown here for period 1860 also refer to the massacre as "led by John D. Lee." It may be that the claimant had no chance to win redress without the term "Indians," for while the federal government (U. S.Indian Agency) might be held responsible for what the Indians did, the government could not be held responsible for actions of the Mormons. After all this, the claim was denied.
54. Lee had taken pride in the fact that Brigham considered him an "adopted son." The practice of taking in "adopted" Church members fell out of practice after

the mid 1800s. JDL, p. 122. The main point is that Lee
was at one time a trusted "son" of Brigham and
appointed keeper of the sacred Nauvoo Temple
records; Lee was entrusted with many other important
Church duties as well. JDL, pp. 72-3.

55. JDL, pp. 341-42. Emma undoubtedly bore a terrible
brunt of her husband's excommunication and execution.

56. Godfrey, p. 4.

57. Brind letter to "Brother Lund-Wall," U.S. Geological
Survey under Capt. Clarence S. Dutton, 1870-72.
Corbett, pp. 330-34,

58. Fremont, *Pathmaker of the West*, Nevins, p. 418.

59. "Dudley was somewhere close around." *Dudley Leavitt*,
p. 33.

60. No one involved in the MMM claimed that Latter-
day scriptures encouraged what took place at
Mountain Meadows.

61. Lee seems sincere in this assessment. Statement of witnesses to this effect can be found in the TLT.

62. Hamblin had often successfully persuaded natives to
give up some habit or tradition, including how they
competed for wives, stole what they wanted, punished
offenders etc. See Chapters 3,4.

63. Little, pp. 46-47. The Muddy region Indians were more
warlike than the Piutes. Missionaries Ira Hatch and
Dudley Leavitt were condemned by the Mohave
Indians to die on one occasion as they tried to save
emigrant trains but the chief's heart softened after listening to Hatch's prayer. Little, pp. 50-52.

64. Little, pp. 50-52. The herd amounted to four hundred
and fifty-eight head, except for a few the Indians had
already killed. See also Dudley Leavitt, p. 34.

65. Hamblin Diary, 1854-57, p. 49.

66. In want of food, the Indians quickly turned a few cattle
to beef. Yet, Hamblin said he convinced them to turn
over all remaining stock.

67. *Dudley Leavitt*, p. 34.

68. The monument says 300 emigrants headed for
California in 1861 were reported killed in a "horrible
Indian massacre." Five escaped. Historical accuracy of
the monument, erected in 1938, is now in dispute.
Historians can find no written reports from the 1861
period about any such massacre.

Chapter Seven

The Second Trial of John D. Lee

By the time John D. Lee's trial came up in 1876, Jacob had long since begun lengthy missionary expeditions across the Colorado River. (The details of those journeys appear in later chapters.) But let us conclude here the aftermath of the Mountain Meadows Massacre, with emphasis on how it impacted the life of Jacob Hamblin. Many questions were answered in the trial not only for a waiting world but for Hamblin himself.

Depositions that had been denied Brigham Young and George A. Smith in the first trial were now allowed. Both men said they were too ill to personally make the trip to the trial site at Beaver. President Young said he was an invalid. (He died a year later.) Young testified in the deposition that he learned of the massacre "through floating rumor." Hamblin had reported it, of course, but he was not an eyewitness. Young emphasized that Lee had spent much time giving bloody details—the Indians "being stirred up to anger and threatening the settlements of the whites." Note that Young testified Lee told him not that whites participated—rather that the white settlers "were threatened."[1] After hearing many gory details about how the Indians conducted the blood-letting, Young said he did not want to hear any more. As for dividing of the property stolen from the Fancher party, Brigham stated at this second trial that he knew nothing about its disposition.

Smith's statement said that he had no knowledge of the massacre until it was over, and was then sent by Young to gather facts. He joined Brigham in emphasizing he did not condone in any way what happened.[2]

Entered into evidence were all of Young's and Smith's letters and communications to southern Utah Church leaders for the past year. The defense could find nothing in them, apparently, which might implicate either man on charges of sending out instructions to harm passing emigrants. One line from Young's declaration of martial law, Sept. 14, 1857, (geared to the coming of Johnston's Army) contained a sentence which said, "We do not wish to shed a drop of blood if it can be avoided."[3]

Many historical analysts agree it was Jacob Hamblin who "provided the most damaging evidence" which convicted Lee.[4] This might seem strange, inasmuch as Hamblin wasn't there, and witnessed nothing. Yet, the fact he had no part in it and therefore nothing to hide, plus his general reputation for veracity, weighed heavily with the court. In concluding arguments, defense attorneys made no attempt whatsoever to discount Hamblin's honesty. They could find nothing to attack other than his memory, at which they hammered prodigiously. It had been nineteen long years. Even there Hamblin proved frustrating by openly acknowledging he could have forgotten some details. The damage came in what Hamblin could not forget.

Some have charged that Hamblin went out of his way to see Lee convicted. Brooks describes Jacob as eager (he "volunteered" information) to tell what he knew about Lee's role. She says (MMM, p. 198) "His [Jacob's] whole purpose was to convict Lee without involving anyone else...like the others, [Hamblin] could not remember what he did not want to tell."

What was it Jacob did not want to tell? What was there to hold back? This statement by Brooks, in view of all facts, seems unduly harsh. The reader can be the judge of this after scrutinizing Jacob's testimony. It would appear that Hamblin did, indeed, implicate Lee deeply, but he did not "volunteer it." He seems to have simply answered questions honestly under repeated probing by the prosecution. Any other response under oath might well have constituted perjury.

If Jacob was under orders from Brigham Young (as Brooks charges) to see that Lee, and Lee alone, was convicted, then Hamblin suddenly abandoned a long practice of following his conscience. True, he had been known as a dutiful and obedient Church servant. But never had there been any precedent of him being manipulated or coerced into anything; he was his "own man." Had he ever lacked the courage or willingness to tell the truth as he saw it? Why would Hamblin suddenly change character, as charged by Brooks, at the second trial of John D. Lee? On the contrary, in places most critical to Lee, it appears that the prosecution had to extract every damning statement from Hamblin.

Truly, Jacob had long sought punishment for the guilty at Mountain Meadows. He stated under oath, "I felt a great crime had been committed." There is also no doubt, based on his testimony, that Hamblin believed Lee to be one of the guilty. Yet, throughout the trial, Jacob treated his old neighbor and Church co-worker with every respect, as we shall see in examining Hamblin's role in the courtroom more fully.

Held in Beaver, the trial site was close enough to Parowan and Cedar City to readily draw on witnesses from those communities; yet Beaver was also far enough away to be considered a change of venue from the abode of most massacre participants. Ostensibly, it was removed because of local prejudice, although it is true that Beaver then and now cannot be considered outside Mormon influence if that was to be a factor in the trial.

Opening as it did in September, the Indian summer might well have offered a beautiful horse and buggy ride within panoramic view of the nearby lofty Tushar Mountains, graced at that time of year by golden aspens, scarlet maple and oak. The trial itself would offer a startling contrast to the scene of beauty outside. A curious audience, comprised of many new LDS converts from Europe and England, many of whom were not present in Utah in 1857, listened as a terrible drama of bloodshed and horror unfolded before them. Chief Judge J. S. Boreman seemed content to let both sides tell their stories with little interruption. Never mind that some nineteen long years had gone by. All that could be remembered now gushed out in a floodwash of horror. In many ways it is lamentable for the mental health of all southern Utah, as well as relatives of the victims in California, that they could not have experienced the catharsis offered on this day many years before. At the same time, as usual, in such probings of carnage, many who didn't know the details of the incident might now become ill in listening to the proceedings. Nevertheless, Judge Boreman seemed determined that all the truth come out.

Indicted with Lee were William Dame, Isaac C. Haight, John Higby (sic), George Adair, Jr., Elliott Wilden, Samuel Jukes, Philip K. Smith (sic) and William Stewart. The focus centered initially on Lee, who pleaded not guilty. Prosecution of the others would hinge on Lee's testimony.

As usual in any trial, there were many irrelevancies and much repetition. At times, as in court proceedings today, "legal egos" and rhetoric delayed justice.

The entire story unfolds in the transcript of Lee's second trial (Lee Transcript) as follows:

Sumner Howard, U.S. Attorney for the Territory of Utah, called Laban Morrill as an early witness. Morrill testified that he attended a meeting in Cedar City and found the participants "excited." An emigrant train had "issued many threats concerning us," and had claimed to participate in the killing of "Old Joe Smith."

Objection: "Lee was not present at that meeting."

Howard then explained the purpose of this questioning: to determine what conspiracy might have occurred later involving Lee. Defense deferred.

Morrill testified that many strenuously objected to the plan presented to attack the Fancher wagon train, including himself. It was determined a message of inquiry should be sent to Governor Young instructing them what to do. Morrill "thought it was unanimous" that all present would wait for Brigham's response. But, said Morrill, he left the area on business; later, he learned that the terrible "job was done."

Cross-examination asked who seemed to be the main conspirators. Morrill replied, "Klingonsmith [sic] was the hardest man I had to contend with." Haight was also named, although he wasn't present when the attack occurred. When Morrill was later asked specifically to help in the massacre, he refused. He would do nothing "without explicit written instructions from Dame," i.e., the top military authority. Dame apparently issued nothing in writing to Morrill. Morrill said he thus refused to cooperate. This was an act of some courage on Morrill's part, for he said he was later viewed suspiciously by the conspirators who didn't like the idea of someone who knew about the plan not playing a role in it.

So far, Lee had not been named as an active participant. The defense must have felt relieved at this point; but it would not last.

Klingensmith repeated what he said in the first trial...he knew not where top orders might have originated. But he was certain Lee did not act on his own. Again, more ammunition for his defense.

When Haslam took the stand he clarified the confused messages sent to the battlefront. Before riding to Salt Lake City seeking Brigham's instructions, Haslam said he heard Haight tell Joseph Clows to take a message to Lee that "the thing should be stayed." Haslam said he heard the words, "Tell him [Lee] to use all his influence to keep back the Indians...back from the emigrants, until Haslam came back from Brigham."

Joel White, who was apparently with Clows, or knew of the message, testified that Lee rebuffed the dispatch: White said Lee told him, "I'll have something to say about that." It was the first testimony implicating Lee.

Nephi Johnson, age twenty at time of the massacre, testified he had seen Lee kill, or try to kill, one of the emigrants. He said that "Klingonsmith and Lee seemed to be engineering the thing" [massacre]. There were others present. But John D. Lee "was the most conspicuous man in the whole thing. He acted like a man who had control." Samuel McCurdy testified much as had Johnson. Things suddenly began to look bad for Lee.

When Hamblin was called to the stand as sixth and final witness, he was asked, "After the massacre, did you have any conversation with John D. Lee about it."

Hamblin: "I don't know as I did after I got home."

Question: "Did you see him after you got home."

Hamblin: "I met him at Fillmore."

Hamblin's complete statement is repetitious, but the gist of it is: "He told me about it. They [the Indians] came to him and made him lead the attack...he had to go and lead the next attack...had to decoy them out...he justified himself in this way, that the Indians made him go and lead the attack...called on the Clara Indians and that he decoyed them out and they massacred them...the Indians could not be restrained."

Hamblin explained that Lee told him the emigrants came through and threatened to take their outfits [steal horses and wagons]. He said Lee told him he was there to keep watch on the emigrants to make certain they did not do this. After trying to help the Indians, Lee moved in closer to check on the wagon train and received bullet holes in his hat and shirt; Lee got some more [bullet holes] and this made him angry. Hamblin said Lee told him, "There was an army on our borders, that they would lead to give the people much trouble. It was thought best to use them up."

Hamblin said Lee told him, after being repulsed by the emigrants, that the Indians were still very mad and he didn't know how to keep them down. Hamblin said he was told by Lee that he sent a message to either Haight or Dame, Jacob didn't remember which, asking what to do. This was most helpful in Lee's behalf for it indicated he awaited further orders from the person(s) who sent him to the Meadows in the first place. Where would the message come from?"

Hamblin: "If from Cedar City, it would come from Haight; if it was not, it would come from Parowan." At this point, no mention was made of William Dame.

Howard: "Tell what else he [Lee] told you."

Hamblin: "Well, he spoke of many little incidents."

Howard: "[Did he] mention any of these incidents?"

Hamblin: "There was two young ladies brought out."

Howard: "By whom?"

Hamblin: "By an Indian chief at Cedar City and he asked what he should do with them. And the Indian killed one."

Howard: "Tell all you heard and remember about it. You say the chief brought him [Lee] the girls?"

Hamblin: "I think I have told it about all."

Howard: "What did Lee tell you he replied to the chief?"

Hamblin: "According to orders he had, that they was too big and too old to let live."

It can be noted at this point that if Hamblin had simply wanted to implicate Lee alone, or was merely "following orders" from Brigham to make Lee bear the scapegoat role by himself—involving no one higher up—Jacob would certainly not have used the words "according to orders he had." It was the second time Jacob had so testified.

After it was established that the aforementioned Indian chief killed one of the girls, prosecutor Howard asked: "Who killed the other [girl]?"

Hamblin: "He done it, he said."

Howard: "Who?"

Hamblin: "Mr. Lee."

Howard: "How?"

Hamblin: "He threw her down and cut her throat."

Asked how he knew details about the killings not attributed to the Fillmore conversation with Lee, Jacob said, "The Indians told me a good many times." Jacob also related how his son Albert led him to the girls' bodies, apart from the other victims.

In cross-examination, Bishop asked Hamblin if he was certain Lee told him he had killed one of the girls.

Hamblin: "Yes, I am positive of that or I would not have told it."

Bishop: "How long has it been since you told anybody that John D. Lee told you that?"

Perhaps a little annoyed by now, Hamblin replied, "It has been about three seconds."

Bishop backed off at that point and asked Jacob how long he had lived at Mountain Meadows.

Hamblin was asked repeatedly if Lee had implicated anyone else in conversations between the two. Hamblin testified that Lee said others were involved; but Lee gave no names. Thus, Hamblin could give no names. When pressed for names anyway, Hamblin replied: "I don't know that he [Lee] mentioned any names of others...he said there was no one with him."

Howard: "Don't you know that Lee lied about it?"

Hamblin: (No answer).

Jacob later testified that he heard his brother Oscar was at the Meadows, bringing in Indians as ordered; also he had heard that Klingensmith and Higbe were there, although it was not known for what purpose. In cross-examination, perhaps to see if

Hamblin could be caught in a contradiction, Bishop asked many questions about the witness's work and missionary activities. Counsel asked such irrelevant (and likely also embarrassing) questions as, "Did the Indians have a name for Lee?" Hamblin answered that they did: "crier" or in Piute, "Yah guts."[5]

Bishop then asked what Lee had told Hamblin about "the council." Hamblin answered that he knew nothing about the council in Cedar City. The question was rephrased to specify the council at Mountain Meadows, i.e., talk of decoying the emigrants out.

Jacob replied, "We had a good deal of conversation about it."

This time when counsel asked who might have given the orders to Lee, Bishop took a new direction. He asked who might be considered superior to Lee. Hamblin said if Howard meant immediate ecclesiastical authority, it would be Klingensmith, Lee's bishop.

Bishop pressed for the top military leader in Iron County.

Hamblin answered, "Dame was in charge of militia."

This has been used by some historians to say that Jacob named Dame as the mastermind behind the massacre; but Hamblin simply answered counsel's question. If in Iron County, "Dame was in charge of militia."

When questioning moved to three men who somehow escaped the circle of Indians at the Meadows (one by the name of William Aiden), and sought help from local white settlements, Hamblin explained how Lee told him the MMM ringleaders couldn't let anyone go on to California. They would implicate whitemen. Hamblin quoted Lee as saying that Aiden was gunned down "because it was the best thing to do." In this, Lee does not sound as if he questioned orders. He gave his opinion that it "was the best thing to do."

Hamblin was the only witness who said Lee confessed to him about slaying two girls, murdered apart from the other emigrants.

Question: "He [Hamblin's foster son Albert] told you where those two bodies could be found?"

(Note: were these the two girls mentioned by Rebecca Dunlap? See pages 84-85.) Is it possible Albert could have watched them killed and later knowing where their bodies were located, have given the impression to the young Dunlap girl that he had caused their death?)

Hamblin: "Yes sir." Asked for more information, Jacob explained that the sight so horrified him that he took only a brief look and left the scene.

He was asked if there were any "bodies lying about" at Mountain Meadows, a question seemingly posed to determine full parameters of the crime. Jacob was further asked, "Were they dead or alive?"

Hamblin: "I didn't see any live ones there."

Rather late in his testimony, Jacob was asked if he had ever spoken to his superiors about his testimony regarding Lee.

Hamblin: "I did speak of it to Brigham Young and George A. Smith."

Question: "When?"

Hamblin: "Pretty soon after it happened. I was advised by Brigham Young not to talk about it until a court of justice was convened. I kept it to myself after that until it was called for in its present place."

Question: "You feel the proper time has come?"

Hamblin: "I do, indeed."

Here again, it would appear that if Hamblin was concerned only about clearing Brigham from delay of justice, it isn't likely Jacob would mention the foregoing "not to talk about it until a court of justice was convened." Brigham had said in his deposition that he left justice to the courts and except for excommunicating Lee, left punishment for the MMM perpetrators to the U.S. legal system. The only explanation Young ever gave for waiting so long to do that was, "I didn't have all the facts until now," as quoted by Lee in *Confessions*.[6] But it is significant that while Jacob might have shielded his Church president from further criticism about delaying justice—and it picked up noticeably after this testimony—Hamblin apparently decided no good would come from talking about the massacre until the matter could be untangled in a court of law.

Hamblin probably saw some pragmatism in it, for even though much disturbed by the massacre, to pursue blame outside the legal system could cause wrangling among the very people he had to work with on a daily basis. For example, Hamblin and Lee often had to cooperate at Lee's Ferry to get missionaries across and prevent Navajos from doing so. Brooks says that Hamblin also (JDL, p. 302, no footnotes or references) brought food and news to Lee and Haight while they were in hiding. Jacob wouldn't testify under oath that the two were innocent; yet, he cooperated with them to accomplish what he, Hamblin, considered the Lord's work. There were also land exchanges and temporal matters involving the two. Brooks says Hamblin also promised Lee the latter would "never be captured" (JDL, p. 313, no source listed), apparently in an effort to brighten Lee's spirits. It does not sound like a prophecy Hamblin would dare make. If so, Jacob was wrong this time.

At another time in the trial, Hamblin mentioned that a freight hauler named Bishop (same last name as defense counsel) was at Fillmore when he talked with Lee.

Defense counsel Bishop: "Not me?"

Hamblin: "No, he had two good eyes."

Jacob's touch of humor in a somber trial is not clarified or discussed. Apparently, defense counsel Bishop had one bad eye.

In summary of Hamblin's testimony, Brooks seemed incensed (MMM, p. 198) that Jacob would not name superiors giving orders to Lee. But Hamblin was not there; all he could do was repeat what Lee told him; Lee himself would not say who gave him orders. The only other knowledge Hamblin had was what Indian leaders and Albert told him. They had no idea who was behind what they saw. They only knew they saw Lee help in the massacre.

Toward the end of the trial, Bishop said something which angered the prosecutor Howard. It implicated upper echelon LDS Church officials in the massacre. Bishop had made the charge in the first trial and repeated it now.

Howard answered: "I challenge John D. Lee to bring one iota of evidence that will saddle it [the Mountain Meadows Massacre] upon the leaders of the Mormon Church...it will require something else than his own excuse given to Mr.

Hamblin to satisfy this jury of it...if he is to prove the Church committed the crime, bring on the evidence."

U. S. Marshal William Nelson also said after the trial: "The authorities of the Church were entirely innocent of the Mountain Meadows Massacre. I know more about that affair than Brigham Young. I have hunted up the evidence."[7]

Bishop chided Howard at becoming "so excited," but offered no direct rebuttal. At times, Bishop even lauded Howard for his eloquence, adding that he had rarely known anyone "to be so talkative."

Following Hamblin's testimony, Nephi Johnson was summoned to answer additional questions. After being asked if anyone present at the Meadows objected to orders given from military leaders, Johnson answered, "Yes sir, a good many objected, but they didn't dare say anything." In this, he agreed with Klingensmith that it was seen as a military organization; all were expected to obey a higher command.

Johnson also cleared up another mystery. Who was it that had been sent, following the Mountain Meadows Massacre, to plot against other wagon trains coming through?

Johnson: "Lee asked me to take a company into the mountains in the Santa Clara and he would follow with the Indians and kill them." Johnson was asked if Lee gave him the authority by which he made this request.

Johnson: "No sir. I said I would not do it. I was sent [most likely from Dame who was known to send orders protecting companies after the massacre] to bring them through the country and I would do it or die. There had been enough blood spilled at the Meadows. He [Lee] called me a great many names and passed on."

The "calling of names" would seem to indicate Lee strongly desired Johnson's participation, whether under orders or acting on his own.

This would explain at least in part Hamblin being told by two men they had "secret orders" to follow a wagon train and help the Indians kill emigrants for the spoils. Johnson was the only witness to implicate Lee in this way. It is not known if

Hamblin learned before this second trial who gave contrary orders to his own. In any event, if Johnson's testimony can be trusted, the mystery was now more fully resolved.

It should also be noted that Brooks suggests men sent to plunder emigrants following the massacre were ordered there by Haight. Since Haight had apparently taken a heavy hand in the massacre itself, this could well be true, as stated on p. l3l of MMM. But Brooks includes no references or sources to pin down this conclusion or verify the source.

In any event, Jacob had been much put out on the Muddy in learning that orders were given to stir the Indians once again to warpaint. Here he was risking his life to save emigrants while someone in his own backyard was, ironically, issuing orders to destroy them! It must have been especially galling that those sent were missionaries to the Lamanites who should have been under Hamblin's direct charge. Indeed, a civil war was waging in Dixie, Church leaders against the missionaries.

In time, this was resolved from Salt Lake City. Companies fearing another MMM got passes from President Young to get through safely. These were usually addressed to Jacob. It is no coincidence that not a single emigrant was harmed when Jacob personally intervened or sent out missionaries to accompany wagon trains after September, 1857. Interestingly, Hamblin called Indians and emigrants together (Little, pp. 50-5l, Roberts, p. 308), on one occasion advising a wagon train leader to reward two Indians with supper and a shirt in turn for watching out for their stock overnight. The emigrants expressed considerable skepticism over this unusual arrangement. But in the morning, not a single cow had been lost. When it became clear that President Young himself did not equate passing wagon trains with military enemies, white-directed attacks in Dixie ceased.

Some have charged in print that Hamblin and mission-airies Leavitt, Knight and Hatch were part of a conspiracy to help Indians drive off emigrant livestock and share in the loot. The conspiracy theory does not bear up. Hamblin spent con-siderable time rounding up livestock, as explained in his "Journal and Letters," which was later returned to rightful owners. In some cases, these intervening whitemen barely escaped with their lives at the hands of angry Mojave Indians. Why so if in league with them?

It is not clear, however, whether all Indian-stolen stock remaining alive was returned. A letter from Brigham Young instructs Jacob thusly about surplus cattle: "To control them and use them for the best interest of both the missionaries and the Indians." But it is not altogether clear in this letter what cattle are being discussed.[8] Did this mean to steal immigrant cattle and disperse them for the Mormons' use? There is no evidence of this, although some cattle found roaming around might have been appropriated by southern Utah settlers. It is known that some of the Fancher cattle were appropriated by MMM conspirators but there is no indication Hamblin or official Church spokesmen had a part in it.

After Hamblin's testimony, Bishop stated that as there had been "an unexpected turn of events," not fully explained, he was not prepared to counter or ask for any more testimony; "the defense rests." In their summation speech later, however, Bishop and his colleagues did launch into a lengthy argument in behalf of Lee. Bishop said that he was called on to save an innocent man in the midst of a "peculiar people." Every witness, save Hamblin, was called into question as having been an accomplice in a conspiracy, each merely trying to protect his own neck. Concerning Jacob, counsel said: "I have no doubt in the world that Hamblin is a truthful man…but nineteen long years have passed."

Counsel finally argued that "at the very least" the jury should not return with a first degree murder conviction.

Another member of counsel, referring to Hamblin several times as "Jake," suggested the "right time" had come along for him to testify only because Brigham Young was no longer a defendent. This could be true.

In their summation, the prosecution, apparently concerned that Lee might prove himself a mere pawn in the tragedy, pounded away at two points: (1) Lee could be led to the scene of the battle but could not be coerced into killing if it was against his will; and (2) he was not, or should not, have been under complete control of the Indians. For proof of the latter, Howard's team extracted words from Lee's letter to Young explaining the massacre. These were civilized Indians, exclaimed the prosecution. They could have been controlled. After all, Lee had written to Brigham of "friendly feelings" between the settlers and natives. Emphasis was given almost derisively to this one sentence in Lee's letter: "Much grain has been raised by the Indians." Did this not prove them somewhat civilized?

Prosecution then asked, "So why didn't Lee constrain those Indians? Was it they who made him, or him who made them?"

Since Lee was local Agricultural Adviser, by Church assignment, to the Indians, he was likely the one assisting them in raising that grain and should have had control over them. In truth, it is more likely the grain was raised under tutelage of Hamblin.

In addition, as already mentioned, the emigrants were about to pass on into a "blank wilderness," away from the Mormon settlements and would have been soon gone. One of the more damning summation statements was this: "The Indians might have been civilized, but the whiteman that was over them was not."

The prosecution emphasized that witnesses indicated Lee seemed to show too much zealous enthusiasm for what he was "required" to do. Howard pointed out that the crime was a particularly reprehensible one. "Never has there been brought into court such a crime...it has lain silent nineteen years." Lee "was guilty of not just murdering one or two men but more than a hundred." And "if you find him [Lee] guilty of just one-tenth of what he is charged with here you will find he is guilty."

Howard stressed that Lee had refused new orders to cease and desist—he was afraid the new message would be to let them pass through but he now had them there. "He didn't want to follow the latest orders."

The prosecution seemed in this summation to overplay its hand. Lee was described as a man "greedy for the spoils" of the emigrants. That might have been a secondary motive but most certainly, revenge for the Missouri years and fear of further depredations at the hands of gentiles were far greater motives, a fact that every Mormon juror surely understood. The crime was not perpetrated for a few material goods, although it appears Lee would not let them go to waste afterward. Most likely, the stolen possessions indicated control over a perceived enemy.

Prosecution also dwelled heavily on John D. concocting the idea of the slaughter entirely on his own. But if Hamblin was to be believed, this could not possibly be true. Jacob said repeatedly that Lee told him he acted on "higher orders." Hamblin consistently said Lee did not name names, but he never faltered in the claim Lee did not act alone.

The defense then properly pointed out that it can be dangerous business to accept one part of a man's testimony, while discarding another. Certainly, if Hamblin reported truthfully what Lee said about "taking orders," those who gave them should have also faced trial for murder in the first degree. In addition, the testimony of Klingensmith, Johnson and others made it clear they were not there on their own. It remains one of the great mysteries of the U.S. legal system that no one other than Lee stood trial for this crime. Even if Lee could be singled out as the one who deceitfully decoyed emigrants under a white flag of truce, or carried out orders zealously, witnesses relied on by the prosection said Lee did not act alone. One must also ask why only Lee was excommunicated from the LDS Church. Hamblin and everyone else who testified agreed that Lee followed orders from a higher authority, militarily and more important, ecclesiastically.

Why did not Lee provide names of those higher-ups while in court? Why did he wait until writing his memoirs in prison? Quite possibly, it was just as he said—he had taken an oath not to. After being convicted, it was different; names poured out in volume with the publication of *Confessions* of John D. Lee.[9]

One reason no others were tried might be that Howard argued so vociferously that Lee concocted the idea on his own. Howard, representing the U.S. Government, seemed satisfied when Lee was convicted.

But Klingensmith had already implicated himself and Higbee. To a certain degree, Hamblin did also by saying he heard they were present at the massacre. Brooks always questioned why Dame was never tried, since all agreed he was the only one in Iron County who could have possibly ordered a military attack in the year 1857. At the same time, why did Haight sign that affadavit in the Church hearing at Parowan clearing Dame of any wrongdoing? Why was it that Haight always wanted Lee to report directly to him? On confidential matters like taking the massacre message to Brigham, why did Haight insist on talking it over personally with Lee? Was it because Haight was making the decisions and Lee was the ideal, obedient emissary who did what he was ordered to do with few questions? It had seemed so; now, during this second trial, it seemed even more so.

Before concluding, counsel refuted the idea of Corn Creek or any large spring of water being poisoned wherein someone might come along later and be affected. Howard did not agree. Bishop was likely correct, but it was a point that could never be proven one way or another. Howard also ridiculed the idea that one Indian tribe (north of Beaver) would come down and join another Indian tribe (south of Beaver) to fight their battles. Bishop countered that he "knew Indians" and "this was entirely possible." It was a minor argument that seemed to be aimed more at enhancing attorney egos rather than actual justice.

In her analysis of the second trial written primarily for students of law history, Faye E. Reber (*Trials of John D. Lee*) suggests the evidence was so overwhelming against Lee that defense counsel lost heart, especially after Hamblin's testimony.[10] As for Lee saying nothing under oath in his behalf, it might well be because John D. would have to face cross-examination by a relentless Howard. Still, with so little to lose, why did Bishop not counsel Lee to say what he had maintained all along, that he was merely a pawn in the military system? Was it because Lee was determined to be a martyr to his cause, or did he really have nothing to say in his behalf? One must also question Bishop's defense strategy at several points. Court records show counsel made this statement: "We will always claim that the defendent did not do it." Why say this when Lee never denied taking part? He simply claimed to have followed orders.

Certainly Brooks is right when she says that once Lee had been excommunicated and six witnesses, one of them Jacob Hamblin, testified against him, conviction was something of a foregone conclusion. Clarence Darrow, the famed defense attorney, could not now save Lee, even with the exaggerated claims of the prosecution in summation argument.[11] The all-Mormon jury required but four hours to reach a verdict: "guilty of murder in the first degree." The sentence which followed, death by one of several different means, found John D. selecting the firing squad.

During this period, petitions were circulated and signed by more than 500 persons in Beaver and Panguitch to save Lee from the death penalty. The petitions mentioned that he was now "past 64 years old...in poor health...only one of the guilty...it was a military act," etc. (The original petitions, lost for a time, are now on microfilm at the Utah Historical Society, Salt Lake City.)

When the verdict was appealed to the U.S. Supreme Court, it affirmed action of the lower court on Feb. 10, 1877. Lee awaited the end within the high walls of the stone-fortressed territorial prison at Sugarhouse on the southeastern edge of Salt Lake City. Brooks documented Lee as a model prisoner awaiting death, the same eager-to-please individual within the legal system that he had been before as a Church member.

Let us digress from the trial temporarily to discuss the issue of loyalty to other Church members, including Brigham Young.

Shortly after the trial, Lee wrote Emma about Jacob's "villany," mentioned earlier. Lee complained about a number of witnesses, but none more vehemently than his one-time neighbor, Jacob Hamblin. Lee also wrote that he felt he would be "rescued" by Church authorities. Bishop had claimed as much in pre-trial "straw" polls. This would fly in the face of those who claim the trial outcome was never in doubt.

As for "feeling betrayed" by Brigham at his second trial, this was nothing new for Lee. If *Confessions* can be believed (p. 196)

Lee had long before been at little-known odds with his Church president. Lee is quoted as saying in 1846 while the saints were at Winter Quarters that Brigham sent him on a "dangerous mission to the Indians" but didn't take care of his family "as promised" while he was gone. Lee was furious to return and find his wife and family living in tents during cold weather while others "enjoyed warm cabins." Lee blames no one but Brigham. Lee says Brigham's "excuse" was that others were asked to build a home for the Lees but provided for their own families first. Young was "going to see to it" that a cabin was built for Lee's family but failed to do so. In this, betrayal by Church leaders is a constant theme of *Confessions* which claims on the title page to be the "true and only true...genuine and only genuine" life and confessions of John D. Lee.

Certainly pledges of help to Lee or his family could have been left unfulfilled in the Winter Quarters incident. It seems strange, however, that Lee would continue to follow Brigham if dealt with so treacherously. Perhaps Lee felt this was all necessary dues in order to receive a "Celestial reward," a favorite subject of Lee's. But to believe this would first necessitate believing that Brigham Young served God, i.e., Lee believed him to be a prophet who could guarantee Lee's future exaltation.

Whatever epithets Lee threw at Church leaders after receiving his death sentence, before and after publication of *Confessions*, Hamblin seemed to lose no confidence whatsoever in Brigham or the Brethren. Yet, he certainly passed through trials ("dangerous Indians" etc.) equal to or beyond Lee's. To his last day of life, Jacob obeyed all explicit spiritual directives of his captain—including at least twice when they seemed certain to lead to his death. The continued loyalty of Jacob Hamblin to Brigham Young, despite many complaints growing out of the MMM incident, indicate an insight to Jacob's personal feelings about the integrity and judgment of his Church leader.

This does not prove Brigham's infallibility one way or the other. Much of the difficulty could simply lie in attitude. Hamblin returned from the "Lord's errand" more than once to find loved ones materially in need. He laments about it on occasion. Yet, he seems to waste little time in placing blame. If he was in his opinion doing the Lord's will, nothing else seemed to matter. Reward was in knowing duty was done. If there was benefit to be reaped, it would be a by-product of following one's conscience.

If there was anything which set Jacob Hamblin apart, it was that he did not serve any man per se. He accepted a few designated humans as God's spokesmen on Earth to speak for the Church as a whole. Yet, he seemed to act on his own inspiration in all matters for which he felt personally responsible.[12] That way, there was less disappointment all the way around.

There have always been serious gaps in Lee's arguments. Why would Lee say (*Confessions* p. 252) that Brigham told him "It was the worst thing that ever befell the Church" and then say that Brigham told him "It was alright, he condoned what we had done"? Even if Brigham commanded Lee to lay the blame solely on Indians, how can anyone say with the slightest logic, "It is the worst thing that ever befell the Church..." but "I condone it"? Lee's Brigham Young is contradictory here. Is Lee guilty of simply wishing too earnestly for authorative approval that never came?

In addition, on p. 252 (*Confessions*) Lee says he "killed six wounded men"? If so, why does Lee lash out so bitterly at Hamblin for saying Lee told him he killed one girl?

Some other questions remaining from the trial: why did Lee reveal so much of his personal role in the massacre to Jacob Hamblin? Did he seek Hamblin's approval, a respected peer, to assuage to some degree growing feelings of guilt? Bailey's account of this meeting between Hamblin and Lee at Fillmore attributes biting sarcasm on the part of Hamblin. Bailey has Jacob openly rebuffing Lee's depiction of the Indians saving younger children.[13] True, it is a fictional account (there is no record of Jacob using those precise words) but the tenor of the conversation is likely correct. Jacob never displayed any sympathy for "excuses" that the natives should be feared rather than benevolently directed. If Hamblin allowed himself to believe this, he could forget proselyting and simply sit back to enjoy the daily comfort of home and family in Santa Clara, or tend to farming.

As Bailey says, Hamblin also knew that the Piedes and Santa Claras were no match for the emigrants' long rifles. Many more Indians would have been killed if acting without outside help.

On Lee's behalf, in *Confessions* (p. 388) he advises his posterity after his sentencing to live exemplary lives, to treat one another kindly. While Lee complains he has been sacrificed in "a cowardly, dastardly manner," he also maintains, "There are still thousands of people in this Church that are honorable and good-hearted friends." He affirmed that he knows he will receive a Celestial reward. "I am a true believer in the gospel of Jesus Christ. I believe in the gospel taught in its purity by Joseph Smith."[14]

Lee's story is one of the most enigmatic in western Americana. Some felt he "possessed too much blind obedience;" at times he was charged with "too much ego." Indeed, he voluntarily vacated several Church positions in Harmony because members said they could not get along with him. Historian Birney Hoffman says of Lee that he dwelled with his brethen in "constant turmoil and strife." Wherever he dwelt, there he made enemies." Quoting Lee, Birney says, "Men acted like demons toward me and mine." Birney says Lee was almost excommunicated in Winter Quarters but for Brigham "who blessed him and restored him to favor."[15]

Unfortunately, Birney does not include footnotes to trace these quotes in *Zealots of Zion*, published in 1931. Yet, to see how Lee was perceived at the time one need only examine the old memorial plaque placed at Mountain Meadows in 1932 (by several historical associations) which included the phrase, "John D. Lee, who confessed participation as leader." Lee might have confessed to being a participant; never "as leader." Nevertheless, this seems to be the perception which has persisted for many years.

If Lee was a killer, he was a most benevolent figure to many, including Emma, who visited him in prison and remained faithful to him until the end. That came when John D. Lee was executed at the crime scene on March 23, 1876 atop his own casket. Witnesses said he voiced no audible complaint.[16]

As a postlude to the Massacre, Congress appropriated $10,000 for the victims, more than $500 per child, in those days a fair amount of money. With the help of then sub-Indian agent Jacob Hamblin, the children were gathered up from LDS homes in southern Utah and returned to the mid-West where relatives were allowed to raise sixteen of the children as their own.[17]

Evidence exists, however, that one of the children remained in the Utah-Arizona area and was reared as a Latter-day Saint.[18]

LDS Church leader Orson F. Whitney also wrote that in 1912 a relative of the slain Alexander Fancher, living in Cowley, Wyoming, told a Mormon congregation he had "shared in a bitter prejudice" felt by his family toward the Mormons. He then met and married an LDS girl, became active in the Church, and became convinced the massacre was the work of a "few hot-headed zealots." He said "his conversion to the gospel was genuine." His faith was "stronger than ever" despite intially fierce opposition from an unforgiving father. The man told assembled Church members that he "hoped to continue faithful to the end."[19]

Jacob Hamblin never again after 1876 mentioned Lee or the ill-fated massacre. His face was turned toward the southeastern "wilderness" where he faced a trial of his own at the hands of a warring Navajo Nation. There he very nearly met the same end as did John D. Lee.

End Notes, Chapter Seven

(Note: Except as described below, all data in this chapter is taken from the second trial transcript of John D. Lee, Church Historians Office, Church Office Bldg., SLC, Utah, microfilm, Call No. MS 8192, Access No. 33217-ARCH-88.)

1. Cowley, *Wilford Woodruff Journal*, p. 388. *Confessions*, p. 252.
2. See Appendix B for full depositions of both Young and Smith.
3. Letter from Young to Colonel William Dame. "Church Letter Book" No. 3, pp. 858-60. Also found in Young's letters, second Lee trial.
4. Reber (*The Trials of John D. Lee*, p. 29) used these precise words.
5. This was a name the Piutes gave Lee after occasionally finding him in tears when things didn't go his way in the early Harmony years. While Lee never gave any indication how he felt about this label, it is doubtful Hamblin would bring the name up here except under direct questioning. Why Bishop did so is not clear. Perhaps Bishop wanted Hamblin to disclose some animosity toward Lee in order to show bias in testimony about him.
6. *Confessions*, p. 265. If Bishop did alter Lee's diaries, he let this statement remain which helps explain Brigham Young's reason for being slow to excommunicate Lee.
7. *Desert Saints*, p. 305, footnote no. 20. "Joseph Smith Journal," Oct. 2, 1876.
8. *Journal History of the Church*, Feb. 10, 1859. Also, Little, pp. 51-52. In MMM, p. 123-5, Brooks questions whether the LDS Church was properly accounting for these cattle taken from passing wagon trains.
9. "Higbee said I was resisting authority." Lee names White as "helping to kill one of the massacre escapees" etc. *Confessions*, pp. 231-235. Many names not given while Lee lived are presented here after Lee's death.
10. Reber, p. 30.
11. Clarence Darrow was the lawyer who successfully defended John Scopes against a charge of teaching evolution in the Tennessee schools, 1925. Darrow brilliantly opposed William Jennings Bryan, champion of the Bible and a popular figure of his day. Darrow became famous for taking (and usually winning) difficult cases. *World Book Encyclopedia*, D, p. 31.

12. There is no record of Jacob ever complaining that his "inspiration" was different than that of the Church president. Hamblin's greatest "test" (see further chapters) was to meet with hostile Navajos at Brigham's request when they sought his blood to atone for the death of three tribal members. Under Young's direction, Jacob returned a second time to meet with the angry Navajos.

13. Jacob asks, "Why didn't the Piedes want older children?" Lee asks, "What you trying to imply?" Baily, pp. 165.

14. *Confessions,* p. 388.

15. *Zealots of Zion,* p. 161.

16. MMM, pp.209-10.

17. "$10,000" figure, *Desert Saints,* pp. 305-06. Disposition of children, MMM, pp. 101-06, Appendix XI, pp. 265-278.

18. Ibid, pp. 104-5.

19. Cited by Roberts, pp. 179-80, from LDS historian Orson F. Whitney's *The Making of a State* .

Note: Photostat copies of several original Lee diaries can also be found in the Henry E. Huntington Library, San Marino, Calif. ; some typewritten copies are in the Utah State Historical Society, SLC, Utah. Some originals and copies are in the BYU Lee Library, Special Collections.

– Chapter Eight –

Realization of a Dream

With the spring of 1858 transforming into the greenery of summer, Hamblin must have become restless. The Mountain Meadows Massacre was behind him. There were some repercussions, such as the San Bernardino saints being threatened with expulsion after southern California residents learned of Mormon participation in the massacre.[1] But with the coming of Johnston's Army, those saints were summoned home by Brigham to help defend inner Zion. Many of these migrating Church members decided to settle in Santa Clara,[2] physically bolstering the white population there, and doubtless, also bolstering the spirits of Rachel, Priscilla and the other women fearful of unpredictable Indians with their men gone so much.

Hamblin does not say much in his journals about this period. Some of his journals are badly weathered and smudged after the period when he recorded taking the Indian chiefs to Salt Lake City. Thus, we turn to the journals of Thales Haskell, who provides domestic insights to the period 1856-8. He says somberly, "The Indians would boast that they could massacre all who were left [at home] and take away everything they wanted before word could be sent to the men who were away...We always advised the people at the fort [Santa Clara]...to be very careful not to leave their axes or anything else lying around which an Indian could use to kill a person."[3]

Haskell says that after the Mountain Meadows Massacre the Indians became "saucy and impudent;" but in addition, the Indians very much feared an invasion from federal troops. "It took time to convince some of the leaders of those tribes that neither they nor we were in any immediate danger from soldiers coming in..."[4]

Perhaps the Mormons had done too good a job of preparing the natives to fight their battles. By the summer of 1858, with President Buchanan's pardon, in effect, it was now necessary to convince the Dixie Piutes to gear up with shovel and hoe to a field of crops rather than bow and knife to a field of battle. Haskell says it was also often necessary "to call out every able-bodied man...to help recover livestock stolen by the Indians or to protect companies of emigrants whose safety was threatened,"[5] following the MMM.

One entry of Haskell describes an Indian massacre in the Las Vegas region that doesn't seem to be reported elsewhere. Fire had been set to the wreckage of an emigrant train "to destroy what evidence they could of their savage deed."[6] Burned bodies lay about. This is obviously not the Mountain Meadows Massacre, for that was described by Haskell (and labeled as such) in previous entries. It is included here to provide an idea of the risk that all whites faced in the Southwest Indian Territory of the late 1850s. Settlers were in less peril, of course, than emigrants because of the former's clout with local militia. Yet, the settlers never knew from day to day what might rile the redmen they little understood.

Hamblin obviously had more insight into their daily moods than anyone else, but that would be of little comfort to Rachel and Priscilla with their husband gone so much. Besides, while Jacob might be certain no aborigine could harm him, did that same protection extend to his family members? Women and children could easily become frustrated if detecting any cavalier attitude on the part of Jacob as to precisely what hazards the local Piutes posed to others. It would be easy to understand their much greater concern when Jacob began talking about going among the more fierce and warlike Navajos. In addition to that, there were the many physical dangers associated with climbing unknown mountains and crossing rivers or vast deserts even the hardened Spanish explorers were careful to avoid.[7]

Nevertheless, with security at home beefed up with the influx of San Bernardino saints, everyone in Santa Clara knew that to try holding Jacob back from visiting the faraway Lamanites would be like trying to halt swirling Santa Clara Creek during spring flood stage.[8]

But at least Jacob could now feel that families of men making the inevitable journey were safe, or at least safer than they had ever been since being called to the southern Utah Indian mission. He could finally pursue his long-held dream. He could visit the "higher civilization" of Moqui Lamanites, the so-called "Town Indians" across the Colorado.[9]

In actual preparations, Jacob's writings indicate that while he may have little comprehended the historical significance of what he was about to do, he felt the surge of a new era about to begin.[10] Hamblin would soon enter uncharted territory. As Birney put it: "At that time, 1858, considerably more was known of the geography of the moon than of the desert regions that lay on either side of the Colorado River from the mouth of the Green River to the Virgen (sic). Men knew that the Colorado had cut its way to the sea through the most stupendous chasms on the face of the earth, but beyond that fact there were only the half-forgotten tales of wandering trappers and the garbled traditions of the Indians."[11] Into this unknown and seemingly forgotten no-man's land Hamblin would begin the work for which he would be most remembered and long revered. Indeed, from which many legends were born.

In chapters about Hamblin's journeys across Colorado, both Birney and James McClintock use James Fenimore Cooper's term from "Last of the Mohicans."[12] Jacob is "Leatherstocking," a name that Dellenbaugh had used for Hamblin. Jacob himself would never have endorsed the term; he would have been embarrassed by it, since there is no indication he ever wished to call attention to himself.

James McClintock, a non-Mormon, says: Jacob was "serene in his faith and confident that his footsteps were being guided from on high...the Author has found himself unable to write the history of northernmost Arizona without continual mingling of the name and personal deeds of Jacob Hamblin."[13] The author of *Mormon Settlement in Arizona* need not be so conservative. Hamblin's explorations and activities went well beyond "northernmost Arizona," southeasterly beyond the Grand Canyon region all the way to the New Mexico border.

In receiving instruction (permission) from Brigham to at last visit the Moquis (Hopis), Jacob was charged to "learn something of the character and condition of this people, and to take advantage of any opening there might be to preach the gospel to them and do them good."[14]

Much preparation, no doubt in prayerful supplication, would be needed in dealing with the Navajos who might be encountered while enroute to the Hopi. Rumor had it that the Navajo brave was particularly adept and cunning in the art of horsemanship, firearms, and battle. Even if one did not directly encounter the Navajos, one must still guard carefully all horses, stock and other possessions. Tribal members had raided smaller Utah settlements like Hebron west of Harmony, running off horses and cattle. Haskell explains some of the Navajo skills at theft and deception: "These Indians would cut down a small tree and with one hand hold the tree up and crawl along, and drive off a herd of cattle or horses before we could imagine Indians anywhere around...they would skin a yearling calf, leave its head and hooves on, get inside of this hide and leisurely let down the bars of our fields or corrells (sic) and drive off our animals."[15]

Knowledge of such surreptitious mischief likely caused no small apprehension among those Jacob might choose to go with him. In spite of it, Jacob knew he could likely get willing men together almost anytime. Some would go for the adventure of it. Others would go out of duty. Yet, it would be prudent to wait for the end of flood season on the Colorado. And with summer's searing heat and lack of water in the vast desert eastward, it would be better to wait until mid-autumn.

There had been a reason why the Old Spanish Trail skirted nearly 200 miles north of the Arizona Strip. The route through central Utah to (today's) Manti Mountain and southwesterly through the highlands near Beaver, thence to Parowan and Mountain Meadows, provided a relatively consistent source of water. Jacob had been told there was little which could be counted on enroute to the Moquis. It required crossing the heart of a forbidden landscape which had been meticuously avoided for years. But one must also not go too far south. It would bring one to the impassable grand gorge described by the Indians. This was the great mistake of the Escalante-Dominquez explorers, who learned the hard way they should have taken advice of native guides. Instead, they wasted some ten days wandering around in a desperate search for water which nearly killed them if lack of food didn't.[16]

Even the Navajos did not take permanent abode in any one segment of the country to be traveled. Rather they wandered where water and game took them, often raiding settlements as widely scattered as northern Mexico, New Mexico, eastern Arizona and any white holdings in between. These Indians were not afraid of armed soldiers, although the latter would be more of a force to reckon with in the next decade. The Ute Walkara had also stolen thousands of horses in California with great stealth and cunning. It wouldn't take that many to break the small Mormon ranchers. Even a few head could make a difference between profit and ruin. The marauders generally tried to avoid confrontation in Utah's Dixie because they were outnumbered. Some of the Navajos had even acquired firearms from unscrupulous traders, although most likely, none of them Mormons. Brigham had with an iron hand forbidden trade with the Indians save through specified men who could be trusted.

Could Jacob assure his companions they might return to their families in this mission-adventure? Ira Hatch and Dudley Leavitt had very nearly lost their lives trying to assist white emigrants. Only Hatch's prayer, softening the heart of a Mojave chief, spared them on one occasion. In escaping ambush, Hamblin could only thank a divine providence for "mericles manifested for which I feel to thank the Lord, my Heavenly Father and his Son, Jesus Christ," as recorded in his 1854-57 diary, p. 48. But if any failed to prepare adequately to provide for themselves, would God save them nevertheless? If any died, would Hamblin be blamed?

Hardship and danger dogged every pioneer saint. It was a common saying in Mormondom that perfection could not come without suffering. Every soul was expected to be doing something to serve the Church. For example, when the missionaries were not directly proselyting (or fighting) Indians, they could be busy at a number of things such as mining iron and lead. Jacob and his companions (Little, p. 56) found a way to successfully smelt lead ore, finding many uses for it, including making bullets.

President Young had said often that gold and silver and all precious minerals would corrupt the saints and turn their heads and hearts from the more precious things of the Lord's kingdom—but there were many uses for lead. Iron had also been mined, making enough impact on the lives of the settlers at Cedar City to name their newly organized county after the metal. Although falling well short of today's steel in terms of strength and malleability, iron of the middle 1800s found many uses in wagon parts, wheel rims, shovels, etc.

The missionaries' mining and smelting efforts might have been far easier without horse-thieving Iyets around. The missionaries were forced more than once to walk long distances in the Nevada desert. On one of these forays, Jacob grew desperately hungry, roasting and eating pods from a cactus. As he described it, "I soon became satisfied that I was poisoned. With no help near, I felt that my earthly career was nearly terminated unless the God of Israel saved me, as I knew he had done many times before. I knelt down and earnestly asked Him to be merciful to me in my extremity and save my life."[17] Jacob then consumed the meager water in his canteen which was soon "ejected," lying down on a troubled stomach to either die or sleep. Awakening in the morning, Jacob found it to be the latter.

Despite many spiritual experiences, there were many reminders for Jacob that he lived in a physical world. One day while cutting wood from a cottonwood tree near home, he fell 20 to 30 feet from a tree and hit his head. "I was badly bruised and was carried to my house for dead, or nearly so." Jacob said he came to his senses about 8 p.m. and threw off from his stomach "quite a quantity of blood." He then lost consciousness and "it seemed to me that I went up from the Earth and looked down upon it, and it appeared like a dark ball. The place I was in seemed very desirable to remain in...I thought I saw my father there, but separated from me. I wished him to let me in his compartment but he replied that it was not time for me to come to him." Jacob inquired why. "He answered, 'Your work is not yet done.'" In a moment said Hamblin, "I was back to Earth."[18] After that, he was fed a diet of goat's milk and recovered.

Jacob named the day for departure as Oct. 28. All of Santa Clara buzzed with the preparations. The weather most likely had cooled down before then, but it likely took more time than expected to mend clothes, recobble old boots, repair bridles and harnesses, pick beans and corn to take along, bake foods with loving care, finish the fall harvest in general and package scriptures to withstand the long journey. Without any stores to purchase goods, all must be repaired to make do. For example, the leather harness on a pack animal might be falling apart at every connection. Strong rope or wire (if available from Salt Lake City) must be used to make a harness or bridle last another 50 or 80 miles, and if possible, 500-600 miles. A few converts coming from England might have brought machine-made wire with them which was becoming available by the middle 1800s.[19] Wire might have been made from iron mined a few miles west of Cedar City, but there is little mention of the same.

It is interesting that while those of the modern era think of our own as an advanced age, almost any pioneer possesed far more individual self-reliance and ingenuity to face the challenges of daily life than most of us do today. That self-reliance and ingenuity was put to a stern test in October, 1858 to ready these men for their new adventure.

To go with him, Jacob chose his brothers Frederick and William, and Samuel Knight, Ira Hatch, Andrew Gibbons, Benjamin Knell, Ammon M. Tenney (Spanish interpreter), James Davis (Welsh interpreter sent along by Brigham), and the Piute guide, Naraguts. "A Spanish interpreter was thought advisable" because many of the Indians were thought to speak that language."[20] Thales Haskell (who for some reason did not join this first expedition to the Hopis) offers an insight into the Welsh connection when he accompanied Hamblin on the second expedition across the Colorado: "It had been reported that included in the Moqui language were some Welsh words and this led to the belief that these particular tribes were of Welsh origin." McClintock says that President Young (p. 63) "had heard that a group of Welshmen, several hundred years before, had disappeared into the western wilds." Davis was a Welshman, familiar with the language of his native land. Tenney, then only fourteen, knew a number of Indian dialects, as well as Spanish, the last learned in San Bernardino."[21]

Tenney, easily youngest of the group, certainly would not have been taken along if he was not a rather mature lad physically as well as intellectually. He not only kept up with the others in every way, but kept a diary which will be referred to later.

Haskell says Davis found no links between Moqui and Welsh people on either his first or second trip across the Colorado. But some years later, about 1878, "A Mormon missionary by the name of Lleweln Harris (himself of Welsh extraction) visited the Zuni tribes, a pueblo dwelling people living east of the Hopi and reported that this people had a great many words in their language which resemble the Welsh and have the same meaning."[22]

The Mormon missionaries would also be interested in checking out any linkage, in language or otherwise, to the Holy Land, since The Book of Mormon taught that Hebrews fled destruction in Jeruasalem. It was accepted by every Mormon that they crossed the ocean in about 600 B.C., safely reaching South America.[23]

Haskell also explains that some whitemen were thought to have reached Mexico even before Cortez' conquest of Mexico in 1519.[24] "They say that from these whitemen came the ancient kings of Mexico from whom Montezuma descended...these whitemen are still remembered...in the traditions of the Zuni Indians...in time these white people became mixed with the Indians until scarcely a relic of them remained."[25]

Of course, Hamblin sought any connection he could find between Indians of his day and those written about in The Book of Mormon. In that context, links between Welsh and Hopi were of less religious significance to him than any Hebrew links he might find.

Because of this, one might ponder which specific scriptures were of primary importance to the missionaries. Certainly Hamblin would explain, or have an interpreter explain, The Book of Mormon title page, "Written to the Lamanites, who are a remnant of the House of Israel." For Jew or Mormon, it was understood an Israelite had been a believer in a pre-existent world...or was expressly born into the House of Israel because he was considered by Deity to be a believer. The latter might be quicker to "remember" the familiar spirit of the gospel, or to recognize it. This didn't automically show favoritism; a man could be adopted into the House of Israel, although outsiders or "gentiles" were lumped with those who might not believe as readily. A fine line separated many whites and all Indians for the Latterday Saint; both would usually show up in a patriarchal blessing as descended from Joseph. Most whites would come through the line of Ephraim; for the Indian, Mannassah.

For unbelievers there were key scriptures like Alma 32: 27-8: "But behold, if you will awake and arouse your faculties, even to an experiment upon my words, yea, even if ye can no more than desire to believe, let this desire work in you, even until ye believe in a manner that ye can give place for a portion of my words. Now we will compare the word unto a seed. Now... a seed may be planted in your heart...behold if it be a true seed or a good seed...if ye do not cast it out...behold, it will begin to swell within your breasts." Alma then gives the conditions to nourish the seed: watering it, exposing to the sun's light, weeding, etc., until the plant begins sprouting and growing. By analogy, water and sun are compared to prayer and exertion of faith. Weeding out doubt is also necessary, i.e., trusting in the process long enough for the testimony within to sprout and grow as would the plant.

As with most Mormon missionaries of that time, the teaching process would have likely ended with Moroni 10: 4, "And when ye shall receive these things, I would exhort you that ye would ask God the Eternal Father, in the name of Christ, if these things are not true; and if ye shall ask with a sincere heart, with real intent, having faith in Christ, he will manifest the truth of it unto you, by the power of the Holy Ghost."

The role of Jacob Hamblin has often been emphasized in visiting the Lamanites as exploring, colonizing, peacemaking, adventuring; but any reading of his diaries reveals his primary purpose—to reach out to the Lamanites and lift them spiritually. Love? Yes, the type of love exemplified by the Apostle Paul which launched so many dangerous journeys to spread the Word. Perhaps the major difference was in the mode of travel; Paul shipboard and Jacob in the saddle.

True, the Mormons had angered some in claiming to be "the only true Church upon the face of the earth" with a "full restoration of all things once had in Christ's early Church." But this was not a boast for most of the faithful. It was a burden and a responsibility. The challenge was one of work accompanying faith, for in Hamblin's philosophy salvation did not come without much labor. One can read the sum of it in 2 Nephi, 25: 23. "It is by grace we are saved, after all we can do." Christ would provide the "grace," to resurrect all men but members must be doing "all they can do" to bring about good works. The question for Jacob seemed to be, "Am I doing enough?" If he had, indeed, built up a personal trust in the Lord over the years, he must now bolster up others who had not. And who would need his help more than a people who had once held that trust and lost it?

But what about trying to teach a people so barbaric that they lied and stole and killed the innocent, openly displaying scalps of their victims? The Indians were guilty of it, yes; but did not some of Jacob's peers, Christian men they called themselves, do the same at Mountain Meadows? Did they not steal, lie, kill innocent souls, and allow their unburied bones to be openly displayed? (Bailey, p. 315, likened renegade Navajos who kill to renegade whites who participated in the MMM.)

Who was to say Indians were more inhumane than their white brothers? The natives were often in violation of whitemen's standards, yet acknowledged a supreme being who controlled the mysterious workings of nature. The natives' Great Spirit was often confused with magic, superstition or even witchcraft; but few Indians thought themselves creation's apex as did many whites.

Birney said of Hamblin and his feelings about proselyting among the natives: "He was absolutely unswerving in his devotion to Mormonism, though far more tolerant than the majority of the missionaries in his attitude toward the religious beliefs of the Indians..."[26] Why should any whiteman claim himself more redeemable than such red brethren who sought humbly to know their place in the universe?

Inasmuch as Hamblin did not believe he could be harmed by Indians, this first trip east provided an interesting insight. One Piute showed Jacob the skeleton of an Indian Hamblin knew well: "There are the bones of Nahguts [not to be confused with Hamblin's present guide, Naraguts], who killed your ox on the Clara. He came as far as here, was taken blind, could not find the spring and died."[27] Hamblin would meet more redmen like Nahguts who threatened at one time to kill him

As explained by Jacob, he and his plodding horsemen were watched by many curious eyes as they ventured into the desert beyond Hurricane Mesa. Fortunately, those eyes belonged to friendly Kaibab Indians (Hamblin called them "Kibab").[28] As they neared Buckskin Mountain, the owners of these watchful eyes contacted their chiefs and marshalled forces to welcome the missionaries. Upon their arrival, a huge feast of roasted rabbit was prepared. One of the chiefs "thanked the Father for success of the hunt" as Hamblin wrote it.[29] Then they divided the meat equally among white and redmen, while the former shared bread brought along from home. All seemed peaceful for the time being.

Then, Hamblin noticed an Indian sitting moodily alone and eating nothing. "I sat down by him and asked what he was thinking about. Said he, 'I am thinking of my brother, whom you killed with bad medicine.' I told him that his brother had made his own bad medicine, that he came to Clara, killed an ox, and had brought a curse on himself. I advised the Indian to eat with the company, and not make any bad medicine and kill himself. This very prevalent idea of good and bad medicine, among these Indians, gives evidence of a very general belief in witchcraft."[30]

Hamblin said the Indian finally took a piece of bread, saying he did not wish to die. "I was told by our guide that this Indian had said that in the night, when I was asleep, he intended to chop an axe into my head, but being afraid it would make bad medicine for him, he did not do it."[31]

Hamblin consumes only one paragraph in telling about crossing the fearsome Colorado. He says, "After climbing dangerous cliffs...on the tenth day out from home we crossed the Colorado River, at the Ute Ford, known in Spanish history as 'The Crossing of the Fathers.' The trail beyond the river was not only difficult, but sometimes very dangerous."[32]

The next day one of the animals carrying provisions ran off. Three days later, the group came across a garden of onions, peppers, and other vegetables and squash. "We appropriated it to our use. It tasted delicious and we supposed it be a better variety than we had before known, but we afterwards found that hunger had made it taste sweet."[33]

Four miles farther, they arrived at their destination, an Oriba (Oraibi) village of about 300 dwellings. Coming in peace, the travelers were immediately made to feel welcome, quite possibly smoothed along with Naraguts knowing a little of Hopi customs and language. "We were invited to dine with different families," says Hamblin. "The hostess made a comfortable seat with blankets, and motioned me to occupy it. A liberal repast was provided. It consisted of stewed meat, beans, peaches, and a basket of corn bread which they called peke." Hamblin was shown how to convey the soup to his mouth without a spoon. "Then she motioned me to eat. Hunger was pressing and a hint was sufficient."[34]

Religious response from the Hopis was mixed. One aged Hopi thought these men were an answer to prophecies that men would come from the west and "bring them great blessings."[35] Others were not so sure. At stake were many centuries of tradition. To embrace these Mormon missionaries meant placing themselves under their direction and quite possibly forsaking some of their past religious practices.

Hamblin felt it advisable to leave some of the brethren behind to live with the Hopis and learn more about them—and "as they are of the blood of Israel, offer them the gospel."[36] Selected to remain with them were William Hamblin, Andrew Gibbon, Thomas Leavitt and Benjamin Knell. Had Hamblin been aware at this time of a Hopi tradition that three men would come among them who should be heeded as bearing a heavenly message, perhaps one less man might have been left behind. Some of the Hopi leaders talked it over and could not decide if these four whitemen were those prophesied to someday visit them.

When it came time to depart, Hamblin felt troubled temporally as well as spiritually. He had expected to refurbish supplies at the Oraibi villages. The missionaries were almost devoid of food. The Hopis had little and had already shared generously with their guests. Snow had fallen by now and grass was difficult to find for the animals. After a few days out, Jacob had to kill a horse and "lived on this rather objectionable kind of food for two days."[37] Interestingly, while Hamblin and his men were to nearly starve on a subsequent expedition, they said at that later date they "had never eaten anything sweeter than horse-flesh." The missionaries, even though hardened frontier types, were just beginning to become acquainted with the full realities of traveling long distances in harsh country. It was especially difficult on the return trip with less food in colder weather.

John C. Fremont had shown a strange propensity for exploring western mountain country in winter; it had nearly killed him more than once. But with federal subsidy, Fremont could choose when to go. For Hamblin and crew, lengthy travel must in most cases come after the autumn harvest. Spring meant floods. Summer travel in the desert was prohibitive.

On pages 67-68 of the Little edition Hamblin enumerates many hardships encountered on the return home. All were all the result of natural adversity. No hostile Indians were confronted on this expedition coming or going, but the physical challenge was itself quite harsh.

On arriving home, Jacob says it was "very pleasant to find a change of diet and our families and friends all well." There had been some problems with the Santa Clara Indians. "I visited the natives and found that there were no bad intentions. They were all pleased to have the matter understood and settled."[38] Ever the diplomat and peacemaker, Hamblin felt white and redmen could live in full harmony.

As for the brethren left with the Hopis, they did not remain long. They "returned home the same winter. A division arose among the people as to whether we were the men prophesied of by their fathers." The missionaries had sought to have some of the Hopis return with them across the Colorado to live among the Mormons, but "they had a tradition from their fathers that they must not cross that river until the three prophets should visit them again."[39]

End Notes, Chapter Eight

1. Birney, *Zealots of Zion*, p. 91
2. B.H. Roberts, p. 245
3. Thales H. Haskell (A. E. Smith), p. 30
4.. Ibid, p. 29
5. Ibid, 29
6. Ibid, 32
7. There is no record of any whitemen exploring the Arizona Strip north of the Grand Canyon prior to this time save the Dominguez-Escalante party who tried to circumvent the region and found they couldn't.
8. Even in modern times "gulley washers" thrust heavy floods down Santa Clara Creek, but much is now held back by Gunlock Reservoir.
9. Little, p. 61
10. Author's conclusion from Little, pp. 61-62.
11. Birney, p. 113.
12. Birney, calls Jacob "Leatherstocking of the Desert," p. 111. McClintock, *Mormon Settlement in Northern Arizona*, also calls Jacob "Leatherstocking of the Southwest," p. 59.
13. James McClintock, p. 59
14. Little, p. 61
15. "Haskell Autobiography," p. 20
16. D & C 101:35. The idea is also expressed by Latter-day Saint pioneer Mary Fielding Smith, 1837, *Women's Voices*, p. 64.
17. Little, p. 57
18. Ibid, pp. 60-61
19. Machine-made wire, *World Book Encyclopedia*, W, p. 289-90
20. Little, p. 62
21. THH, pp. 30-31. This rumor seemed generally prevalent in the United States at that time among more than the Mormons.
22. Ibid, p.30. Haskell and Little used the term "Moqui" for some time. But Little explains in a footnote, p. 61:"There is no tribe acknowledging that name. They were known even at that time (1881) as Hopi."
23. Ancestors of the American Indian. 1 Nephi, *Book of Mormon*.
24. WBE, Ci-CZ, p. 854
25. THH, pp. 30-31. Haskell is doing some theorizing here.
26. Birney, p. 22
27. Little pp. 62-63

28. "The travelers knew that their movements were being watched by curious Indians." Corbett, p. 151, concluded from Little, p. 62

29. Little, p. 62.

30. Ibid, p. 63

31. Ibid

32. Ibid. It is typical of Hamblin here that he mentions items of considerable danger in a very few words.

33. Ibid, pp. 63-64. Note Hamblin's unique oblique humor.

34. Ibid, p. 65

35. Ibid, p. 66. Hamblin's personal journals say nothing about this period, probably because he was so busy with travel and the fact he recorded his visits to the Moqui (Hopi) in the Little account.

36. Ibid. This could only be labeled "Mormon duty." It would appear there was no remaining adventure in it.

37. Ibid, p. 67. The Dominguez-Escalante group had also killed a horse for meat in 1776. It would be almost a regular ritual with Hamblin's party.

38. Ibid.

39. Ibid, p. 68

Chapter Nine

Across the Colorado: Physical Challenge

Only with a personal inspection of the vast distance between Santa Clara and Oraibi can one begin to comprehend the physical challenge faced by Jacob Hamblin in his missionary efforts to the Hopi Indians. Not only did Hamblin have to travel some 600 miles round trip to complete this journey but it led through both pine-jungled plateaus and barren deserts, with a temperature change from freezing to heat-seared, waterless sand. Then came the most formidable challenge of all: crossing the Colorado River. If you went in the late fall-early winter, the only time the stream was low enough to ford, you encountered ice-slick cliffs and ledges. They caused the death of at least one Hamblin party pack horse and constantly threatened the same to anyone making the slightest mis-step.

In addition, only on the first expedition did Hamblin have a guide. After that, there were hundreds of places to take the wrong game trail. One could wander about for days before locating either the correct direction, or life-preserving water.

To shorten this distance, Jacob moved to Kanab. From there, the trek was some 160 miles less. But it also required a different route to reach Lee's Ferry on the Colorado, and thus, new landmarks (often no more than a gulley or rockface on Buckskin Mountain) had to be learned.

If one got too far east going over Buckskin (named by the Piutes for an abundance of mule deer) it meant looking down from more than a thousand feet atop the Vermillion Cliffs. To get an idea of the danger represented, one can look at the westward Vermillion Cliffs as they tower above present-day Kanab. Yet, if Hamblin led his party too far west, they would find a long delay in descending the 6,500 foot high Kaibab Pleateau; if venturing too far south, the Grand Canyon blocked their path.

Hamblin never mentioned making a map through this country, nor did he or any of the party personally with Jacob, ever mention getting lost. Hamblin and his crew had to be con-summate outdoorsmen to negotiate such wild terrain repeated-ly, and more importantly, to be persevering and dedicated to Jacob's perceived plan of teaching the Hopis. Hamblin was most certainly all this, or he would have remained comfortably home to teach the local Lamanites.

Interestingly, Hamblin's men used a route from Kanab which crossed the path the Escalante-Dominguez party forged in 1776. Jacob's route was closely approximated in the late 1800s by Mormon couples heading to and from the St. George Temple. This came to be known as the "Honeymoon Trail" and ironical-ly, modern maps mark it that way rather than the "Hamblin Trail."

Today, one can view several places where all three trails converge, or nearly so, at Pioneer Gap, some 15 miles east of Kanab. Most of this area is under control of the U.S. Bureau of Land Management and can be traversed by the public today, although stock fences might cause detours if venturing to the base of Buckskin Mountain. The Gap is exactly 5.5 miles east of Johnson Wash just south of U.S. 89. Hamblin and group were almost certainly the first whitemen to use the Gap route as they headed for the Colorado River via House Rock Valley in the early 1860s. One often reads in Jacob's diaries about stopping at Navajo Wells, a key watering hole just west of the Gap, but in private ownership today. Yet, there are few landscape changes. The terrain looks as seemingly remote and lonely today as it must have 150 years ago.

When living in Santa Clara, however, Jacob's straightest and shortest route to the Colorado would have been what is now called the "Mid-Mountain" trail. This led past Pipe Springs,[1] a valuable source of water, directly over the Kaibab Plateau (today only the northern end of the Kaibab is called Buckskin Mountain) near present day Jacob Lake. From Hurricane Mesa some 20 miles east of Santa Clara, this route followed the basic line of today's Utah 59-Arizona 389 to Pipe Springs.

That route was far more sensible than the one taken by Francisco Atanasio Dominguez and Francisco Silvestre Velez de

Escalante. The Catholic Fathers did not trust local Indians' advice to steer more east than south from Hurricane Mesa,[2] thus peering into the sheer abyss of the Grand Canyon. Part of that distrust could have been the Shivwits' condition and temerity. As Escalante put it: the Shivwits were "extremely low spirited." They wore only loin cloths and the women little if anything at all "...barely covering what one cannot gaze upon without peril."[3] One Indian guide had deserted them a few days earlier "without an adieu" after watching two of the exploring party argue and grapple.[4] The physical confrontation, ironically, was about praying the Virgin's Rosary. The fathers watched in dismay as the frightened native (who had guided them all the way from Utah Lake) hurried out of camp, presumably to return to his home in Utah Valley. As Escalante put it, "We knew nothing about the country ahead, not even from hearsay."[5]

A new guide that they didn't fully trust took them into a defile near Hurricane Mesa which was apparently so narrow it alarmed the Fathers into thinking they were being led astray or into ambush. They acted against the guide's advice and headed south into what they apparently thought was less rough terrain. No Indian would follow. Escalante says it this way (page 81 of his journal): "They told us that in two days we would reach El Rio Grande, but that we could not go by the route we intended because there were no water sources, nor could we cross the river by this route for its being very much boxed in and very deep, and having extremely tall rocks and cliffs on both sides." But Escalante adds: "We did not want to give up going south toward the river no matter what..."[6]

The mistake cost them dearly. The friars continued until encountering the Grand Canyon near what would be later called Mt. Trumbull, dry, desolate and forbidding then as now. The group's leader, Dominguez, then turned sharply eastward. The group killed one of their horses for food. Then, they spent some 10 days wandering about the North Rim wilderness perilously close to death. Finally, they made their way into the present-day Kanab area, apparently found water there, and proceeded toward Buckskin Mountain just southeast of Pioneer Gap.

With much difficulty and suffering, the padres crossed the Colorado and made their way to Santa Fe, completing the first white exploration into the wilderness of southern Utah and northern Arizona. Looking for a route to Monterey in California, they proved one thing: the way they went wasn't the best way to go. The dire circumstances faithfully recorded in their journal, particularly the lack of water, could well have had much to do with the Spanish Trail later shunting far from the Arizona Strip.

Jacob, too, had noted the poor living conditions of the natives, their scant clothing and timid manner, as recorded by Escalante. (There is no indication that Hamblin saw any of Escalante's writings.) But after spending much time talking eating, dancing, smoking,[7] and living among the Indians, Hamblin learned who he could trust. And they learned to trust him. Jacob placed much confidence in the Piute guide Naraguts for the missionaries' first venture east. The latter led Hamblin on a line roughly paralleling today's Utah-Arizona border. Naraguts got Hamblin's group to the Kaibab region in less than half the time (and in much better health) than Escalante's group managed. Hamblin knew Indians. His confidence in Naraguts was obviously well-placed.

In later years, a wagon road wending all the way from Kanab to the upper Little Colorado River replaced the trail Hamblin's group pioneered.[8] But it was too rough a route for later highway builders, who opted to build through what is now the Jacob Lake area atop the Kaibab, miles from Pioneer Gap.

Today, looking at the Gap in late autumn when Jacob most often passed through, one sees that things haven't changed much since the l860s. A vast panorama of silver-blue rabbitbrush unfolds below Buckskin Mountain. A few golden leaves are conspicuous toward the summit overlooking Coyote Wash. From there, a black labyrinth of pinyon-pine, bathed in north slope shadows, climb up Buckskin Mountain which does not descend to lower elevations until reaching Cockscomb well to the north, opposite the Hamblin route to House Rock Valley. One does not fully comprehend until reaching the foothills just how steep and formidable the natural barrier looms. There is no easy canyon passage now; there was none then.

November in this country is cool by day, frigid by night. Yet, once Hamblin entered hostile Indian country, he and his men did not dare build a fire. They went weeks without cooked meals, or even a warming and cheerful campfire. By January, when Hamblin often returned fron Hopi country, temperatures turned bitter cold. Only once in all his writings does Jacob lament cold or snow, and only then when fearing frostbite for his men. Hamblin does mention lying in the cold once on Buckskin Mountains while experiencing the apprehensive dream about his family explained in Chapter Two.

Hamblin, of course, had to worry about possible Indian ambush behind thousands of boulders and pinyon thickets. Rocky outcroppings and deep washes offered multiple dangers.

Hamblin's entourage had horses most of the time, of course, but there were occasions when a horse had to be shot for food. Jacob tells of times when he developed painful foot blisters, when his party had to double up on horseback, or walk long distances, carrying limited food and water.[9] Since they didn't dare be without their firearms, walking was indeed a heavy burden.

Hamblin took pride (if not always comfort) in surviving without complaint. He rarely mentions hardships. Yet, his company faced many of the same hardships as their LDS Church peers in the Willie-Martin handcart companies who died in Wyoming, September-October, 1856, due to confrontation with the physical elements.[10] Cold and wind buffeted the Hamblin adventurers, as it did the handcart companies, at nearly every turn. The fact that not a single Hamblin associate trekking through unmapped wilderness (with one exception) ever died due to purely physical causes indicates the preparation and savvy of their leader, Jacob Hamblin. The lone loss to physical hazard was Lorenzo Roundy, who drowned on a makeshift raft while crossing the Colorado at Lee's Ferry in 1876, an event which nearly cost Jacob and others their lives as well. Neither the loss of vital supplies nor death of a friend, however, halted Hamblin. After the drowning, he writes: "We gathered up what was left of our outfit, visited the missions of Mowabby and Moancoppy and...settlements of the Little Colorado."[11]

Interestingly, to show their respect for Hamblin, the Piute Indians declared House Rock Valley a gift to Jacob, although it is not known if it was theirs (or some other tribe's) to give.[12] Hamblin never did spend much time at House Rock, but journeyed through frequently. A spring of water there still shows on some maps as Jacob's Pool.

The Mid-Mountain route taken by Hamblin when departing from Santa Clara does leave a few place names to remember him by, including "Jacob's Lake" on Alt. U.S. 89. The name was first given to a pond and then to the nearby junction stop, now popular with summer tourists enroute to the North Rim of the Grand Canyon. There is also Jacob's Canyon (roadless), on the west side of the Kaibab Plateau.

Arriving at what is now known as Lee's Ferry, water proved too deep and swift to ford. There were no materials nearby to build a secure raft; a poor one could be swept downstream and one would be forever doomed after entering the Paria Rapids. Below that were swirling torrents such as Soap Creek and Badger Falls in upper Marble Canyon, entirely unknown until Major John W. Powell's first exploration in 1869. It is said that Hamblin named these two rapids (if so, a rarity, since he left few place names as did Major Powell) because he shot a badger near one; the other name emerged because, when trying to cook the animal, a soap-like and totally inedible substance filled the pot.

To cross the Colorado, Naraguts took Hamblin and his men where Escalante-Dominguez had gone in 1776. First, one had to climb the Paria Canyon, a twisting and tortuous gorge killing anyone caught there in time of flood. They proceeded along ledges high above the treacherous Colorado to a place some 30 miles north of what is now Lee's Ferry to a place long known to the Indians as "Ute Ford" or "Ute Crossing."

Hamblin traveled to the Ute Crossing many more times than he negotiated its waters. The main reason was to keep a watch on rogue Navajos crossing over to steal livestock from Mormon settlements. Jacob saw it as his duty to maintain vigil at the crossing to prevent such thievery.[13] After Lees' Ferry came into use, the settlers dynamited the narrow ledges surrounding this crossing, forever putting an end to it as a viable crossing for crafty natives to steal stock.[14] Later, of course, Lake Powell inundated Crossing of the Fathers (Padre Bay) under more than 200 feet of water.

Hamblin's group often brought along dozens of cattle for sustenance on their long journeys. One of the more amazing feats they accomplished was to get all cows and horses herded (alive) across the river. It was one thing to get a man and his horse across the Colorado; quite another to push reluctant oxen up the narrow Paria Gorge, down the precarious ledges to the Ute Crossing, then across the river with its tricky quicksand bottom and frightening currents.

Escalante went so far as to call the Paria Gorge impassable in his journal,[15] even though he and his peers had just managed somehow to get through. The missionaries' struggle at getting stubborn stock across the Colorado is best told by Thales Haskell. He says one time an ox went partway across but when the men looked again, it had returned to the opposite bank.

"One mule...being heavily packed with meat, got off balance and went rolling over and over down the stream. He finally struck bottom and lay with his feet sticking up kicking. All hands gave him up for lost and the meat supply with him, but he suddenly made a desperate struggle, raised up and came to shore much to the satisfaction of us all." When an oxen started over several times and turned back, the company "decided to let the ox go until tomorrow." The next day Haskell chose Brother Young, "he being a good swimmer," to help him go back for the ox. "We got him safely over this time...me behind brightening up his ideas with the spike pole."[16]

After all their work, some stock was inevitably stolen by Indians. After the first few expeditions, Hamblin and his crew seemed more content to leave the beef behind and eat rabbits. Once they ate six crows.[17] After crossing the muddy Colorado, whether at Ute Ford or later at Lee's Ferry, many difficult miles of jumbled cliffs and gullies awaited the men enroute to Hopi lands. From Lee's, one had to circumvent steep sandstone ledges and lava rock to reach the plateau above. Floating (before the ferry was built) usually meant going far upstream to allow for swift current coming down. Several routes were used from the eastern bank, depending on where the crude skiffs or rafts finally beached. If one reached the other side near the perilous Paria rapids, it meant a steeper climb, as can be viewed now from Navajo Bridge. Or one could be lost forever within the deep walls now known as the Grand Canyon.

After emerging from the incessant shadows of the Colorado River, the men faced many sun-weary miles to Tuba City and Moancoppy (shown on modern maps as Moenkopi). After that, it was nearly 100 miles through hostile Navajo country. Because of it, much travel was done at night in arroyos and washes, without fires. If the missionaries got too far east they would encounter Black Mountain with its many steep cliffs; almost certainly they took a route to the south. It is doubtful even Naraguts had been through here often enough to make no mistakes. Hopi villages in the distance must have been a joyous sight.

No matter which way they went, water was a major problem. On one expedition to the Hopis south of the Grand Canyon, Hamblin wrote, "Brother Jehiel McDonnell was so far gone he could only whisper. Men and animals suffered severely."[18]

Birney says that "Hamblin's self-confidence, his courage, and his calm assurance that he would survive any hardship cannot be exaggerated...Hamblin scouted all of northern Arizona in search of a route that would be less hazardous, less exposed to the Navajo menace, than the Crossing of the Fathers and the long trek across the Kaibito. To him belongs the credit for the discovery of the easier road [crossing] at Lee's Ferry, the building of the first boat at that point, and the development of the wagon road that made possible the colonization of the Little Colorado [River] Valley."[19] But all that would come nearly a decade later.

The terrain to Oraibi via Tuba City and Hotevilla on today's Arizona 264 toward Keams Canyon and south to Holbrook hasn't changed much in 150 years: a dull grey and rather bleak landscape. Large game animals which might feed dozens of men were and are scarce in this monotonous country. Hamblin once described shooting pronghorn antelope for sustenance until reaching Oraibi, cited as "among the oldest continuously occupied settlements in the United States.[20] The Hopis undoubtedly built there because an intruder would find access difficult up forbidding cliffs. Access is most difficult from the south where soldiers and white marauders usually approached. A Hopi could quickly find security by climbing to a second or third story and pulling up the ladder.

Cultivating friendships with the natives from one domain to the next was likely the major reason for Hamblin's survival on these treks across the Colorado. Only the seemingly lowly Kaibabs and other local tribes knew location of the precious rock cavities holding recent rain. These rain pockets could be widely scattered, however, and not easily located.[21] The critical lack of water on the Arizona Strip is told by Jacob's frequent traveling companion, Thales Haskell with a touch of humor:[22] "Thursday 20th: Got up, took breakfast, packed up and...traveled 12 miles to a dry wash where the Indians told us we would find water, but we found none. We went on about 15 miles...camped for the night without water...Friday 21st: Got up at daylight and started following an Indian horse track, the Indians having told us it would lead to water...got off our course and rather bewildered...it was very hot; some got to quoting Shakespeare, when one of the boys remarked that he wished Shakespeare was in hell and that he was with him if they had such a commodity as water there."

Perhaps the use of the word "hell" caused the missionary to feel apologetic. In any event, he added: "I write this to show how savage men felt traveling in the sand without water."

According to Haskell, the party was often scattered out in search of water. In one instance, Thales wrote that the group "finaly came together at the mouth of a kanyon which headed in the Buckskin Mountains." Some hours later, fellow missionary Marion Shelton arrived in camp with a canteen of water he had located at a small spring about three miles away and "treated the crowd." Haskell concludes: "...the idea of finding a spring cheered us up amazingly..."[23] The group lost little time in packing up and riding to the spring. Pressing on, of course, they had to locate water repeatedly before reaching their destination.

Haskell says they often fired guns when separated to locate one another, but even then "wandered around" at times in a constant search for water. Haskell, better than Hamblin, allows his feelings to be known about journeying so far away from families into the unknown. On the eve of departure from Santa Clara, he writes: "Friday 7th:...that night I got to thinking of my misfortunes...could not sleep and finally I believe I had what some people call the blues. After a short time the scene changed and I was happy. The riches of this world and the ups and downs, disappointments and sufferings of life seemed like nothing compared to the work of God...though a few minutes before I had dreaded to go, having been once before and suffered a great many hardships."[24]

Those venturing into the Grand Canyon region today between June-September find temperatures well over 100 degrees. All it takes to suffer severe dehydration or death is to lose one's way for a day or two. One must also be careful not to drink just any water. Longstanding water in particular, or even streams large enough for animals, then and now, might carry *Giardia*.[25] Hamblin never mentions being poisoned by bad water, but the threat was always there.

Where Hamblin hiked into the present Havasupai Indian Reservation below the south rim of the Grand Canyon is nearly 150 (paved) miles today from Las Vegas through a remote desert to Haualapai Hilltop. From there one hikes eight miles deep down into the Indian Village of Suapai, the secret hideaway which Hamblin promised never to reveal to the outside world. Ironically, while Jacob kept his word, the tribe itself now publicizes its tropical-like paradise, attracting many tourists.

Two miles below Supai are three spectacular waterfalls, which Hamblin must surely have visited, yet never mentioned in all his writings. The highest, Mooney, spills some 210 feet. Even more spectacular is Havasu, thundering through lush emerald ferns and limestone terraces. White sand beaches beckon. Swimmers cannot resist plunging in, although the water is not warm, and most don't stay in long.

Hamblin does mention Cataract Creek [today's Havasu Creek] several times. One reference says it was a "bright silver thread glittering in the sun." Another, "It was rapid and clear and skirted with cottonwood timber growing on rich bottom land."[26] He mentions no waterfalls. And he says nothing about how to get there.

Traveling across Navajo Bridge over Marble Canyon (upper Grand Canyon near Lee's Ferry, one finds a monument to John D. Lee honoring his vigil at "Lonely Dell" on the Colorado River. He and wife, Emma, who receives no mention on the monument, deserve some sort of recognition for their long service in operating the ferry, and warning settlers when Indian danger approached from the east. But there is no roadside monument at all in northern Arizona honoring Jacob Hamblin, even though he had more to do with exploring and settling this region than anyone else.[27] As one historian puts it, "They should have named the bridge after him."[28] A wider bridge has been constructed alongside Navajo. But it was not named "Jacob Hamblin Bridge."

Fortunately, the terrain from the Gap to House Rock Valley is on public land. Perhaps some day an annual trail ride or at least a monument will commemorate the historic figures who went there.

End Notes, Chapter Nine

1. This historic spring and ranch, given national monument status in 1923, is located 14 miles west of
   Fredonia, Ariz. The Kaibab Indian Reservation is to the
   north; another historic spring listed on maps as
   Moccasin is to the northeast. The monument is referred
   to as "springs" by Pearson Corbett in *Jacob Hamblin,
   Peacemaker* and some maps. Historian David Lavender
   makes it singular, "Pipe Spring and the Arizona Strip."

   Lavender states (p. 49) that the name came from a
   legendary feat of marksmanship when William
   Hamblin, Jacob's brother, won a bet by shooting the
   bottom out of a (regular) smoking pipe at 50 paces
   "without touching the sides." Legend also had it that
   William first attempted to hit a silk handkerchief but,
   of course, the bullet merely pushed the flimsy cloth
   away. Lavender asks, "Would a pioneer Mormon be
   likely to carry a silk handkerchief on a tough trip
   through rough country?"

   Pipe Spring(s) has been preserved as it was in the
   late 1800s, with a large edifice known as Winsor Castle
   named for its builder Anson Winsor.
2. Escalante says the group "talked [with Indian guides]
   for more than two and a half or three hours" about the
   best direction to take. P.82 explains lengthy attempts of
   local guides to steer the Fathers eastward.
   "Dominguez-Escalante Journal," p. 81.
3. Ibid p. 75. See also p. 78.
4. Ibid p. 69. "As he [Don Juan Pedro Cisneros] was
   scolding him [Simon Lucero, a servant] for his laziness,
   and lack of piety [Lucero was slow in praying the
   Virgin's rosary with Cisneros] the servant took him on,
   grappling with him arm to arm."
5. Ibid p. 69
6. Ibid p. 82
   Note: According to the *World Book Encyclopedia*, G, p.
   299, Spaniards from Francisco Vasquez de Coronado's
   expeditions in 1540 were the first whitemen to discover
   the Grand Canyon. But it is not likely that Dominguez
   or Hamblin learned much from any writings about the
   canyon. Hamblin probably learned all he knew about
   the canyon from local Indian and personal exploration.
7. While the Mormon Word of Wisdom today is interpret-
   ed as placing tobacco off-limits, it was not necessarily
   so in Hamblin's time. (Interview with Dr. Thomas G.
   Alexander, BYU History Dept., Oct. 14, 1994. (See also
   his *Mormonism in Transition*.) Hamblin mentions in

journals of smoking the "peace pipe," with tobacco, among various Indians. A few missionaries also mention drinking (alcoholic) wine. Brigham Young preached strong discourses, however, about the evils of drunkenness: "I will say who drinks wine to excess-- stop it." Bleak, 1874, Book B, p. 262.

8. P. T. Reilly, "Roads over Buckskin Mountain;" Reilly says Isaac Riddle drove the first wagon over Buckskin but credits Hamblin as a primary factor in blazing the first permanent trails through the area.

9. "I started for the Colorado on foot, carrying my gun, bedding and provisions with me....I can scarcely walk my feet are so very sore." "J-C Summary," p. 9: Also, "Could not have a fire. Passed a cold night." In J & L, p. 70, Hamblin says many in his company nearly froze to death.

10. In the Willie Company, some 66 of an estimated 500 emigrants died enroute to Salt Lake City, mostly from hunger and exposure, some of disease. Of an estimated 575 in the Martin Company immediately behind the Willie group, 135 died. (Preston Nibley, *Church History Charts*, 1967.)

11. Corbett, p. 390. There is no endnote for this statement attributed to Hamblin. It could be conjecture.

12. Hamblin muses, "What will I do with House Rock Valley?"J & L, p. 66. Jacob mentions "starting a ranch in the valley," Little, p. 127. There are no further details given; so far as is known, Hamblin did not live there for any length of time although passing through with frequency.

13. "Indian Charly came in from Ft. Sevier. Brought letters from St. George news that the Navajos had taken all the horses from Little Pinto to Minersville. They have not gone this way." J-C., Sect. 1, p. 9: Reference to "this way" was likely Lee's Ferry. Hamblin decided the Navajos must be taking the stolen horses through the Ute Ford and thereafter watched it more closely.

While this site on the Colorado River was known as "Crossing of the Fathers" by whitemen following Escalante's historic 1776 expedition, Indians continued to call it Ute Ford or Ute Crossing.

14. Birney, *Zealots of Zion*, pp 116-17: "The actual crossing cannot be made today...the trail up the western cliffs was dynamited nearly half a century ago [early 1900s] by Mormon settlers of southeastern Utah." Corbett says (Endnote, p. 509), "The Navajos knew that ford too well…"

15. D-E Journal, English translation, pp. 95-96: "It took us more than three hours to climb it [Paria Canyon] because it has...extremely difficult stretches and most

dangerous ledges and is at the very last impassable."
Nevertheless, the padres passed it and reached
Crossing of the Fathers.

Hamblin lost a mule on a dangerous ledge here. On
another like it, his horse rolled over in a creek; Jacob was
fortunate in surviving, but he and his blankets became
wet; afterward, he was "sick all night." J & L, p. 55.

16. *Autobiography of Thales Haskell*, pp. 13-14; Haskell later
explains that this stubborn ox recrossed the river during the night; Hamblin and a companion went over the
river to return it, this time for good.

17. "....cooked six crows to help out our rations," Little, p.
87.

18. Hamblin said that he and his men "had gone 56 hours
without water." Little, p. 94.

19. Referring to northern Arizona: "...between 1858 and
early 1870s, Jacob Hamblin, the Mormon's greatest
trailblazer, made several reconnaissance missions,
locating river crossings, water holes, and suitable
trails." From "Diamond in the Rough."

20. Oraibi (also spelled Oraibe and Oraiba) "is one of the
oldest continuously inhabited villages in the United
States," according to *The World Book Encyclopedia* (H, p.
301). It says that the Hopis there "live in 11 self-govern-
ing villages perched on three high, barren mesas."
Under a listing for Pueblo, including several groups of
Indians in Arizona and New Mexico ("P", p. 769), it
says that the Spanish discovered the Hopi mesas in the
1500s but after failing to find the gold they were looking for, they began to subdue the Indian villages. "In
1680 the Indians revolted under their leader, Pope, but
the Spanish put down the uprising."

21. The missionaries suffered much for water, J & L, p. 58.
On one occasion, Jacob could hear running water in a
deep gorge below him but couldn't reach it. J & L, p.
36. Indians often insisted there was no drinking water
enroute between Hurricane Mesa and the Colorado
River. J & L, p. 59.

22. Haskell, Missionary Diary, pp. 7-8. In the same humor-
ous vein, Haskell tells of difficulty getting a cart over
the Kaibab: "...the cart capsized plumb bottom
up...righted her...went about 30 steps and capsized
again...our faith in regard to the cart going to the
Colorado now began to weaken..." (p. 2) Thales says
that one mule became so ornery they named him
"Devil." One mule bucked awhile but "getting pretty
well acquainted with a pair of American spurs, concluded to give up and be gentle." (p.4)

23. Approximate horseback distance from Santa Clara to Oraibi.
24. Haskell, under date of Oct. 7, 1859, p. 1.
25. *Giardiasis*, causing stomach nausea for several weeks or more, is picked up from animal droppings in water. Giardia could have been the cause of illnesses in Hamblin's group attributed to something else.
26. Little, pp. 90-92. Jacob says it required six hours to reach the stream after first viewing Cataract Creek. Meeting local Indians, Hamblin says: "They desired that I would not lead anyone into their hiding place and particularly a stranger, without their consent."

    Describing the origin of Cataract Creek, Hamblin says, "It boils from the bottom of the canyon in a large, beautiful spring." Corbett, endnotes, p. 515. Jacob never once mentions any aesthetic propensities of the Grand Canyon. Perhaps he simply viewed it as a giant obstacle in his travels.
27. While Arizona has no major historical markers along its roadways honoring Jacob Hamblin, there are two in Kanab, Utah. Jacob's two-story rock home on U.S. 89 on the east side of Santa Clara is open to the public under auspices of The Church of Jesus Christ of Latter-day Saints.
28. "If any man's name should have been attached to the wonderful bridge across the canyon of the Colorado River, it unquestionably should have been called the Hamblin Bridge." *Arizona Characters in Silhouette*, including reprints from the *Arizona Republic*.

Chapter 10

Across the Colorado: Spiritual Challenge

Hamblin had been impressed with the craftsmanship of Hopi pottery for years, even though he only looked at fragments. On his first trip to the Hopi mesas, he also witnessed a zeal for self-supporting agriculture rarely seen among the other Indian tribes. Most native Americans were nomadic, wandering about to take what nature imparted to them, or partaking from the industry of others. The Utes at Meeker, Colorado refused so vigorously to sustain themselves through farming that it led to the "Meeker Massacre" in 1879.[1] This was years after Hamblin first visited the Hopis in 1858, but the seeds of rebellion had sprouted much earlier.

The Hopi had resided in one place for years in a close-knit familiy enterprise, building their adobe pueblos into comfortable and secure villages. Labor and thrift among each family member were not only part of a daily regimen but a discipline and trust; all must labor to avoid becoming a burden upon others. Indeed, the measure of a Hopi man or woman was his or her ability and devotion to render service within each family and clan unit which in turn, built up the entire community.

Helen Sekaquaptewa, born at Oraibi[2] in 1898, barely a decade after Hamblin last visited the seven-mesa villages, tells about the work-ethic of her people from childhood days. She was taught that "The sun has much work to do, warming the whole earth and making things grow. Do not add to his burden by making him have to get you up. Get up before the sun comes up."[3]

These Indians had a physical health regimen more strict in some ways than the Mormon "Word of Wisdom" found in the *Doctrine and Covenants*, Sect. 89. The section mentions the value of eating whole wheat and grains, etc. and emphasizes the value of healthy exercise; but it does not specify daily physical routines to the extent of the Hopi. Helen describes on p. 4 of *Me and Mine* how the Hopis developed a habit of "running out to the water" before sun-up; "they would dash cold water on their bodies and run back to the village." This was done not only to build a "strong physical tabernacle" to house the spirit, as emphasized in the D&C, but for practical community protection. Helen says Hopis must always be prepared to do battle against their enemies. Strong arms and leg muscles were needed in order to shoot an arrow swift and straight. One of their traditional enemies was the Navajo. Says Helen, "Everyone watched for signs of raiders, especially at harvest time."[4]

Religion was not merely a token oblation to be filled one day a week, but woven into a Hopi's daily discipline. Jacob had noticed even before arriving at Oraibi many examples of Hopi religious devotion. He wrote in his "Journal and Letters," "They never send out any of their people in the public interest, without sending one of their religious teachers with them. The position of these religious men is probably a traditionary remnant of the pure priesthood held by their fathers." Hopi holy men also carried consecrated meal, eagle feathers and other objects placed in a sack. "They were used daily to keep a memorandum of the number of days spent on their journey." It was as if they could do nothing without seeking divine approval, even journeying day to day. This was much like the Mormons, whose scriptures taught daily prayers.[5] It was also customary in the LDS Church to consecrate certain items to the Lord; olive oil was used in healing of the sick. Homes and farms were "dedicated" for temporal success as well as for serving deity.

Noticing these similarities attracted Hamblin again and again to the Hopi people. These were not heathen as the other aborigines, even though they did not speak the name of God or Christ. Yet, Jacob likely had no idea when he visited them just how hostile the Hopi could be against those they deemed an enemy. According to Ken Sekaquaptewa, Helen's grandson, the Hopi rebelled much more violently against religious oppressors than is mentioned in any current encyclopedias or history books. An example is the account he passes on—told among his people from one generation to the next—about how the Hopi overthrew Catholic control during the 1600s in the village of

Awotovi in eastern Arizona. The Hopis killed not only all the padres of the village but all Indian converts who embraced the outside faith. "After some 25 years of corruption, with money and young women siphoned away for use of the non-Hopi clergy, the entire village was destroyed. It does not exist today. The male converts who would not renounce the white religion were killed, the women and children removed to other Hopi families so that every segment of 'brainwashing' might be expunged."[6] Ken adds that since that time, the only white churches gaining a stronghold among the Hopi are the Mennonites, Baptists and Mormons, "and among them only those serving with an example of discipline and piety."

What happened at Awotovi was unusual only in the extreme. Catholic priests were thrown off a cliff to rid their village of spiritual contamination, according to one history.[7] In another, the Zuni Indians did not kill but terminated the presence of a Catholic priest who had resided among them for years. At the time the history was written in 1877, some sixty years had gone by without allowing his return.[8]

There were also many periods of Arizona history where white and redmen broke trust with one another for reasons other than religion. Twenty Indians were killed in Yavapai County when suspected of stealing several mules. The mules were later found. In revenge, the Indians went on a murderous rampage, "killing at every opportunity," a thing not uncommon in the 1800s in Arizona.[9] That this did not happen to Hamblin or his peers stands as a monument to his rare understanding and treatment of the natives. Indeed, Helen records that the Indians were always treated as equals by Hamblin, not as "dogs who can't eat at the same table" with the others.[10] Treating the natives as inferiors was a mistake clergymen weren't always allowed to make twice among unforgiving Indian tribes.

Says a story in *Arizona Highways*, "The Indians trusted Jacob Hamblin. He never betrayed that trust." The story credits this trust with Jacob being allowed to come and go safely and make way for later Mormon pioneers to come unmolested into the most rugged and terrifying part of the western frontier."[11]

It must also be said that Jacob knew Indians. He usually brought trinkets or presents along for the more primitive tribes and treasured gifts like blankets for the natives in more advanced cultures. And for the Hopi, he brought tools such as hoes and shovels, as well as new dyes for their wool carders and sheep shearers.[12] By this, the Indians saw Jacob's interest in them as they were, not necessarily how they might be changed to fit some white culture's image of what they ought to be. "He probed deeper and deeper into their psychology," as one historian put it.[13]

This was true not only among the Hopi, but the Hualapai. One history recounts long chapters of trouble between this tribe and whitemen.[14] But Hamblin labored much among this tribe, and his name is never mentioned.

Ken Sekaquaptewa, who served in the LDS Southwest Indian Mission (Holbrook, Ariz.) after his grandmother and father were baptized Mormons, said he felt he was watched closely among members of his Hopi Eagle Clan to see if he helped in their culture and causes—or detracted from them. "My father put out a newspaper called 'Cry of the Eagle,' championing Hopi rights in obtaining fair land acquisition from the government, etc., and maintaining all that was dear and important to our people." Doing so, Ken said he and his father seemed to be considered by most as "good citizens."

At one time, after his father had lamented the poor showing of the Hopi nation in a traditional, annual foot race in which the prize was a quarter horse, Ken won and "enjoyed a greater rapport" among his people. For years the race had been won by Navajos and whitemen; Ken's victory was viewed by his father as "an indication of what can be done by living up to Hopi standards." The concept sounds very much like modern Mormonism.

It was Ken's observation that the two religions were so identical some felt they might live by either. If social ostracism did occur because a Hopi chose the Latter-day Saint religion, one could stop attending LDS services and go to the Hopi Church, without renouncing beliefs of the Mormons.

Although the Hopi are not considered a Christian Church per se, Ken says their long-awaited personage to usher in a millenium of the future is a Christ-like figure named "Masaw," pronounced very much like the English "Messiah." To keep all Hopi youth in remembrance of their heritage and unique values, meriting acceptance by Masaw, an uncle, usually on the maternal side, assumes the role as keeper of all that is sacred to the Hopi. While males held this "priesthood," it was the wife who carried the responsibility for the family's social and spiritual welfare. If the wife or mother felt that her husband was not performing his husbandly or fatherly duties, she could divorce him by simply setting his clothing and belongings outside the home. The Hopi, like the Jews, deeply cherished their heritage and determined never to depart from it. This made conversion to Mormonism or any other religion difficult.

Hamblin probably never realized just how traditionally entrenched the Hopi were in every facet of their religion and had been for centuries—and how improbable it was they might change. Perhaps Hopi and Mormon sprang from the same Hebrew ancestors came from the same origin. And if the Hopis embraced the prophesy that whitemen would visit them from the west and bring their people great spiritual blessings, why should the Hopi not believe that the Mormon missionaries came to fulfill that divine promise?

Ken relates that when the first Catholic fathers arrived, they were treated by the Hopi as likely fulfillers of the prophecy. The Hopi elders even had a specified greeting by which they were taught the prophets would respond in kind. But says Ken, when the Hopi leader placed out his hand, the puzzled white newcomer placed money in it.

Not getting a second chance to make a favorable first impression, the Catholics were to fail other tests as time went by. Did the Hopi later greet the Mormons in this special manner? Ken says it was believed they did not, instead becoming extremely wary and skeptical, determining to judge the whiteman by demonstrated character and repeated honesty. Thus, Jacob Hamblin and his missionaries were watched closely. The

Hopi would not tolerate any attempt to further exploit them as they had been exploited in the past, or, most specifically, any attempt to crush their rich religious heritage. If the Mormons had attempted to do that, who is to say they could not have met the same fate as earlier Catholics.

Still, the Hopi seemed willing to maintain an open mind. In his history, LDS record-keeper James Bleak quotes Jacob as giving details about their reception among the Moqui (Hopi). They had "a neat 40 by 30 foot room prepared for the reception of whites...whom they had been expecting for years."[15]

It must have been obvious to the Hopi elders that these newcomers were also dedicated to spiritual matters. Indeed, Hamblin wrote often in his journal that he read from his *Book of Mormon* frequently on his long missionary journeys. There were instances there of whitemen (Nephites) taking a gospel message to the Indians (Lamanites). As Jacob put it, he was "taking the olive branch" to the Hopi. "I felt humble and had a great desire to fill my Mision exceptable [acceptable] before the Lord."[16]

On one occasion, Jacob counts the many ancestors for which he did temple work. In his handwriting, he says (the spacing is his) "Was baptized for my Mother''s gran father David S. (?) Stoddard grand uncles Jonithan and Moses Haynes grand cosen Marten Haynes my uncles on my fathers sided Sylvanny Hamblin Asa Hamblin Jeneral Haynes of South caraline Jeneral Francis Marion of South caroline." On another line he writes, "was ordained Elder for Barnebas Hamblin allso for Wm Haynes went throu the endouments for Wm Haynes John oakley for gran Father Hamblin."[17] The next twenty pages of Jacob's journal were left blank and some pages, which might have mentioned more temple work completed for ancestors, were too smudged to read.

While few if any of the Hopi would know about these spiritual activities, they undoubtedly influenced Jacob's activities and demeanor. His devotion was not one of weekend piety, but of a consuming passion. This would be true of his expeditions to the Hopis; if there was much adventure in his travels, it was probably less of a factor on the eighth or ninth trips.

The Hopi knew that Jacob and the missionaries traveled from afar. Of course, so had the previous whitemen from Santa Fe. Yet, as Helen Sekaquaptewa puts it, Jacob was different than his white predecessors. She says he did not come to take anything of material wealth from them but rather to share matters of spiritual value. The *History of Arizona*, Vol. III, says the Hopi "found that this man Jacob Hamblin was not like the soldiers and other whitemen...he kept his word and seemed genuinely interested in their welfare."

Further details of Jacob's dealings with the Hopi (and other Indians) is provided by the diary of Ammon Tenney, the 14-year old boy who first accompanyed Hamblin as a Spanish interpreter to the Hopis in 1858. Tenney's granddaughter Winn W. Smiley, who had access to Ammon's diary, wrote: "Hamblin's friendly attitude toward the Indians deeply influenced Tenney, and the young man developed strong personal feelings of affection and paternal concern for them. He communicated with them in Spanish which he had learned as a child in San Bernardino, California." When the Tenney family moved to Cedar City in 1857, Hamblin became aware of the young boy's language skills. Marlene Taylor Mott, of Thatcher, Arizona, where Tenney lived his later years and was buried, says Tenney's skills were honed by having a foster brother who was raised in a Spanish family before the Tenneys took him in.[18]

Tenney's diary provides insight into Hamblin's character on the first trip: "My loving parents arose early from a sleepless night, their hearts had been swollen with emotion over my departure...for I was only 14 years old...our journey was tended by many hardships which for me were grievous to bear...my feelings were often lacerated or wounded but I had some friends in the company, especially Jacob, who fully appreciated my labors." Tenney wrote that it was Hamblin who sustained him on these difficult expeditions with the words, "This little man has been our eyes and tongue."[19]

The words "lacerated" and "wounded" indicate what appears to be an emotional struggle on journeys with the older men, possibly about who would take care of which tasks, locate water, get food, etc. It may also be that through his inexperience young Tenney did not know what was expected of him. He was almost certainly more vulnerable to danger. As an older man, Tenney became a seasoned traveler among the Indians, having several narrow escapes among the Navajos, including one that put arrows into a traveling companion.[20]

After being introduced to Lamanite missionary work via Hamblin, Tenney maintained a firm devotion to the Indians. At one time, Tenney even risked his life to save a Piute who members of the Southern Utah Militia seemed bent on torturing. Only when Tenney vehemently appealed did the militia cease burning the Indian with campfire embers.[21] (Why this should have taken place among this militia was never explained.)

Tenney's spiritual acumen was obvious when he wrote after crossing the Colorado: "We were in no-man's land, for the land had not been blessed and dedicated yet...I felt lonely and the longing that always follows homesickness."[22] The fact that he went along at all is an indication of the dutiful devotion this Mormon family felt in sharing what members knew from The Book of Mormon with their Lamanite brethren. Tenney went on the first two expeditions to the Hopis, but after starting on the third, a sense of foreboding on Hamblin's part sent him back.

Hamblin was likely much perplexed by the Hopi resistance to change. Yet, he probably also perceived that it was their very dedication to spiritual duty which made accepting new religious beliefs so difficult. By contrast, the Shivwits knew little of the Restored Gospel of Mormonism, yet after a few weeks of casual discussion, demanded baptism. Pictures exist showing dozens of Shivwits waiting in line to be baptized. Some Shivwits sought rebaptism, inasmuch as the missionaries gave them presents and clothing the first time.[23] These more lowly tribes seemed to have less to give up spiritually. But every Hopi chant, song, custom and saying carried down from their fathers seemed sacrosanct. To change would be to engender the displeasure of forefathers who it was believed, watched on with the gods to ensure that a precious heritage was not wasted.

Thus, when invited by Jacob to come with the missionaries to visit the Mormon settlements, the Hopi elders said that "they would make no move until the re-appearance of the three prophets who led their fathers to that land and told them to remain on those rocks until they should come again and tell them what to do."[24] The Hopi had heard of Indians being mistreated at the mercy of whitemen in New Mexico and across the Colorado. They would stay where they were for now.

Yet, Hamblin and Haskell both seemed to feel a certain degree of security among the Hopi. They tell of leaving considerable meat to dry within sight of these Indians and having not a single piece stolen.[25] But one couldn't put his guard down. If a horse or saddle was stolen, by Hopi or a visiting Navajo, the whitemen would have difficulty returning to all they had left at home.

One history of Arizona, written in 1877, had little good to say about the Navajos. "The Navajos are an Apache band...naturally inclinded to rob, murder and steal, and before their subjegation lived by war and plunder." But some bias against the Indian may be present in such a conclusion, for this same history, *Arizona as it is*, adds: "Most of this vast section of country [White Mountain Apache Reservation northeast of Globe] is quite useless to the Indians and can never be utilized for their civilization and should be opened to the use of whitemen."[26] That reservation, of course, has remained in Apache hands to this day and has brought much economic and aesthetic value to tribal members in mining, logging and tourism revenues.

In a history of Araivapa Canyon (southern Arizona) an account is given of an Apache named Eskiminzin who stopped to see a rancher named McKenzie who had befriended all Indians. The rancher invited Eskiminzin and his men to eat with him. They did and then killed McKenzie. Said the Indians, "Anyone can kill his enemy, but it takes a brave man to kill his friend."[27] One must wonder about the meaning of that word brave as used by Eskiminzin. Fur trappers as well as Indians lived in an environment of daily violence, kill or be killed; courage was often measured by physical resolve and combat readiness. The history of Aravaipa Canyon cited above mentioned everyone living the "Law of the Canyon," i.e., "fist and guns prevailed."[28] While violence in "the Old West" has been severely over-dramatized today, it should be remembered there was, indeed, a time when there was no legal authority other than those immediately present. That the Mormon and Hopi religions taught a higher standard of behavior during this era set them apart and bonded them more closely. If red or whiteman were to enjoy social interaction, it must be by extending and receiving trust, a commodity won hour by hour, day by day.

But for the redmen there was perhaps cause for considerable concern. Both Hopi and Navajo were witnessing more and more whitemen, miners, missionaries, soldiers, and others encroaching upon their lands. Fortunately for the Hopi, the U.S. government did not force them from their cherished haunts. According to Ken Sekaquaptewa, the Hopis settled where they did (being first on the Southwest scene possibly as early as the 1100s with initial choice of where to settle) because they considered it the "center of the universe." They would likely have fought to the death before being removed from it. As for the Navajos, they were marched enmasse to Basque Redondo in New Mexico after being subdued by the armies of Kit Carson, but in an almost unprecedented move, were allowed to sign a peace treaty and return to the land of their fathers.[29] Yet, these tribes never knew what subterfuge the palefaces might have in mind.

It was known among most Indians that the Mormons had serious differences with the "gentile Mericats" but still, were not the Mormons also whitemen? That this was overcome in the developing friendship between Hopi and Mormon is in many ways remarkable, a friendship rarely solidified between Navajo and Mormon, as we shall see in later chapters.

Yet, the LDS missionaries quickly became frustrated in trying to teach the Hopis their Mormon version of Christianity. The problem was not spiritual only, for there were many social differences. Consider, for example, the Deseret Alphabet.[30] Brigham Young had promoted the idea of teaching all non-Mormons this "more perfect language." While it might well have been an improvement, it was never accepted by the gentile world. Like the U.S. school system's past attempts to replace American math with the European metric system, the new

"Adamic" alphabet "didn't take." The Hopis were satisfied with their own language and its mesa-by-mesa dialects. In time, of course, all Indians found the English language forced upon on them in whiteman's schools. Ironically, the white culture made a special effort in the 1970s via the University of Arizona to help preserve the Hopi language by recording and taping many of the old songs sung by Helen Sepaquaptewa in her childhood days.[31]

The Hopi language is stated by several sources to be derived from the Shosonean Indian culture. John D. Rhodes, Safford, Arizona, a longtime student of native languages, indicated in an interview that the Apache and other Arizona tribes were of Athapascan (northern Canada) descent.[32] The *World Book Encyclopedia* agrees with this theory, saying "the most adventurous of this Athapascan family, the Navajo and Apache, reached the Southwest." If so, as the Santa Claras and Piedes suggested, the Hopis derived their language from the same source as the Shoshone. Most historians have also insisted that Central and South America were inhabited by Indians crossing from northern Asia via the Bering Strait route on a then existing land mass into Alaska and thence southward.

But Ken says the Hopi have always refuted this idea. "We believe we moved northward from Central America. When I visited Guatamala, I was struck with how similar the cultures and languages are. There is no way we have as much in common with tribes to the north as we do those to the south. Word of mouth is strong in the Hopi culture (like Navajo, there is no written language)," says Ken and "that word says we came from the south."

Hamblin would have agreed with this concept, for The Book of Mormon taught that the Lamanites (Indians) settled in South and Central America after arriving from Europe in boats. The native tribes then moved northward into the rest of America. It was this concept which repeatedly drew Hamblin across the Colorado.

What did the Hopi think of Jacob? Helen says her elders reiterated that "Jee-co-ba" was "an honest and kind man...in contrast to the abuse and exploitation at the hands of the other 'Pahonas' who had come."[33] But Helen says the elders couldn't agree on exactly what Jeecoba's coming to them meant. Some said he was one of the promised prophets who should come. Others disagreed. The Hopi would later split into factions on several matters, including what kind of education their children should receive. The federal government insisted by the early 1900s that Hopi children should be taken to the boarding school at Keams Canyon. After hiding her from the officers for a time, Helen says her parents finally decided not to fight the inevitable any longer. She was sent off with the other youngsters for months at a time "to get an education"—whiteman style. The children divided up; there were the "Hostiles" berating those who cooperated in going to class and the "Friendlies" who did as the whites told them, often assisted by Navajo policemen.[34] Resistance was not so much a matter of fierce and stubborn pride, according to Helen, as genuine concern that the Hopi would lose all of great value handed down by forefathers. Older parents in particular feared loss of revered culture and religious tradition by a younger generation. It became a Hopi crusade to prevent erosion of religious beliefs, a crusade which is still very much alive today.

Helen says on pages 4-5 of her book that the Hopis had kivas, or "a good-sized room, partly underground, for sacred and ceremonial use...for the male members of the specific society." It appeared to carry the remnants of some sort of priesthood. "In winter evenings the men go to the kiva, taking their sons with them, to learn and practice ceremonial songs and dances, and to retell their traditional stories and give moral and civic training. A high standard of dignity and decorum is religiously maintained...Hopi legend tells that long ago the kachinas (messengers from the gods) came and delivered instructions and admonitions." These events are relived. The priests would put on masks and assume the authority and character of the kachinas. A priest "would become that kachina," and "due respect is given him as such." This is one reason why the Hopi today do not want kachina dolls or masks sold and/or displayed publicly and or insensitively; to them it is demeaning and sacrilegious.

According to Ken, Hopi activities among family members bonded them together in a "warm relationship" which gave the children "a feeling of being loved and of having a purpose in life." Children learned to work hard but carry a smile. Even daily toil fraught with drudgery, such as weeding or grinding corn "gave one a feeling of worthwhileness because he/she was contributing to the family's well-being and happiness." The goal was to work, pray and play in family units, within a clan of relatives.

This might seem perfectly suited to proselyting by Mormon missionaries who themselves placed great emphasis upon family values. But it didn't quite work out that way, according to Thales Haskell. He explains in his journal how he came to live among the Hopi and how he felt among them: "That night after supper, Brother Hamblin said he would like to talk with me a few minutes. He said that I had been among the Indians so much he hated to ask it of me, but that if I was willing, he would like me to stay with Brother Shelton one year among these Indians, learn all we could about their language and customs, and teach them the gospel if possible. I told him I was willing…to do the best I could."[35]

On pages 37-39 of his journal, Haskell tells about the "cold and disagreeable room" left to them for living quarters and of persuading the Hopis into giving them a more comfortable place to live. Making a ladder to reach their new room, the missionaries ripped open a cottonwood log with their axes. "This attracted the attention of the natives and they gathered around in large numbers and had great remarks to make." Haskell does not elaborate on what those "great remarks" were. But being a progressive people, the Hopis appeared ready to learn all possible from their white guests.

After selecting Haskell to remain with Shelton (whom Brigham had sent because of his knowledge of the Welsh language), Hamblin visited other Hopi villages, then said goodbye to Haskell and Shelton on the outskirts of Oraibi. Says Thales: "I wended my way back to the village with such a feeling of utter loneliness, I never have experienced before. If you searched the wide world over, I do not believe you could have found a more bleak, lonesome, heart-sickening place for human beings to dwell. Here we are–Brother Shelton and I–with strange Indians who talk a strange language and their village situated hundreds of miles from the busy haunts of men. Who but Mormons would make up their minds to stay in such a place for a year? Who but Mormons would do it?"

Haskell soon found himself in culture shock as he "dipped [his] fingers into the same dish with six or eight natives. It requires a good appetite for a fellow to go in and fill himself in this manner. A few days of fasting however, will accomplish this purpose."[36]

Nevertheless, Haskell and Shelton pitched in to learn more about the people, helping with daily work such as cording wool, braiding rawhide ropes and bridles. In some matters, such as the making of bear and wolf traps, and pounding out rawhide for moccasins, the Hopis displayed a high degree of sophistication. Haskell reports that when he and Shelton went hunting with the braves, the latter carried small images to "prosper" them. But Haskell gives it as his opinion that they were "not really image worshippers." They believed "that the sun or some great spirit who dwells therein is the Supreme Being and overrules everything."[37]

Thales said he and his companion made a special effort to learn the Hopi culture. Their dances, with a rattling of gourds, seemed utterly primitive at first. But they turned out to be more than that: a "snow dance" seeking winter moisture. At the heart of the Hopi's industrious lifestyle was raising, watering, weeding, cultivating and harvesting corn, ground as a flour, made into meal or dough, etc., with many uses in a Hopi household.

As Haskell describes it, the two found the Hopi way of life rich in simple song and rhyme, often related to nature in some way; there was the owl song and the prairie dog song and many other songs. Some were sung while churning corn or other daily chores.[38] (Several of these have been preserved today by Helen Sekaquaptewa, who recorded the ditties and chants of her childhood.)

Shelton also played his violin for a people who obviously loved music. Even though the two never did learn the words to many of the Hopi songs, the missionaries joined in singing them. The songs were never boisterous but seemed to convey a feeling of unity and worship.[39]

However, a feeling of strangeness in the language and surroundings plus lack of success in teaching the Deseret Alphabet, caused the two missionaries to contemplate more and more how much they missed their families. Finally, on March 9, 1860, after a meal of "panther soup" at the hands of their Hopi hosts, Haskell and Shelton decided to go home.[40]

Haskell wrote that they "started for home feeling that we had accomplished about all the good we could for the time being." They had hoped to remain for a year but started for home after some three months. The Hopis wished their friends well, cautioning them to "beware of the Navajos" on their long journey back across the Colorado. The two returned safely to the arms of loved ones a few weeks later.

Hamblin did not seem dismayed, but resolved to return again with the same missionaries. In fact, three years later, as explained in pages 87-88 of his autobiography, Jacob left three missionaries to spend the winter with the Hopis and departed for home. Hamblin was happily surprised when three Hopi men caught up with him and said they had been sent by the tribal elders. But when the party reached the Colorado River, the Hopis remembered their tradition never to cross it until the promised prophecy was fulfilled. They were "visibly affected," in Hamblin's words. Showing again the depth of his understanding of Indians, Hamblin says, "Anticipating that they...might not proceed farther, I forwarded their blankets and provisions by the first ones that crossed over." Soon thereafter, they expressed a desire to go home "but upon finding their things had been taken over, they concluded to follow." Finding no harm had come to them in the crossing, "they returned thanks to the Father of all for their preservation." White and redmen proceeded on, going without food for several days.

However, Mormons along the way shared flour and all they had. For this, the Hopis thanked the Great Father. Jacob's next comment is typical of his attitude toward the redmen: "To see these Indians, who are looked down upon as barbarians, so humble and childlike in their reverence to the Great Father, seems worthy of special notice."

Jacob took them to Brigham in Salt Lake City and "all possible pains were taken to instruct these men concerning our people, and to show them that which would gratify their curiosity, and increase their knowledge. They said they had been told that their forefathers had the arts of reading, writing, making books etc."[41] Jacob concludes: "As Lehi had promised his son Joseph that all his seed should not be destroyed, it was the mind of the brethren…that in the Moqui people this promise was fulfilled."

The three Hopis were returned safely to their people, and were immediately "sprinkled with holy meal."[42] Thales Haskell, Jehiel McConnell and Ira Hatch likely breathed a sigh of relief. It is not likely that these three would have lived had anything happened to the three natives across the Colorado. In fact, Haskell and the others met Hamblin about two miles out from the villages. "They rejoiced much in seeing us…" says Hamblin.[43] Haskell's journal gives his feelings in third person: "The missionaries who were held as hostages were found well but somewhat homesick."[44]

Hamblin's persistence to teach Christian principles to the Indian in the face of repeated hardship and danger is probably one reason that historian Hoffman Birney said of Jacob: "No more distinctive proponent of Christianity ever lived in America."[45] But the attention paid to the Hopis by the Mormons did not escape the attention of the Navajos, through whose terrain the missionaries had to pass. Were the Mormons and Hopi forging some kind of an alliance against the Navajos? The Mormons seemed to lend moral support to the Hopi in resisting Navajo marauders, and in fact, would later bring rifles and better weapons to the Hopi. If need be, Hamblin might even join his Hopi friends in the fight. After all, Hamblin had done as much for the lowly Piedes when Utes threatened to raid them for their children.

But Jacob would find trouble of his own with or without the Hopis. There had been none in his first two visits across the Colorado. On the third, he would not be so lucky.

End Notes, Chapter Ten

1. Dee Brown, *Bury my Heart at Wounded Knee*, pp. 374-389

2. *Me and Mine*, p. 4. (as told to Louise Udall) was published in 1969. Helen grew up in Oraibi, "one of 11 villages, each with similar charcteristics and mores, yet each a separate city-state...known to have been inhabited continuously since the time of Columbus."

3. Ibid

4. Ibid

5. *Book of Mormon*, lll Nephi: 19:17; 20:1

6. Lengthy interview with Ken Sekaquaptewa, April 4, 1995. At age 45, Ken had at that time worked for 15 years in Brigham Young University's Multicultural Center (Provo, Utah) in daily contact with Indians of various tribes. All references in this chapter with Ken are from this interview.

7. There are several references to hostility between Hopi and white. William Smart, *Old Utah Trails*, says: "Escalante warned in 1875 that the Hopi were sullen and inhospitable." After saying that four Spaniards were killed in Indian villages, Smart adds, "Indians of the desert had had their fill of whitemen." Also, "The Hopi threw more than one overzealous Spanish missionary over the cliffs of their mesas, and resisted white culture and religions long after other tribes." Hopkins, *The Colorado River*, p. 92.

8. Hodge, *Arizona As It Is*, p. 168

9. Farish, *History of Arizona*, Vol. 111, p. 254

10. Sekaquaptewa, p. 238

11. *Arizona Highways magazine*, April, 1943, pp. 31-35

12. Ibid.

13. Farish, pp. 89

14. Ibid, pp. 45-46

15. Bleak, Book B, p. 111

16. "Journal-Contents," p. 7

17. "An account of what I Jacob Hamblin hav don for the dead," *Journal and Letters*, pp. 57-58. (This would have been in the St. George Temple after 1876.)

18. Interview with Marlene Taylor Mott, Thatcher, Arizona, March 28. All references with Mott are from this interview.

19. Smiley, "The Journal of Arizona History," Vol. 13, Summer, 1972, No. 2, Arizona Historical Society, pp. 82-108.

20. McClintock, *Mormon Settlement in Arizona*, pp. 70-71

21. Smiley, p. 88.

22. Ibid, pp. 86-87.
23. McClintock, p. 67
24. Little, p. 70
25. T.H. Haskell journal, p. 38
26. Hodge, p. 165 (Published in 1877.)
27. "Claridge, Klondyke and the Aravaipa Canyon," p. 10.
28. Ibid
29. Brown, pp. 35-36.
30. THH journal, p. 40. For a better understanding of the subject, read John A. Widstoe, *Gospel Interpretations*, p. 265. "Classes of instruction in the Deseret Alphabet were held throughout the territory... however, the alphabet was found difficult to read...the Deseret Alphabet represented a noble experiment with a thorougly worthwhile objective... [but] the whole subject fell into disuse...the letters are now literary curiosities." Widstoe says the alphabet died out completely shortly after Brigham Young's death. Widstoe suggests the alphabet's value was not to further isolate the Latter-day Saints but to rewrite offensive material— "to eliminate much of the unworthy literature on the market."
31. Video tape, University of Arizona, Tucson, Ariz., 85717
32. Interview with Rhodes, March 28, 1995. The Hopi language derived from Shoshonean culture discussed, WBE, I, p. 134. See also Birney, p. 115.
    For a discussion of Navajo migrations via Bering Strait between 800-1400 AD, see Hopkins, p. 82.
33. Sekaquaptewa, p. 237
34. Ibid, 13. "The labels were later changed to "Progressives" and "Traditionalists," probably at government request.
35. THH, p. 37. Hamblin wrote a slightly more enthusiastic response for Haskell remaining behind than Thales had given. Little, p. 70: "He [Haskell] replied he was the man for it."
36. Ibid, p. 40. Once again, Hamblin's trusted friend, Thales Haskell, tries to make the best of a difficult situation via pioneer humor.
37. Ibid,
38. Video titled *Native Literature from the American Southwest*, University of Arizona, Tucson, Ariz.
39. Author's conclusion from TTH, p. 40
40. THH Journal, p. 40. In his personal diary, p. 32, Haskell provides many more insightful details. "This is the best people [Hopi] I ever saw, but it is such a lonesome country that it makes it a heart sickening place to stay." At one time Haskelll says the Hopi danced and howled all night "in all the fancy rigging that their wild nature

and ingenuity can invent." The two ate often of "corn mush," sometimes in a sort of progressive dinner from one Hopi home to another. The "panther soup" mentioned by Haskell seemed just one more difference (personal diary, pages 33-36) between Hopi and Mormon cultures. The main problem was mounting homesickness. Haskell says poignantly, "spent the day wishing the Piutes would bring us some letters or some news from home…felt low spirited all day."

Note: while this diary has been quoted in a few historical journals, it has never been published. It includes daily entries of Haskell's journey and stay among the Hopis, but does not cover the period in which he, Hatch and McConnell lived with the Hopi.

41. Little, p. 88
42. THH, p. 44
43. Little, p. 93
44. THH, p. 44. Since the journal was edited, some of it in the third person, this statement may have been paraphrased by A. E. Smith. As for "being hostages," neither Hamblin nor Haskell mention the Hopi saying anything specifically about being killed if harm came to the natives across the Colorado. But past tradition would indicate this to be a most likely circumstance. No wonder the Mormon hostages welcomed safe return of the Hopis accompanying Hamblin.
45. Birney, p. 132

Note: McClintock, p. 81-82 writes of a "sacred stone" of the Hopis, but it is never mentioned by Hamblin or Haskell. The 15x18 inch stone was shown several guests of Chief Tuba, says McClintock. It was covered by hierglyphic markings but the Hopi had no translation for the red-clouded marble, "entirely different from anything found in the region." Being as close to Chief Tuba as he was (Tuba and his wife accompanied Jacob to Salt Lake City) Hamblin would surely have known of the stone. However, since neither Hamblin nor Haskell found it worthy of mention in their journals, it forms no major part of this chapter. Apparently neither man saw any religious connection between it and The Book of Mormon.

Chapter 11

Tragedy Amid Triumph

After a season of relative tranquility, trouble came in clusters for Jacob during the early and middle 1860s. In chronologial order, they included the death of young George A. Smith at the hands of Navajos while in Hamblin's party; the death of sons Duane and Albert; and, following a flood which destroyed years of cooperative toil for both white and redman, the most personally crushing blow of all: the death of his wife Rachel who had so loyally been at his side since Iowa.

In speculation, there are several reasons why Hamblin's third expedition to the Hopis might have met with disaster. One is that the Navajos readily suspected the Mormons would show up in late autumn; that was when the Colorado ran at its lowest and crossing the river was safest. That was when missionaries had shown up the two previous years. Navajos themselves usually chose to cross the river in the fall when raiding Mormon settlements.

But the major cause of trouble on this occasion was more likely the *who* than the *when.* The Navajos that Jacob encountered on this third trip were from the east side of the Painted Desert, knowing nothing of Hamblin nor the peaceful intent of his missionaries. To understand the mind-set of these Indians at this time, we need only look at their experiences with whitemen. The U.S. Army "greycoats" had by 1860 moved into what is now eastern Arizona and began building Fort Defiance [in defiance of Indian claims]. The soldiers weren't there long until they turned their livestock out to pasture on land long grazed by the Navajo.[1]

Soldiers told the Indians that the pastureland belonged to the fort; no Indian stock would be allowed on it. So, when Indian ponies were found on this pastureland, the greycoats rode out and shot all animals belonging to the natives. When the Indians retaliated, the battle for Arizona Territory was on.

According to historian Dee Brown, the Navajos attacking Fort Defiance were "determined to wipe it off the face of their land...and came very near succeeding."[2] Considering the attack an act of war, the Army declared every free-ranging Navajo to be an enemy; they could be shot on sight without provocation or question.

According to Haskell's journal, three Indians had been killed by these soldiers and comrades had it fixed in their mind to make atonement by killing three whites.[3] Quite likely, the wandering Navajos encountered by Hamblin had considered killing soldiers to get this atonement but thought it too risky. Now, before them were a handful of whitemen, non-combatants, seemingly brought by the hand of providence. This handful of civilians was, to be sure, somewhat armed, but nothing like the greycoats; the nine of them were no match for many angry Navajos painted and ready for battle.[4]

Jacob announced shortly after departing Santa Clara that he felt a premonition that something "gloomy" lay ahead for them on this trip. He explains his feelings and the reasons for them in pages 71-81 of his autobiography (all information in this chapter about this expedition among the Navajos is from those pages unless otherwise referenced): "What it would be I did not know. Whether we would ever see home again or not, I did not know, but I knew we were told to go among the Moquis [directions from Brigham Young] and stay for one year, and that I should do so if I could get there."

Noting Jacob's discouraged demeanor, his brethren asked him about it. "They wished to know if there was any one in the company that I did not wish to go on." Jacob said he assured them this was not so, "but I knew there would be something happen that would be very unpleasant, and that there would be hard times for some of us."

With that, says Hamblin, 15-year old George A., son of the LDS apostle George Smith who spent so much time among the southern Utah settlers, spoke up and said, "You will see one thing, that is, I will stick to it the last. That is what I came for."

In the afternoon of the second day after crossing the river, the missionaries could not find water where it had been before. Four friendly grey-haired Navajos showed up, sent from their aging chief, Spaneshank, who knew of Jacob's reputation for honesty and held friendly feelings toward the Mormons. The chief also considered this territory within his domain of control, although such things might be disputed at times among members of the same tribe. Spaneshank's emissaries warned Jacob that hostile Navajos waited ahead; they offered protection if Jacob would turn about to the north. Hamblin says, "We counseled about the matter and concluded that the animals were too nearly famished for want of water to reach Spaneshank's camp...as the [expected] water was but a short distance ahead on our route, we concluded to push on and risk the consequences."

When they did so, it was precisely as Spaneshank's braves had warned. The missionaries were quickly surrounded by many Navajos dressed for war. Hamblin learned through his Piute interpreter, Enos, that the warriors were determined not to let the Mormons any deeper into the heart of Navajo country on their way toward the Hopi villages. Enos relayed to Hamblin that the Navajos were not quite certain, however, exactly what to do with the whitemen, "whether to kill us or let us go home." As it turned out, their intentions focused more on the former.

In his journal, Thales Haskell says the missionaries "tried to make peace with them by offering articles of trade but they refused and demanded that three men be given to them to kill because some white people had just killed that number of their men a few days travel east of here." It must have been clear to the Navajos that their tribesmen murdered east of here could not have been the work of Mormons; they always came from the west. But in the redman's mind, whitemen were whitemen; it mattered little who they were. Three palefaces must die.[5]

As fate would have it, one of those whitemen was to be young George A. Smith. Seeing his horse wander off, George A. apparently feared it might wind up in Indian hands. Hamblin says: "As he started after it, I told him that he had better not go alone, to which he made an indifferent reply. Something else immediately attracted my attention, and he was forgotten until the Navajos in our camp suddenly left, when I learned that he was after his horse alone and out of sight." Jacob sent two men after the lad. "They went about a mile and found him lying by the trail, with three bullet wounds through the lower part of his body, and four arrow wounds between the shoulders." Hamblin quickly mounted a horse and rode to the spot. There he learned of the treachery done against the boy who lay paralyzed. A Navajo had asked to look at Smith's gun, and when he trustingly handed it over, the lad was shot with his own revolver. Another Indian added the four arrows. Hamblin took the dying man to a blanket near camp where he asked "to be left alone that he might die in peace."

Jacob then demanded to know why the Navajos had done this. They did not give him the courtesy of an answer, replying only, "Tell Jacob that he need not bury him for we will eat him, and the women and children will help do it." Thus, Hamblin had a choice: he could remain, or leave the dying young man behind for the Navajos to quarrel over—allowing the missionaries a head start toward the Colorado. Smith was already bleeding heavily by now; it was just a matter of time before he was dead. But to the surprise of no one in his party, Hamblin refused to depart without the dying boy.

Jacob was then asked by the others, "What are you going to do?...the query was an earnest one with us all...What can we do? The Heavens seemed like brass over our heads and the earth as iron beneath our feet. It seemed utterly impossible to reach the Moqui [Hopi] towns which were almost in sight and like certain death to attempt to escape in the night with our jaded animals." The Navajos offered a compromise: "We want to kill two more; and if Jacob will give them up or let us quietly kill them, the rest of the company may go in peace."

Noting two Indian females with the Mormons, the Navajos suggested they would do for now in place of two whitemen. They happened to be the wives of Ira Hatch and Jacob Hamblin. Jacob explains it this way: "We had taken two Indian women with us, thinking that they might be of a great help in introducing some things like cleanliness in cooking among the people we were going to visit. The Navajos said we might go home if we would leave them. I directed the interpreter to tell them that one of the women was Brother Hatch's wife, and the other was mine. They replied they would not kill the men who had married them."

The marriage of Jacob to Eliza, one of several adopted children in the Hamblin household, has been hushed over by some biographers. Eliza, by now a young woman, is listed in some indexes as "Hamblin, Eliza, servant." Historian Corbett says that according to Hamblin's sons and daughters and friends "Jacob...never married an Indian squaw."[6] But it is Corbett himself who says that Jacob took adopted Indian maidens Eliza and Ellen to Salt Lake City, as taking a polygamous Lamanite wife could be done only by direct authority from Church headquarters. "[Jacob] was married to Eliza by Daniel H. Wells. When it came Ellen's turn to be married, she changed her mind. Eliza, seeing what happened, changed her mind and refused to live with Jacob."[7]

Hamblin had argued in most instances against marrying Indians, partly because a maiden might have a jealous buck for a boyfriend. But knowing this was not so in Eliza's case, and that she might enjoy a higher status in the community as a legal wife rather than being labeled a "servant girl," Hamblin seemed willing to make an exception.

It may also be that Jacob never consummated the marriage to Eliza, for she seemed torn by her decision soon after Ellen backed out.[8] But on this occasion, she was introduced to the Navajos as Jacob's wife. It is entirely possible that Jacob did so to save her life, or at least to impress on the minds of oppressors that it was useless to press demands to take women the missionaries were married to. The Piute interpreter did not agree with Jacob's decision, arguing that "It would be better for two of the company to die than for all to be killed."

Hamblin did as might be expected, directing Enos to give the Navajos this reply: "I would not give a cent to live after I had given up two men to be murdered; that I would rather die like a man than live like a dog." Hamblin then told Enos, by now likely badly frightened, in something of a courageous ploy, that, "There were only a few of us but we were well armed, and should fight as long as there was one left."

Hamblin continues in his autobiography: "As the interpreter turned to go, the two Indian women we had brought along with us wept aloud, and accused us of bringing them along to be murdered." In addition, wrote Hamblin, "Some thought it was certain death whether we went or remained where we were...I went a little way off by myself and asked the Lord to be merciful and pity us in our miserable and apparently helpless condition, and to make known to me what to do and say to extricate us from our difficulties."

Jacob seems to have received the answer he was looking for. He told the men to prepare to ride "as soon as possible," then made a rather startling statement: "I told them, however, that there would not be another one of us injured." It would be an incredible assumption to make on his own volition given the predicament he was in, one Hamblin surely would not have made without a deep feeling of inspiration behind it. Jacob had no time now for long explanations, but the assurance he received likely meant the men would have to do their part in reaching safety.

"We left our camp kettles over the fire containing our breakfast untouched, and all our camp outfit that we could possibly do without. The Navajos who had been guarding our trail beyond the camp, started after us, coming down like a whirlwind. Some of our party predicted that in ten minutes there would not be one of us left, but there was no flinching, no wilting in the emergency."

Trying to transport by pack mule the now nearly lifeless George A., one man holding on to the body, slowed the missionaries down considerably. At last, Smith, seeking not to be a burden to his comrades, asked a final time to "be left in peace to die." He did die soon afterward; but where could they bury him? Hamblin writes, "I said to the company, 'what shall we do?'...what can we do...only lay the body on the ground and leave it."

About sundown, the missionaries wrapped the body of George A. Smith in a blanket, placed it out of sight of the trail and pushed on. At one point, the Navajos "came within sight of our rifles and then turned suddenly to the right." As they did, a pack mule laden with provisions bolted and followed the

Indians. According to one account, trinkets (probably meant as gifts for the Indians) fell from the panicked pack animal and as Indians stopped to pick up the items scattered over a wide area, Hamblin's group gained ground.[9] Some Indians undoubtedly wanted the Mormons' horses and packs even if unwilling to face a shootout. Hamblin says, "We then rode on as fast as our jaded animals would carry us, until late into the night."

When stopping with a guard to allow their horses to graze, Hamblin says: "I…leaned over my saddle but could not sleep. The scenes of the past two days were before me in vivid reality. The thought of carrying the wounded man with his life's blood dripping out of him…leaving of his body to be devoured by wolves and vultures, seemed almost too much to bear."

"My imagination pictured another scene. South of us, in the distance, we could see a large fire, around which we presumed the Navajos were having a war dance over the scalp of our brother." Jacob pondered the difficulty of conveying the terrible news to the parents who had left their son in his trust. "The thought pierced me like barbed arrows and caused me the most bitter reflections that I have ever experienced in my life."

There was no time to mourn. Even with Spaneshank's trusted four guarding the rear flank, the mischief-bent Navajos might yet burst upon them. Traveling as silently and swifty as their mounts could carry them, the missionaries finally arrived at Spaneshank's camp. Even then, pursuing Navajos demanded that the whitemen be given up but Spaneshank stated he was "chief in that country" and as Hamblin wrote it, "we should not be hurt." Although among valiant friends, Hamblin found sleep impossible.

Keeping an eye on their backtrail the next day, Hamblin and the others quickly crossed the Colorado, riding to the familiar conifers of Buckskin Mountain where hospitable Kaibabs and Piutes sustained them with pine nuts. After arriving home, Hamblin sadly informed Apostle George A. Smith his son had been killed. Smith went soon thereafter to Santa Clara. He made it easier for Jacob by telling him that the family was shocked but "upon reflection, we all in the Historian's Office came to the conclusion that the Lord wanted the young man in just the way he took him." Wrote Jacob: "President Young also looked upon the matter in the same light."

The young Smith boy had been especially well liked in the Mormon community, as indicated by these lines penned in a long eulogy by Haskell titled "My Beloved Companion, George A. Smith, Jr.[10] It is not a good poem in the literary sense, but like much of Haskell's writings, it carried poignant feelings:

"Young George…went quietly for the mare that was gone.
He had not gone far before he was met
By some five or six of the treacherous set
Who robbed him, then shot him…
We'll take him to camp, to his wounds we'll attend,
Everything in our power we will do for our friend."

Following Haskell's poem are these words: "All the Mormon people and especially the parents of this fine young missionary were greatly shocked to hear of this savage act perpetrated by these Navajo Indians with which great effort had been made to be friendly and peaceful."[11]

One line in Haskell's poem says, "We numbered but nine, and could not contend With a force of two hundred desperate men." Hamblin does not give the number of Navajos, but says one pass was guarded by about forty; there could have been some two hundred as Haskell says. But even allowing some poetic license, the missionaries felt, indeed, vastly outnumbered, enough to once again give thanks for divine deliverance. Haskell also writes that the Smith family "naturally…desired that the remains of this, their son, be brought back home for burial. To accomplish this, Jacob Hamblin led another group in which many of the same persons who were along when the incident happened were sent to recover the body and bring it home for burial." Haskell journal editor A. E. Smith says Thales was one of those who went along to recover the body.[12]

Hamblin tells it differently in his autobiography. "Brother Smith gave me a note from President Brigham Young, in which was a written request to raise a company of 20 men, and bring in what we could find of the remains of Brother George A. Smith, Jr. Winter having set in, I considered this a difficult task. It was necessary to go to Parowan for men and supplies, a distance of 70 miles. This accomplished, we were soon on our way."

Note that Jacob's response refers to it only as a "difficult task." Then, as is typical of him, he sets about fulfilling it.[13]

Most likely, Jacob was under the necessity of gathering his posse from Parowan because the citizens there knew less than those at Santa Clara about the inherent dangers of returning to the warring Navajos. If Haskell did go, or anyone else from Hamblin's home region, it is not mentioned by Jacob.

The posse raised by Hamblin managed to locate some of Smith's bones and transport them west across the icy Colorado River without mishap, although they had to wait until mid-day for sun to melt ice along the ledges towering above the river. Hamblin writes that one pack mule was almost lost, sliding near "the edge of a chasm below." "We fastened a long lariat to the animal, and saved it and the pack." Fortunately, no hostile Navajos were encountered this time. A chief and his wife came to Jacob at his last camp to say that "if he had known what he afterwards learned about us, he would have protected instead of injuring us."

Once home, Jacob wrote: "This completed one of the most trying series of circumstances in my life. That the misfortune was no greater is due to the kindly Providence of our Heavenly Father and the faith in Him and confidence in each other, of the brethren involved in it." Hamblin added that "President Young proffered to pay us for our trip. I replied that no one who went with me made any charge, and as for myself, I was willing to wait for my pay until the resurrection of the just."

It is rather typical, however, that upon returning home, Hamblin found his family out of provisions. "I had left my family with plenty of food, but they had lent it to their neighbors." These neighbors were likely families of those accompanying Jacob across the Colorado, an indication the wives and children left behind might well have benefitted had an "idealistic" Hamblin and the missionaries accepted some of the "proffered

pay." Such apparent refusal by Jacob to accept pay for his sacrifices—and more particularly in behalf of the many missionary
families—might have led to the criticism later that Hamblin was
gone too much and didn't "provide for his family." This will be
examined in a later chapter.

Some questions remain about Smith's murder. Why was he
the only member of the party killed? Was it soley because he
was young and alone, i.e., more vulnerable? That was certainly a
major factor, for Hamblin warned him about leaving the others.
But Smith's tender age seemed to also be a consideration. Jacob
had sent young Ammon Tenney (about the same age as George
A.) home after feeling misgivings early on this third trip. If
Tenney had gone, would he, too, have been singled out and
murdered by the Navajos at the first opportunity? Quite possibly.

Hamblin had prophesied that no one would die after Smith
was taken, a thing which proved to be true. Skeptics might ask,
"But why was it that Hamblin could not foresee Smith's death
and leave him home as he did Tenney?" Only Jacob, if he was
here, could answer that question. Hamblin might have been
considered infallible by some Church members who saw him
come and go safely so many times among unfriendly aborigines.
Likewise, it might be inferred that anyone with Hamblin was
safe. The news of Smith's death quickly dispelled this idea.

Others, assuming that Hamblin could tell "by the Spirit"
what to do in any given dilemma, must now admit a harsh reality—anyone going among the Indians, especially those across the
Colorado, did so at great risk, notwithstanding they went with
Jacob Hamblin, or as missionaries in the name of peace.

A strange incident also later mentioned by Hamblin was
that the day after Smith was killed, a Navajo rode up to Jacob
and asked for a gift. As Hamblin gave a trinket, he noted
Smith's revolver in the Indian's belt. Jacob later noted that the
Navajos who killed Smith were told by other tribesmen that the
Mormons "were good people;" it could be proven by asking one
of them for a gift. If it was given, that would suffice as proof. If
so, Jacob's present did not end trouble between Mormons and
Navajos.[14]

After the death of Smith, many Church members felt no more good could be accomplished across the Colorado. But time began to heal the memory of young Smith's murder, and in the autumn of 1862 (as written in pages 89-108 of Jacob's autobiography) it was "recommended" by President Young that Hamblin go again to the Hopis. This time Brigham suggested the missionaries explore a different route by proceeding south of the new village of St. George "with a view to finding a more feasible route than the one we had before traveled." After crossing the Colorado (downstream from today's Grand Canyon), the group found themselves without an Indian guide. His reason, says Hamblin, was "that we were going into a country destitute of water." But it snowed sufficiently that the missionaries found standing water until reaching seeps and springs on the flanks of the 12,000-plus foot-high San Francisco Mountains north of today's Flagstaff, Arizona.[15]

Jacob saw evidence on this trek that his reputation was beginning to precede him. The Havasupai Indians were friendly and said they "had heard of Jacob." It was then that they besieged him not to publicize their hideaway among the scenic waterfalls of Havasu (Cataract) Creek, a promise Hamblin kept to his death. He was also entreated at this time by Lewis Greeley, a nephew of the famous Horace Greeley of the *New York Tribune*,[16] to join the newsmaking Mormons in their explorations. After deciding Greeley would be no burden to them, and that he might help get out the gospel message Hamblin was ever eager to share, Jacob agreed. Hamblin never does mention Greeley again, save for one reference that Lewis discovered water in a volcanic crater on San Francisco Mountain.

It was also on this trip that the Hopis consented to send three of their number with the Mormons, three missionaries remaining behind with the Hopis. Returning via Ute Ford (Crossing of the Fathers), Hamblin completely encircled the Grand Canyon, the first whiteman known to do so.

On the return home, Jacob was informed by a man among the group (unnamed) "that he had heard that one of [Jacob's] sons had been killed at Santa Clara, by the caving in of a bank of earth and he thought it was Lyman. That night I had a dream or vision. I learned that it was Duane instead of Lyman, and I told the brethren so in the morning."

This declaration by Hamblin indicates just how certain he was of inspiration and answer to prayers, for there appears no doubt whatsoever which son had died. To announce the same as a fact next morning to many others indicates Hamblin felt himself in tune with the Spirit of the Lord, which he talked about often. His inspiration was just as he had announced it. He was informed upon reaching home that Duane had died Dec. 17, or about a month earlier, when a water headgate he was working on caved in about him. Duane was Hamblin's oldest son and as Corbett sums it up, "He had been a faithful boy and would be greatly missed."[17]

In March after deciding to visit the Hopis again (Hamblin's first spring trip across the Colorado), Jacob had an unusual conversation with another son, Albert, as recorded in his "Journal and Letters."

Jacob: "I remarked to him that the peach trees had begun to bloom, and it would be warmer than it had been."

Albert: "Yes, and I shall be blooming in another place before you get back. I shall be on my mission!"

Jacob: "What do you mean by that?"

Albert: "That I shall be dead and buried when you get back."

Hamblin writes of the trip later that the hooting of an owl attracted their attention. The men determined it to be "counterfeit." But too late. Indian thieves took ten of their sixteen horses. With little water to be found, and some men having to walk on blistered feet, the group suffered terribly. Being slowed to this extent, the trip consumed fifty-six days.

Not much was mentioned about missionary accomplishments. But Hamblin says, "We had explored a practicable, though difficult route for a wagon from St. George to the Little Colorado... and explored some of the country around the San Francisco Mountain." This would prove to be a major factor in later Mormon settlement throughout eastern Arizona.

Once again in Santa Clara, Hamblin says: "I found on my return home that my Indian boy, Albert, was dead and buried, as he had predicted he would be when I left home. I supposed his age to be about 10 years when he came to live with me; he had been with me 12 years, making him 22 years old when he died. For a number of years he had charge of my sheep, horses, and cattle, and they had increased and prospered in his hands.

"Some time before his death he had a vision, in which he saw himself preaching the gospel to a multitude of his people. He believed that this vision would be realized in the world of spirits. He referred to this when he said that he should die before my return home, and be on his mission. He was a faithful Latter-day Saint; believed he had a great work to do among his people; had many dreams and visions, and had received his blessings in the house of the Lord."

During the next year Hamblin visited myriad Indian bands from the Kaibab to the lower Sevier River Valley, all hovering within striking distance of the white settlements. Jacob noted that more and more settlers were moving in, the Lamanites being impacted: "When the natives resorted to…gather seeds, they found they had been destroyed by cattle…only the poor consolation was left them of gathering around their campfires and talking over their grievances."

Jacob visited many of these Indian campfires, and sympathized with the natives. "Those who have caused these troubles have not realized the situation. I have many times been sorely grieved…trying to get our people to understand their [southern Utah Indians circumstances], without being able to do so. Lank hunger and other influences have caused them to commit many depredations."

On one occasion when planning to visit Indians gathering to plunder north of St. George, Hamblin was asked how many he wanted go with him. "I replied only one, and that I did not want any arms, not even a knife, in sight." Hamblin observed that these Indians had prepared for hostilities, as was their custom, by secreting their women and children. He visited many camps, and "by talking with them, a better influence came over them, and the spirit of peace triumphed over irritation and a sense of wrong."

At another time, a band of Piutes joined with Indians driven out of California; they threatened small settlements from the Fillmore region to Shoal Creek, near Hebron. "Our people had manifested as much hostility as the Indians, having killed two of their number." Hamblin roasted an ox, and invited all redmen to the feast, listening to their many grievances. "I could not blame them, viewing matters from their viewpoint. I rather justified them in what they expected to do, but told them in the end it would be worse for them to carry out their plans than to smoke the pipe of peace." He reasoned a course of action with them thusly, "I told them that the seeds were gone which they once needed for sustenance but that...they could get more food by gleaning from our fields than they had before we came into their country. The talk lasted for hours. The difficulty was settled and we returned home."

These unorthodox methods likely made the white settlers uneasy. Here was Hamblin's collaborating with the enemy rather than shooting them. During this time, Hamblin also went to Oraibe once more to foster friendly relations with Navajos and Hopis. Jacob says little of this particular trip but apparently felt it helpful in letting the Indians know Mormons wished to be their friends.

In the winter, after his return from this trip, Navajos raided the Whitmore Ranch at Pipe Springs and killed owners Whitmore and McIntyre, mentioned in a previous chapter. Hamblin was quickly "drafted" into a militia seeking to punish these Indians, but "was taken sick" and turned back to go home. His health was so poor for a time that family and friends "thought that I was dying." Hamblin says, "I was willing that it be so, for I had only been in their way for nearly a year; but my little children were crying around me, and the question came into my mind: What will they do if I am taken away? I could not bear the thought of leaving my family in so helpless a condition." Hamblin says he asked the Eternal Father in the name of His son Jesus Christ, "to spare my life...and I would labor for the building up of His Kingdom." After that, says Hamblin, "I...felt a desire for food" and "slowly recovered."

The statement that he had "been in their way for nearly a year" is worth examining more closely. It seems revealing of Jacob's intense sense of Church-community duty that if he wasn't away from home meeting trouble head-on that he "was in the way." But even if not crossing the Colorado, he was constantly guarding it at the Ute Ford to turn back raiding Navajos. When Hamblin did later cross the river again, it was at a new place, Lee's Ferry, where rafts were fashioned out of driftwood.[18] On arrival at the Hopi towns, Jacob felt "some of the people received us rather coldly." It might have been that, as with the Catholic priests of old, the Hopis were concerned about losing their more cherished traditions to this new religion. Or it could have been that the Navajos raided more often out of jealousy after seeing Hopi-Mormon friendships possibly attract more whitemen to the region. Hamblin wanted to return home via the Ute Ford on this last trip, but other white members of the party insisted on using the Lee's Ferry route again. "I told them if I knew anything about the mind and will of the Lord, it was for us to go that way."

Afterward, Jacob discovered that the Navajos escaped with much Mormon cattle across the Ute Ford; he was angry with his brethren for not listening to him. "I felt vexed that I did not take the Piutes with me and save this valuable lot of stock for our people."

Hamblin slept out many cold nights in the 1860s, watching and guarding with the Piutes to keep Navajo raiders from crossing. At one time, the Piutes under Hamblin's direction trapped some Navajos in Paria Pass and prevented a large loss of livestock. The Navajos were allowed to flee for their lives, but without the stolen booty.

Chasing other marauding Navajos, Hamblin was "fired at several times...one bullet just missed my head...the Navajos lost three of their men." Hamblin expended much energy during this time trying to guard the frontiers, sometimes crossing Buckskin Mountain when the snow was waist deep, "passing many sleepless nights." From his "Journal Contents," p. 8, we read: "Slept in the Rocks where we fought the Navajos, cold and lonesome night...all well, no Navajos seen yet."

In the spring of 1865 Jacob returned home to learn his beloved wife Rachel was gone. She had been dead and buried for nearly a month.[19] This fact is never mentioned by Jacob in his autobiography. As usual, Hamblin chose not to tell of matters deeply private and personal in his own writings unless they somehow dealt directly with his missionary activities among the Lamanites.

Corbett says (p. 246) that Jacob realized Rachel had not been the same since the night of the flood.[20] This had occurred several years earlier when heavy winter rains left Santa Clara Creek so swollen it washed out Fort Clara and took with it to the raging Virgin River all the toil of a decade's work. As Jacob describes it, the fort was 100 feet square, with walls 12 feet high and two feet thick—a considerable distance north of the original bed of the creek. Inside the walls were rooms occupied by families, and "we had considered it safe from flood."

In the middle of the night, Jacob and the others discovered otherwise. All were evacuated safely at first, but as Jacob attempted to remove some personal property, the bank fell beneath him and he was washed into a muddy torrent. "The thought flashed through his mind "that I had one chance in a thousand of my being saved. I heard someone say it was 'of no use to try to save me.'" Hamblin says he shouted at the top of his voice, "It is of use to try to save me!"[21]

A rope soon settled around him and he pulled himself up. Minutes later, he almost drowned a second time when a woman seemed soon to be swept away. Hamblin used the same rope as before to pull the woman, who had a child standing outside the fort, toward land. At one point, the woman's hold on Jacob's neck nearly strangled him but he "reached the shore safely...to the great joy of the husband and children."

When the flood was done, "grist mill, and most of the houses and cultivated lands of the settlement had disappeared." In the flood's aftermath, Rachel, who had brought Jacob so much solace and peace since crossing the plains to Salt Lake Valley, lay wet and sick. Corbett says, "Still ill with a baby eight days old, she had been carried to the top of the bluff and laid on a mattress on the ground exposed to a drenching rain and chilling winds."[22] By this time, of course, there were no structures or buildings in which to find protection from the elements

Rachel's personal loss to Jacob was only part of the story. She had been the first source of succor to many in the community, especially small children, ever since the Mountain Meadows Massacre, when she had taken in some sixteen homeless youngsters. She had been the school teacher and daytime mother to many children in the village. She and polygamous wife Priscilla had been extremely close, relying on each other as only frontier mothers and wives can, nurturing a large household of both white and Indian children. When Jacob was gone, which was often, the two had to cooperate in every endeavor, throwing aside any jealousy (if there had been any temptation to such luxury) for the simple reason that there was no way to meet the daily challenge of both households if the women did not work together in every facet of mind and spirit.

Priscilla tended to Rachel's every need as she lay dying, apparently due to complications from recurring pneumonia. No doubt, the two women thanked one another for their trust, charity, love and spiritual strength over the years. Corbett, who had interviewed many Hamblin family members while preparing his biography of Jacob in 1952, says Rachel told Priscilla, then pregnant, that she would have a son and that she should name the boy Jacob, which Priscilla did.[23]

Corbett also says that "Jacob had been concerned about [Rachel's] health and warned her about over-working."[24] This could have been so, but with Jacob gone so much, and with the domestic chores facing her every day, it is doubtful Rachel could have done anything else. Most likely, if Jacob ever did warn Rachel about over-working, it would have been met with rebuff, or at the least, sarcastic humor. If Jacob was as wise and diplomatic at home as he was in the camps of faraway redmen, it is doubtful he would ever make such a statement. Nevertheless, theirs was a tender love story, reminiscent of Jacob and Rachel in the Old Testament, who provided the world with a well-known love story of their own.[25] And with their faith in a hereafter, Jacob and Rachel Hamblin could dream of the time they might be together again without the pain of an oft-times harsh western frontier.

End Notes, Chapter Eleven

1. Brown, *Bury my Heart at Wounded Knee*, pp. 14-15
2. Ibid, p. 15
3. Smith, T. H. Haskell, p. 41
4. Hamblin does not give the number of Navajos. But he says some forty guarded one pass that no move might be made toward the Hopi villages.
5. The custom among the Navajos and other tribes that a like number of whitemen (or offending non-Indians) must die to atone for redmen killed was apparently not arbitrary; the concept seemed rigidly fixed to a meticulous sense of justice. Hamblin would encounter the concept again.
6. Corbett, p. 215. But there is a serious time discrepancy here. It is well documented that the only trip in which Hamblin took Eliza (announcing her as his wife) was in 1860. Recorded in the Salt Lake Endowment House is a marriage document showing the two married on Feb. 14, 1863. (BYU Lee Library Computer Room Family Search, IGI, North America Dish 2, lists the ordinance as a sealing, Nos. 1-2; AFN 37CX-QC lists it as a marriage.) The point is, if Eliza were married to Jacob Hamblin in 1863, how could she be his wife in 1860? It is possible that Hamblin claimed Eliza as a wife to save her life when the Navajos threatened, and then simply included that statement in his autobiography. As for disclaimers by anyone that Hamblin never did have an Indian wife, the evidence indicates otherwise. Brooks says further, "The fact [Hamblin] had married her was never any secret until later years." *Utah Historical Society*, Jan.-April, 1944, Vol. X11, Nos. 1-2, p. 42, "Indian Relations on the Mormon Frontier."
7. "Eliza left the Hamblin household. Soon after, she married…a Shevwit [Shivwit]. Later she returned to live with the Hamblins with her baby. Jacob refused to take her back." Corbett, p. 215.
8. The author's statement that the marriage may not have been consummated is based on Corbett's statements: "Eliza refused to live with Jacob" and "on their return home [from the wedding in Salt Lake City] Eliza left the Hamblin household."
9. Isaac Riddle Journal, p. 17
10. T.H. Haskell, p. 42
11. Ibid.
12. It is not likely Haskell went along on this mission, or Hamblin would have mentioned it. The idea may have been added by an editor.

13. Compare to the "Message to Garcia," a legendary story of a man who could be trusted to do all asked of him by superiors, without hedging or asking questions. Seemingly that was the case here and in other instances with Jacob Hamblin.

14. It was 1872, some dozen years after the death of young George A. Smith, before Hamblin learned the full meaning of the "gift incident." Hamblin says: "Some Navajos came to us to trade for horses. We camped with a party at the rock where young George A. Smith was killed. One of them said he was there when young Smith was killed. Most of them contended that the Mormons were a good people." The man who did the killing was told to go and ask for a present and this would prove the Mormons were 'good people.'" The Navajo went after Hamblin and returned with a gift Jacob gave him. Hamblin adds: "We were told that the murderer died a miserable death, and the Navajos believed it was because he had killed a Mormon." Jacob also learned that the Navajos did not do a war dance around Smith's body because some of the Indians felt they should not have killed a Mormon. Little, pp. 126-27.

15. Some exploration had been done by this time around Arizona's highest mountain (elevation, 12,670 feet at Humphrey's Peak) including a wagon route known as Beale Road used by Hamblin's group for a short distance toward Oraibe.

16. Haskell says of Greeley: "Some resentment was voiced toward bringing along this New York dude, but he represented that he was physically fit and would do any service required of him…after some consultation, agreement was made to take him along." Added in a footnote is this: "Greeley proved to be a real scout and pioneer and found many things and had many experiences of which to write about when he returned home." T. H. Haskell, p. 44. It was Greeley's uncle, of course, who made famous the statement, "Go west young man, go west." *World Book Encyclopedia*, "G," p. 372. There is no mention in the encyclopedia of Lewis, and no mention in Hamblin's writings about the man's opinion of his trip.

17. Corbett, p. 212.

18. The first rafts were very crude and dangerous. But by the time John D. Lee settled at what was to become Lee's Ferry, rafts were more than wood scavenged from the Colorado River banks. This safer and more convenient crossing basically replaced the old ford

some 30 miles northward known as Ute Ford or
Crossing of the Fathers, which is now, of course,
beneath Lake Powell.

19. Rachel was born Sept. 15, 1821 and died Feb. 18, 1865 at
the rather young age (by today's standards) of 44.
20. Corbett, p. 246.
21. For a more complete story of the Santa Clara flood, see
Hamblin's Autobiography, pp. 82-84.
22. Corbett, pp. 246-47.
23. Corbett, p. 247
24. Ibid.
25. Genesis, *Bible*, Ch. 29.

– Chapter 12 –

Troubleshooter

In the mid 1860s, Hamblin seemed to be constantly in the saddle, putting out frontier "brush fires" among the Lamanites. He did not state whether he used up several mounts, but his activities would seem to wear out considerable horseflesh, if not the rider himself. One trip of note was to the Muddy and Cottonwood Islands (apparently on the Colorado River) where Indians were making trouble for settlers, who planned on moving to California until Jacob "had profitable talks" with the local natives. Part of the problem could have been caused by Navajos whom Hamblin came across far from their normal haunts, quite possibly up to no good.[1] Hamblin also found time to make an exploratory trip down the Colorado River below the Grand Canyon into the Black Gorge near and below today's Hoover Dam. While the voyage was to explore possible settlement in that region, the expedition had its perilous side. Hamblin pushed off with two other missionaries from Grand Wash and floated in a 16-foot skiff some 45 miles downstream to the mouth of the Virgin River, mapping the countryside as they went to Call's Landing. On the way, they undulated through rapids in narrow canyon walls estimated as high as 1,500 feet—"walls shutting us in from light and hope," wrote Hamblin.[2]

Apparently, it was the first exploration by whitemen; the crew had no idea what to expect around the next bend. It should be remembered that this voyage was two years before Major Powell's first exploration down the Grand Canyon of the Colorado in 1869.

Hamblin mentioned no near-escapes. If it seemed in the interest of missionary work or Mormon expansion to ignore them, negative aspects were rarely mentioned. The entire expedition was apparently under the auspices of President Erastus Snow, regional LDS presiding authority, for immediately following the expedition, Hamblin met with Snow and others in St. Thomas and the Muddy areas (Nevada) for Church meetings before returning home.[3]

Desiring to be with his family more, Jacob decided in 1867 to go into a mercantile business partnership in St. George. Hamblin took out a large loan at a bank in Salt Lake City, with his cattle herds as collateral. His partner allegedly didn't do his share of paying it back, according to historian Corbett,[4] who also suggests that Hamblin was much more the forgiving Christian than he was a good merchant, extending credit too generously. When some of his neighbors couldn't pay, Hamblin forfeited many of his cattle, leaving his family in a precarious position financially. It was doubtful from the first that Hamblin really had his heart in becoming a businessman, for the store never flourished. Within a year, Hamblin went from merchant to missionary, the latter quite obviously his real love.

It wasn't long before he was back to "troubleshooting" along the frontier, particularly among vexatious Navajos in the Kanab region. It must have become apparent to Jacob that he could spend more time at home if he moved to Kanab. It was some one hundred and fifty round trip miles to Kanab and back to Santa Clara. Perhaps slowly at first, then with more enthusiasm, Hamblin discussed the idea with his household. It must have seemed to them that their husband and father couldn't stand prosperity. He must always be going off someplace where life was at greater risk, more difficult and more challenging.

At that time in 1869, Fort Kanab had been dug from the red clay above Kanab Creek only a few years earlier. It was but an outpost compared to the comfortable settlement at Santa Clara. Santa Clara also had several other LDS communities within a day's ride, while Fort Kanab could only be termed a lonely and remote frontier.[5]

Although no known formal complaint was ever lodged by any member of Hamblin's families against the move, it can be assumed without diligent imagination that Priscilla didn't think too highly of starting anew.[6] Second wife Louisa, however, would have no lengthy memories of life in Santa Clara; it would be different for her. Jacob had married Louisa Bonelli a few years after Rachel's death. Louisa was 22 to Jacob's 46, seemingly too young and small to accept rigid frontier duties. But she had displayed a hardy disposition when her family accepted the restored gospel in Switzerland. She was baptized in a pond where the ice had to first be broken, her wet clothing freezing on her before she could change.[7] It likely made little difference now where she might live as Mrs. Hamblin.

The reason for taking another wife had seemed obvious. Priscilla needed help in raising her own and Rachel's children. Although perhaps accompanied by a sigh, she saw the practicality of sharing her abode with two more willing adult hands. Jacob first talked things over with Louisa's father, George. As Corbett puts it, "It looked like a business proposition; if there was any love shown no one noticed it. The purpose of the coming marriage was well understood; love could wait."[8]

Making it even more a business arrangement was the fact that Louisa's mother accompanied the two to Salt Lake City for the proper marriage ceremony before Church authorities. She also accompanied the pair in the long wagon ride back to southern Utah, a honeymoon Jacob spent with both bride and mother-in-law.

This assessment of the nuptials may be a little harsh. But when he had married Rachel, there was no time for wooing or courtship. Jacob was a man of duty. Not only were there many children to raise, there was much work to be done in planting gardens and protecting against the elements while Jacob was on the Lord's errands.

The Hamblin house on the little hill overlooking Santa Clara Creek was a beautiful and sturdy edifice, thickly insulated against cold or rain and summer heat, secure against Indian or other trespasser. The fields had yielded an ample harvest for most of a decade; life was beginning, as much as possible for anyone tied in with Jacob Hamblin, to become pleasantly routine. The children had many friends, were learning much in school and new settlers were coming from Salt Lake Valley to bolster the community's security and services. The local Lamanites had become more acclimatized to whiteman's ways and were beginning to be less troublesome. The uprising at Mountain Meadows was all but forgotten.

In moving, Hamblin would leave behind many close friends, including Thales Haskell. Jacob would miss daily association with many other missionaries who had bravely accompanied him on visits to the Hopis. There were his several brothers[9] and relatives as well. But once Hamblin decided it was his duty to change residences, he seems not to have lost much time pondering the matter.

Before departing Santa Clara, he had to find someone to handle the government mail contract between Santa Clara and Cedar City. Jacob says nothing of mail delivery challenges of that day, but it was definitely not for the timid. Hamblin had gotten the job in southern Utah because few others wanted it.[10] Indian hostility along the route was entirely possible. Jacob felt a responsibility to find a replacement who wasn't cowed by the prospect of meeting a few painted aborigines along the way.

Snow had written to Hamblin on occasion that if the Indians prowled around "like wolves" that "we shall kill as many of them as possible," but he also told Hamblin he expected that "you will act upon your own judgment."[11] Snow's hard line made it clear he would countenance no mischief from lethal Lamanites in the territory under his jurisdiction.[12] A militia could be readily raised for the Mormon cause if needed. But it was this very military posture which Hamblin had tried so diligently to avoid over the years.[13]

Snow also warned Hamblin when going forth on his missions "to look into every hiding place where there would be the least possibility of a lurking enemy."[14] Of course, there were so many rocks and crevices encountered in crossing the Colorado River Plateau that little progress could be made if one searched behind "every hiding place." To do so all about them, they would have breached another unwritten commandment of the wild, to keep together for safety in numbers. Hamblin might have chuckled at the practicality of such advice; yet, he knew his regional president cared about the missionaries as did Hamblin. But even living on the frontier at this time carried with it certain inherent risks for all inhabitants.

Jacob well realized, however, that if he was not effective in forging a peace without arms, his white peers would send an overwhelming force against the Indians. Then, many of his friends, red and white, would die.

But for the time being, both Snow and Young had placed great confidence in Jacob to handle the Indian problem with trust and talk instead of military terror. Over the years, Hamblin had rarely failed to reach the ear and heartstrings of the main chieftains, even though there were yet young factions among the Navajo Nation beyond anyone's control. Snow and Young could be assured, too, that Jacob would be fair in all his dealings with the Lamanites, from proudest Navajo warrior to humblest Piede beggar. Jacob would not buckle down to any of them; he seemed constantly in search of stolen livestock among the Indians. He was never known to hesitate in demanding the return of plundered horses from an entire band of raiders in war paint. He would also teach them the orthodox "restored" gospel regarding honesty and truth, Mormon virtues exemplified in the religion's "Thirteen Articles of Faith."[15] He would seek to convert Lamanites to all Christian principles, forever on the alert to help build up the Lord's kingdom on earth. With intrepid energy, Jacob could also pave the way for further Mormon colonization in one of the West's last frontiers, eastern Arizona. If and when Jacob declared routes open for LDS expansion, Brigham could confidently follow with mission calls to settle the entire upper Little Colorado River valley.

Thinking about it, Jacob's family would readily agree he was the ideal man, probably the only man, who could resolve the mounting Indian problems in the Kanab region. The Piutes and Utes in Long Valley along the upper Sevier River country north of Kanab were growing cunningly belligerent, and at best, totally unpredictable. From Skutumpah[16] near present-day Alton in northern Kane County, to Circleville and north along the Sevier, Indian depredations were generating much fear among the white settlers. Hamblin mentions in his journal an abandoned community on the Sevier which held promise before acute white-Indian conflicts.[17]

Many of the settlers, repeatedly attacked by anti-Mormon mobs in Missouri and Illinois, longed now for the opportunity to live in peace. The threat of Indian attack was especially severe for travelers from Johnson's Wash, ten miles east of Kanab, to Lee's Ferry. Whitmore and McIntyre had been recently murdered, as had the Berry family, by Navajos or Piutes or both, in the vicinity of Pipe Springs. Travel was not as safe in southern Utah anymore, probably because the influx of whitemen seemed endless, making game and other food scarce. Some Piute and Navajo raiders were even making excursions into the Minersville region and Pinto, some thirty miles north of Santa Clara. The settlers managed to kill seven Indians there on one occasion.[18] On another, seventy-nine Navajos stormed into Kanab at a time when most of the men were gone, demanding food and horses. Citizens offered food but could not part with the horses. Women and children were much alarmed. They sent a frenzied message to President Snow, "What can we do for protection?"

Via a new telegraph line which had been recently connected between Toquerville and Salt Lake City, Snow asked the governor for help. The cold response was: "Governor Woods refuses to give an answer, or any reason. Says he will do as he pleases."[19] Apparently, Indian troubles in southern Utah were too inscrutable. It was not his problem. But if someone didn't resolve the growing tensions, the entire frontier could soon explode. History says citizens welcomed Jacob to Kanab in early September, 1869.[20]

Was Jacob called directly by Church hierarchy to make the move? Corbett does say that, "Jacob had talked it over with Erastus Snow. After due deliberation, because of the mounting Indian troubles, President Snow gave his consent."[21] No doubt, Snow conferred with Brigham, for by now, the Southwest Indian Mission was the most productive and promising in Zion, providing it was safe to continue proselyting. It appears Jacob made the initial decision, while Church authorities reasoned, "Why rein back the most influential Indian mediator in the history of this Church?" If Jacob was willing, and felt his domestic affairs to be in order, why delay making the frontier safer? By now, Young and Snow knew the mind of Jacob, that their "Apostle to the Lamanites" accomplished peace without bloodshed. He espoused the same concilitory position preferred at Church headquarters.

History records that as soon as Jacob hurriedly put in a few crops at his new home in Kanab, he departed for the Sevier. He says, "I sought out places where the Indians were gathered in the largest numbers. I had many long talks with them which seemed to have a good effect. Although some of the bands were considered quite hostile and dangerous to visit, I felt that I was laboring for good and had nothing to fear."

One reason Hamblin dared "labor for good" when no other whiteman would was that he sincerely cared about the growing plight of the redman. While many of his peers regarded the Indians as a nuisance which couldn't be reasoned with, Hamblin tried to see life from their point of view. President Young had sent Jacob a letter in which he acknowledged that Hamblin possessed "greater endurance" than others; so much was asked of him that it was needful he have more "forebearance" than others.[22] For example, Choog, chief of the Kaibabs, prophesied that disaster would strike Kanab in the near future; perhaps coincidentally, a fire soon broke out in the cabin of Hamblin's neighbor which killed six in one family.

This would seem mere superstition to most of the settlers. Hamblin listened to the chief. He sincerely believed that Choog had the spirit of prophecy and deserved an audience. "The more intelligent part of the Indians believe in one Great Father of all; also in evil influences, and in revelation and prophecy; and in many of their religious rites and ideas, I think they are quite as consistent as the Christian sects of the day."[23]

In "sects of the day," Jacob did not include Mormonism; it had always claimed to be more than that, a reason he was attracted to it. But it was clear in this statement that he considered the redman as much a child of God as any human being. If one truly cared about the welfare of the Indian, then perfect love could cast out fear, as emphasized in 1 John 4:18.

Hamblin wrote in his "Journal-Letters" concerning troubles on the frontier, "I cannot blame the Indians more than the white people." He did not strive to remove the Indian problem so much as to resolve it. Only by that approach could a long-lasting solution fair to all be found.

LDS Church historian Bleak wrote of Hamblin at the time, "He has faithfully devoted himself to friendly relations among the Pah Utes, Shebits [Shivwits]...his 16 years' service proves to be of inestimable value to the region."[24] Bleak also writes, "Our always reliable and faithful Jacob Hamblin, who had rendered much efficient service...was again called to make another trip to the Moqui [Hopi] towns to learn if other Navajos are engaged in the present raidings."[25]

Some say Hamblin should have been called into Salt Lake City to serve as a full-fledged apostle; but if so, his great value to the frontier would have been lost. Historian Charles Peterson notes that, "In ordaining Jacob Hamblin apostle to the Lamanite, Brigham Young bestowed a high but hollow title...Neither his title nor the work with the Indians provided Hamblin with the social position and access to power that assignment to the regular hierarchy of Mormon leadership carried."[26] But it is doubtful if Hamblin would have wanted it any other way. He was where he could serve most effectively, among a struggling minority people of God; they needed his help as much as the whites. Jacob would have almost certainly argued against a position in Salt Lake City; it is quite certain that he would have withered emotionally under the constraints of city social life. His place was on the frontier.

Petersen continues: "Heavenly prompting early gave Jacob the heart of a friend...quiet determination to get to the 'real mission' soon won him the special designation of 'Indian's friend.'" Peterson quoted Dellenbaugh's statement that "Jacob Hamblin knew the Indians of Utah and Arizona better than anyone who ever lived."[27]

These comments about Hamblin are given here rather than in an end tribute because they particularly exemplify his life during this period. His reputation as a powerful force among the Indians had grown immensely since the days on the Muddy. Hamblin himself seemed to understand that no one had more influence with the Indians. If he remained comfortably at home, who would talk with the natives and turn away their wrath?

It should also be mentioned that throughout this period Hamblin often worked or stood guard in the Paria area with a gun "strapted to my back."[28] He knew that the Indian respected a rifle and a man behind the firearm who knew how to use it. It was just that he much preferred amicable settlement whenever possible. Good marksmanship was not entirely for protection against Indians, for there were outlaws about in such country with no established law enforcement yet in place.

With his families in the fort at Kanab until he could build his own cabin, Hamblin made another visit to the Hopi Nation. This time, he persuaded friendly Chief Tuba and his wife to cross the Colorado River and become his guests for several months. It must have been with much excitement that Jacob learned they trusted their lives to him and would accompany him to the land of the whiteman. But on the trip home, Hamblin encountered several difficulties. After descending a cliff, just one of many obstacles in reaching the Colorado River, Jacob became so sick that he lay for some time in pain. It is not known what caused the malady. But unable to continue, he asked a Brother Terry to administer to him. He gave thanks to his Father in Heaven and was then able to get up and press on toward home.[29]

As Tuba first prepared to cross the Colorado, he asked Jacob to join him in a religious cermony. Tuba "then knelt with his face to the East, and asked the Great Father of all to preserve us in crossing the river."[30] Tuba prayed for the safety of the Hopi and the Mormons, "to preserve unto us all our food and clothing, that we need not suffer hunger or cold on our journey." Jacob concluded, "He then arose to his feet. We scattered the ingredients from the medicine bag [carried by many journeying Hopi religious men] into the air, on the land and into the water of the river."

Hamblin was much moved by the spiritual sincerity of his guests. "To me, the whole ceremony seemed humble and reverential. I felt that the Father has regard to such petitions. The

scatterings of the ingredients from the medicine bag I understood to be intended as propitiary sacrifice." Safely on the other
bank, Tuba thanked the Great Father that he had "heard and
answered our prayers."[31]

A few days later, they arrived in Kanab. By now, Priscilla
may not have not known exactly who her husband would bring
home to dinner but was ready on short notice to cook extra
meals and find an extra bed. Like the three Hopis who had preceded them, Tuba and wife Pulaskanimki accompanied Jacob to
visit Salt Lake City and learn more about the Mormons' industry and hopes for peace between white and redman. No doubt,
Tuba and wife learned more about The Book of Mormon and the
Latter-day Saints' beliefs that the pre-Columbus Indian was a
child of the God who communicated closely with them through
His prophets. As Hamblin put it, he wished for Tuba and all
Hopis willing to visit Mormon civilizations to "get acquainted
with the spirit and policy of our people, and become a truthful
representative among his people."[32]

It undoubtedly pleased Hamblin that Tuba and his wife visited a factory at Washington, east of Santa Clara, where some
300 spindles were in motion at once. Says Jacob, "It spoiled him
for being an Orabi. He could never think of spinning yarn again
with his fingers, to make blankets. His wife, after looking at the
mill, thought it was pity that the Hopees (meaning the Orabi
women) were obliged to work so hard to get a little meal to
make their bread, when it could be made so easily."[33] Tuba and
his wife also gleaned cotton in the Mormon fields and President
Young gave him a suit of clothes made from LDS cotton.[34]

In Kanab, Hamblin says they found some eighty Navajos
who had come there to trade. One Indian wife told Jacob that
her people had little left after being marched by the soldiers to
Bosque Redondo. "We were taken prisoners and carried to a
poor desert country, where we suffered much with hunger and
cold...we want to get a start of horses and sheep, and would like
you to tell your people to give us as good a trade as they can."[35]

Hamblin says the Indians traded for fifty horses in Kanab,
then went to St. George and other settlements and traded all the

blankets they had for horses. They "went back to their settlements quite satisfied." It should be remembered that Jacob had encouraged the Navajos while at Fort Defiance to cross the river and "trade with the Mormons," a thing they now began doing for the first time. Hamblin makes no mention of any conflict between white and redman at the time he was returning Tuba to his people. He concludes only that "[the Navajo traders] went back to their own country quite satisfied."[36]

During these trading sessions, an incident never mentioned by Jacob was reported by his son, Jacob Jr. and has been retold many times since. The 10-year old boy was determined to get the very best deal he could for his father in a trade with the visiting Piute chief, Frank. Young Jacob wouldn't give up a horse until the Indian piled up many blankets. Taking them to his father proudly to show him how sharply he had traded, his father shook his head. He had made too good a bargain. Jacob Sr. made the lad return two-thirds of the blankets. The Indian smiled and said, "I knew you would come back. I knew Jacob would not keep so many. You know Jacob is our father as much as your father."[37]

After returning Tuba and his wife to his people, Hamblin went to the Navajo Agency and attended Sunday Church services conducted by a Methodist minister. Jacob says he was invited to speak and talked about the "coming forth of The Book of Mormon, and about the ancient inhabitants of the American continent."[38]

It should be mentioned that Thales Haskell accompanied Jacob on one of these trips across the Colorado, although it almost ended in tragedy for him. The account is written by Hamblin as occurring enroute to Buckskin Mountain: "The brethren engaged in freely shooting at a mark, in order to try their new breech-loading guns furnished by President Young. As there were several men working about the target which the boys had been shooting, [W.B.] Maxwell pointed to a small knot in the second bottom log of a cabin in the northwest corner of the fort." The men called out in case someone was inside but heard no response. "Maxwell fired, hitting just above the knot.

Soon after Ira Hatch made his appearance supporting Thales Haskell and called for help, stating that Haskell had been shot in the head. The blood was streaming from his right temple and his hair was clotted with blood."[39]

Upon examination, it was found that Haskell was lucky. The ball only grazed his skull. He and Hatch having served guard duty, went inside the cabin to get some sleep. Hamblin wrote that the ball passed through a log five inches thick, three folds of an overcoat and through the rim of his hat before striking his friend. Although Haskell was not seriously injured, it cast a "feeling of sadness over the whole camp" for the remainder of the trip across "famed Buckskin Mountain."[40]

As fortune would have it, Hamblin's group was met by a band of Piedes who had one of their warriors accidently injured by gunshot. Jacob said the Indian's thighbone was badly broken; all he could do was to obtain a wagon and send the wounded Indian to Kanab. Ten warriors offered to go along with Hamblin as guides. Jacob could accept only three, "that being all that we could feed."[41]

After returning home, Jacob was soon gone again, helping in the settlement of Pahriah (on the Paria River), laying out a ranch in House Rock Valley, and building a small boat at Lee's Ferry. He also explored a route for a wagon road from Lee's Ferry to San Francisco Mountain. "I procured the assistance of a Piute who lived on the east side of the Colorado, and was somewhat acquainted with the country. We readily found the desired route."[42]

After that, Hamblin piloted the first ten wagons of a group of settlers headed for the Little Colorado, or to some of the tributaries of the Gila. The latter was settled as Thatcher, Ariz., where many Latter-day Saints, including the forefathers of later Church president Spencer W. Kimball, homesteaded.

But at this time, many saints had apprehensions about going into such a new and untamed country. After Hamblin had guided them to Moancoppy near present-day Tuba City in northern Arizona, the would-be colonists looked at the barren nature of the country, became apprehensive about what might be beyond, and turned back. Hamblin showed little sympathy for their temerity. "They all returned to Utah and the great effort to settle the country south of the Colorado was, for the time being, a failure. The failure was evidently for want of faith in the mission they had been called upon to fill by the Lord, through his servants. They lost out on an excellent opportunity, for later, the best locations were taken up by others."[43]

During the time that Navajo depredations occurred in southern Utah, Hamblin sought to gain help from officials across the Colorado. It was known that some stock was taken into New Mexico. But contacting the governor there, Hamblin was told that the governor informed Navajos within his jurisdiction that "they might keep the stock" already taken but should try to stop raiding in the future.[44] It must have seemed a matter of weak character to the people of Utah to hear such talk.

The Piutes could also be trouble. One of them in particular, the renegade chief Patnish, caused the Utah settlers many problems with his thievery. Hamblin attempted to meet with all such troublesome Indians, but could not get Patnish to talk. The Utes under Chief Walker (Walkara) had been troublesome in the so-called Black Hawk War, but with his death, there had been fewer problems.

During the fall and winter of this period, when the Colorado was low enough to cross at Ute Ford, Hamblin spent many nights sleeping in the cold, accompanied by a few hardy Piutes, watching for mischief-bent Navajos. Although Hamblin rarely provides any details of suffering, there was bound to be much of it during times of long vigilance. Jacob seemed determined not only to stop the Navajo depredations but to talk with the primary trouble-makers. Their raids could only lead to their own downfall in the long run. Besides, there were accounts in The Book of Mormon of war-like Lamanites laying down their weapons.[45] Why not these Navajos?

After noting in his journal that Kit Carson's war against the Navajos had attempted to place many of them on a reservation, Haskell provides this insight: "A large number of [Navajos] escaped into the wild, rough Colorado River country and formed themselves in small groups of raiding parties which came across the Colorado River to steal provisions and livestock, especially horses which they moved back into rough country where it became almost impossible to track them down."[46]

The wild nature of the Navajos and the same wild character of their homeland made them more difficult to subjugate than other Indian tribes. In addition, Carson's war in Arizona and New Mexico stopped well short of pursuit to the west side of the river. The Army attacks had also caused many Navajos, especially the younger bucks, to be more determined than ever in protecting their traditional, warring lifestyle against all white intruders. If they were unsafe among the soldiers in eastern Arizona, the renegade bands became mobile. They could move west, just as they had in 1860 when G. A. Smith Jr. was killed—only in greater numbers now.

Why did U.S. troops at the new Army post known as Fort Defiance, Arizona make no attempt to protect U.S. citizens west of the Colorado? It was as if the soldiers considered the Mormons part of some other country. Yet, had the latter not been U.S. citizens ever since the Mexican War? Did they not, in fact, render loyal service during the war with Mexico? And was Utah Territory not a part of the United States?

Some day, Jacob must have a pow wow with the government at Fort Defiance.

End Notes, Chapter Twelve

1. Pearson Corbett, pp 250-5l, no footnotes, referring to settlers' trouble with Indians. Bleak, Book A, p. l92, referring to wandering Navajos.
2. In Jacob's words, Bleak, Book A., p. 261-62
3. Corbett, p. 260. Very little has been said in these pages about Jacob's Church activities at home. Although he had once held the office of bishop in Santa Clara (Bleak, Book A, p. 5l) he was then freed of any local responsibilities which might hinder freedom of travel to the various Indian tribes. When his reputation as a powerful influence among the Indians grew, he was a popular speaker at Church meetings. But he was home infrequently and rarely scheduled in advance to speak.
4. Corbett, p. 256.
5. There are two historical markers in Kanab commemorating Jacob Hamblin at this writing, one at the north entrance to town on U.S. 89 and another south of town near the airport exit road. But the data can be confusing. One marker says Jacob Hamblin helped build Fort Kanab; another says he moved there after construction of the fort. Historical accounts elsewhere say Kanab was settled in l865 and Hamblin moved there in l867.
6. Corbett says, "When Jacob mentioned these things, Priscilla flared up and said she hoped he wasn't getting any ideas about moving the family there. She loved her home and was content to to spend the rest of her days there. To Priscilla, Jacob's desire to travel and move was due to something else besides the urge to 'do missionary work.' It was a habit." Corbett suggests that moving constantly had caused Lucinda to leave Jacob; but in that instance, it had much to do with her husband moving to join the Mormons.
7. Corbett, p. 265.
8. Corbett, p. 248-49. He includes no footnotes with this data, but in the mid l950s he says he was able to interview members of the family who knew Jacob, Priscilla and Louisa personally. Prior to Jacob's marrying Louisa, Priscilla was the lone mother of nine children under l5 years old.
9. Jacob's relationship with his brothers is somewhat enigmatic. He undoubtedly enjoyed having them with him in southern Utah but he writes of them rarely. "Gunlock Bill" is mentioned on earlier missionary expeditions, but there is little other reference to the brothers. It was also typical of Jacob that he mention

no personal acquaintances if they did not directly
relate to missionary labors.

10. According to an unpublished diary kept by Enoch
Bartlett Tripp, mail delivery was received almost daily
in 1868 in Salt Lake Valley, without hindrance from
Indians. It was not always so in southern Utah.
Tripp's handwritten diaries with unnumbered pages
(see entries for 1868) were in the hands of a relative, J.
R. Johnston, Spanish Fork, Utah, at this writing. The
Pony Express from St. Joseph, Missouri to California,
of course, had terminated in 1861.

11. Bleak, Book, B, p. 10.

12. Snow had written previously, "Tell the Navajos not to
let their thiefes (sic) visit us again unless they make
satisfaction for the horses they have stolen from our
people, lest some of our angry men slay them." (Bleak,
Book A, p. 150).

13. It will be recalled that when various militias were called
up to go against the Indians, including one punitive
expedition which killed two Piutes found with some of
the clothing and effects of Whitmore and McIntyre,
Hamblin found some excuse not to be present. It was
quite possibly Jacob's greatest contribution to the frontier that he found a way to make peace between redman
and white without spilling considerable blood, as was
the case almost everywhere else in Arizona.

14. Bleak, Book B, p. 21.

15. No. 13, "We believe in being honest, true..." *Pearl of
Great Price*, p. 61.

16. *Utah Place Names* , p. 80-81. (Listed by an alternate
name, Clarkdale). Walcott says Skutumpah is a Piute
word meaning "where squirrels and rabbitbrush are
plentiful."

17. "Journal and Letters," p. 52. "Came up the Sevier
alone. The deserted houses at Circleville looked lonely
and dead. Here I reflected upon the deeds of cruelty
perpetrated both by the Indians and brethren...the
killing of the women by the Indians and then the murder of the Indian women and children by the brethren
at Circleville." Hamblin gives no other details.

18. Bleak, Book A, p. 259.

19. Ibid, Book B, p. 111.

20. Corbett, p. 266. Little, p. 103, says Hamblin planted
crops earlier.

21. Ibid, p. 123.

22. Hamblin did not include his own LDS faith in this
summation.

23. "Perfect love casteth out fear."1 John 4:18.

24. Bleak, Book B, p. 28.
25. Ibid, p. 10.
26. *Journal of Mormon History,* Vol. 2, pp. 21-34.
27. Ibid.
28. "Journal contents," p. 11.
29. Little, pp. 119-120.
30. Ibid, p. 121.
31. Ibid.
32. Ibid 119. The reference to a "truthful representative among his people" indicates Hamblin felt Tuba was an influential priest among his Hopi people. Much good could be generated through such a man for Mormon efforts to Christianize and civilize the Hopis.
33. Ibid, p. 134. In this, Tuba and his wife clearly saw the vastly superior technology of the whitemen. Hamblin undoubtedly reasoned that with the Hopi emphasis on learning and progress, the Hopis would want to cultivate a closer relationship with these Mormons.
34. Ibid. Nothing more is said of the suit of clothes. Whether he wore them among his people is not stated. But given Hopi customs, it is unlikely. It did prove another form of Mormon industry.
35. Little, pp. 124-25.
36. Ibid, p. 125. While this trade may have been satisfactory to all sides at the time, it was not always to be so with visiting Navajos. Still, in Hamblin's mind, it must have seemed better than having the Indians prowling around at night.
37. Corbett says this data was obtained from an interview with Jacob's son, Walter. See Corbett, p. 520. After being published, the story has been been told for many years in the LDS Church Historian's office and in Mormon sacrament meetings.
38. Little, p. 126.
39. "Journal contents," p. 15.
40. Hamblin says no more of the mishap. T.H. Haskell Journal (edited) says, "Members of the party dressed the wound the best they could and in time it healed without leaving a very noticeable scar."
41. "Journal contents," p. 16.
42. Little, p. 127. With Hamblin's known penchant for optimism, mentioning few problems if his desired goal was reached, one might take the word "readily" to mean no insurmountable obstacle was encountered.
43. Little, p. 128. This represents one of the few times Hamblin was so openly critical of his LDS peers. One reason, undoubtedly, was that he had personally reported to Church leaders the land in question was

highly desirable; he wanted the Saints to get an early foothold in it.   44. Bleak, Book B, p. 63.
45. *Book of Mormon*, Alma 24:19.
46. T. H. Haskell Journal, p. 47.

The close association of Thales and Jacob ends here, for in 1867, Haskell was called to a mission among the Lamanites at Moancappy (Moenkepi), Ariz. A daughter, Irene, says that in making the move, "We traveled hundreds of miles and never saw a white-man." p. 48. Haskell's ability to speak "five or six" Indian languages likely made him invaluable at Moancappy, just as he had been when accompanying Hamblin on mission journeys to various native tribes.

– Chapter 13 –

Powell's Right Hand Man

Seeking a man who could guide him among sometimes unfriendly Indians of the Grand Canyon region, it didn't take long for Major John Wesley Powell to settle on the name of Jacob Hamblin. Rumors had circulated in the Southwest that some of those Indians, the Shivwits, murdered three of Powell's men. The major now needed to make certain his crew would not be killed on a second expedition down the Colorado. He also needed to find access points into the deep bowels of the canyon where his men could pick up much-needed supplies enroute.

On his initial exploration of the Grand Canyon in 1869, Powell and his crew suffered much from lack of food, almost starving during the nearly four-month journey. Food like flour and bacon spoiled quickly after becoming waterlogged by whitewater rapids. Powell knew of only two supply points on the lower Colorado, the Crossing of the Fathers and Lee's Ferry, too close to one another to be of separate value. Powell needed some one who knew Southwest Indians and their trails in and around the Grand Canyon. He needed him before his next scheduled voyage down the canyon in 1871, one year away.

In Jacob Hamblin, Powell knew he had found the right man.[1] In Chapter 12 of his *Exploration of the Colorado River and its Canyons*, Powell says: "This evening, the Shivwits…came in, and after supper, we hold a long council. A blazing fire is built, and around this we sit—the Indians living here [probably the Kaibabs] the Shivwits, Jacob Hamblin, and myself. This man, Hamblin, speaks their language well and has a great influence over all the Indians in the region round about. He is a silent, reserved man, and when he speaks it is in a slow, quiet way that inspires awe. His talk is so low that they must listen attentively to hear, and they sit around him in deathlike silence. When he finishes a measured sentence the chief repeats it and they all give a solemn grunt."[2]

After being introduced by Hamblin, Powell explains to the assembed natives that he comes in peace. He does not come to take away their lands or harm the people, but to learn about the land and the people; that he seeks knowledge, a valuable thing for all people of all races. He adds: "Heretofore, I have found it very difficult to make the natives understand my object but the gravity of the Mormon missionary helps me much."[3]

The chief replies: "Your talk is good, and we believe what you say. We believe in Jacob, and look upon you as a father." Referring to Powell as Kapurats (Piute for "one arm missing"),[4] the Indians welcome the Major to partake of their game, water, friendship.

Then the Shivwit chief makes mention of Powell's three men. "Last year we killed three whitemen. Bad men said they were our enemies. They told great lies. We thought them true. We were mad; it made us big fools. We are very sorry...it is done; let us be friends. We are ignorant—like little children in understanding compared with you."[5]

Hamblin was able to take one of the Shivwits aside, and again acting as interpreter, told Powell more about the slain men: "They came upon the Indian village almost starved and exhausted with fatigue. They were supplied with food and put on their way to the settlements. Shortly after they had left, an Indian from the east side of the Colorado arrived...and told them about a number of miners having killed a squaw in drunken brawl and no doubt, these were the men; no person had ever come down the canyon; that was impossible; they were trying to hide their guilt."[6]

Normally a docile tribe if left alone, the Shivwits were "worked into a great rage," caught up with the trio and filled them with arrows.[7]

According to Powell's account, he had been extremely desirous that the three men, brothers O. G. and Seneca Howland and William Dunn, remain with the group to finish out their scientific canyon voyage. When the three exhibited a determination to hike out of the canyon rather than face the next formidable rapid, Powell's cook prepared them biscuits and Powell offered them more of the meager food supply which was left. But the men insisted on taking only two rifles and a shotgun, declaring they could shoot game for sustenance, striking toward the high cliffs rimming Kanab Creek Canyon. After successfully negotiating the rapid that the trio feared—ever afterward known as Separation Rapid—Powell said he waited some two hours for the men to rejoin the crew.[8] The Major never saw the three again. Only rumor explained their fate until Hamblin's conversation with the Shivwits cleared up the mystery for Powell.

"That night I slept in peace, although these murderers of my men…were sleeping not 500 yards away. While we were gone to the canyon, the pack train and supplies, enough to make an Indian rich beyond his wildest dreams, were all left in their charge, and were all safe; not even a lump of sugar was pilfered by the children."

Before departing the Shivwits camp, the Major named the great mountain nearby Mt. Trumbull, "in honor of the senator" (a name, like most of Powell's labels, persisting to this day)[9] and climbed the summit. There, the Major broke into poetic outburst: "What a view is before us! A vision of glory! The vermillion Cliffs to the north, with their splendor of colors; the Pine Valley Mountains to the northwest, clothed in mellow perspective haze; unnamed mountains to the southwest, towering over canyons bottomless to my peering gaze, like chasms to nadir hell; and away beyond, the San Francisco Mountains, lifting their black heads into the heavens."[10]

Admittedly, Major Powell had a way with words. Hamblin trod almost daily among the same geographic grandeur described by the Major but for reasons of his own, never ventured to pontificate upon their magnificence. The Major, a geologist, was also more interested in rock formations and volcanic residue. Yet, despite these differences, Powell and Hamblin had much in common. They were both patient, gentle men, truly interested in the natives; Professor Powell (as Hamblin often called him) more for scientific reasons, as shall be obvious later, Hamblin for his religious purpose. Both were extremely eager to learn all they could about the little-known aborigines of the Southwest. And Powell's writings throughout *The Exploration of the Colorado*

River make it clear that he had entered a wonderland both geo-logically and ethnically.

In many chapters of his Hamblin biography,[11] Bailey shows a euphoric relationship between Jacob and John. Although the precise wilderness conversation must be considered speculative (only the two of them could possibly know precisely what was said), it is undoubtedly true that a deep bond of trust developed between them. Mormon and Gentile, total strangers just a few weeks previous, these men making Southwest history devel-oped a deep respect for one another as they pursued a greater comprehension of the first Americans.

For Hamblin it seemed a time fondly remembered; his fami-ly could benefit materially while he carried out his first love, missionary work among the Lamanites.[12] While his own people had made many sacrifices to visit the Indians of the Arizona Strip, Jacob found few so eager to learn intricate details about the Indians' heritage and lifestyle as Professor Powell. It must also have been refreshing for the natives, for here were two whitemen who did not wish to exploit them, but who made an energetic effort to visit their people solely to gain a better under-standing and forge a closer friendship among them.

In this regard, it is interesting to see what another author, James R. Ullman, has to say about the meeting of Powell with Hamblin and the Shivwits. "[Powell's] only companion was Jacob Hamblin, a famous Mormon frontiersman who knew the plateau country even better than Powell, and also the nature and whereabouts of the Indian tribes." But then inexplicably, Ullman adds: "And the Indians looked after him—this stranger named Kapurats—with awe and wonder, for he was the first whiteman they had ever met who treated them as free and equal human beings."[13] Either the author forgot that Hamblin had spent years building trust among the Shivwits, or supposed that Jacob himself was an Indian. It is typical of the treatment Hamblin often received from later historians. Powell was the man remembered as "taming" the Southwest Indian, yet quite obviously could have gotten nowhere without the presence of Hamblin, a thing the Major said repeatedly in his own writings.

Hamblin says of his meeting with Powell, "He wished to employ someone who understod Indian character, and spoke their dialect, to go with him, and President Young had recommended me as a suitable person. He offered me liberal terms, and as I was desirous of seeing the Indians myself, a satisfactory arrangment was made. We left Kanab…in September, 1870…[w]e found some Indians gathering cactus fruits which grew there in great abundance. I requested them to bring in some of the party who took a part in the killing of Powell's men the previous year."[14]

Since Powell's explanation was based upon Hamblin's interpretation of conversation with the Shivwits, it follows that the two accounts are alike. However, Jacob includes two explanatory items omitted by the Major—that Indians on the east side of the Colorado floated across the river on a raft (swimming could be very dangerous) and that the Indians warned "if any mines were found in their country it would bring great evil among them." Hamblin does not elaborate on this statement, neither pursuing the implication that a discovery of mines per se would bring a flood of palefaces among them, nor perhaps reflecting some of Brigham's well-known biases against the idea of getting rich quick via mineral wealth. In any event, Powell does not repeat this warning about the "evils of mining," given by Hamblin in his autobiography.[15]

Jacob concludes: "The Indians further stated that they believed what I told them, and, had they been correctly informed about the men, they would not have killed them."[16] It is only speculation but it would seem quite likely that if the Howlands and Dunn had been so fortunate as to have Hamblin present among the Shivwits after climbing out of the Grand Canyon, they would have lived to tell about it.

In weeks following the "treaty at Mt. Trumbull," as it was later called, Hamblin and various Indian guides led the Major along primitive trails from the head of Paria Canyon near Utah's present-day Bryce Canyon National Park across the Arizona Strip to the Colorado River of the Grand Canyon. It is obvious from this trip that Powell wanted to learn much more about this little-known country than just that adjacent to the Grand Canyon. In the process, he and his men placed the Henry Mountains on the map for the first time, 1871, the last major mountain range in the United States to be so mapped. All of this is explained in vivid detail in Powell's writings about his Grand Canyon explorations.[17]

Aesthetics now behind him, Powell sought dropoff points where Hamblin could leave supplies for his next expedition down the canyon. After being satisfied that Hamblin could provide the supplies, Powell invited Jacob to an important meeting of the federal government with the Navajo Nation at Fort Defiance, Arizona. Some 6,000-8,000 Navajos would be gathered there to receive their annual annuities in the autumn of 1870.[18] Going with Hamblin was his old friend, Spanish interpreter Ammon Tenney, now age 26. Tenney had compiled statistics showing that some million dollars worth of Mormon cattle, horses and sheep in Utah had been stolen by Navajo raiders, proof that a serious problem persisted.[19] The council in Ft. Defiance was "tremendously dramatic," according to Tenney. Many whitemen wondered why payments should be continued to a Navajo Nation which couldn't control those committing such continued depredations.[20] In addition, there were a number who had made no agreement to comply with regulations set forth by the U.S. Army in and around Defiance. Kit Carson had starved out some renegade Indians by destroying their horse pasturage and peach tree orchards at Canyon De Chelly. Many Navajos were marched to the barren plains of Bosque Redondo, New Mexico.[21] Those who wanted to return to their homeland were allowed to do so if they signed a "cease war" document. But as later events would indicate, many Navajos deeply resented the whiteman's intrusion and refused to take a subservient role in his encroaching world.

Hamblin describes the Defiance conference as one in which Major Powell was "extremely helpful" in the pursuit of peace. As historian McClintock explains, "It was found that the gathering was entirely hostile,"[22] no specific reason was given for this conclusion.

McClintock says, "Powell and Hamblin led in the talking. The former had no authority whatever, but gave the Indians to understand that he was a commissioner on behalf of the whites and serious chastisement would come to them in a visit of troops if there should be continuation of the evil conditions complained of by the Mormons."[23] This was a critical and very timely statement made by Major Powell in the hearing, perhaps, of the Indian Agent, Captain Bennett. Powell suggested the agency needed to pay more attention (few had before Bennett or afterward) to the west side of the Colorado. Basically, the Army had sought to protect citizens on the east side, letting the Mormons take care of themselves. In fact, on several of Jacob's expeditions to the Hopis he had even been told that the soldiers suggested killing the Mormons rather than let their missionaries proselyte among the Indians.

Enroute to Defiance, Hamblin and Powell had stopped among the Hopi villages and the Major no doubt saw the high regard in which the Hopi chiefs held Jacob, as had Indian tribes all along the way.[24] It was the Hopis and their high level of civilization which most interested Powell, just as it had Hamblin on his first visit twelve years before. The Major wrote several chapters about the Hopi festivals, dances, level of civilization in building homes, skills as pottery makers, industry in utilizing corn in so many ways, etc. Powell also witnessed a primitive side, which included the handling of rattlesnakes in religious ceremonies (a thing which neither Hamblin nor Haskell journals mention, possibly to avoid alarming those back home). It was also learned that the Hopis had driven their arch enemies, the Navajos, over cliffs in a fiercely militaristic manner. Neither Hamblin nor Haskell had previously mentioned this aspect of the "peaceful Hopis" in their journals.[25]

Powell spoke to the assembled Navajos first, according to Hamblin's autobiography, pages ll3-ll8. "He stated that he had lived and traveled with these people [Mormons] and formed a very favorable opinion of them. He said that they were an industrious people, who paid their quota in taxes in common with other citizens of the United States, from which the Navajos received their annuities."

Then Jacob spoke of the "evils of war" which make for "a bad policy." He said that much Mormon stock had been lost to the Navajos. "That our young men had wanted to come over and drive them, but had been told to stay at home until all other means for obtaining peace had been tried and failed. I see much grass and many watering places on each side of the river. If we could live at peace with each other, we could take advantage of all the land, grass and water...and have all we need. We could sleep in peace, awake in the morning and find our property safe...What shall I tell my people, the Mormons, when I return home?...I have now grey hairs on my head, and from my boyhood I have been on the frontiers, doing all I could to preserve peace between the whitemen and the Indians. I despise this killing, this shedding of blood. I hope you will stop this, and come and visit and trade with our people. We would like to hear what you have got to say before we return home."

As Jacob took his seat, he said "noticed the tears start in the eyes of Barbencita, the Spanish name of the principal chief of the Navajos. He slowly approached and put his arms around me, saying, 'My friend and brother, I will do all I can to bring about what you have advised. We will not give our answer now. Many of our Navajos are here. We will talk to them tonight, and will see you on your way home.'"

Hamblin seemingly touched the heart of Indian Agent Bennett, who told Jacob that he "could not have talked better to bring about peace with the Navajos. He manifested much good feeling, and furnished us liberally with supplies for our journey home."

A little wryly, perhaps intended only for LDS faithful among his readers, Jacob added, "This was probably the first time that the chiefs of the Navajo Nation ever heard a gospel discourse adapted to their circumstances...the hearts of many of them were open to reciprocate to it."

On his way home, Hamblin met with an old Hopi Indian who repeatedly refused to return stolen Navajo sheep. The Hopi was in a "surly mood." Hamblin reminded the Indian they had done some trading previously and that the man had said he thought the Mormons were a fulfillment of prophecy. Said

Hamblin: "You told me you believed we were the men your father meant [who would bring peace] and I hope you will not prevent peace from coming into your country for the sake of a few sheep." The man gave up the sheep.

Enroute home Hamblin and Tenney also met some Navajos not present nor a part of the "treaty" at Fort Defiance. They told Hamblin, "We have some bad men among us...but if some do wrong, the wise ones must not act foolishly like children." A chief by the name of Hastele was introduced to Hamblin as a man who never lies or steals. "He is a truthful man; we wish all difficulties settled before him." Jacob would have later dealings with this Hastele. Jacob notes, "The peace treaty talk with these Navajos ended by some of them saying, 'We hope we may be able to eat at one table, warm by one fire, smoke one pipe, and sleep under one blanket.'"

It was a fitting end to an historic alliance, one undoubtedly providing Jacob with a deep feeling of satisfaction as he made his way back to his family. It would surely bring greater peace between at least some whites and some Navajos. But not all.

End Notes, Chapter Thirteen

1. pp. 289-90.
2. Ibid, pp. 320-21.
3. Ibid. p. 321.
4. According to *Utah Place Names*, p. 211, the Kaiparowats Plateau in southern Utah's Garfield County is likely the result of a corrupted form of the Piute word for "Karaputs." This was the name given the whiteman who had lost half of his right arm in the Battle of Shiloh in the Civil War.
5. J.W. Powell, p. 322. The tone of this statement indicates an intense desire by the chief to be certain that Hamblin, and to a lesser extent, Powell, are not disappointed in the moral integrity of the local Shivwits.
6. Ibid. It would be easy to imagine how impossible this story might sound to Indians. A person could float across the raging Colorado in some selected spot on a raft, but even to try floating the length of the (Grand) Canyon would be sheer madness.
7. Ibid. There has been speculation that Indians with home-made bows could not overwhelm Powell's men armed with two rifles and a shotgun. Powell says the Shivwits "surrounded the men in ambush." In addition, Indian bows of the region may not have been as primitive as supposed. Powell explains local Indian bow-making. "The best are made of the horns of mountain sheep. They are soaked in water until quite soft, cut into long strips, and glued together; they are then quite elastic." Powell, p. 319.
8. For an account of weapons and provisions taken, see J.R. Ullman, pp. 155-158. Also Powell, pp. 280-282. The Major is known to have "strained" the truth in writing of his Grand Canyon explorations (for example, combining incidents from both his 1869 and 1871 voyages as if they occurred in the earlier expedition) but the fatherly concern that Powell expressed for his men here seems genuine. Powell says he did not think of the trio as deserters but faithful comrades in a dangerous journey. He was most anxious to learn of their fate when employing Hamblin to talk with the Indians of the North Rim about their demise.
9. Powell, p. 323. This reference is apparently to Sen. Lyman Trumbull, whom Abraham Lincoln helped get elected in 1854. *World Book Encyclopedia*, L, p. 278.
10. Powell, p. 325. It is not known why Powell would refer to "unnamed mountains" to the Southwest; he normally

named any new geographical discovery immediately. The other scenic vistas mentioned must have taken distracted his attention.

11. Several middle chapters of Bailey's biography include folksy dialogue between Hamblin and Powell which must be considered apocryphal. Still, the conveyance of a deep friendship seems accurate.

12. Little, p. 112. Exploring the countryside "east, north and south… afforded me an excellent opportunity to carry out my mission to the Lamanites."

13. Ullman, p. 180.

14. Little, p. 110.

15. Ibid.

16. For another viewpoint on the murder of Powell's men, see chapter 16, "Answering the Critics."

17. The first 374 pages of Powell's *Exploration of the Colorado River and its Canyons* include many expeditions outside the Grand Canyon, and Colorado River drainage. This would include forays to the upper Sevier River which drains into the Great Basin.

18. That the "treaty" in Ft. Defiance occurred in 1870 is well documented. On p. 113 of his autobiography, Hamblin incorrectly recalls the date as 1871.

19. Quoted by McClintock, p. 76. The latter stated he had a personal interview with Ammon Tenney in 1920. Since Tenney acted as interpreter for Hamblin at the Defiance conference, he would have been a direct participant with almost all Hamblin or Powell said or did.

20. Neither Tenney nor McClintock make this statement directly. It is the author's speculation on why Indians gathered to receive needed supplies and annuities but were "distinctly hostile" as McClintock later puts it. Powell sheds no light on the subject, saying only that there is "gambling…feasting…at night, the revelry is increased." Hamblin has nothing negative to say about the Navajos' mood but they may well have been "distinctly hostile." Jacob could be a decided optimist in describing Indian behavior.

21. This attempt to teach agriculture to Navajos on barren soil turned out to be so costly, with such loss to Indian life, that the government mercifully abandoned it, allowing the Navajos to return to their native land. They were one of the few U.S. Indian tribes allowed to do so. See Brown, *Bury my Heart at Wounded Knee*, "The Long Walk of the Navajos," pp. 140-36. It should be noted that this was a particularly sympathetic treatment of the American aborigine by the U.S. Government.

22. This seems to be McClintock's conclusion, not that of Tenney.
23. McClintock, p. 76.
24. Powell, pp. 336-44.
25. Ibid, pp. 346-47. The snake dance was performed at Walpi, less than a day from Oraibi. Powell says the medicine men or priest doctors placed the rattlesnakes in their mouths; then "they engaged in a dance." Another Indian tickles the snake's head with a feather to keep attention away from the handler. After the ceremony, the snakes are given their freedom.

– Chapter 14 –

Condemned to Die

When Jacob Hamblin promised safety to all Navajos willing to cross the Colorado and trade in Utah, he likely thought such dealings would be with Mormons like himself. He knew most everyone in the Kanab area and could vouch for their willingness to deal honestly with Indians coming in peace. But unknown to Hamblin, the McCarty brothers had made their home in Grass Valley. The rights of others, whites or Indian, meant little to them. They had, in fact, thrown in with Robert Leroy Parker, alias Butch Cassidy, who later led a Wild Bunch of outlaws.

While western romanticists insist that Parker, raised by Mormon parents in Circleville, was "careful" to rob only corporate trains and banks, intending to harm no one, the McCartys were clearly a different breed of bandit. Tom and Bill McCarty had settled on a small ranch in Grass Valley north of the present-day Antimony, but ranching apparently yielded too little profit. Their stay in Utah launched a career of violence which would soon make them wanted by the law throughout most of the West.[1]

It was at Grass Valley, while the McCartys were temporarily away, that four young Navajos came to trade in the early winter of 1874. Caught in a snowstorm, they took refuge at the McCarty Ranch. According to historian Charles Kelly, the Navajos "are said to have killed a calf belonging to the McCartys. They then entered the cabin, forced the two whites out [names not given] and helped themselves to breakfast and left with a horse belonging to James Clinger. The McCartys followed them and killed three. The fourth, greviously wounded, somehow lived to return to his family. When he reported the death of his comrades, the Navajos declared war on all whites in Utah and began raiding Mormon herds around Kanab."[2]

Kelly says the McCartys moved soon after that from Grass Valley and apparently kept horses belonging to the Navajos.

Hamblin attempted to get the horses returned. A statement in his "Journal and Letters" (interspersed with other items dated March 12, 1874) stated: "Would like if possible to have the horses that belonged to the Navajos sent...would like to get counsel from the First Presidency."[3]

Hamblin seemed to feel personally responsible because it was he who had promised safety to the Navajos if they came into Utah to trade.[4] Jacob meant it as a gesture of peace and friendship. While Kelly asserts that the Indians did not come in peace, the Navajo who escaped to his homeland presented a much different story. He insisted that he had permission to cross the Colorado, and that his companions merely attempted to find refuge in the storm; they abused no one, stole nothing. Hamblin accepted this report; it was the only one he ever referred to in any of his writings.

How accurate is Kelly's report? He is known to have erred in one minor fact. He stated that the killings occurred in the fall of 1874; it was, in fact, the previous winter. But he was certainly not amiss in concluding that the death of three Navajos fomented a major uprising against the white settlers of southern Utah in general, and Jacob Hamblin in particular. Corbett described the event as "rocking the foundations" of the Utah-Arizona border.[5] Racial conflict such as that generated by the McCarty killings had exploded into major warfare between whites and Indians in many other sectors of Arizona.[6] Hamblin was determined that this should not happen here between white and Navajo.

For the Indians, there was only one way of looking at it. Hamblin had been taken at his word; now, three promising young braves lay dead. News of the Navajo somehow making his way home after thirteen days with a "bullet hole in him" spread like wildfire among the tribes. Corbett says that after friendly Chief Tuba received word of it, he sent messengers to the closest white outpost which might be affected, Lee's Ferry. From there, John D. Lee rode with his son all through the night to Kanab, and located Jacob as the one who could best decide what ought to be done. If so, the ride suggests considerable valor on Lee's part, for he was by then a much sought-after fugitive from the Mountain Meadows Massacre.[7]

Kelly summed the matter up this way: "Hamblin visited the Navajos in their own territory" to talk over the matter and was "threatened with death."[8] In fact, a hastily summoned Navajo Council (which included Ketchene, mourning inconsolably for his three slain sons) condemned Jacob to be burned immediately at the stake.

Hamblin explains it this way. "A party of four young Navajos went to the east fork of the Sevier River to trade…they encountered a severe snowstorm which lasted three days. They found shelter in a vacant house belonging to one McCarty. He did not belong to the Church and had that animosity towards Indians too common with whitemen, which leads them to slaughter the savages as they are called, on the most trifling pretenses.

"The Navajos, becoming hungry during the delay, killed a small animal belonging to Mr. McCarty. In some way he learned of the presence of the party on his ranch, gathered up some men of like spirit with himself, came suddenly upon the Navajos and, without giving them an opportunity of explaining their circumstances, killed three of them and wounded the fourth. The wounded man, after enduring excessive hardships, made his way across the river, and arrived among his own people.

"Telling the story of his wrongs, it aroused all the bitter spirit of retaliation, so characteristic of the Indians from tradition and custom. The affair taking place in 'Mormon' country, where the Navajos naturally supposed they were among friends, and not distinguishing McCarty as an outsider, the murder was laid to the Mormons.

"The outrage created considerable excitement among both whites and Indians. When President Young heard of it, he requested me to visit the Navajos and satisfy them that our people were not concerned in it."[9]

Hamblin left Kanab by himself. No one could much blame his peers if they chose not to provide company on this occasion. The mission seemed little short of suicide. The bishop of Kanab, Levi Stewart, the top ecclesiastical authority in that part of the world, attempted to stop Jacob from going. Stewart said he had learned from the Piutes that the Navajos were prepared to "retaliate the first opportunity," i.e., kill the first whitemen on sight, and specifically Jacob Hamblin. If not for him, the young Navajos wouldn't have ventured into "Mormon country" in the first place.

"My son Joseph overtook me about 15 miles out, with a note from Bishop Levi Stewart, advising my return."

But even though Stewart undoubtedly felt he had pertinent information, President Young had sent Jacob on a mission—and in Hamblin's mind, he still outranked the local bishop. "I directed my son to return to Kanab and tell Bishop Stewart that I could not make up my mind to return."

The remainder of the story is taken from *Annals of Southern Utah Mission*, Book B, as recorded by LDS historian Bleak:

When President Young heard of it, he requested me to visit the Navajos, and satisfy them that our people were not concerned in it. Feeling that the affair without great care, might bring on a war, I started at once for their country to fill my mission…My son Joseph overtook me about fifteen miles out with a note from Bishop Levi Stewart advising my return, as he had learned from the Piutes that the Navajos were much exasperated and threatened to retaliate on the first opportunity. I had been appointed to a mission by the highest authority of God on the earth. My life was of but small moment compared with the lives of the Saints and the interests of the Kingdom of God. I determined to trust in the Lord and go on…

Arriving at the settlement of Pahreah, I found Lehi Smithson and another man preparing to start for Mowabby. We remained overnight to procure animals for the journey. That night, my son Joseph came to me again with a note from Bishop Stewart, advising my return, and stating that if I went on I would surely be killed by the Navajos.

When we arrived at the Mowabby, we found that the store house of two rooms which had been built there, had been fitted up in the best possible manner for defense. This had been done by three or four miners who had remained there, on account of the excitement, for which there appeared to be considerable reason.

I felt that I had no time to lose. It was important to get an interview with the Navajos before the outbreak. My horse was jaded…wishing to go to Moancoppy, ten or twelve miles farther, that night, brothers by the name of Smith, brought in three of their riding horses, offered me one, and they mounted the others to accompany me.

At Moancoppy [Moenkopi] I hoped to find some Oribas who could give me correct information about the temper of the Navajos. Arriving there, we found only a Piute family and one Oriba woman. From them I learned that the young relatives of the Navajos killed in Grass Valley were much exasperated, but the older men expressed a desire to see me before anything was done, or anyone hurt. This news was encouraging to me. It being now evening, we lay down and slept till morning. Tuba had been living at Moancoppy and had left on account of the excitement. Some of his effects were lying around in a way that indicated he had left in a hurry.

I was informed that Mush-ah, a Navajo with whom I was somewhat acquainted, and in whom I had some confidence, was camped at a watering place twelve miles east of Moancoppy. I hoped to see and have a talk with him, and get up a conciliatory feeling without exposing myself too much to the ire of the Indians. Arriving at the water where we expected to find Mush-ah, we were disappointed. The place was vacated. We met a Navajo messenger, riding fast on his way to Mowabby, to learn of affairs at that place. He appeared much pleased to see me. After a little talk, he pointed in the distance to a high mesa, and said the Navajos were camped at that point, and wished to see me. We arrived at the lodges after sun-down. In the neighborhood were gathered a large number of horses…Two or three gray-headed men came out to meet us good naturedly, but did not appear as friendly as formerly. I told them my business. Soon afterwards some young men put in an appearance, whose looks bespoke no good.

There being a good moon, a messenger was soon on his way to inform those at a distance of my arrival.

I enquired for Hastele, who had been shown to me by the principal chief in our final peace talk, three years before, and for whom

I was directed to enquire in case of difficulty. I got no answer, which indicated to me that they did not wish for his assistance.

I communicated to the old men the circumstances connected with the killing of the Navajos in Grass Valley, as I understood them. They replied that they were not ready for a talk, or council and said, 'When the relatives are all in we will talk.'

My spirit was weighed down with gloomy forebodings, and I would gladly have left the place could I have felt justified in doing so. Unless the Lord was with us, what were we to do with all these against us?

The night passed and a part of the forenoon of the following day, when the Navajos who had been sent for began to gather in. About noon, they informed me they were ready for talk. A lodge had been emptied of its contents for a council room. It was about twenty feet long by twelve feet wide, constructed of logs, with one end set in the ground, and the top ends leaning to the center of the lodge, and fitted together. The outside was covered with about six inches of dirt. A fire occupied the center of the Lodge, smoke escaping through an opening in the roof. There was but one entrance, and that was in the end.

Into this lodge were crowded some twenty-four Navajos, four of whom were councilors of the nation. A few Indians gathered at the entrance. The two Smiths and I were at the farther end from the entrance, with apparently not one chance in a hundred of reaching the outside, should it be necessary to make an effort to save our lives.

The council opened by the Navajo spokesman asserting that what I had said about the murder of their relatives was false. He stated that I had advised their people to cross the great river and trade with my people, and in doing so they had lost three good young men, who lay on our lands for the wolves to eat. The fourth, he said came home with a bullet-hole through him, and without a blanket and he had been thirteen days in that situation, cold and hungry. He also stated that I need not think of going home, but my American friends might, if they would start immediately. I informed the two Smiths of the intention of the Navajos concerning the disposal of myself. I told them they had been obliging to me and I would not deceive them; the way was open for them to go if they desired to do so. They replied they would not go until I went.

Our three revolvers were hanging over my head. It was desirable to have them as well in hand as possible. I took hold of them, at the same time saying to our Piede interpreter, 'These are in my way; what shall I do with them?' As I spoke I passed them behind to the Smiths: not wishing to give any cause for suspicion that I had any fears, or expected to use the weapons. I told the Smiths not to make any move until we were obliged to.

The Navajos continued to talk for some time, when I was given to understand that my turn had come. I told them of my long acquaintance with their people, and of my labors to maintain peace. I hoped they would not think of killing me for a wrong with which neither myself nor my people had anything to do; and that strangers had done the deed.

I discovered that what I had said the day before had some influence with the gray haired men. None of the gray haired men belonged to the council, but were allowed to speak.

The young men evidently feared that the council would oppose their desire for revenge. They evinced great intensity of feeling. The wounded man was brought in. His wounds were exposed to the council, and a stirring appeal was made for retaliation by a young warrior. It stirred up the Indian blood from its very depths. He closed by asserting that they could do no less than put me to death. For a few minutes I felt that if I was ever permitted to see friends and home again, I should appreciate the privilege. I thought I felt one of the Smiths at my back grip his revolver. I said to him quietly, "Hold still! Do not make the first move, and there will be no move made. They will never get ready to do anything.' This assurance came by the whisperings of the Spirit within me. When the excitement had died away a little, I spoke to the Piute interpreter. He either could not, or would not, answer me. Neither would he answer the Navajos but sat trembling, apparently with fear.

The Navajos brought in another Piute and recommended him as a man of much courage and said he would not falter; but he was soon in the same dilemma as the other. After some further conversation, they appeared a little molified, and, in lieu of blood revenge, they proposed to take cattle and horses for the injury done them. They required me to give them a writing, obligating me to pay one hundred head of cattle for each of the three Navajos killed, and fifty for the wounded one.

This was a close place for me. I could go home by simply putting my name to the obligation. I reflected; Shall I acknowledge by my act that my people are guilty of a crime of which I know they are innocent, and neutralize all the good results of our labors among this people for fifteen years? Shall I obligate the Church to pay three hundred and fifty head of cattle for a crime committed by others? It is perhaps more than I should be able to earn the rest of my life. The sacrifice looked to me more than my life was worth. I replied that I would not sign the obligation. One of them remarked that he thought I would by the time I had been stretched over that bed of coals awhile, pointing to the fire in the middle of the lodge.

I answered that I had never lied to them, and that I would not pay for the wrong that other people had done. Let the Americans pay for their own mischief, I will not sign a writing to pay you one hoof.'

Here the new Piute interepreter would not say anything more. A Piute Chief, standing in the door of the lodge, spoke to him in an angry tone, and accused him of having a very small heart and little courage.

The Chief then asked me if I was not scared. I asked, 'What is there to scare me?' He replied, 'the Navajos.' I told him I was not afraid of my friends. 'Friends!' said he, 'You have not a friend in the Navajo Nation. Navajo blood has been spilled on your land. You have caused a whole nation to mourn. Your friend Ketch-e-ne, that used to give you meat when you were hungry, and blankets, when you were cold, has gone to mourn for his murdered sons. You have caused the bread he eats to be like coals of fire in his mouth, and the water he drinks, like hot ashes. Are you not afraid?'

'No,' I replied, 'My heart never knew fear.'

The Navajos wished to know what the Piute Chief and myself were talking about. The Piute repeated the conversation in their language. They then conversed among themselves; at times they manifested considerable warmth. I was asked if I knew Has-te-le. Replying in the affirmative, they asked, 'What do you know about him?' I answered, 'I know that Bar-ben-ce-ta, and others of your leading men said, at the great peace talk, that he was an honest man, and that all important difficulties between you and our people should be settled before him. I knew this affair should be settled before him, and have known it all the time we have been talking. I came here on a peace mission. If you will send Has-te-le into our country to learn the truth concerning what I have told you, let as many more come along as you like. I wish you would send the best interpreter you have along with him. It is no use to ask me about pay. In the meantime your people can trade among the Mormons in safety. They will be glad to see you if you will come in the daytime, as our people come into your country—not to prowl around your lodges to steal and kill. I came to do as I agreed to, after the good talk at Fort Defiance.'

I felt that the last I said had the desired effect. Their feelings began to soften.

After some further conversation among themselves, the interpreter said, 'They are talking good about you now.' I replied, 'I'm glad; it is time they talked good. What have they said about me?'

'They say you have a good heart. They think they will wait until they see their greater chiefs, and believe that the matter will be settled before Hastele.'

It was then agreed that I should come to Mowabby, in twenty five-days, and they would see if it was not advisable to send someone over, and satisfy themselves of the truth of my statement. Twenty-five notches were cut in a stick, and when all were gone by cutting off one notch each morning, I was to be at the Mowabby. The history of my intercourse with the Indians on the east side of the Colorado, for fifteen years, had all been talked over. In fact, I had been on trial before them for all my sayings and doings that had come within their knowledge. I was able to answer all their questions, and give good reasons for all my acts.

My mind had been taxed to the utmost all this time. I had been at the farther end of a crowded lodge, with no reasonable probability of getting out of it if I wished to, and without the privilege of inhaling a breath of fresh air.

Some roasted mutton was brought in and presented to me to take the first rib. The sight of the roasted meat, the sudden change of affairs, together with the recollection of the threats of a very different roast to the one I had on hand, turned my stomach. I said to those around me, 'I am sick.' I went to the door of the lodge. It was refreshing to breathe in the open air, and look out into the glorious moonlight. I thought it was midnight; if so, the council had lasted about twelve hours.

A woman's heart seems kindlier than man's among all people. A Navajo woman, seeming to comprehend my condition, came to me and asked me if she could not get me something I would like to eat. She mentioned several varieties of food she had on hand, none of which I desired. She said she had been at my house in Kanab, and she saw I liked milk, and she would get me some. With a dish in her hand she went about among the goats stripping them by moonlight. She brought me about a pint of milk, which I drank; went into the lodge, and lay down and slept until some of the party said it was light enough to see to get our horses.

I asked the Navajos to bring up our horses. I felt it was safer for me to remain in the lodge, than to be out hunting horses, and liable to meet some of the angry spirits who had been about the council. The horses were brought, and the Smiths and I were soon in our saddles, and leaving behind us the locality of the trying scenes of the past night.

Again was the promise verified which was given me by the Spirit many years before, that if I would not thirst for the blood of the Lamanites, I should never die by their hands.[10]

Following "Hamblin's trial" by the Navajo Council, John. E. Smith, who was with Jacob, wrote the following letter to the *Pioche (Nevada) Record*, which was re-published in the *Salt Lake*

City Deseret News. Little is known of the Smiths but they were obviously courageous in remaining with Hamblin during his ordeal. They give this account of what happened:

"Mowabby, Mohave Co., Arizona, February 5, 1875. On the third day, a Piute Indian, sent by the Navajos arrived. After a long talk, we gathered that the young men of the tribe were at first determined on war, but that the chiefs were opposed to it, for the present, at least; and that they desired to await the arrival of Jacob Hamblin, who had acted as representative of Brigham Young, in all negotiations of importance with the Indians for the past twenty years, and learn what settlement of the affair he was willing to make.

"We communicated to Mr. Hamblin the message from the Navajo chiefs, and merely pausing to take some refreshments, he started at once for the nearest Moqui village, to send a messenger to them to notify them of his arrival, and request their presence, my brother and I accompanying.

"We reached there about sundown, and found, to our extreme disappointment, that all the Indians had gone to a big dance at the Oriba villages, sixty miles distant, with the exception of one lame Piute.

"We remained there that night, and the next morning started for the Oriba villages, taking Huck-a-bur the lame Indian, who is a good intereperter, along with us.

"We had not ridden over fifteen miles, when we met the Piute who had acted as the Navajo envoy on the former occasion. He said he was going to see if Hamblin had arrived, and expressed great delight at seeing him, saying that the Indians were extremely anxious to see him, and urging him to go back with him to the camp of the nearest Navajo chief, which he said was not more than fifteen miles distant, and talk the matter over there.

"After consultation, being anxious to lose no time, we consented, and after riding some twenty-five miles, instead of fifteen, we reached the Navajo camp, which consisted of only two lodges. A tall, powerful Indian, on whose head the snows of many winters had rested, welcomed us with impressiveness and an embrace like the hug of a grizzly bear and invited us to enter.

"The lodge (wick-e-up), which was substantially built of heavy cedar logs about fifteen feet long, was circular in form, like the skin lodges of the Indians of the plains, with an opening near the top to give vent to the smoke, and, being covered with bark and dirt, was very warm and comfortable, which was nonetheless agreeable to our party, as it had been snowing hard all the afternoon. There were three Navajos and three squaws, one of the latter a very pretty girl, and two Piutes.

"After a friendly smoke, they furnished us a good and substantial supper of broiled and boiled goat's flesh and corn meal mush, the squaws grinding the meal in the old-fashioned way, between two stones.

"Then the talk commenced. Hamblin, be it remembered, though perfectly familiar with the Piute tongue, knows nothing or very little of the Navajo language, so the services of our Huck-a-bur were called into requisition. The chief we came to see, I forgot to mention, was not there, but was only, so they said, distant a few miles. As we were anxious to get back, we got the Navajos to dispatch the Piute to him that night, so that he might be there early in the morning, and the business be closed that day.

"After his departure the talk went on. The Navajos present expressed themselves anxious that the affair should be settled without further bloodshed, and said that was the wish of the principal men of the tribe. They said the Navajos had long known Hamblin, and they believed he would do what was right.

"Everything looked promising, and we retired to rest on a pile of buffalo skins and Navajo blankets worth a horse apiece, and slept soundly and well.

"The next morning the Indians gave us an excellent breakfast and we passed the morning sauntering about examining such articles of Indian manufacture as were new to us, and endeavoring to while away the time till the arrival of the chief.

"A little before noon twelve Navajo braves, armed with bows and arrows and rifles, rode up on a gallop, and dismounting, entered the lodge without shaking hands, and called in an insolent tone of voice for tobacco. We gave them some, and after smoking awhile, they threw everything out of the lodge, saying there were more Navajos coming, enough to fill the lodge. Sure enough, there soon rode up some more Navajos, making nineteen in all, but still no chief.

"To our inquiry as to his whereabouts, they replied he was gone to Fort Defiance. We took our seats, completely filling the lodge, and all hands smoked in silence for some time. Then the Indian whose lodge we occupied commenced talking, and spoke with only an occasional momentary interruption from the others for about an hour.

"After him, five or six others talked in rapid succession and from their earnest tones and impassioned gestures, so different from the usual manner of Indians, we could see they were much excited.

"We could not, of course, understand much of what they said, but could gather enough to know that the temper they were in boded no good to us. One old scoundrel, of brawny frame and hair as white as snow, talked in a stentorian voice, and his frequent use of the gestures of drawing his hand across his throat looked particularly ominous.

"In about an hour more they ceased speaking, and, after a pause, told their interpreter to talk. He arose slowly and walking across the lodge, seated himself by Hamblin. He was a Piute, a slave of the Navajos, and as they have the unpleasant habit of sometimes killing their interpreters when they don't interpret to suit them, and as was what he was about to reveal was not calculated to render us very amiable, I could excuse the tremor that shook him in every limb.

"He finally commenced, in a low tone, to speak to the following effect: The Navajos believed that all Hamblin had said the night before was a lie, that they thought he was one of the parties to the killing, and with the exception of three, our host and two others of the old Indians, all have given their voice for death.

"Most of them were of the opinion that it was best not to kill my brother and myself, as we were 'Americans,' but to make us witness the torture of Hamblin, and then send us back on foot. As we were not likely to desert a comrade at such a time, this was but small comfort.

"Hamblin behaved with admirable coolness, not a muscle in his face quivered, not a feature changed, as he communicated to us, in his usual tone of voice, what we then fully believed to be the death warrant of us all.

"When the interpreter ceased, he, in the same even tone and collected manner, commenced his reply. He reminded the Indians of his long acquaintance with their tribe, of the many negotiations he had conducted between his people and theirs, and his many dealings with them in the years gone by, and challenged them to prove that he had ever deceived them—ever spoken with a forked tongue. He drew a map of the country on the ground, and showed them the impossibility of his having been a partici-pant in the affray.

"To their insolent query, 'Imme-cotch na-vaggi?' (Aren't you afraid?), he replied with admirable presence of mind, 'Why should we be afraid of our friends? Are not the Navajos our friends, and we theirs? Else why did we place ourselves in your power?'

"He spoke for a long time, and though frequently and rude-ly interrupted, his patience and nerve never gave way, and when he ceased, it was apparent that his reasoning had not been without effect in their stubborn bosoms. But the good influence was of short duration.

"A young Indian, whom we afterwards learned was a son of the chief, and brother of two of the slain Indians, addressed the assembled warriors, and we could see that the tide was turning fearfully against us. He wound up his impassioned harrangue by springing to his feet, and, pointing to an Indian who had not yet spoken, called to him to come forward. The Indian came and kneeled before him, when with one hand he took back his buckskin hunting shirt, revealing the mark of a recent bullet wound, and with the other pointed to the fire, uttering, or rather hissing, a few emphatic words, which we afterwards learned were a demand for instant death by fire.

"The effect was electrical. The sight of the wounded brave roused their passions to the utmost fury, and as we glanced around the savage circle, our hands involuntarily tightened their grasp on our six-shooters, for it seemed that our hour had come.

"Had we shown a symptom of fear, we were lost; but we sat perfectly quiet, and kept a wary eye on the foe. It was a thrilling scene. The erect, proud, athletic form of the young chief, as he stood pointing his finger to the wound in the kneeling figure before him; the circle of crouching forms; their dusky and painted faces animated by every passion that hatred and ferocity could inspire, and their glittering eyes fixed with one malignant impulse upon us; the whole partially illuminated by the fitful gleam of the firelight (for by this time it was dark), formed a picture not easy to be forgotten.

"The suspense was broken by a Navajo, our host, who once again raised his voice in our behalf, and after a stormy discussion, Hamblin finally compelled them to acknowledge that he had been their friend; that he had never lied to them, and that he was worthy of belief now.

"The strain was over, and we breathed freely once more. We smoked the pipe of peace, and a roasted goat being shortly produced, we fell to with a will, and gnawed ribs together as amiably as if it had not been just previously their benevolent intention to roast us instead of the goat.

"By this time it was past midnight, the discussion having been prolonged for eleven hours. I never was so tired in my life. Eleven hours in a partially recumbent position, cramped for room, with every nerve strained its utmost tension, and momentarily expecting a conflict which must be to the death, is tolerably hard work.

"After supper, it was arranged by Hamblin that we should be home in the morning, and await the arrival of the chief, for whom they promised to dispatch a trusty messenger. We slept by turns till morning broke, when we bid our amiable friends good-by, and started for Mowabby, where we arrived about eight o-clock in the evening, to the great joy of Boyd and Pattie, who had given us up as lost.

"This was five days ago, and today the Navajo chief arrived, and, after a long discussion, agreed to settle the matter for a certain number of cattle and horses; but their demands were so exorbitant that I am sure they will never be complied with.

"Mr. Hamblin leaves tomorrow morning for St. George, to lay the matter before Brigham Young, and he is to meet the chiefs here again, with the answer to their demands, in twenty-five days from today.

"In conclusion, I wish to give my testimony to the bearing of Mr. Hamblin during the trying scene I have endeavored to depict. No braver man ever lived.–J.E.S"[11]

This account by John E. Smith describes a much narrower escape for Hamblin than described by himself. At one point, save intervention by a single old Navajo, Jacob appeared condemned to die.

Historians have long wondered what it was that took the Smiths along with Hamblin among angry Navajos. They are listed only as "miners" and their presence later at the mining community of Pioche would seem to confirm the same. Since they were not LDS and seemed to have no interest in proselyting among the Indians, it is likely the Smiths were concerned in finding out if it was safe to continue prospecting in Navajo country.

An account by Elizabeth J. Smith, age 87 at the time she was interviewed in Henrieville, Utah, adds some details to the other two reports. She was age 13, living in Pahreah east of Kanab, when Jacob rode off to meet the angry Navajos. (Her interview by son T. W. Smith, unpublished typescript, is titled "A Brief History of the Early Pahreah Settlements" LDS Historian's Office.) Her account provides significant insight to an historic moment. As Jacob rode out, "war between Mormons and Navajos seemed inevitable. The entire village mourned."

Mrs. Smith said the townspeople didn't think any of them would return because there were three whites (Hamblin, her brother, Nephi Smithson and husband-to-be James E. Smith) to atone for three dead Navajos. "It was an Indian custom to demand an eye for an eye and a tooth for a tooth."

Before departing, Hamblin promised the villagers that if they would "all pray and exercise your faith in our behalf, I will promise you in the name of God that we will all safely return."

According to Mrs. Smith, her husband kept a diary after the three left Pahreah. She says it was found later worn but legible.

The diary records that Hamblin was careful not to be seen when approaching the hogan where they were supposed to meet with the Navajo chiefs. When nearing the hogan, "they ran quickly inside." This was apparently to avoid being confronted by any vengeful Navajos acting on their own before the council could meet. The diary said that the party watched an Indian cat jump in the food pot, but was cautioned by Hamblin not to say anything which might rile the Indians. Elizabeth also said that the three left Pahreah unarmed; this does not agree with the other accounts, as both Jacob and the two miners specifically mentioned having firearms with them.

With so many persons by the name of Smith present, plus one Smithson, the account can be confusing. Hamblin does not mention having anyone with him but the two miners named Smith. However, significant details all agree in the three accounts. Hamblin's venture into the lair of the Navajo Nation at this time constituted a rare devotion to duty.

But the most difficult challenge for Hamblin lay ahead: keeping his promise to return after 25 days. It is not amiss to imagine loved ones at home pleading with him not to return. He was home. He was safe. He had been fortunate. He would not be so lucky next time.

The reasoning would go something like this: even if the older Indian "grey heads" had the wisdom to settle things without bloodshed, what was to prevent the young bucks, perhaps friends or relatives of the three slain Navajos, from exacting the revenge they had already expressed? The answer Jacob gave is that the above was not material. He must go because he had promised to go. There may well be no examples in history of a more courageous act.

Attempts to reason with McCarty got nowhere. President Young sent a man to Grass Valley to talk with McCarty, but the latter replied that he "would kill any Indian found on his property unless accompanied by whitemen." He also refused to return the horses belonging to the three dead Navajos "unless ordered to do so by the Indian Agent in Salt Lake City."[12] For some reason, this did not happen,[13] and the Navajos' horses were never returned. Not only did this deprive a poor people of what right-fully belonged to them but carried with it a mean-spirited tone from the white nation across the river. Proud Navajos would not be insulted in this manner. They must get even.

Just how incensed the Navajo Nation was over the three young dead men—and how determined they were to exact jus-tice—can be seen from this ultimatum delivered via telegraph from Pipe Springs directly to Brigham Young April 18: "Navajos are very angry and demanded 250 head of horses and 100 head of cattle. They give until June 13 to satisfy their demands; and if we do not comply, they will kill the brethren over the river and never cease raiding on our settlements until they are satisfied. Can the property be obtained and forwarded that was taken in Grass Valley? It would result in much good."[14]

Hamblin made every effort to recover the horses and prop-erty kept by McCarty. He wrote as follows to the man who had subverted peace on the frontier:

Mr. McCarty: Dear Sir:

I deem it proper to open a comunication with you concern-ing the unhappy occurrence of the killing of three and wounding one Navajo Indian at or near your place. I have traveled some eight or nine hundred miles and exerted myself to prevent, if possible, anymore bloodshed and settle this unhappy affair.

I have just returned from the Navajo country, where the rel-atives of the persons killed lived. After the labors and pains I have taken this far, we have come to the conclusion that it would be just and prudent at least for you to forward to the father and the relatives of the Indians killed, the horses and other property they left behind them; or, if you will forward them to me, I will be responsible that the relatives get them. I herewith forward you an account of the before named property, as described by the Navajo...

I saw the wounded Indian a few days since. He is nearly well. The three who were killed had their tickets of leave from the agent at Fort Defiance and were of good character.

I think you would do well to comply with this request in returning the before mentioned property.

(Signed Jacob Hamblin, Indian Agent)[15]

Learning of the Navajo threats, Brigham sent his son, regional Church official John R. Young, to inform the settlers of Moenkopi, the closest Mormon settlement to the Navajos, to return to Utah. They were putting in crops and orchards, and were understandably reluctant to leave. Jacob was determined they need not. He left immediately for Fort Defiance to meet with Navajo chieftains soon to gather there. Hamblin had gone only twelve miles when a messenger arrived telling him to drop any attempt to further meet with the Navajo Nation. He was to return home. The settlers of Moenkopi were to vacate and return to safety across the Colorado. The order came from President Young.[16]

Obviously, the action was taken by Brigham to protect Jacob and the settlers and to express his concern for their welfare. But for the first time in his life, Hamblin disobeyed a direct order from his ecclesiastical leader. He decided headquarters was not in possession of all the facts as he knew them, and that he could be instrumental in resolving the problem. It was not a spiritual, but temporal matter. If he succeeded, the settlers of Moenkopi would not have to give up their energetic efforts to wrest a living there. Mormon colonization might proceed into eastern Arizona. Hamblin likely also wanted to prevent the hostile element among the Navajos from gaining favor with their nation.

How could he give in to their unrighteous demands to deliver the horses? For one thing, his people did not possess such wealth; most importantly, it would be an admission of guilt, and the Mormons were blameless in the matter. Besides, it was one of his nine rules for managing Indians that one not bow to demand (see end of chapter 17). The Indians would surely see it as a sign of weakness, and seek more and more advantage at every perceived slight or grievance.

Hamblin might have also suspected that the idea of making amends for the three dead Navajos (with Mormon livestock) originated with the Piute interpreter attempting to save his own neck. He, too, must not be rewarded for chicanery. If allowed, he, Hamblin, could be forced to contribute to a falsehood.

But Jacob's peers saw only that his life was at stake. When he attempted to meet with Navajos at Defiance, friends besieged him a third time not to go. John Young's party caught up with him at Oraiba to make the request. He refused to back down. He did agree to see the Indian Agent in Wallapi before meeting with any Navajos at Defiance.

If these refusals seem headstrong on Jacob's part, it should be remembered that he had sacrificed much over the years to help settle white-Indian grievances. If he stopped now, all such efforts would be futile. He could not quit until finished.

Longtime friend Ammon Tenney agreed with Jacob and they pressed on. When they arrived at Wallapi, Thales Haskell was there to sit in on the meetings. Hamblin said Indian agent Rollins warned them that they might as well not go to Fort Defiance, for the new agent held no sympathy for the Mormons. Rollins opened discussions by saying: "I have been in the Navajo councils. The relatives of the murdered men are very mad." He said feelings were mixed about whether the Indians should go to war.[17] In the midst of this disappointment, Hamblin noted a familiar face, a Navajo he had long known. The latter invited the men to his home where blankets were spread and he gave them a good meal. Afterward, the chief asked Jacob a hard question: "Why did you not punish those young men [the three murdered Navajos] if you thought they were doing wrong...they had just arrived in manhood and becoming useful in the nation; they were honorable and honest and were not stealing. The Navajos are mad and are going to raid until they are satisfied."[18]

Then Jacob reminded him the Navajos had killed young George A. Smith, yet the Mormons had not declared war even though Smith was the son of a good and great captain. The Navajos had also killed Whitmore and McIntyre. (Piutes were found with their clothes and belongings, but it was determined that Navajos did the killing.) Jacob then gave the chief a letter.

"To the Chiefs of the Navajo Nation:

Three years ago we had a great peace talk with you. We offered you the Olive Branch, which you accepted, in good faith as we verify, and believe from the course you have taken since in returning stolen property.

We have felt to rejoice in the hope of living in peace with you as with all other people, which I am confident we would have done had it not been for one Mr. McCarty killing three of your people and wounding one. This man is a stranger to us, and is not one of our people. We have tried very much to satisfy your people of this fact, but they will not listen to the truth, and demand of us three hundred head of cattle, in payment for a deed our people never committed.

Now, under existing circumstances, we shall expect you to keep on your side of the river Colorado, and we will keep on our side until this thing is amicably settled and well under-stoood by both parties.

If a few of your good men will come over the Colorado, with a good Spanish interpreter, we will meet you at our Ferry Boat, where we will be happy to see you, and satisfy you that what we have said is true. But, should any attempt to cross the Colorado above our Ferry Boat we shall look upon them as enemies.

We have written to your agent in hope and in good faith that he will explain this fully to your understanding. We don't want war, but greatly desire peace with all men; but we will defend ourselves, our wives, our children and property.

In conclusion we send our respects to you and all good men.

Hoping you will not delay your visit, this being by the assent of your agent."[19]

(Signed Jacob Hamblin)

Note in this letter the firmness manifest by Hamblin. He makes it clear his people will accept no Navajos save those who come in peace and only those who come to Lee's Ferry. In addition, he thinks the Navajos are bluffing about their threat to raid Kanab. He will not be intimidated.

Hamblin then sent the following letter to John R. Young, regional Church official:

"Dear Brother Young, we feel to offer to you our views in relation to the affairs.

It is our opinion that they don't intend to raid, judging it of Indian character on account of their numerous threats.

We believe that had we reached the chiefs we would have accomplished our mission in that respect. All the Moquis say, it is nothing but talk, in hopes of their demands being met. In all of our talks from the beginning, the Spirit testified to us that what the Moquis said was true, and invariably upon separating or in conclusion, they would say, 'We think you ought to, at least, send our property, which is according to the treaty, for we have done the same by you.'

In conclusion: We know but three places where they can cross the River. Major Powell's survey can be had; which will show that with careful and prudent watch at those places and at proper times together with the services of our native brethren offering the latter a reward for information concerning raids from the East, peace and safety will be secured for our frontier settlements. The river at present secures us from them for awhile; the probability is, it will be August before they can cross, which affords us plenty of time to secure ourselves against any hostilities.

We offer these suggestions for your consideration and shall await your reply.

We will probably be at St. George conference where we can explain more fully."

(Signed Jacob Hamblin)[20]

While in Hopi country at Wallapi, Jacob learned that the settlers at Moenkopi were in possible danger. An Indian friend told Jacob the chiefs had met and that Peakon and some other Navajo leaders had calculated precisely how they would attack the settlers of Moenkopi. Only when they found the settlers had fortified defenses and prepared for war, did the angry Navajos back off to revise strategy.

Peakon made an observation at this time, relayed through the friend near Oraibi mentioned above, which greatly reflected the thinking of the entire Navajo Nation. "[Peakon] saw no difference between the Mormons and Americans. They travel with, eat and drink, and sleep with Americans, are the same color; therefore, he saw no difference. And further, if any Navajos took from the Mormons, the latter would hunt behind every rock, look in every stream, search the top of every mountain for the stolen property and take it back as they had done in several cases since the treaty."[21]

Peakon reasoned along racial lines, as did many whites. It was generally true that whitemen basically classified all redmen as the same. If an Indian stole from the whites, the latter caught up with and punished the first native who appeared guilty. In the Whitmore incident, Thales Haskell tells us that a [white] posse looking for the murderers of Whitmore and McIntyre "surprised some Indians just as the sun was coming up," killed two of them and upon finding some wearing clothing of Whitmore and McIntyre, "dealt with them according to frontier justice."[22] There was no proof they had committed the actual murders. But the whiteman's posse considered justice done nonetheless.

Hamblin sought justice outside such irrational thinking. Wisely, as it turned out, he placed his trust in Hastele, as a fair and open-minded leader among the Navajos to visit Grass Valley and see for himself if the Mormons were guilty. Hastele could persuade the Navajo chieftains to differentiate between Mormons and non-Mormons as culprits. This would buck a longtime Navajo tradition of exacting revenge. Nevertheless, Jacob was determined to try.

The following is Hamblin's account of returning to the Navajos in 25 days as promised:

"Soon after arriving at Kanab, I went to St. George and visited Presidents Brigham Young and George A. Smith. I then returned to Kanab, and worked about home until it was time to go over the river to meet the Navajos as I had agreed to.

"Through hardship and exposure my health was somewhat impaired, I endeavored to get a light wagon, that I might travel more comfortably than on horseback, but without success. I set out with a horse and three blankets. Soon after a blowing, chilling storm of rain and sleet commenced, and I became thoroughly wet.

"I rode twelve miles to Johnson, when I was scarcely able to sit on my horse. I could proceed no farther, and stopped with Brother Watson, who was living in his wagons and a temporary camp prepared for winter. Sister Watson cared for me as well as circumstances would permit.

"The storm continued the next day until afternoon, when the weather appeared a little more favorable. I was scarcely able to mount my horse, but I did, and started on my way.

"The storm soon came on again, and again I was thoroughly wet. I traveled until after dark, and stoppped at a vacated house at the Navajo Wells, ten miles from Johnson. In dismounting I fell to the ground.

"It was in a place where travellers on that road usually camped, and the wood had been gathered for a considerable distance around; and had there not been fuel I would not have been able to go after it.

"It was a dark, dismal time, and it appeared to me that I could not live until morning. I prayed to the Lord to have pity on me and save my life. I succeeded in getting myself and horse into the house out of the storm.

"I felt my way to the fireplace, and was much surprised to find some good, dry wood. I soon had a fire, and, leaning against one side of the fireplace, with my blankets drawn closely around me, and with a small blaze of fire, I was soon warm, and slept until morning.

"When I awoke I felt well, and quite able to pursue my journey. I went by the Pahreah settlement, and from there Brothers

Thos. Adair and Lehi Smithson accompanied me to Mowabbby. There I found Ketch-e-ne and a deputation from the Moqui towns.

"Ketch-e-ne renewed the former demand for three hundred and fifty head of cattle for the injury done himself and his people. I told him that when I went home I might talk with the chiefs of my people about it, but would make no promises.

"Hastele, whom I wished to see, did not put in an appearance.

"I went on and visited all the Moqui towns, and told the people the object of my visit. I requested them to tell all the Navajos they had an opportnity of seeing that I had come there according to agreement, and as they had failed to meet me as I had expected, if they would come over the river, I would be on hand to show them that I had told the truth. Feeling satisfied that things would work out all right, I returned home.

"Some of the brethren who went to Moancoppy visited the Navajo, and talked unwisely about affairs. They in turn, talked and threatened in a way that frightened our people, because they found they could do it, and the mission was broken up.

"I had passed through many perils to establish a mission among the Indians on the east side of the Colorado, but on account of the sayings and doings of unwise brethren, the time came for it to be broken up. The Moancoppy was ordered to be vacated, and I went to assist in bringing the people away. They brought away the feeling with them that there would be another Navajo war.

"I attended the quarterly conference at St. George, in May. The war question and the necessity of putting a guard at the crossing of the Colorado were agitated.

"In speaking in the tabernacle on Sunday, I told the congregation there would be no trouble with the Navajos, and as soon as the summer rains commenced, there would be a party of them over. I felt an assurance of this from what I knew of circumstances, and the whisperings of the Spirit within me.

"It was decided to establish a trading post at one of the crossings of the Colorado, east of St. George. For this purpose a party was sent out under the direction of Bishop Daniel D. McArthur.

"As I was acquainted with both crossings, I was called upon to go with them...In traveling with Brother McArthur to the Ute crossing, thirty miles above the ferry, and back, I gave him a detailed account of our affairs with the Navajos.

"I told him that I considered the breaking up of the Moancoppy mission as unnecessary; there would be no trouble with the Navajos, and some of those among them who had authority to settle their difficulties with us would be over as soon as the first rain fell.

"That night there was a heavy shower. The following day I started for home by way of the Pahreah settlement, and Brother McArthur went on to the ferry.

"Before separating, I told the brethren they would meet the Navajo peace party that night at the ferry, and they would travel to Kanab together.

"They asked me how I knew. I told them I knew they would be over, for they would just have time to get to the ferry since the rain.

"Arriving at Kanab I found Hastele and his party, including two good interpreters.

"I had been away so much, that my family seemed badly in need of my help at home, and I, at the time, thought I was justi-fied in remaining with them. I requested Brother Ammon M. Tenney to go with Hastele over on to the Sevier River, and satis-fy him of the facts concerning the murder of the young Navajos.

"After the party had gone I began to work in the garden, but everything went wrong, and I felt that I had done wrong in remaining behind.

"I continued to try to accomplish some necessary work, until I was seized with such a violent pain in one of my knees, that I had to be assisted into the house. I sent for my horse, was assisted into the saddle, and was soon on my way to overtake Hastele. The pain left my knee and I was soon all right.

"I overtook the Navajos sixty miles from Kanab. Everything worked well for showing the facts connected with the murder. The brethren we fell in with rendered all the assistance in their power.

"I had talked with the Navajos and explained to them the locations of the Mormons and the Gentiles, and what took place at McCarty's ranch. I had telegraphed to Bishop Thurber, of

Richfield, and Brother Helaman Pratt to meet us at the lower end of Circle Valley. We arrived there before them and waited. I told Hastele there would be two Mormons there that evening, who knew more about the affair than I did, and they were men of truth.

"We were camped near the road, where men were passing both ways, on horseback and in wagons. When the two brethren were approaching, and still a considerable distance off, Hastele arose to his feet, saying, 'there come the two men we are waiting for.'

"As they drew near, he remarked, 'Yes, they are good men, men of God.'

"As the brethren dismounted, Hastele embraced them in true Navajo style.

"I mention this as one of the many circumstances that have come under my notice, which prove to me that many of the Indians, and especially the honest-hearted, are blessed with much of the spirit of revelation and discernment.

"The following morning, when arranging to visit the spot where the Navajos were killed, Hastele spoke as follows: 'I am satisfied; I have gone far enough; I know our friends, the 'Mormons', are our true friends. No other people we ever knew would have taken the trouble they have to show us the truth. I believe they have good hearts. Here is Jacob; he has been traveling about to do good all winter and spring, and is going yet. When I get home I do not intend my tongue to lay idle until the Navajos learn the particulars of this affair.'

"Hastele started for Kanab; Brothers Thurber and Pratt, a Mr. Boyd, who was sent by the agent at Fort Defiance to accompany the Navajo delegation, the two Navajo interpreters and I went to Grass Valley, to see the place where the Navajos were killed. Having satisfied the interpreters, we returned by way of Richfield.

"Returning to Kanab, we found Hastele and his companion waiting for us. It was thought advisable for me, with Brother A. M. Tenney as Spanish interpreter, to visit the Indians on the east side of the Colorado River, and go to Fort Defiance and have matters properly understood there. We visited the Moqui towns, and had much interesting talk with the people.

"Arriving at the Navajo agency, we found there a Mr. Daniels, who had been sent out by the government to inspect the Indian agencies. He had called on the agent at Fort Defiance to report the condition of his agency. Learning of the Utah difficulty with the Navajos, he made an effort to throw the blame on the Mormons.

"The Indian who escaped wounded from the massacre in Grass Valley was there. Mr. Daniels examined him very closely. He also heard the report of Mr. Boyd, who accompanied Hastele, to learn the facts of the case. All the facts elicited gave a favorable showing for our people. Mr. Daniels was disappointed and evidently vexed. He gave me to understand that I did not belong to the council, and was not wanted there."[23]

This account makes it clear Hastele had greater influence with his people than did Indian Agent Daniels. With his reputation among the Navajos for honesty and fairness, Hastele seemed to have convinced his people the Mormons could not be held guilty. Hamblin concludes in his autobiograpy: "Matters were settled between the Mormons and Navajos on the basis of our great peace talk at the same time [the treaty at Defiance in 1870]. The truth was brought to light and those who wished to throw the blame of murdering the young Navajos upon the Saints were confounded."

Hamblin said he later had occasion to introduce one of his sons to Ketchene, who "turned away and wept, apparently much dejected. His friends told me that the loss of his sons was killing him."[24] Jacob learned two months later that Ketchene had died.

On Aug. 21, 1875, Hamblin declared himself satisfied that the matter of war was closed. "The Navajos expressed themselves as fully satisfied that I had told them the truth…I felt that the Lord had greatly blessed me in filling the mission assigned me, of convincing the Indians that we had not injured them, and thereby maintaining peace…at the close of these labors, I found myself three hundred miles from home, rather jaded and careworn, but full of thanksgiving for the happy termination of my labors."[25]

Most Navajos thereafter came over the river in peace. Hamblin was finally able to declare, "Doubtless, a war had been prevented."

End Notes, Chapter Fourteen

1. Charles Kelly, *Outlaw Trail*, pp. 15-50.
2. Ibid, p. 16.
3. "For at least fifteen years, he [Tom McCarty] had terrorized the West." Ibid, p. 5.
4. Bleak records that the promise came about this way: After Navajo chief Barboneta suggested his people might be killed on the other side of the Colorado, Hamblin said, "I guarantee safety on the other side of the river." Barboneta: "In case any should come to trade for horses, could they do so?" Hamblin: "Yes, come to my house and I will assist you." Bleak, Book B, p. 63. Bleak also says that Navajos crossing the river must have passes from Indian Agent Bennett, friendly to the Mormons for the time he was in charge at Fort Defiance. He was later replaced by unfriendly agents.
5. Corbett, p. 343. This is an opinion rendered by Corbett minus any footnotes.
6. *The History of Arizona*, T. E. Farish, has a long list of Indian-white killings and massacres on the Arizona frontier during the late 1800s. See specifically pages 254-355.
7. Corbett, pp. 344-45.
8. *Outlaw Trail*, p. 16.
9. Little, pp. 128-139.
10. Bleak, Book B, pp. 223-232.
11. Little, pp. 140-147.
12. Bleak, pp. 284-85.
13. Hamblin does not mention any response from the Indian agent in Salt Lake City. This is strange, since Jacob was an Indian agent in southern Utah urgently seeking return of the three Navajos' horses. It is likely, however, that efforts were made by the Indian agency in Salt Lake City to contact McCarty but were either rebuffed (in spite of McCarty's statement to yield therein), or McCarty could not be reached.
14. Bleak, Book B, p. 283.
15. Ibid, pp. 232-33. The Navajos' property was substantial (including 10 horses and many saddles and bridles) as they had just completed a good trade with the Ute Indians. All is itemized by Hamblin in the letter, showing the extent to which Jacob went in seeking to have the property returned.
16. Bleak says a telegram was sent by Brigham Young saying the brethren "had better come in from the Moencoppy. Still, hearing it, Jacob felt as though he would pursue his journey." Bleak also states that John R.

Young and others "rode all night to Oriba" but Jacob "still expressed his opinion and remained." Bleak, B, p. 287.

17. Ibid, p. 290.

18. Ibid. Bleak does not mention Peakon by name. But the Navajo chief named is most likely Peakon.

19. Ibid, pp, 291-92.

20. Ibid, pp. 292-93.

21. Ibid, p. 288. Peakon further stated that the Navajos "did not like being told they should have to go to the man" in Grass Valley to recover their stolen horses and effects. Yet, Peakon also proved himself a friend of the Mormons, according to Bleak (B, P. 288.) He quotes Bishop Levi Stewart as reporting Peakon had, on occasion, returned Mormon property stolen by the Navajos at Kanab. It should be noted that Grass Valley is sometimes referred to as Circle Valley, although the latter is some 15 miles to the west. Many who ranched in Grass Valley actually lived in Circle Valley.

22. T.H. Haskell Journal, p. 47.

23. Little, pp. 149-155, 157.

24. Ibid, 157. It is a tribute to Ketchene that while he so greatly lamented the loss of his young sons, after a period of mourning he no longer sought revenge. Undoubtedly, Hastele influenced Ketchene after deciding Hamblin told the complete truth about the Mormons being guiltless in slaying the three Navajos. McCarty was never captured and tried for the murders. There was some question in frontier Utah (and remainder of the West) at that time whether he could have been convicted of killing three Indians on his own property. Hamblin and the southern Utah Mormons might have had an even greater problem on their hands if McCarty had been brought to trial and found innocent.

25. Ibid.

– Chapter 15 –

Taming the Frontier

Although some renegade bands of Navajos yet roamed the Southwest—indeed McCarty and other non-Indian outlaw gangs were causing trouble in corners of the frontier—the middle 1870s was a time of focus on expansion and settlement. Several wagon trains of emigrants from Utah had made it as far as Moenkopi, then turned back until the Navajo troubles were resolved. But with the Navajo Nation finally convinced Hamblin told the truth about the murders of three young braves in Grass Valley, Indian animosity toward the Mormon people began to subside.

The Mormons wasted no time in preparing emigration to the green valleys of the upper Little Colorado River which Hamblin had explored and described to Church leaders. Mission calls were given from Salt Lake City to settle all the way across Arizona to the New Mexico border.

About this time, the brethren in Salt Lake City, perhaps concerned Jacob might retire, issued a clarion call emphasizing that he remain as president of the Church's Lamanite program among the Southwest Indians.

The official letter dated Dec. 28, 1874 read:

Dear Jacob Hamblin

"We wish you to remain as a missionary to the Natives, and call upon such of the brethren from time to time as you feel will render you suitable help.

"We appreciate the labors of all the brethren who have worked with you during the year, at the River, and since you first came on your mission.

"We have written to Brother Tenney and Hatch to meet your calls according to their ability, and it is for you according to the spirit of your appointment to determine from time to time when to make moves in crossing the River and continuing your labors in preaching to and teaching the Indians. We fully appreciate your labors in the past and feel to encourage you to persevere.

"We have suggested to Brothers Hatch and Tenney, that in regard to their outfitting, they are privileged to meet their own wants; and it will be needful for you to have forbearance with such as have not the same endurance as yourself.

"According to your present appointment with the Navajos, meet them and strive to continue your friendly relations.

"In regards to the Ferry and Boat it is our mind that Mrs. Lee and family stay in their place, continue the Ferry and have the avails of the transient travel; taking particular care and charge of the boat that it be not lost.

"We recommend that you take a course to have some families go into the vicinity of the Post and utilize the farming land there and build up the place.

"In regard to the safety of the boat, it may be well to assist Mrs. Lee to put the boat in the safest place possible.

"Asking the blessings of God to continue with you.

We are truly, your brethren in the Gospel."

Signed

Brigham Young
George A. Smith[1]

References to the ferry boat, of course, were crucial, for it was the sole means of wagons crossing the Colorado safely. Emma Lee had done a dutiful job of operating the ferry while her husband was in hiding from the law after the Mountain Meadows Massacre. It appears Brigham wanted Hamblin to look after her from time to time in her key role at Lee's Ferry.

The letter repeating Hamblin's mission responsibilities gave him great latitude, indicating the confidence Church leaders had in him. He might have been relieved that he did not have the responsibility of such things as sawmills and factories. President Erastus Snow had said, "There is no revelation as to how we shall manage cooperative institutions."[2] The Saints must use their own understanding in operating the sawmill north of Kanab, those at Pine Valley, the cotton factories from St. George south to the new settlements at Bunkerville, Nevada (adjacent to present-day Mesquite), etc. For Hamblin, it might be easier to run the Lamanite program where one could expect daily inspiration.

During the winter of 1875-76, Jacob would have remained at home with his family except that his long sojourns away had left the family with little cash to purchase needed supplies. "My family was destitute of many things. Some mining prospectors came along and offered me five dollars a day to go with them, as protection against the Indians. To go with them could not injure the interests of our people. It seemed like a special providence to provide the necessaries for my family, and I accepted the offer. I was gone 60 days, for which I received three hundred dollars."[3]

The money put out by the prospectors was a fairly large sum in those days but none too much to ensure remaining alive. Even the gentiles had noticed how Jacob Hamblin went among the most antagonistic of Indians and always returned safely. In addition, no one knew the region roundabout, including the formidable Arizona Strip, better than he. It is interesting that even as late as the 1940s, the area was referred to as "America's Tibet."[4] Truly, one could become lost, or die from lack of water and game, as well as at the hands of Indians, in much of the wilderness surrounding Kanab, and even Santa Clara.

The bottom line for Hamblin's family was that he had to be gone from them once again. Some of the older children had married by now, but many were still quite small. Only Joseph, 21, and Benjamin, 17, Rachel's sons, were large enough to do a major share of heavy work.[5]

While Hamblin had made peace with most of the natives, the frontier was not without its physical dangers. In May, 1876, Jacob led an expedition across the Colorado which proved as much. The group included Erastus Snow, Daniel Wells, and other leading LDS men. Crossing the Colorado at Lee's Ferry on crude skiffs in May flood stage, Hamblin nearly drowned, along with several others. The rapid current near the confluence of the Paria River swept men, wagons and luggage swiftly toward the Grand Canyon. Hamblin was able to save his life by finally grabbing an oar with one hand and hanging on until he could pull himself ashore. One wagon hung on an island and was saved; two others were lost. When men and equipment clambered ashore on the east bank, it was discovered that Lorenzo Roundy was missing. Although known to be a good swimmer, his body was never found.

Said Hamblin: "We gathered up what was left of our outfit, and visited the missions at Mowabby and Moancappy [Moenkopi], and the settlements on the Little Colorado."[6]

Making their way along the barren, nearly waterless south side of the Grand Canyon, the group suffered much before arriving on the Little Colorado. It was on this journey that Hamblin was to entirely circle the Grand Canyon, for he did not return on the south side of the gorge as intended.

Hamblin visited his daughter, Louise, there among the colonizing Saints, whom he "was very much pleased to see. One is likely to appreciate friends and relatives when found by traveling in the desert."[7] Hamblin then headed homeward. This time, in spite of so many successful journeys across the vast wasteland, Jacob and his crew faced disaster. A massive snowstorm caught the men, delaying their return to the place where they had earlier cached supplies. Out of food, Hamblin did something he had rarely done. He sought help among the gentiles.

"We went to a military post called Camp Apache, and asked for supplies. We were refused, as it would break orders from the government to let us have them. We applied to a Mr. Head, who kept a sutler's store. He thought we ought to know better than to travel without money. I prayed to the Lord to soften the heart of some one that we might obtain food."[8]

Jacob explained that they had been forced to return by a different route from their food cache. "'Oh,' said he, 'you are Mormons, are you! What do you want to last you home?'"[9] Hamblin promised to send money for the rations received and presumably did, although he never mentioned the same in his writings. After arriving home, Hamblin gave President Young a full report of the challenges and accomplishments of the assigned trip.

He received this response from the Church president: "I know your history. You have always kept the Church and Kingdom of God first and foremost in your mind. That is right. There is no greater gift than that. If there are any men who have cleared their skirts of the blood of this generation, I believe you are one of them, and you can have all the blessings there are for any men in the temple."[10]

This was a special moment for Hamblin: "It was the last time I talked with President Young. He died the following August. The assurance that the Lord and his servant accepted my labors up to that time has been a great comfort to me."[11]

With time he could now spend at home, Jacob says, "I thought I would try to raise a crop. I found that the land had been so divided in the Kanab field, that what was considered my share was nearly worthless. I sowed some wheat, but it proved a failure."[12]

While Jacob was about the Lord's business, it appears that his family did not prosper as well economically as some of his neighbors remaining at home. At the same time, it can be ascertained that local reasoning went something like this: "Why should choice land be allotted to a man who is seldom there to till and cultivate it?"

Bleak records a period of prosperity for Hamblin's missionary efforts (a thing never mentioned by Jacob himself): Nearly all of the Shivwits tribe was baptized, some 90 males and 80 females. "A goodly number of Indians met in the St. George Tabernacle March 21, Sunday." Bleak says some 170 had been baptized the week before."[13]

He follows, "Some 30 Navajos had lately been baptized by Jacob Hamblin." Many of these conversions appeared to come about because of, if not an intellectual understanding of Mormon Christianity, a liking for what they saw: the newcomers had a plan, knew where they were going and worked to carry it out. Good "fortune" seemed to follow Mormon technology in producing food and fiber. The deity they prayed to seemed to be God; indeed, a God who answered prayers. No doubt the warmth and caring expressed by Jacob and his peers, treating Indians as equal human beings, meant much to the natives. Obviously, the missionaries also sacrificed much in order to share their religious beliefs with the various tribes.

However, it did not mean the Indian problem had vanished among all local Indians. At that same period, Haskell records: "If some wandering Piedes can't get a good trade, they will plunder...some 300 Navajos are nomads, roving part of the Nation."[14]

Much was likely due to sheer desperation. Changing an Indian's mind did not necessarily alleviate the hollow feeling inside his stomach.

Besides that, the Saints must be ever vigilant that the government leaders at Fort Defiance did not stir the Indians to plot and raid anew. Following the days of Captain Bennett, agency leaders had expressed intolerance bordering on hostility against the settlers to the west, U.S. citizens or otherwise. Haskell had gone so far as to say in 1875 (recorded by Bleak, Book B, p. 411): "We believe that government officials [at Fort Defiance] are seeking excuses to incite the natives against us."[15]

Thus, Hamblin had to be among the Navajos and other tribes frequently to assess their attitude. It was true the Hopis much resisted baptism; but with Tuba, his wife and others who had been guests of Hamblin and his people, it was likely they would always maintain a leveling influence among any of their people who might feel animosity toward the Mormons. In that sense, the friendships Hamblin made among key tribal members were of such immense value to frontier peace as to be almost incalculable.

Ever sensitive to Lamanite disposition, Hamblin continued to visit the tribes for many miles around, assessing their needs and problems. If any were hungry, he must help alleviate the same to keep the peace. If he could not directly provide food, he talked over the dire consequences of raiding and pillaging the settlers. As he said in Little, p. 148, he "reasoned with an Indian as an Indian."

Some might say he was more visibly concerned with the welfare of the aborigines than with his own family, but Hamblin's personal point of view seemed ever to be that: "I have been called by the Lord's top representative on earth to be president of the Southern Utah Indian Mission. I must be about my duties. What I am doing is of benefit to my family and all the Saints. The Lord will provide."[16]

On one of Hamblin's trips to Fort Defiance in his later years, he had occasion to talk with a minister who, as Jacob says, was there by "by government appointment." The Reverend Mr. Trewax invited Hamblin to his room, "saying he would very much like to talk with me. I replied I had no objection to talking with him if his object was to obtain correct information." The reverend asked Jacob about his religious faith and from what source he derived it.

"I told him we prove the truth of our religion by that book (pointing to a *Bible* that lay on the table). If you will read what Christ taught, you will learn what our principles are. They are from Heaven."

Hamblin says the minister asked, "Is it possible...that your people believe the *Bible*?"

"I replied, 'We are the only people I have met during the last 40 years that do believe the *Bible*. Many profess to believe it, but when I open and read it to them, I find they do not.'

When the minister said he believed every word of the Bible, Jacob replied, "Then we are brethren." Spending nearly half a day with the reverend (Hamblin never divulged the man's religious persuasion, except that he was obviously Protestant), Hamblin explained the Stick of Judah (*Bible*) and Stick of Joseph (*Book of Mormon*) as explained in the 37th chapter of Ezekial. When the minister asked where the Stick of Joseph was today, Hamblin went out and brought him a *Book of Mormon*. After examining the testimony of the Three Witnesses in the book, Jacob said he exclaimed, "Surely this book is the best or worst thing that ever was."

Hamblin "allowed him to keep it." Before Jacob departed, the reverend had read thirty pages and "found nothing contrary to the *Bible*."[17] This exchange between the two would seem to showcase the sincerity of both men. It was typical of Jacob that he was tireless in teaching the religious beliefs which he espoused to all men, Indian or otherwise. Yet, he would not force his opinions on others. Apparently, Powell and his crew asked little about Jacob's ecclesiastical persuasions, at the same time respecting that they were precisely what made Hamblin who he was. Hamblin does not record any attempt to explain the Mormon's "Restored Gospel" to Powell or his men.

Jacob could well have grown somewhat restless in the middle 70s with no new frontiers to conquer. But it wouldn't be long before he had a new one. In one of President Young's last acts before dying, he called Jacob to join with other Mormon emigrants to settle on the upper Little Colorado. The "invitation" to join them came in this letter dated Dec. 1, 1876:

"As you pass from this city [St. George, where Brigham Young had begun spending his winters], look out as good a tract for a wagon road as you have to time...as you are so well acquainted with the country that you can be of some use to Brother (Harrison) Pearce (Pierce), who is building a ferryboat on the Colorado for crossing people...then proceed south near the west of the San Francisco Mountain to what is called the Beale Road, then easterly to what is called Sunset-Crossing, on the Little Colorado...when you return to the Kanab [creek], we would like to have you take your stock and such ones of your family and friends as you would like to have go with you and locate and take possession of a little place called Surprise Valley near the Colorado River and report to us your success.

"We feel to caution you against the Mexican robbers that infest the country where you are going. Be always ready for them, and keep your little company together. We pray the Lord our Father in heaven to bless you and give you success, and return you in safety."

(Signed by Brigham Young, Wilford Woodruff, Erastus Snow and Brigham Young, Jr.)[18]

There it was, an invitation Jacob couldn't refuse. Becoming too comfortable usually meant less accomplishment anyway. Besides, it was an official call from Brigham himself. Reluctantly, Priscilla and Louisa, with their children, resigned themselves to leave their known world behind once again. It would be the beginning of a long sojourn into eastern Arizona, perhaps now safe from marauding Navajos, but "infested" with Mexican robbers, not to mention the warlike Apaches. Hamblin does not mention any trouble with Apaches, although they were known to move northward at times from their stronghold in southern Arizona. Nor does Hamblin ever mention the rebel Apache chief Geronimo, although the latter was not persuaded to surrender to the U.S. Army until years later in 1886.

At least the polygamist-hunting feds wouldn't find Hamblin at his long established residence in Kanab. Even if he did remain domiciled there, he wouldn't dare show up at home.

Being a restless man who sought constantly to be doing something of value for his Church and community, Jacob might have tried to do too much. In one instance, a sheriff's deputy found Jacob on the way to grind grain for his family and told him he needed his help as a guide in catching a fugitive who had escaped. Jacob was under no legal obligation to help, but as one who seemed inclined to accept civic duty, left immediately to help search for the runaway. The search took the men in the heat of August across the Colorado to the Hopi villages. From there, Hamblin went to the Indian agency at Fort Defiance to leave a description and alert for the missing man. He was not found. Jacob makes no mention of receiving or asking payment for his services.[19]

One thing he did accomplish is described in this manner: "Several Hopis came to me and requested that I would pray for rain, asserting that I used to help the Piutes to bring rain, and they thought they were as much entitled to my prayers as the Piutes.

"I felt to exercise all the faith I could for them, that they might not suffer from famine. In all their towns there fell, the following night, an abundance of rain." Later, he said, "We noticed that in and around their towns and fields it had rained very heavily, but on either side the ground was dry and dusty."[20]

All, however, was not as well at home. "On my return home, I found that the fall crop I had planted was too far gone with drought to make anything, but through the blessings of the Lord, I was able to provide necessaries for my family."[21]

Hamblin closes his autobiography at this point: "I desire this narrative to be a testimony to all who may read it, that the Lord is not slack concerning any of His promises to His children. My whole life, since I embraced the gospel, proves this fact. If this little book shall leave a testimony of this coming generation, I shall be satisfied."[22]

The autobiography does not take us past the year 1877. Beyond that time, we must rely on other sources for the next decade of Jacob's life. Bleak had this praise for Hamblin's influence among the Lamanites: "Jacob Hamblin in his quiet but persistent manner has continued his peaceful ministry amongst the Indians in the southern and southeastern regions; and using the more friendly among them to assist in watching for marauding Navajos."[23]

It is quite likely that Bleak met with Hamblin periodically to record Jacob's latest missionary journeys and activities, for a faithfully-chronological account is given by the LDS historian for several decades. Of special interest to Bleak were Lamanite attitudes leading to baptisms. In one instance, he wrote that the Indian Mokeok "asks white people to bear with the weaknesses and ignorances of his people."[24]

During the early 1800s, Hamblin attempted to spend more time at home with his family. He was entering his 60s now, a time to slow down and be with his children. But other matters demanded his attention. The frontier could not part with him. An interview Corbett had with one of Jacob's daughters, Mary, illustrates. She recounted a particularly cold winter day as Jacob attempted to get his battered livestock sheltered and fed: "About this time, three of our prominent citizens rode up and asked for father. They told him the Indians were on the warpath again. They were coming to wipe out the small settlement. They said, 'Brother Hamblin, we hate to ask you to take this trip; it is full of danger, not only from the Indians but the freezing weather, but so many lives depend on it and you are the only one who can handle the old chief. We are asking you to go for the sake of the women and children.'

"Of course, father's family began to plead with him not to go...[but soon] mother got his warm clothing...the boys saddled the horse." When Jacob left, the children played a game, with glowing sparks on the fire representing Indians and father.[25] When it was over, their father had won in the fireplace, just as he did with the old chief.

In 1883, Jacob was called to settle the Alpine, Arizona area. Many Mormon settlements had begun to spring up east of the Colorado now that it was safe to travel in that region. Hamblin might well have felt the challenge and adventure of the frontier was gone. But he may not have had much time to think about it. Pioneering still another homestead had its problems. Jacob also had various local (ward) Church assignments.

Federal troops were in the area seeking to capture Geronimo, but Mormons and feds appeared to have no conflicts, at least if the latter were not looking for "co-habs," as practicers of polygamy were scornfully called. In fact, some of Hamblin's family befriended and assisted the troops in that part of eastern Arizona-New Mexico.[26]

In 1884, Jacob moved his wives and families, forever uncomplaining and dutiful to Jacob's keenly-felt duties, to Pleasanton, New Mexico. Amarilla, his 24th child to live under his roof, was born there. She would be his last.

The next year, Hamblin was forced to turn his attention both from proselyting among the Lamanites and from his family. He said in his journal, "In the winter of 1885, I thought it best to leave home for my own safety as the feeling in Arizona and New Mexico was to arrest all those...living in polygamy and send them to prison."[27] Some of the words in Jacob's journal were smeared but can be made out to say he traveled to Mexico hoping to find a new home for his families where U.S. agents would leave him alone.

Since the end of the Civil War, the government had turned greater attention to internal matters, especially the West. Rumors of federal officers plaguing Mormon polygamists north of Kanab indicated it was dangerous for Jacob, now that he had more time, to remain at home. The Little Colorado country beckoned, for its uncivilized wilderness would harbor fewer "co-hab" agents. The thought of being placed in a prison chamber for months at a time was likely something Hamblin could not reconcile himself to doing. He was a man who had always shunned violence; now he did not want to be placed in a situation where it might be necessary. Historian Bailey said that the "Indians likely hindered Hamblin less" than federal agents.[28] It was not long before Hamblin left eastern Arizona for Old Mexico, a nation with no anti-polygamy laws, a place where the Latter-day Saints might take religious refuge.

As Hamblin's entourage traveled the strange countryside, dust was seen in the distance. The children looked on in horror as they saw what appeared to be hundreds of mounted Indian warriors on the horizon headed directly toward them. Corbett describes it this way: "When the leader, a grey-haired old chief galloped up and saw who it was, he yelled, 'Jacob!'" It was Hastele, the Navajo chief who had become such fast friends with Jacob in settling the difficult Grass Valley affair. Jacob and his old friend jumped down to hug one another.[29]

The children must have heaved a giant sigh of relief. It turned out that the Indians had been spread out over the horizon because they were hunting antelope on their return home. They had been enlisted by the government in running rebellious Apaches out of the country into Mexico.

History records that Hamblin did not remain long in Ascension, Mexico. Land was supposed to be purchased for the Saints to settle, but Jacob learned it would take months before they could build homes and till the earth.[30]

Some progress was made, but Hamblin seemed to have grown impatient[31] and made the 700-mile round trip home. Upon his arrival at Priscilla's house, Jacob said one of his little ones asked, "If I had come home to stay now. I answered, [and] the little girl wept and said when will you come to stay?"[32] Jacob explained that he had to leave his family again and go to St. George to do temple work and meet with Church officials.

While there, Hamblin would have noted that the imposing white edifice (the first LDS temple to be completed), wrought by the devoted hands of so many Latter-day Saints, was now available for members to receive their endowments, be baptized for the dead and partake of celestial (eternal) marriage, as given in revelation by Joseph Smith. Hamblin also spoke to a Church congregation in St. George as follows: "I found myself...in the Republic of Mexico, seeking for the religious liberty sought for by my forefathers and denied me in the United States."[33]

Shortly thereafter, he was given the following document:

"To The Twelve Apostles, High Priests, Seventies, Presidents of Stakes and Bishops and their counselors And all whom it may concern:

"This is to certify that Jacob Hamblin is here appointed a missionary to labor among the Lamanites in any part of the United States or Old Mexico to preach the Gospel to them, and teach them the principles of self-sustaining industry, and peace toward all men, and as far as they receive his testimony of the Gospel of Christ, to baptize and confirm them as members of The Church of Jesus Christ of Latter-day Saints, and where no organization as members of the Church exists, to organize such as may be baptized; doing so in conformity with the revelations and the usages of the Church."

There is a paragraph about not interferring with established authorities in existing Church organizations. The certificate then concludes: "It is desired that all Saints who have the opportunity should assist Brother Hamblin as far as they can, to carry the Gospel to the Lamanites who are an important branch of the House of Israel."[34]

This call could be called a blessing more than a certificate, for the language does not give him new authority so much as it broadens already existing responsibilities. It is a recognition from the top echelon down of his dedication as a missionary to the Lamanites. It was signed by Wilford Woodruff, then LDS Church president.

It is interesting that in his journal, Hamblin referred to this document as a "noat" (note).[35] Much more than that, it indicates the reverence in which the Church leaders held Hamblin at the time.

John Pulsipher wrote in his journal, "Jacob Hamblin, our long tried, true and faithful missionary and frontiersman is with us, resting from his wicked persecutors who are determined to fine and imprison every man that has more than one wife."[36]

Indeed, the federal government did appear overly zealous. Before the Civil War, polygamy had been billed with slavery as a "twin evil." In March, 1882, Congress had passed the Edmunds-Tucker Bill which in effect, deprived polygamists of U.S. citizenship, for they could not vote or hold office. Hundreds of homes were broken up in Mormondom as husbands and fathers were treated the same as criminals who robbed or maimed the helpless.[37] As federal agents began to hound Latter-day Saints who believed they were simply faithfully living their religion, Hamblin must have had reason to believe that the federal marshals were more a thorn in his side than was ever any savage. It was ironical, too, how a few years before, he had at considerable sacrifice, assisted a lawman from Richfield to help find a fugitive fleeing from justice. Now he was one.

Always one focused on duty to others, Jacob now had to be concerned about himself. While he seemingly couldn't do his family much good far away talking to Indians, he could accomplish even less sitting in a jail cell for several years. Others of the brethren like Rudger Clawson had done so. The mood in Washington appeared somber, with penalties growing ever more severe. In 1884 a "segregation ruling" had been made law which might find a man guilty for every day he lived with a plural wife.[38] Under such a statute, a man could be sent to prison for the rest of his life.

At 66 years of age, and perhaps facing the continued hardships of a rugged life, Jacob told Patriarch (no first name given)

McBride that "I was called on a mission in my old age and I wish he had a blessing for me."

Brother McBride asked Jacob to come to his house and gave him a blessing, which included the following passages: "I confirm upon thee all thy former blessings...thou has been called on many missions and I know thou will be faithful because thou has been true to thy trust, though thou art now called to one of the greatest missions that hast ever been given to Man in the dispensation in which we now live...to carry the gospel from the Jentiles [gentiles] to the Jewish House of Israel and in so doing thou mayest expect some obstacles in thy way, but the Lord will be with thee. And when thou art alone, thou shall not be alone, for the Angels of the Lord shall be with thee and round about thee...thou shalt be led and directed by the Holy Spirit of Prophecy to the Branch of the House of Israel and they shall know thee...the power of the Holy Ghost shall fall upon them and shall be with thee as it was with Peter when he carried the gospel from the Jews to the gentiles."

One line read that Jacob "shall prepare the way for the establishment of the kingdom of God upon the earth and of restoring peace" to it. This was a blessing that had obviously been Hamblin's most of it his life. Jacob was told he was from the lineage of Joseph who was sold into Egypt, and that "there is a crown laid up for thee of eternal life."[39]

Strangely, Hamblin's "Journal Contents" ends with a remedy for blood poison and malarial poison. There is some conjecture whether he himself wrote it in the journal which bore his name. That is possible, since he and his family became so ill with what was apparently malarial infection during the latter years of his life.[40]

For a time, Jacob's whereabouts were unknown, as he fled from federal marshals. When he did reunite with his family, his health had declined noticeably. The end came quickly and without ceremony. One evening he asked a son to go with him from Alpine to his families in Pleasanton. Jacob said he "would take the young man fishing." Enroute, the pair took refuge in a rainstorm under a building with a roof which leaked. Jacob became wet and cold, falling ill. He arrived in Pleasanton weak and found many members of his family in the same condition.[41]

Three days later, he lay so sick that family and neighbors rallied to his bedside, praying and administering every possible remedy for his recovery. This time, the man who had gotten up so many times and rallied against so many odds, who had survived so many hostile Indians, did not get up again. He died Aug. 3l, l886.[42]

With many members of the family ill, the man known as "Apostle to the Lamanites," was buried with only a few family members present. There was no comforting eulogy, no funeral. If he had died in Kanab or Santa Clara or almost any other community where he resided for so many years, the funeral chapel would not have been able to hold them all. Instead, he was dead and buried before most people who had known him ever knew he was gone. It was like Jacob, some might have said, to go without any fanfare, no speeches, no calling attention to himself.

Word that he died was sent to the *Deseret News* which wrote in an editorial, "Oh how hard it seems, after having spent his whole life in the interest of the work, to be deprived of a burial by his brethren!"

Another statement by the LDS Church newspaper, Sept. 20, l886 reads: "The faithful old veteran and pioneer Brother Jacob Hamblin, whose name is so well known among the Latter-day Saints, died of chills and fever at Pleasanton, N.M. His death and burial occurred under pathetic circumstances. His wife was obliged to prepare him for burial…they had to send thirty miles for a coffin and passing strangers dug his grave."[43]

The *News* also explained that when departing to Mexico, Hamblin had leased his stock to a man who was to make improvements and later relinquish the land. He showed up later with papers to declare the property his and evicted Jacob's widows and children. Summed up the *Deseret News*: "Two wives and a number of children are left without any means of support."

If success in life is measured by the ceremony at its conclusion, then Jacob Hamblin's inglorious ending marked a life of failure. But his legacy would not be forgotten. Material accumulation comes and goes, but the ideas and principles Hamblin lived by seem more vital and inspirational today than ever before. They particularly gain momentum in an age when so much is shallow and self-serving. All that Jacob Hamblin believed in and stood for gain greater value in comparison. This is seen in the many tributes reviewed in the next two chapters. His is a legacy that can never be forgotten.

End Notes, Chapter Fifteen

1. Bleak, Book B, p. 376. One history, "The Activities of Jacob Hamblin in the Region of the Colorado, No. 33," p. 30, says that Hamblin, now age 57, asked to be released at this time, but President Young wouldn't do it. Hamblin was "irreplacable." The same is stated by Bailey, p. 371.
2. Bleak, Book B, p. 328.
3. Little, p. 158.
4. The name "America's Tibet" was used in a Provo, Utah *Daily Herald* newspaper article dated May 28, 1995, referring to the Arizona Strip of the 1930-40s. Author J. R. Paulson describes an interview with the family of DeLaun Heaton who spent lonely weeks on the remote Strip during that era tending sheep. The same account was given this author by DeLaun's brother, Alma Heaton, of Provo in September, 1994.
5. "They cooperated in every way...but still, the family needs were more than could be adequately provided for." Corbett, p. 388. No footnotes.
6. Little, p. 160.
7. Little, p. 162.
8. Ibid, p. 163.
9. Ibid. The inference seems to be that Mr. Head relented after Jacob's prayer and broke government rules in doing so.
10. Ibid. The phrase "cleared their skirts of the blood of this generation" was one used often in LDS literature, meaning "remained clean" and "kept the faith." Taken in its entirety, this statement would seem to say that all of the blessings in store for any Latter-day Saint would be Jacob's. It seems to have a special meaning in that Hamblin had so little time to attend the St. George Temple, even though then complete.
11. Ibid.
12. Ibid, p. 164. Inasmuch as Hamblin seldom mentioned personal hurts or slights, this seems to have been a par-ticularly difficult time for him. Lack of community help for his family seemed a personal affront.
13. Bleak, Book B, p. 409. Bleak also said earlier that Tutsegonit, a Hopi, "had been spreading a good influ-ence among the Apaches...he had been ordained by Brigham Young to preach to the Indians." Book A, p. 119. Since Young never did go personally to the Hopis, Tutsegonit was likely influenced by Hamblin. The Indian was possibly among those Jacob took to visit Salt Lake City.

Another indication of success in baptizing the Shivwits is mentioned by the *Salt Lake Herald* in a story from St. George, March 20, 1875: "The next marvel was the arrival, last night, of about 200 Shebit [Shivwit] Indians, who came and demanded baptism."

14. This statement by Haskell is recorded in Bleak, Book B, p. 411. By "roving part of the Nation," Thales likely meant the entire Southwest which the Navajos considered the domain of their tribe. Dellenbaugh assessed the local situation around Kanab thusly after the crisis was broken with the Navajos in 1874: "The natives are harmless, except for Patnish [the rebel Piute chief], thanks to Jacob's wise management." *A Canyon Voyage*, pp. 166-68.
15. Bleak, Book B, p. 411
16. A frequently quoted LDS concept likely stemming from, "And it is my purpose to provide for my saints…but it must needs be in my own way." Explained is how each member must do the Lord's will. *Doctrine and Covenants*, 104:15-16.
17. Little, p. 156.
18. Ibid, p. 160. Young said, "Our people will want all the choice places where there is water and grass." This statement does not appear, however, in the presentation of Hamblin's "Journal and Letters," p. 73. It is likely the statement was made to Jacob verbally. The name Pierce's Ferry, in honor of Mormon Harrison Pierce, persists to this day on the south bank of Lake Mead. It is a take-out point for Grand Canyon river runners.
19. The account is given in Little, p. 164.
20. Ibid, p. 165.
21. Ibid. Jacob said many times upon return from proselyting journeys that "all was well at home." As he became older, such was not the case. It is not known whether his families' fortunes changed for the worse, or whether Hamblin simply became more realistic (with time) in his reports. Yet, he also added that the "Lord provided for" him and his loved ones.
22. Ibid. Hamblin deserves literary recogition as a writer in his own right. His written memories are rich in thought, lucid and insightful. Why he is not more fully recognized for this is lamentable.
23. Bleak, Book A, 263.
24. Bleak, Book B, 410.
25. Corbett, p. 410.
26. Ibid, p. 412.
27. *Journal Contents*, p. 16.
28. Bailey, p. 315.
29. Corbett, p. 414.

30. "They [who were] expected to make the purchases made a failure and thought it would take from 3 to 6 months to accomplish the purchase. My son Lyman went home with his team. I was not able to do much. I then started for Utah." "Journal Contents," p. 16.
31. One factor rarely mentioned may have been Hamblin's health. "Went into Old Mexico...on my way down was hurt in my breast and side...was not able to work much in putting in a crop." Ibid.
32. "Journal Contents," p. 17.
33. Corbett, p. 415.
34. J-C, p. 17.
35. Ibid.
36. Corbett, p. 417.
37. Berret, *The Restored Church*, p. 440
38. Ibid, p. 441.
39. J-C, p. 18.
40. "Use hypro Sulphite of Soda, take 2 ounces to a pint of cold water and keep well corked...dose one spoonful every 2 hours until a movement of the bowels..." Ibid, p. 19."
41. Corbett, p. 422.
42. While Jacob Hamblin died in Pleasanton, N. M., and was initially buried there, his body was moved a few years later to the cemetery in Alpine, Ariz. where he spent more of his life. A large marker was placed at the latter site by family members in June, 1947; nearby are smaller markers for wives Priscilla and Louisa. Rachel had been interred earlier (with a small gravestone) in the Santa Clara Cemetery, southwest corner.
43. *The Deseret News* story resulted from a long letter sent the newspaper by Emma Coleman of Pleasanton. Corbett, p. 422-23.

– Chapter 16 –

Answering the Critics

While the accomplishments of Hamblin are obviously considerable, few people who attempt as much as he manage to
escape any criticism. It must be said that Hamblin is not without
a few detractors.

They are mentioned here in order to tell the complete story
of Hamblin. However, even trying to detract from Jacob's
accomplishments only shows how regionally well-known he
had become.

Most criticism can be dismissed with little comment. For
example, a writer for *True Frontier* magazine calls Hamblin a
"Cowardly Saint in Buckskin." In its 1969 story, Maurice Kildare
refers to the "Leatherstocking of the Southwest" as one who
"allowed" a person entrusted to him, 15-year old George A.
Smith, to be killed by the Navajos.

It appears that Kildare and *True Frontier* magazine wanted
to write a shocking story and they did so. It is also a left-handed
compliment to Hamblin that his reputation for courage was so
well known by then that Kildare felt a need to attack it. More
likely, it was done for no other reason than to titillate readers, as
are most grocery store tabloid stories today.

Hamblin himself relates the incident in which young Smith
was pierced by Navajo arrows, and shot with his own revolver.
But a careful reading of the account by Hamblin also indicates
he attempted to stop young Smith from going out alone to locate
his horse; when Hamblin found Smith dying, he took the boy
with him in spite of pursuing Navajos. After young George A.
died on the trail, Hamblin was forced to leave him behind. But
at risk of his own life, Jacob returned to locate the bones and
take them home for a decent burial.

In hindsight, should Jacob not have allowed the young man
to come along? Hamblin also allowed Ammon Tenny at age 14
to join the missionaries as an interpreter. Certainly Jacob could

be more optimistic than were his peers. Danger seemed a foreign word to the Mormon missionary. On one proposed visit to a belligerent and threatening Indian chief, Hamblin could find no one who would go with him save Thales Haskell. No harm came to either man.

But did Hamblin place too much confidence in divine providence to protect those with him? In many ways, it is remarkable that no one other than Smith was killed by hostile Indians while accompanying Hamblin on his lengthy journeys, considering the myriad physical and Indian dangers. The entire frontier of the time was filled with perils, for those venturing beyond the borders of known civilization. What if something had happened to the three Hopis Hamblin took with him to Salt Lake City...would Haskell and those left behind with the Hopis find their lives forfeit? Quite probably.

Hamblin prophesied their safe return and that is exactly what happened. Was Jacob just lucky that his prophecies came true time after time? Remember that in the expedition with Smith, Jacob had a dark foreboding, a premonition of serious injury or death. It was no little thing, for it was the only time Hamblin ever mentioned negative feelings before heading into the heart of hostile Indian country.

At times J. Brooks places blame on Hamblin for "railroading" John D. Lee to his execution without implicating higher-ups who issued Lee's orders. But Brooks clearly went too far. If her own bias against Brigham Young (and at times, Jacob) isn't evident in her Mountain Meadows Massacre, Levi Peterson points it out in his biography titled Juanita Brooks. One excerpt says this on p. 246: "Juanita held a lifelong grudge against Brigham Young for having sent her ancestors into an impoverished exile on the ragged edge of Mormonism." Peterson also seems to judge Brooks rather harshly with this comment on page 384: "In keeping with her usual practice, she [Juanita] failed to document her sources closely." Was Peterson possibly alluding to references about Jacob Hamblin? The bottom line is, in any event, that a jury of Lee's peers, not Jacob, voted Lee guilty and sentenced him to execution.

If Jacob committed any crime during his lifetime, it was in refusing to help federal marshals pursue and find Lee. With the assistance of natives within his sphere of influence, Hamblin could easily have found Lee's hideaways and sent marshals after him had Jacob so chosen. He refused to persecute (or help prosecute) local Indian agricultural agent John D. Lee. When it was time to disclose what he knew at Lee's trial, Hamblin told what Lee and Indian friends had told him of the killings. To lie was simply not in his nature. And it would have constituted, perhaps, the more serious crime of perjury.

Some criticism was leveled against Hamblin because he accepted government money in his role as local Indian agent helping care for the children who were spared. If the government money had not been paid to Hamblin, it would most certainly have been paid to someone else. He and his wife, Rachel, went out of their way for months to give assistance to children badly wounded, and badly frightened after watching their parents murdered. They cared for them until next of kin could be located in the mid-West. Jacob's families, with him gone so much, were in too poor a financial situation at the time to help anyone. Should Jacob have denied government reimbursement which would benefit his wives and children? He had already refused numerous offers for payment for his missionary labors from Church headquarters.

Hamblin also allegedly received pay for crossing the Colorado River to find a child declared missing after the massacre. He went but did not find the child, then proceeded to proselyte among the Indians. This is typical Hamblin.

Jacob had many peers who likely thought him too devoted to duty. Quite clearly, orders to teach the gospel from Salt Lake City didn't mean leaving crops unplanted and a wilderness untamed. But Hamblin said they were sent into Dixie to teach the Lamanites. The Lord's work should come first.

That could admittedly be a pain in the neck for those facing scant survival in a harsh land. Yet, for Hamblin, if one had enough faith (or gumption), the gospel work must precede everything else; all needful things would be provided, as per the

Sermon on the Mount in the New Testament, repeated during Christ's ministry to the Lamanites as recorded in The Book of Mormon. If Hamblin had a fault here, it was putting faith before pragmatism. In Jacob's eyes, raising crops for horse and cattle feed would mean little if the latter were stolen by Indian enemies. He would go among them and try to make them friends. And when trouble did come from incorrigibile natives, the settlers knew who to call on.

In addition, Hamblin's known penchant for duty might have caused Church officials to prevail upon him more than on other LDS members and perhaps, unfairly. Such seems to be the case with the call to settle Surprise Valley (see Appendix B) in Arizona. Jacob had already moved his families from Santa Clara to Kanab, much to the consternation of wives and children who were settled and happy in Santa Clara. Now, Jacob was asked to move again to an unsettled and possibly hostile environment in an unknown land. Jacob, of course, was an adventurous sort always ready to explore new lands (as he once went to Mexico with plans to settle there, to escape federal polygamy-hunters) but the call to leave Kanab in 1876 could be considered by some as unfair to his family. Jacob, of course, went with no known complaint.

Jacob Hamblin differed significantly from his peers in Mormon settlements of the upper Little Colorado. Others sojourned many miles and saw only desolation. Hamblin perceived a vision of what could be done with the land a few miles farther on. Accustomed to riding hundreds of miles in a few days, what was another dozen miles or so in finding fertile soil? Besides, they should have filled the mission Brigham sent them on. To not do so was a dereliction of duty.

One of the sharpest criticisms on Hamblin has been from historians who complain of his long absences from home. They seem to feel he should have spent more time making a living for his family rather than merely trusting that the the Lord would provide. It is true that in Pleasanton, just before his death, some type of misunderstanding in leasing out his properties resulted in a cruel takover by an uncaring man who claimed legal rights.

Jacob, it might be argued, should have "nailed down" material assets so that no one could usurp what was rightfully his. Perhaps Jacob took out a mortgage he couldn't later pay, and failed to mention it in writing , or in speaking to his family. But business details are not given and it is not known where the blame should be placed. Years later, the thing far more remembered by family members was this: Jacob's generosity among all the Lord's children seemed boundless. If he went too far in that generosity, well, there were many spiritual blessings which could come from Christ's admonition to "Love your neighbor as yourself."

The statement in Hamblin's autobiography that he tried to work in his garden while others (including a very capable Ammon Tenney) went with Hastele to see if the Mormons were guilty in the death of the three Navajos killed by McCarty carries a touch of humor. Hamblin said his knee hurt, or at least until he was on his horse to join Tenney; then, miracuously, the knee seemed not hurt. It was never mentioned again. Perhaps seeing that frontier peace was finally within grasp, Jacob felt the pain no longer.

It is true that Hamblin wasn't much of a delegator; he usually went to see a matter through personally. But then, he learned that not everyone showed the tenacity to meet and pacify Indians as patiently and skillfully as he. Clearly, Jacob saved many lives on the frontier—quite possibly, some who prospered economically in the fields more than he.

Whether Hamblin was gone so much that he didn't do right by his family materially was for them to decide, not historians who have come along decades later. According to comments by John Hamblin, grandson (Chapter 16) descendants felt Jacob left them a rich legacy and a noble heritage. Hamblin's longest-lived daughter, Amarillo, visited the Hamblin home in Santa Clara before she died in 1982 and praised her father's name in every respect, according to a personal interview with missionary caretakers.

Yet, one must ask, just how important was Hamblin's work outside the sphere of Mormondom? What about all those

Arizona histories on library shevles which barely mention his name? (We would expect Utah histories to praise Hamblin because of connections to the LDS Church.) It is a fact that many Arizona histories perused by the author barely mention Hamblin, or do so with scant praise. Was it a prejudice against the Mormons? Even so, several gentile historians like McClintock and Birney admitted they could not mention a history of Arizona without including his name and that always with labels of "fearlessness" and "courage" and "duty."

Of course, most histories of Arizona focus more on the founding of Tucson, Phoenix and the older communities settled from the south.

But maybe the peaceful negotiations of Hamblin were a major reason for the Navajos living harmoniously with the settlers at an earlier period than say, the Apaches did. Certainly, military operations like those of Carson helped break the spirit of the Navajos, but it is a fact that all the generals and cavalry in the world couldn't on their own entirely placate an energetic generation of Apache and Navajo rebels. Hamblin's adversity to military action against the aborigines appears, in hindsight, to have been wise. Western tribes were subjugated, yes, but those like the fierce and proud Navajos, and the Apaches, might have yielded to the whiteman much sooner had someone gone among them as Hamblin did to learn their ways, and more particularly, their grievances.

Was northern Arizona terrain easier to penetrate than Apache country? Is that why the Navajos "surrendered" to the whiteman (1875 as compared to 1886) earlier than the Apaches? Hardly, considering the Navajos' Canyon De Chelly and the Grand Canyon, as well as the remote Arizona Strip. The Navajos could have held out in their wilderness stronghold perhaps even longer than the Apaches if they had not been greatly influenced by Hamblin.

Maybe Arizona should re-evaluate the role of Jacob Hamblin in northern and eastern Arizona to determine just how effective he was among the aborigines there—not just for Mormons, but for all colonizers.

A letter from the Arizona Historical Assocation seems to indicate part of the problem. One sentence (letter dated Dec. 12, 1994) reads, "While Jacob Hamblin is mentioned in various books, none of the titles in our collection study him in depth." Other sources are given; but perhaps the Arizona Historical Society should lead the way in obtaining the greater "in-depth" data about the man so prominent in its state's history. After all, Hamblin was the primary force in settling some one-third of the state of Arizona.

It is also true that LDS Church histories often say little about Hamblin. If Jacob's work was so intertwined in Brigham Young's vital missionary program for the Lamanites, why is there is not a single word about him in the 553-page *Brigham Young, the Man and the Work* by author Preston Nibley? Quite obviously, much depends on the focus of the history. In proving that one can write a lengthy history of Brigham Young without mentioning Jacob Hamblin, one chooses to emphasize the president's accomplishments outside of the Southwest. As for support given to Brigham, was there ever a more devoted soul in assisting the goals of any LDS Church president than Jacob Hamblin?

If one wanted to nitpick, Hamblin had idiosyncracies. He placed much confidence in Lamanite extra-sensory perception (guidance of the Spirit?) and sometimes in what appeared to be outright, illogical Indian superstition. The idea that the Mormon missionaries had driven the evil spirits from the Hopis, so they must now flee to the west side of the Colorado, was mentioned to Jacob by a Piute. Hamblin gave it credence by stating in his autobiography that a house fire in Kanab killed several members of one family soon thereafter. Many would see no connection. Hamblin did. And in the process, he possibly alienated some of his white brethren.

One must wonder also how much of what is traditionally attributed to Hamblin, or written about him, is in fact, absolutely accurate. A case could be made from known mistakes. For example, in his autobiogaphy, it appears that someone (quite possibly Little) refers to Jacob's wife as "Louise." Everywhere else she is "Louisa." Is this simply a more endearing term used by Jacob, or a discrepancy that copied over and over could conceivably lead to a major error given time?

There are other inconsistenciews, even some made by Hamblin himself such as listing 1871 as the year of the Treaty at Fort Defiance when through Powell's writings we learn the year is clearly established as 1870. (Powell was kept busy floating the Grand Canyon in both 1869 and 1871, and is known to have spent his time with Hamblin in 1870.) In recalling the incident in 1881 for Little, Hamblin apparently remembered the date incorrectly.

There are also fictionalized accounts, dramatized by Bailey, of Jacob's relationship with Major Powell which might be confused as fact.

But the most serious charge against Hamblin is a new one, launched in 1993 with an article first appearing in "Canyon Legacy," a quarterly publication of the Dan O'Laurie Museum in Moab, Utah, inferring that Hamblin lied in saying Powell's three deserters on the Colorado River died at the hands of Shivwits Indians. The article says they were really murdered by Mormons in Toquerville, Utah after the three strangers were mistaken for federal investigators snooping into John D. Lee's role in the Mountain Meadows Massacre.

The story refers to a letter, allegedly lying in a trunk in Toquerville, Utah for more than a century, from William Leany to John Steele, later coming into possession of Prof. Wesley P. Larsen of Cedar City. If the letter is correct and Toquerville Mormons killed the defecting trio, then Jacob Hamblin must have lied in saying a Shivwits chief told him his tribesmen did the deed. Hamblin says the chief told him (Jacob being the sole interpreter for Major Powell of what was said) that William Dunn, and brothers O.G. and Seneca Howland, were murdered on the north rim of the Grand Canyon. Hamblin says the chief told that the three were nurtured by the Shivwits until an Indian came from across the Colorado to say the three must have been those thought to have abused an Indian squaw. The Shivwits then stalked and killed the three men, according to what

Hamblin told Powell. (See Chapter 13.) The same is recorded in Powell's *The Exploration of the Colorado River and its Canyons*, p. 323. Other writers picked up from these sources and repeated the Shivwit story for more than 100 years.

But in stories carried by the Associated Press in the St. George *Daily Spectrum* dated Oct. 22, 1994, Leany is quoted as referring to, "the day those three were murdered in our ward and the murderer killed to stop the shedding of more blood." Leany also refers to the "killing [of] the three in one room in our own ward." Larsen is quoted in the AP story as saying that Leany referred to an incident occuring in the summer of 1869.

This would appear to be a damning statement against both Hamblin's veracity and Toquerville Mormons. In the panicked aftermath of the massacre (even more than a decade later) is it possible three more "anti-Mormons" might be murdered if appearing to probe too deeply into the Mountain Meadows Massacre?

What do we do with this story? The AP account adds, "No bodies of effects were ever recovered, and Powell and others doubted the tale...." But the latter statement is misleading; no bodies were found in the Toquerville chapel either for that matter. Nor is there any mention of Powell ever "doubting" Hamblin's story. After putting his life in Jacob's hands time after time, it is clear from the Major's writings that he trusted Hamblin implicitly. In fact, on p. 323 of *The Exploration*, Powell says, "That night I slept in peace, although these murderers of my men...were sleeping not 500 yards away." That certainly does not sound as if Powell disbelieved or distrusted Hamblin.

There is another mention of Hamblin's visits with Powell to the Shivwits. Brooks says on p. 110 of her *Jacob Hamblin* that Jacob "saw signs of 'Old Toab' with a five-dollar bill pasted across his head for a decoration...a young fellow with a watch suspended around his neck on a rawhide string...another with a pocket knife." These would be effects of Powell's three deserting men. But Brooks has no footnotes or references here and her colorful words could be mere speculation.

Yet, was Powell duped? The following is exerpted from an article written for *Utah Lifestyle* magazine Spring, 1993 (but never published): "Larsen speculates that Eli N. Pace, Lee's son-in-law, could be the murderer as he sought to protect Lee. Pace reputedly said that the three strangers 'came out of nowhere.' That, indeed, could describe men climbing out of the Grand Canyon. Pace died by suicide, according to a coroner's jury in 1870, but some have since disputed the decision...some may have killed Pace to keep him quiet.

"The Toquerville story seems unlikely to Kerry Bate, a Steele descendent writing a family history. He is quoted in the AP story as saying 'There is no question the letter is authentic,' yet Bate questions Leany's soundness of mind at the time. Leany recieved a severe skull fracture in an 1857 beating, according to the AP story, allegedly for providing supplies to the Fancher party annihilated at the Mountain Meadows Masscre.

"There are many questions: how come no mention of the trio's murder in the press of 1869? Friends of Lee trying to keep it quiet? If so, why would Hamblin cooperate to cover for Lee. He and Lee rarely agreed on anything and were almost never in harmony during their entire lives right up until lee was executed in 1877 for his role in the Mountain Meadows Massacre."

In addition, as has been pointed out, Hamblin rarely took the side of peers if he considered them wrong. And for Jacob, Mormon or non-Mormon, certainly any murder would be wrong. And loving the Lamanites as he did, why would Jacob place blame on them for a murder they didn't commit?

The article continues. "Yet another question: how could anyone crawling and clawing their way for some 100 miles up the Grand Canyon north rim [to nearest civilization] have been anything but bedraggled, starving, dehydrated, exhausted? How could they be mistaken for federal investigators?

"Wayne Hinton, an SUU historian who researched the Powell expedition, is quoted in the AP story as saying he is highly doubtful that the three men met death in Toquerville. 'The fact no one mentions it is very curious. Mormons are such a writing people.'"

The story does say, however, that just as in the Mountain Meadows Massacre, perpetrators of such a heinous crime would make a pact to keep it quiet. But could they?

"Adding to the enigma of the missing Powell trio is a highly suspicious telegram received in 1869 by Mormon apostle Erastus Snow. It came from unknown origin. It claimed that two Shivwits trekked from their home on the Grand Canyon Mt. Trumbull area into Washington [near St. George] to report that they had killed Powell's men."

This is highly unlikely. If Indians had something of that nature to report, they wouldn't contact anyone save Jacob Hamblin, a known friend, who might help them if arrested. In addition, the Indians were known to have no horses. Why would they bother to walk so far just to risk being arrested? Neither Hamblin nor Powell ever mention a telegram being sent concerning a confession of the Shivwits.

The story, although receiving wide circulation in southern Utah, seems hollow. The statement of Bate weighs heavily that his ancestor Leany was not of a sound mind in writing such a letter. Inasmuch as Leany received a serious head injury, or could be angry at someone in Toquerville for the violence shown him, it is difficult to trust Leany's memory or his accuracy.

In the late summer of 1995 Dr. David Whitaker, BYU Lee Library, acquired additional letters written to Steel which appear to add to the history of southern Utah's late 1800 period. But there is nothing more conclusive on the murders of Powell's three men than those reports already given. The AP story seems to convey little more than empty conjecture. Unless irrefutable facts turn up in the future, Hamblin's story stands just as he told it some 125 years ago.

Charles Peterson sums up Hamblin very well in the "Journal of Mormon History" article previously quoted: "He [Hamblin] had many detractors, but over the years a bigger-than-life tradition has gathered to the memory of Jacob Hamblin."

– Chapter 17 –

Eloquence in Review

The passing of time has brought an ever greater appreciation of Jacob Hamblin's accomplishments. For starters, he spent
some thirty years almost constantly on the move to bridge the
gap of conflict between his many white and Indian friends. He
did it not by offering trinkets and baubles to the natives, but by
sharing religious ideas and ideals so valuable in his own life.
His was no casual labor of love, but an all-consuming endeavor.

Hamblin's life has been summed up by The Church of Jesus
Christ of Latter-day Saints as follows: "Jacob Hamblin made
nine [recorded] missionary visits to the Hopi villages of northern Arizona and in the process, reopened the ancient Ute
Crossing (also known as the Crossing of the Fathers) on the
Colorado River. He pioneered the Lee's Ferry crossing and in
1862-63 traveled completely around the Grand Canyon. In 1870
he guided Major John Wesely Powell on a survey of the Grand
Canyon."

This information is included in a brochure provided at the
Jacob Hamblin home in Santa Clara. The brochure quotes
Hamblin as saying, "I have greatly desired to gain influence
with them [the Indians]. The Lord has blessed me with the
desire of my heart" (quote given to Brigham Young, Oct. 9, 1859,
Church Historical Dept. Archives, SLC, Utah).

With that determination to make a difference among the
native Americans, it would appear Hamblin helped fulfill a
prophecy of Mormon leader Joseph Smith: "This work will fill
the Rocky Mountains with tens of thousands of Latter-day
Saints and there will be joined with them the Lamanites who
dwell in these mountains" (Quoted from Wilford Woodruff,
"The Lamanites in the Words of the Prophets," p. 281.)

Woodruff is also quoted therein Feb. 22, 1857 as follows:
"The door has already been unlocked to the Lamanites in these
mountains, and they will begin to embrace the Gospel and the

records of their fathers and their chiefs will be filled with the
Spirit and power of God...the Lord has spoken it and made
these promises unto them through their fathers."

From the same reference, Woodruff is quoted as saying on
Sept. 19, 1892, following a conference in St. George, June ll-l2:
There "were quite a few Lamanites in the congregation."

Almost certainly Hamblin was aware of both Smith's and
Woodruff's prophecies, and sought diligently to fulfill them. But
at the time Jacob died, he could have scarcely comprehended the
encompassing results of his work, particularly among the Navajo
and Hopi. Influence with the Hopi was mentioned by Helen and
Ken Sekaquaptewa in an earlier chapter. While few of the Hopis
who so intrigued Hamblin were ever baptized into The Church
of Jesus Christ of Latter-day Saints during his own lifetime, the
seeds were apparently sown to help the Lamanite "blossom as
the rose," as Mormon missionairies often put it.

Historian Corbett says that in an LDS conference in 1940
some two hundred Lamanites were in attendance, including
Navajos, Shosta, Hopi, Tewa, Cherokee, Papago and Shoshone
tribes. "Twelve Navajos and ten Hopis were baptized."[1] Here
the words of Brigham and Wilford were partially fulfilled.

President Young had sent Hamblin into southern Utah for
the primary purpose of teaching Christian doctrines to all
Lamanites, no matter how stubborn or reluctant to change.
Young had admonished the great Indian scout, "Remember the
gospel is for the Navajo as well as for the Moquis [Hopis]."[2] It
would be difficult to imagine what more Jacob might have done
to loyally follow his leader's fondest hopes for success among
the natives. In addition, Hamblin personified in every regard
the scriptural injunction to do good works "without having to
be commanded in all things." Surely there are fewer examples of
greater self-motivated industry anywhere.

One Hopi particularly impacted by Hamblin's message was
Tom Polacca, who was baptized not long after Hamblin discon-
tinued visiting the Oraibi region villages. Polacca reconciled his
Hopi teachings to those of Mormonism, and lived it faithfully
unto his dying day, according to Corbett. Polacca advised his

people "to wait for the return of the Mormon missionaries, who would bring them the true story of the origin of the Indians."[3]

Polacca was not mentioned by any of the Sekaquaptewa family, but could well have been a role model for them in converting to the Mormon faith. Ken Sekaquaptewa told the author that in his boyhood the religious teachings of the whiteman which made the most impression on his people were the "personal" and somewhat "unorthodox" tenets of the Mennonites, some Baptists and Mormons. There were LDS branches in each of three major mesas during Ken's years at home. He emphasizes that among the Hopis, "If you were not participating daily in a religious lifestyle, you were not being spiritual." But he added: "If that participation was not in the Hopi religion, you were in danger of being ostracized."[4]

Thus, it required courage to take on any whiteman's religion after so many years of traditionally following the Hopi priests. It helped that the Hopi and Mormon religions had many parallels, yet it still required more than a little valor to make changes after centuries of resisting them. One reason for this difficulty was the legacy of the Spanish conquistadors, who brought the Indians the *Bible* and took away their gold. It would require a total conversion to the teachings promulgated by Hamblin for any Hopi to embrace the religion of a whiteman.

While there were many similarities between Hopi and Mormon religions, there were aspects of the former which of necessity, must be purged after conversion—such as using poisonous snakes (or other rituals considered pagan by the Latter-day Saint hierarchy) in religious ceremonies. But conversion by Hopis to Mormonism was probably as much a product of Hamblin's honesty and service to the people as anything he carried in a book of scripture. According to Helen Sekaquaptewa, "Jeecoba's" personal daily life had more lasting impact upon the Hopi people of her era than anything ever said or taught by any other whiteman."

The Utah Historical Quarterly, Vo. 5, no. 4, shows a blind missionary baptizing many Shivwits in the Santa Clara area in the late 1800s. Some Shivwits were baptized while Hamblin lived there. Many were baptized later. Certainly there was much residual value in the teachings of Jacob and his missionaries, including constant companion Thales Haskell.

Research by David K. Flake in eastern Arizona shows that much of Hamblin's work among the Hopis began showing results about 1936. Mormon leaders, inspired by Jacob's zealous missionary labors, recalled his prodigious labors and called for the same sort of dedicated effort among their missionairies. Flake says, "Most notable was the efforts of the Snowflake Stake with the Hopis and Navahos. The St. Johns and Young stakes also did some work with the Navahos during this period. In 1943 the Navaho-Zuni mission was organized...[growing] slowly during its first four years, partly due to the wartime situation [World War II] and also because the Church was not fully convinced that the Indians were ready for the gospel. By 1947 most of these problems had been set aside...Indian missionary work with the Hopis, Navahos and Zunis moved into a new era of proselyting and conversion, one that is still going forward."[5]

James A. Little, editor of Hamblin's autobiography, had much praise for his subject and expected much good to be accomplished in having Jacob's work published. "He is such a modest man that he would be content to ever remain in obscurity." Obviously, Little was much impressed with Hamblin. The title page to the Little-edited autobiography reads: "A narrative of his personal experiences as a Frontiersman, Missionary to the Indians and Explorer disclosing Interpositions of Providence, Severe Privations, Perilous Situations, and Remarkable Escapes"–1909 Edition, preface, *Jacob Hamblin.*

Juanita Brooks said of him: "So at his death, Jacob Hamblin seemed a failure, one who had wasted his life in an unworthy cause. Yet, when the word reached Chief Tuba, he called all the people of his nation together, and for one night they mourned the passing of this, their best friend. The old chief told again of the man who always spoke the truth, who respected the Hopi for what he was, who helped...protect them from Navajo and the soldiers."[6]

Thus, the words on his grave marker had special meaning: "In memory of Jacob V. Hamblin, born April 2, 1819; died Aug.

31, 1886. Peacemaker in the Camp of the Lamanites; Herald of truth to the House of Israel."

Corbett includes this insight into the life of Jacob from a daughter. She said she thought Jacob was an oddity: "He just went about the Indians. Later, I cried bitterly as I repeated the words to my mother. She said, 'Are you crying because your father did a good piece of work that not many would or could do? Some day you will be older and wiser and can appreciate, and maybe understand what your father did.'"

When she was older, the girl replied that she realized her father "was one whose philosophy was fashioned of humans, woodlands and brooks; who had a compassion for broken wings; who recognized the greatness of simple things." Corbett added: Hamblin loved a "fallen human race…he had the power to look into the very souls of these red nomads and see mirrored there the historical tragedy of the lost tribes of Israel…his was the pure flame of love…'Blessed are the peacemakers, Matt. 5:9.'"7

A play written and produced by Rock Hamblin, "grandson of the famous old Indian scout" indicates an intrigue for Jacob's legacy. The play, in four acts, can be read today in BYU's Lee Library Special Collections Room.

In Santa Clara, the Jacob Hamblin Home is a must-see stop for all passing through, Latter-day Saint or otherwise. A Mormon missionary couple explain briefly the exploits of Hamblin, and show where he and two wives, Rachel and Priscilla, met the pioneer challenge in Santa Clara with a special brand of faith and fortitude. The home was, of course, built after Fort Clara washed away on lower ground, and where Rachel caught an illness from which she never recovered. All that was in the new home is restored, from spindles to willowback chairs (visitors will find them turned away from the table, as Hamblin's family did, until prayers were said for each meal.) One of Jacob's old saddles, brightly polished but well worn, is there along with many heirlooms, plus a copy of his journal in his handwriting. All are testimonies to his dedication as missionary and frontier peacemaker.

The entire community of Kanab showed its gratitude for Hamblin's many accomplishments in the town's behalf by erect-

ing a marker to his name near the north entrance on U.S. 89.
After enumerating his many accomplishments, it states this:
"The great Mormon frontiersman and Indian Missionary...
began peaceful negotiations with the redmen. He was so suc-
cessful that the officials of The Church of Jesus Christ of Latter-
day Saints sent him to establish residence among the
Indians...His friendship with the Indians saved many lives."
The monument was erected by the Utah Pioneer Trails and
Landmarks Association and Citizens of Kanab (LDS) Stake.
Another marker honoring Hamblin's missionary journeys is
located south of town at the junction of the airport road.

In 1946, a "Jacob Hamblin Park" in Kanab was officially
named and dedicated by the Governor, Herbert B. Maw.
Mention has been made of a large oil painting in Hamblin's likeness (painted by Willard Kirkpatrick) hanging in the lobby of
the Jacob Lake Lodge, Kaibab Plateau, Arizona, U.S. 89 A, some
25 miles south of Kanab.

Many communities in Arizona owe their existence to
Hamblin's exploration and foresight, including Tuba City,
Moenkopi, Alpine, Shumway, Woodruff, St. Johns, Joseph,
Showlow, Snowflake, Springerville, Eagar, Nutrioso, and others
on the upper Little Colorado River, plus Pleasanton, New
Mexico. As stated on p. 80 of *John Hamblin, Heritage and a
Personal History*, Jacob was the first whiteman "to trace the head-
waters of the Little Colorado." He and his peers also paved the
way for the Mormon settlements of Mesa and Thatcher on the
route into Old Mexico. The Mormon system of irrigation as utilized at Santa Clara helped nourish many of these communities.
Jacob and the missionaries under his leadership founded Pipe
Springs in northern Arizona, now a national monument. (The
same is well preserved from pioneer times and offers an excellent opportunity to see how things were done before days of the
horseless carriage.) Both Jacob Lakes, both the body of water
and the community on the Kaibab Plateau, were named after
Hamblin, plus several geographical features in the nearby
national forest.

This author had opportunity in the 1960s to interview many
LDS residents of Snowflake while they were in Salt Lake City

competing at a Church sporting event. Some surprise was expressed that there were so many Mormons "from such a far-away community." The residents answered: "Oh yes, Jacob Hamblin brought our people down. We thank the courage and foresight of Hamblin and the early settlers he brought with him. If anyone complains about so many Mormons in the region, we can point out that we were here first."

In Nevada, "Las Vegas Springs," now a metropolitan city and important tourist center for much of the world, was explored early by Hamblin and his peers. Other communities from Las Vegas to the Muddy were early visited by Jacob and his missionary compatriots. Call's Landing, referred to so often in Hamblin's history (now on Lake Mead), as a crossing point on the Colorado River below the Grand Canyon, still shows on most maps of Arizona-Nevada.

Historian Marshall Trumble paid this tribute to Hamblin as a pioneer into the wilderness: "The trailblazer for the Mormons into Arizona was a kindly frontiersman named Jacob Hamblin...over the next several years, the Hamblin Trail was the main pathway for the Mormon settlers into Arizona." Trumble's *A Panoramic History of a Frontier State* carries a map showing "Hamblin Road" from Lee's Ferry through present-day Tuba City and general area near Cameron to the Little Colorado River. "Overlooked many times by historians was a much-traveled north-south road into Arizona from Utah."[8] There is no Hamblin Road today, but anyone driving U.S. 89 (or 89A) can thank Jacob Hamblin for first marking the way.

According to U.S. Sen. John Murdock (Arizona), the trail through northern Arizona should have become known as the "New Mormon Road," and "if any man's name should have been attached to the wonderful bridge [Navajo Bridge] across the canyon of the Colorado River, it unquestionably should have been called the Hamblin Bridge."[9]

Author Frank Arnold said: "He was the pathfinder of Northern Arizona, its Daniel Boone or its [Admiral] Peery...If you sit on the [Grand] Canyon rim and don't think about Jacob Hamblin, then you are absolutely without piety. You are as hard as a man who visits Mt.Vernon and never gives a thought to George Washington."[10]

The Arizona Guide, Works Project Administration (a federal government-assigned volume on each of the lower 48 states) refers to Hamblin as "the fearless Mormon trailblazer."[11] Other Arizona histories credit Hamblin with "reconnaissance missions."

In the late 1800s, The Mormon "Honeymoon Trail" (wherein Southwest LDS couples headed for the St. George Temple to be married for time and all eternity) followed the general route across the Arizona Strip taken years before by Hamblin. The Honeymoon Trail is well marked on most maps of the Arizona Strip put out by the U.S. Bureau of Land Management and the U.S. Forest Service. (Some of the route near Buckskin Mountain had been taken by Dominguez-Escalante, but had fallen into disuse some 90 years before Hamblin tapped the Piute Naraguts to guide them across.)

Concerning Jacob's attempt in 1874 to make peace with an angry Navajo Nation, writer John Murdock quoted Hamblin: "My heart has never known fear." Murdock interjects: "We wonder whether this was statement of absolute truth–and it was possible that it was–or merely an effort to feign a calmness which he did not actually feel." But the writer adds this: "Let it be understood that in the fulfillment of the condition imposed upon Hamblin, a degree of courage was evidenced by him equal to any that has been renowned in song or story in olden times in Europe."[12]

Murdock likens Jacob to Regulus during the Roman war with Carthage. *The World Book Encyclopedia* says this about Regulus: "He was a Roman hero and military leader whose life story is often given as an example of true patriotism. He was captured by Carthage and was sent to Rome to discuss peace terms. Whatever Rome's decision, Regulus promised to return with that decision. Rome refused to accept peace terms, but Regulus returned as promised, although he bore news which would surely anger Carthage. The latter's army put Regulus to death by torture." Adds the encyclopedia entry, "The story was likely invented to excuse Roman torture of Carthaginian prisoners but it helped make Regulus a national hero."[13] In Hamblin's case, however, it happened in real life. He said he would return. Threat of torture and death would not deter him.

From the beginning, Hamblin had shown a willingness, even a tenacious determination, to sacrifice much for what he believed in. He had written in his "Letters and Journals" while making an early missionary journey that "we were much persecuted for the gospel's sake."[14] He made it clear to Lucinda that he was not a sunshine or Sunday saint. He must join with the other members in Zion. When she could not abide this, he stated, "I would not bend one inch from the order of God to live with her."[15] The latter was not the mark of a man who could compromise principles or beliefs; his refusal to back away from personal conviction would send him into the jaws of many perils.

It was clear with his testimony at the Mountain Meadows Massacre—which Brooks says was the strongest offered against John D. Lee—that Hamblin had already gained a reputation for absolute veracity. He was not an eyewitness to the massacre, yet no one could refute what he said. Bailey summarized throughout his book that Hamblin was a man who could not lie, one who put the cause of truth above his own welfare.

Says Andrew Jensen, *LDS Biographical Encyclopedia*, Vol. 111, p. 100: "He was a distinguished Indian missionary and faithful Church worker." Also from Jensen: "Jacob was a famous frontiersman...he never killed an Indian...the Indians said Jacob never lied."

F. S. Dellenbaugh of the Powell expeditions had a most profound respect for Hamblin. Dellenbaugh said that he knew of a situation where a (white) fanatic on the Muddy concluded to kill a man and declared, "'This man must go.' Jacob answered, 'If he does, I go first, mark that.' The man went free and never knew his danger, for it would have been reckless nature to oppose the wrath of Old Jacob. Had he been at the Mountain Meadows on that awful day he would have saved the immigrants or have died with them."[16]

Few ever used the word "wrath" in connection with Jacob; he was usually described as a man with astute patience. But it is clear that Dellenbaugh, who didn't know Hamblin until fourteen years after the massacre, understood the influence the man wielded with both white and redmen. Dellenbaugh concluded that "Old Jacob was a remarkable character and must hold a place in the annals of Wilderness beside Jedediah Smith, [Jim] Bridger, the [William and associates] Sublettes, and the rest of the gallant band. But he differed in one respect from every one of them; he sought no pecuniary gain, working for the good of his chosen people...seeming to have no ambition for riches. Honest, slow and low of speech, keen of perception, quick of action."[17]

Hamblin, of course, was a missionary and peacemaker which the above adventurers never pretended to be. His honest character and selfless service in behalf of Indians and others would appear to place him on a lofty mountain peak above the bold but sometimes untrustworthy Bridger. (See *Fort Bridger*, Gowans and Campbell, p. 59.) Sublette made considerable money in the fur trade and must be considered an astute businessman. He also helped open Sublette's Cutoff to the Oregon Trail. Smith completed some marvelous explorations across the Great Basin. But none of them served others in Christ-like dedication as did Jacob Hamblin. None of them expended the effort he did to serve a cause outside himself.

In travel to share religious beliefs, probably only the Apostle Paul in ancient times began to approach as many miles logged as Hamblin, albeit transportation via ship was much more difficult in those days.[18] In more modern times, only figures like Dr. Livingstone or Mother Teresa could match time spent in missionary work. It is really as a humanitarian, not merely trailblazer or scout, that Jacob Hamblin made his unique mark on the world's history. Few expended greater devotion and energy to a humanitarian cause. Hamblin's unique vision of what could be saved an incalcuable number of lives, both white and red, along the frontier he served. The same can be scarcely said of Bridger, Sublette, or even Smith.

Jacob seemed not to consider himself as "courageous" or "brave." He simply took the trouble to understand the

Lamanites and cared deeply about their welfare. Consider these excerpts from a letter written to Brigham Young: "I have spent the last 19 years of my life mostly attending to Indian matters; have spent more nights under cedar and pine boughs than in a house; though I do not regret it...I have noticed that the natives in southern Utah live mostly on seeds and roots. When the whiteman settled the country, it is where the redman and his forefathers have subsisted for generations unnumbered. The whiteman's cattle crops the vegetation that produced the seed...year after year [it] causes less to grow. The game also disappears. Grievances are talked over at the campfire...necessity drives the Indian to steal, the whiteman wants to bring the Indian to his standard of civilization, they are both driven to desperation, and all for the want of a little understanding."[19]

Hamblin also recounted in his letter to Brigham how he had heard a whiteman boast that he had fattened his horses from a cache of Indian seeds. Thus, while some have portrayed Hamblin's contribution to frontier peace as a muscle-flexing show of power (somewhat like Kit Carson) seeking to solve the whiteman's problems, Jacob seemed every bit as concerned to solve the Indians' problems. And in finding justice for the redman, he found peace for the whiteman. Quite possibly, Hamblin has no peer on the American frontier in effort expended to learn the Indian mind and heart.

Thus, the word that marked his life's work with the aborigine might be better stated as "insightful" for it seemed to precede even his courage. The latter came via his assurance he would not be harmed while helping the Lamanite. In religious parlance that might be considered "inspired" in that he felt he knew the mind and will of the Lord sufficiently to place his own life in the hands of the Almighty. Who among us would have the "insight" to go among a band of Indians prepared to kill us with such confidence in a higher power that we felt no fear?

In discussing efforts to guard the Southwest frontier, Flake says that Hamblin "was the central figure," and enlisted the assistance of friendly Piutes to prevent the theft of much more livestock by the Navajos than they actually got away with. "The settlers had a small militia which hurried about from one trouble spot to another, but its presence probably had less to do with keeping the peace than the quiet influence of Hamblin and his missionaries."[20]

Flake says that "Southern Utah began to relax after Jacob made peace with the Navajos in 1870 [the treaty at Fort Defiance]... it looked as if peace had come at last to the frontier. This happy state of affairs was brought to a sudden jolt during the winter of 1873-74 by a series of events that rocked Southern Utah [McCarty's irresponsible killing of three Navajos] and would probably have brought war without the cool courage of Hamblin."[21]

Ammon Tenney, who spent some fifteen years of his life accompanying Hamblin in his missionary journeys said this in his diary: "I learned many lessons from that noble and God-fearing man and one who never faltered in performing his duties."[22] Tenney said of the Lamanites Hamblin dealt with, "The descendants of Father Lehi...for many years were a source of peril... the very elements seemed impregnated with the spirit of war and theft and robbery." The Indians of the period were "a term of terror in which millions of dollars were stolen and wasted under the sound of the war whoop." Tenney was, in spite of those hazards, converted as a young man under Hamblin's tutelage to realize the value of the Lamanite; Tenney was an Indian mission leader and later baptized about one hundred and fifty Indians.

Thales Haskell, a constant companion of so many missionary journeys with Hamblin, never questioned the latter's leadership. Haskell made it clear throughout his journals that in following Hamblin, he felt he followed the will of the Lord. One statement from Thales shows the respect the natives also had for his leader: "When Jacob told them [the Havasupai] who they were, they had heard of him and the work of the missionaries and were friendly and provided the party with food and other necessities."[23] From spying on the Ives expedition, to calling on the angry Piute chief, to remaining behind with the Hopis, Haskell did without fail as Jacob asked. This is a tribute to Haskell's duty and loyalty; but it is also a tribute to Hamblin's judgment and leadership. If Thales had been in the Pleasanton region when Jacob died, he might have made a statement at the time regarding his longtime and trusted companion.

Dudley Leavitt, another loyal missionary companion, referred to Hamblin as "like a father to the Indians." Ira Hatch and other missionaries with Hamblin when George A. Smith was killed likely owed their lives to Jacob's decisive action in eluding the Navajos, and his friendship with Spaneshank who sheltered them and saved their lives.

Charles Peterson summed it up: "His gentleness and determination to make peace were among his most appealing qualities."[24] Wallace Stegner was not the first to identify Jacob with J. F. Cooper's intrepid (fictional) Indian fighter (in Hamblin's case, a peace negotiater). Says Stegner: "As Mormon Leatherstocking, [Hamblin] has a permanent and respected place in the history of the West...the Indians were not wolves to be destroyed, but souls to be saved."[25]

Several Hamblin researchers at Dixie College gave these tributes to the man: (from Rexann Sylvester, a relative, 1975): "I hope the people who read this will find Jacob Hamblin to be the great man I have."[26] She recounts his life story as given by Bleak and others.

From Brad Bishop (Dixie College, 1974): "Jacob was a man called of God to do a special task."[27]

Says researcher Del Despain, quoting John R. Young who witnessed the work of Hamblin in ending the traditional Piute custom of fighting for squaws: "It seems to illustrate the influence for good that this wonderful peacemaker [Jacob Hamblin] held over our fallen brethren, the Lamanites."[28]

Even anti-Mormon historians cannot help giving Jacob his due. Charles Kelly said little if anything good about the Latter-day Saints and often castigated the Mormons for various reasons, including polygamy, blood atonement, etc. But of Hamblin he states in words of respect: "To settle this affair [McCarty's killing of three Indians] Jacob Hamblin...visited the Navajos in their own territory, was threatened with death [and] talked his way out. To prove his point, he later took a group of Navajos into

Utah to listen to evidence. This conference, says Hamblin, was the most difficult of his life and incurred the greatest danger."[29]

Hamblin did not term it "danger," however; he didn't seem to know the meaning of the word. Even when Bishop Levi Stewart said he "learned from Piutes that the Navajos were waiting to kill Jacob Hamblin" (Bleak, p. 223), Hamblin would not cower. It wasn't just duty. He seemed to have the sort of faith that overcomes all fear.

Too infrequently mentioned is Hamblin's remarkable skills at diplomacy, Indian or white. In the Mountain Meadows Massacre, he walked a tight line adhering to his keen sense of justice while not condemning his erring peers. Despite statements from some (including Brooks) about his testimony convicting John D. Lee, Hamblin did so with noticeable lack of animosity or personal vengence against the men who had sabotaged his work with the Lamanites. He bore a great burden without complaint, even though innocent, when all living in southern Utah were suspected of hate and revenge which led to murder in the Meadows' tragedy. There is also the example of his restraint in the letter to McCarty, although absolutely firm in the pursuit of justice. There are the letters and responses to superiors in Salt Lake City to apprise headquarters of conditions other than what were sometimes assumed. There was the bold but gentle letter to the Navajo leaders explaining his efforts at peace which they had seemingly spurned. And what more profound verbal answer could be given when his life was at stake among the Navajos than, "I told him I was not afraid of my friends."

Countless times when a rash or fearful act might precipitate bloodshed, Hamblin moved with a wisdom rarely found in a terrestrial sphere. No doubt Hamblin's patient concern for the Indians' welfare assisted his cause. Escalante and Dominguez encountered the same stubborn resistance from the Hopi as all whitemen did. The Hopi were friendly to a point with the padres but refused to listen to their religious views. Wrote Escalante bluntly, "they wanted to be our friends but not Christians." When the padres gave a blanket as a gift, it was thrown back in their faces. (See pp. 108-109 of the Dominguez-Escalante journal.

A footnote on the latter page says, "Throughout the Spanish colonial period the Hopi were referred to as 'the obstinate Hopi.'")

History indicates the Catholics got virtually nowhere with the Hopi even though they had the earliest contacts. Only a man of great patience and love could succeed among them. Hamblin seemed to be that man, more so than any other whiteman, although some colleagues might have thought him too "soft" on marauding Indian chiefs like Patnish. Bleak stated that: "It is evident he [Patnish] would like to break up the treaty Brother Hamblin has just effected with the Navajos."

Jacob spoke not a word of anger at the hostile Indian. He simply tried to work around Patnish and eventually did.

Jacob wrote about some Indians as though they were punished by a Divine Providence when oppressing the Mormons. For example, the Indian who killed George A. Smith died "a miserable death" within months afterward. "The Navajos believed it was because he had killed a Mormon." (Bleak, p. 147) If the Navajos thought this was a sign that they should not harm Mormons, Jacob was ready to let their superstitions work in behalf of peace. As Hamblin put it, his prayers were answered in a way harking back to the miracles of Old Testament times. Or those of The Book of Mormon.

His influence over the Hopis and Piutes in praying for rain cannot be ignored. Either it was supreme coincidence on several occasions, or Jacob had influence with the heavens. The reader can decide which; but clearly, no one else has had such a lasting spiritual hold on the Indians in any age; and Hamblin used it in every instance for the betterment of both races.

It is time, too, to give Hamblin his just place in the realm of literary achievement, not only among his Latter-day Saint peers but in the world at large. Like most men of his time (including Abaham Lincoln) Hamblin had little formal education. But he mastered the art of communication. Consider how beautifully and succinctly he has expressed himself in the most powerful words available to him on the frontier of his time. (Example from his autobiography during trouble with the Indians in

Tooele): "I told them...if there were any shot, I should be the first." From the same period, "I decided the Lord must have a use for them [Indians]." From his journal referring to Brigham Young: "We told him [angry Indian leader] that our chief had sent us there and we should stay until he told us to leave." From his journal at Pine Valley: "I gathered that the brethren would rather have my room than my company." His empassioned speech at Fort Defiance, his Autobiography: "What shall I tell my people the 'Mormons' when I return home? That we may expect to live in peace, live as friends, and trade with one another? Or shall we look for you to come like wolves at night?...I have now gray hairs on my head, and from my boyhood I have been on the frontiers doing all I could to preserve peace between the whiteman and the Indians."

A study of Bleak's history indicates his respect for Hamblin's veracity. On several occasions, he inserts: "Jacob says..." He does this for no one else. Obviously much of Bleak parallels Hamblin's autobiography, especially after death of the three Navajos threatened frontier peace. But Bleak also interviewed many of Hamblin's peers, men like Thales Haskell, Ira Hatch, Samuel Knight, Dudley Leavitt, etc. and never found anything contradictory to what Jacob had told him.

It is apparent Jacob's progeny have long recognized the rich heritage left them. There is this comment by Jacob, Jr., speaking of the Indian Frank story (Jacob's son had made "too good a trade"): "We had a code of honesty to live up to."[30]

The following was a presentation made by John Hamblin, Jacob's grandson, at a family reunion (no date given): "In spite of circumstances, he never forgot that feeling of love and faith and a feeling of serenity toward God and man. It is true that times were very hard for his family but I never heard any member of his household complain about it. His family had love and respect for him."[31]

Adds John Hamblin, "The things that Jacob Hamblin stood for are as important and vital today as they were when he lived upon the earth. No greater blessing could come to his descendants than for them to develop the qualities of character and ideals he possessed. These things we can take with us when our own work is completed here on earth."

In the same book referred above, John Hamblin says his grandfather left this legacy with the family:

1. He left them with a feeling of love and respect and honor toward him.

2. He left them a name free from scandal, deceit, suspicion and pettiness. A name that has made them all known and respected as descendants of Jacob Hamblin. They say it with pride.

3. He left his descendants a testimony of the gospel. He lived up to the admonition of his Church, "Seek ye first the Kingdom of God and His righteousness and all other things will be added."

4. He taught that to steal, to lie and be deceitful, led only to unhappiness, loss of faith and often, violence.

5. He taught that faith in God is a powerful force if exercised for good. It will overcome all our problems.

6. He helped locate his family in settlements that have proven to be the best in the world to raise families in. In these settlements the first things built were homes, Churches and schools. These settlements and communities created environments healthy for young people in their formative years.

7. He taught that patience, humility, kindness, and friendship are greater powers than those of armies.

8. He taught that all people are the children of God. That it is wrong and very displeasing to God to abuse them, rob or murder them. He taught that God's true purpose is peace for all. He demonstrated this in his attitude toward all men by his treatment of the Indians. His rules for dealing with them give an insight into his influence over them." (See end of chapter.)

While some non-Mormons then or now may not have agreed with the religious message Jacob took to the Indians, that message (from the Latter-day Saint concept of Jesus Christ's teachings) undoubtedly helped assuage the savage traditions of redmen who for years had engaged in unhindered child slavery, torture, pillage, and often murder. Jacob taught the redman a new and lasting concept of Christ-like peace which resolved conflict over a longer period of time for all parties than merely placating them for short periods with trinkets and ribbons. In addition, it instilled an inner feeling of self-worth and well-being vital to overcoming life's obstacles for people of all races or ethnic backgrounds, Indian as well as whiteman.

Hamblin accomplished much (especially in his work with Major Powell) to dilute wholesale prejudice against his Church. Whatever one might think of Mormons who participated in the Mountain Meadows Massacre, it became clear in the writings of Powell, Dellenbaugh, several Indian agents, eastern writer Greeley, and other non-Mormons who met Hamblin, that here was a sincere and devout Christian. If the Mormons had strange doctrines and beliefs, such as polygamy and work for the dead, well, here was a "common sense" fellow named Jacob Hamblin who epitomized all that was right and good. He was trustworthy, dutiful (perhaps to a fault), and won the friendship of even the most skeptical individual, including previously prejudiced gentiles. Consider, for example, the letter from the skeptic named Brind, who concluded Jacob was a remarkable man. Prof. H. A. Thompson of the U.S. Geological Survey thought so too: "Jacob was a man I could trust with my money, my life and my honor, knowing all would be safe."[32]

Even hardcore opponents of Hamblin's mission had to respect his plucky spirit, uncomplaining nature in meeting daily challenge, indomitable (physical, mental and spiritual) stamina, woodsmanship, leadership, manliness, frontier know-how, horsemanship, duty and valor in meeting all rigors of the frontier and in living up to his convictions. Certainly the Indians respected him for it, even those who did not share his cause for being there. "I was 56 hours without water,"[33] Jacob said on one mission around the south end of the Grand Canyon; but such hardships never precipitated any thoughts of quitting, or returning home before his mission was completed. He was always ready to return once more to crusade for peace against any obstacles wherever he might be needed, so long as his body held out. Even then, he often forged ahead when sick.

As time went on, President Young saw to it that Jacob was better outfitted for his lengthy journeys; but until the very last, his travels were not without considerable sacrifice. Risk factor among the Indians diminished after his stand-off with the Navajos, but the physical danger in crossing rivers and mountains and deserts was never obliterated unto the end of his days. His indomitable will to carry out difficult missions was never exemplified more than in returning to locate the physical remains of young George A. Smith among what many considered "killer" Navajos.

In attributing all this to Jacob, one must include with his name and accomplishments the persistent support of wives and families. Jacob's achievements would have been impossible without commitment and devotion at home. Rachel, Priscilla, Louisa and their children cleared the way for Jacob to be gone for extremely long periods. His work in carrying out the missionary program of Brigham Young and later, Wilford Woodruff, would not have happened without the shared vision and internal harmony of a devoted homefront. While Jacob speaks little of it publicly, he must have expressed considerable appreciation for his family's devotion privately.

A careful reading of his autobiography would indicate a great love and devotion to wives and children, who would quite naturally benefit along with him in their husband/father's spiritual blessings which he mentioned frequently. Without this uplift shared with the family, it is doubtful Jacob could have remained focused on his many sojourns across the Colorado. It is an intangible thing, the commodity called "spirit," but Jacob talks of it frequently and as openly and matter-of-factly as any of the four gospel writers in the New Testament.[34]

The Hamblin Home brochure in Santa Clara (published by the LDS Church) says of his Jacob's domestic life: "The Hamblins were a deeply religious family. Family prayer preceded meals at their home. During Jacob's absence, his wife Rachel presided. She also supervised family spinning and weaving and served as local schoolteacher, nurse and midwife. Priscilla, head cook for the family, was known locally as the "herb doctor." The children helped with household tasks, and tended livestock, and harvested…peaches and apricots."

Rachel bore Jacob five children…Priscilla was mother of nine children. Louisa…six children. The family adopted three Indian children and two other Piute girls who served as maids. The wives raised their families as one, in peace and harmony."

The one non-Mormon who seemed to recognize the inner strength and disciplined devotion of Hamblin more than anyone else was Major John W. Powell. The latter, of course, needed someone who knew the trails and water sources of the Grand Canyon region, but he also needed someone who could face danger cooly while dealing daily with unpredictable and potentially dangerous natives. Jacob could not have accomplished this if afraid of the unknown, anymore than could have Powell have explored the unknown Grand Canyon, for which the Major was nationally acclaimed.

But Hamblin was no frontier adventure-seeker; within him was an almost tunnel-vision purpose. Only a man like Jacob Hamblin, one they might trust, could have persuaded the reticent and often wary natives to open up to Powell and share their beliefs, customs, religious rituals, inner thoughts. Then could Powell say, "This man Hamblin…has a great influence over all the Indians…I have found it very difficult to make the natives understand my object but the gravity of the Mormon missionary helps me much."[35]

A number of biographies about Powell lend much to the myth of Hamblin, almost bordering on folklore. One romanticized version says, "The Buckskin Apostle was a spare giant of a man who appeared taller than his six feet two inches tall." Elsewhere, Hamblin is an even six feet and never referred to as a giant in the physical sense. Some Powell biographies also refer to "an angel of the Lord" appearing to Jacob to warn him about spilling Indian blood." Hamblin claimed no angelic visitation, just inspiration. But it was a mighty inspiration, not needing exaggerations like this one concerning the country Jacob explored: "The terrain was so terrible that even mountain men like Jim Bridger had stayed away from it." While this might be so, it is more likely that the veteran fur trapper called the northern Rocky Mountains home and simply preferred to remain there.

A more credible account is this one: "Powell could not have turned to a more capable man." Or "He was not afraid of the wilderness." Another: "Powell would always be safe as a friend of Jacob Hamblin."

One scholarly history of Powell points out that the military campaigns of Kit Carson probably made things more difficult for the Mormons and Jacob Hamblin after the Bosque Redondo experience. "Carson starved them [the Navajos] out...they returned [to their homeland] embittered and defiant."[36]

It should be realized that while some of the older Navajos were grateful to finally return home, younger and more rebellious braves did not like being pushed onto a reservation one quarter the original size of "Navajo country." They required greater sensitivity and understanding than ever, the kind only someone like Hamblin could provide.

Historian Robert McPherson observed Hamblin as a man who could understand and reason it out with the angry redman, made even more belligerent, if stories were true, about government agents claiming Mormons "were encouraging Indians to steal from the gentiles," etc. McPherson says, "Jacob Hamblin was a Mormon frontiersman famous for his ability to work with Indians." Hamblin "found Indians eager to hear the history of their forefathers."[37] He worked patiently with them to understand what God had in mind for them.

Hamblin was bestowed with the title "Apostle to the Lamanites." This does not mean that he was ever a member of the LDS Church Council of the Twelve. That is, his name is not included in the Church's historical list of council members. It was meant to mean, as today's dictionaries say it, "One who leads or advocates a cause or movement." His cause was well known; he moved it as no one else could.

Says researcher Roberta Duff, Dixie College: "He was deserving of the name 'Apostle to the Lamanites'. She adds, "I only hope that through this writing I can do justice to a great man."[38]

Brooks says, "It is the title [Apostle to the Lamanites] of which he was most proud...even ignoring his official ordination by Brigham Young, he was really an apostle to [the Lamanites].[39]

It is likely Hamblin might have been ordained officially to be a General Authority if living in or around Church headquarters, or if inclined to supervise many others in the diverse duties he might have. But if Jacob was removed from the frontier, it would not have gotten along without him. The position of Church Presidents Brigham Young and Wilford Woodruff seemed to be: "Let Jacob continue precisely as he is doing. Help him...or stay out of his way." Hamblin required no special title to perform at zenith level; he needed only a verbal approval to proceed. Brigham apparently recognized that, when ordaining Hamblin mission president very soon after Jacob arrived among the Southwest Indians.

From his great-great-grandson, Mark Hamblin of Kanab, who is one of thousands of progeny of Jacob, comes this appraisal: "Stories handed down from family members indicate Jacob was a man of flawless character. He was away from his family for months at a time but it was clear he always tried to do his duty in the Church and community." Asked if he thought Jacob could have prevented the Mountain Meadows Massacre if present, Mark answered, "From all that family members have said during my lifetime, and my own research, I would say, absolutely! Jacob had too much influence with the Indians to allow a siege on the wagon train to get started in the first place."[40]

Jim Schreiner, historian, Kaibab National Forest, Fredonia, Arizona and a member of the Kaiva Plateau Chapter of the Arizona Archaelogical Society says: "We don't know all of the trails taken by Jacob Hamblin going to and from the Colorado River but we do know that nowhere could be found a more energetic and courageous explorer. He gained the confidence of various Southwest Indian tribes and learned what they knew about game trails and location of water. It would appear no one worked harder to bridge the conflict between white and redman in bringing peace to the frontier." In a later letter, Schreiner wrote, "We in the Kaiva Plateau Chapter hope to form a partnership with these agencies [Arizona Archaelogical Society, Forest Service, Bureau of Land Management] to designate the 'Big Canyon' route [on Buckskin Mountain] as an interpretive-historical trail to honor Jacob."[41]

Rod Schipper, U.S. Bureau of Land Management, Resource Protection Specialist, Kanab, says: "In the Southwest BLM, the name of Jacob Hamblin is associated with dauntless energy in exploring the unknown and making peace with hostile Indian tribes. We are continually trying to pinpoint the routes he took on the Arizona Strip, make them known, protect and memorialize them so that future generations can better appreciate all he did."[42]

Here are examples of other tributes to Jacob's life and work:

David J. Whitaker, Curator of the Mormon Experience, BYU Lee Library: "The insight and skill exhibited by Hamblin in dealing with the Indians, as first gained in the Tooele experience, is almost without precedence. As he claimed, it seemed he held special powers to resolve the needs of both his people and the Indians. What he accomplished seems more remarkable with the passage of time."[43]

Marlene Taylor Mott, librarian, Thatcher, Ariz. High School: "The very name of Jacob Hamblin in Arizona stands for integrity and courage. He did not receive as much credit for what he accomplished as have many others in Arizona history."[44]

Stephen Clark, student of southern Utah history: "Jacob Hamblin's name stands out as one who rose above personal anger and grudge. He truly carried with him the message of Jesus Christ in bringing out the best in others regardless of their station in life. The world needs more people like Jacob Hamblin."[45]

Larry Echohawk, Pawnee Indian and LDS Church member: "People like Jacob Hamblin are an inspiration to all Lamanites trying to better themselves and improve their capabilities to serve others. He reminds me of Church President Spencer W. Kimball who shared his great dream for the Lamanites with myself and many others in 1946. 'Rise to a great destiny.'"[46] Echohawk did just that in the early 1900s as he rose to become Idaho's Attorney General, the first American Indian to hold that position.

For other Lamanites, Echohawk urges reading 2 Nephi 26: 15-16, (originally written 550 B.C., according to The Book of Mormon). "After my seed and the seed of my brethren shall have dwindled in unbelief...the prayers of the faithful shall be heard and all those who dwindled in unbelief shall not be forgotten. For those who shall be destroyed shall speak to them out of the ground...their speech shall whisper out of the dust." It is Echohawk's belief that this "voice from the dust" emanated from The Book of Mormon written by ancient Indian prophets on plates of metal, then hidden in the ground until Joseph Smith was directed to them in the latter 1920s. This is, of course, what Hamblin tried to impress upon the mind of the Indian.

Echohawk (and Ken Sekaquaptewa) told the author that the message introduced to the world by Joseph Smith, and carried forth with such dedication by Jacob Hamblin, has been paramount in lifting their lives to meet the Savior's teachings—and to live up to the substantial promises made to their ancestors.

Their testimonies hark back to the experience Jacob had in Tooele. Hamblin concludes that a "special Providence" looked after them to prevent the spilling of blood on both sides: "The Holy Spirit forcibly impressed me that it was not my calling to shed the blood of the scattered remnant of Israel, but to be a messenger of peace to them. It was also made manifest to me that if I would not thirst for their blood, I should never fall by their hands."

Much has been said about the whitemen's lives that Jacob saved. But it is certain that if he had not made peace with the Piutes and Navajos who were pillaging stock and killing settlers who tried to stop them, white militias would have moved in to kill the redmen in wholesale fashion. Hundreds if not thousands of Indians could have been killed by the time of Jacob's death in 1886 if the militia mind-set of revenge had prevailed. According to Echohawk and Sekaquaptewa, Hamblin saved many Lamanite souls as well as their physical bodies.

From the Christian point of view, it must be concluded that Hamblin received one of mankind's greatest revelations for peace, in any age. Not fearing for his life despite the presence of hostile Indians, he went among them when conventional wisdom dictated he remain safely home. One must ponder Hamblin's composure in totally trusting in an Almighty power in marked contrast to many in a hopeless and negative world which seems to have "waxed cold" as stated in scripture.[47]

Hamblin's was a working faith beyond the comprehension of most mortals, akin perhaps only to that of Daniel in the lion's den from the Old Testament. As much seemed perceived by the non-Mormon Smith brothers at Jacob's trial by the Navajos in 1874 : "No braver man ever lived."[48]

Dr. Ron Walker, Smith Institute for (LDS) Church History, and an expert on frontier-Indian relations, put it this way: "No more could be asked or expected in effecting peaceful relations with hostile Indians than accomplished by Jacob Hamblin. He did so without any attempt to bring credit or attention upon himself, in an entirely selfless manner."

Hamblin's accomplishments came about by placing purpose above self. In one instance, providing medical assistance to a lowly Piute, he obtained the confession that the Piute and Navajos had helped kill Whitaker and McIntyre of Pipe Springs.[49] It was a confession, with seeming contriteness and hope of forgiveness, which probably would have been shared with no one but Hamblin.

In 1874, Hamblin's putting lofty resolve above self served a most useful purpose in assuaging angry natives. In his words, "My life was of but small moment compared with the lives of the Saints and the interests of the kingdom of God. I determined to trust in the Lord and go on."[50]

Historian John H. Evans stated that Hamblin accomplished much with supreme confidence in a Father in Heaven. "Although he generally carried a gun...his dependable weapon was prayer and the most absolute trust in God."[51] Corbett concludes: "The passing of time seems to make the work of Jacob Hamblin greater."[52] Another half century has gone by since that statement, and it appears truer now than ever before.

Jacob Hamblin did, indeed, leave behind a rich heritage for his progeny, a remarkable legacy for all mankind. His depth of commitment to a purpose and value greater than himself is to be the more admired in a modern era of unaccountability and chaos. All might seek profitably to emulate the man Jacob Hamblin more closely.

Jacob Hamblin's rules for managing Indians

(It has been suggested every Indian agency manager read them. They were given at the request of John W. Young, and are found on pp. 67-68 of his "Journal and Letters," pp 281-82 in Bleak.)

1. Never talk anything but truth to them.
2. Never let them see you in a passion.
3. Never show fear. This should be observed that you may show your self of a sound heart and strong mind.
4. Never approach them in an austere manner using more words than is necessary to convey the idea in full, nor in a higher tone of voice to be distinctly heard.
5. Always listen to an Indian when he wishes to tell you of his grievances and redress wrongs if they can show there are any.
6. Never use obscene language or take any course of that kind before them.
7. Never submit to any unjust demand or let them coerce anything from you, thereby showing you are governed by the rule of right.
8. I think it is useless to speak of things they cannot comprehend.

(The following paragraph is listed as a ninth rule in some biographies, but neither Bleak nor Hamblin include it as such. It appears to be merely a summation of the foregoing rules.)

I have tried to observe the above rules for the past twenty years and it has given me a salutary influence wherever I have met with them. Many times when I have visited isolated bands upon business and have been addressing them in a low tone of voice around their council fires, I have noticed that they have listened with attention and reverence. I believe if the rules that I have mentioned were observed there would be but little difficulty on our frontier with the Redman.

End Notes, Chapter Seventeen

1. "Mission records, Report of Indian Conference." See Pearson Corbett, p. 439.
2. Ibid.
3. Corbett, p. 439.
4. Interview at Brigham Young University Multicultural Center, Provo, Utah, April 4, 1995.
5. "A History of Mormon Missionary work with the Hopi, Navajo and Zuni Indians," Master's thesis, abstract, 1965, p. 132.
6. *Jacob Hamblin, Mormon Apostle to the Indians*. p. 135. Chief Tuba became well acquainted with Hamblin when he and the missionaries showed the Indians how to plant and irrigate crops other than corn. (The Hopis were very adept at growing corn.) The community of farms was later named Tuba City. (See map northeast of Cameron, Ariz. near U.S. 89.)
7. Corbett, pp. 425-26.
8. "The Mormon road began transporting settlers into Arizona Territory around 1860," p. 116. The WPA Guide credits Hamblin with "laying out" a wagon road from Lee's Ferry to the Beale Road near San Francisco Peaks. Jacob used this route frequently in traveling to the Hopi villages.
9. *Arizona Characters in Silhouette* (See entire chapter on Hamblin).
10. "Utah Piety on the North Rim of the Grand Canyon," 1925 *Improvement Era*, Vol. 29, p. 965.
11. p. 53. The WPA Guide also incorrectly gives Jacob credit for shooting out the bottom of a pipe at what was later named Pipe Springs. The feat was accomplished by Jacob's brother, "Gunlock Bill" Hamblin.
12. *Arizona Characters in Silhouette*, entire chapter on Hamblin.
13. WBE, "R," p. 198.
14. L & J, p. 7.
15. Ibid, p. 11.
16. *Breaking the Wilderness*, p. 312-14.
17. Ibid.
18. Paul's three missionary journeys, as explained in the New Testament's Book of Acts, show that he went from Jerusalem to Greece (twice), and (once) to what is now Turkey. He was also taken to Rome (not technically a missionary journey) to be placed on trial. The combined distances would be approximately 10,000 miles. Additional source: *The Life and Teachings of Jesus and his*

Apostles, pp. 218-19. The purpose here is not to determine devotion by mileage traveled in missionary work, but to provide a better idea of the time (and miles traveled) spent by Hamblin in fulfilling his Church endeavors.

19. Hamblin, letter to Brigham Young, Sept. 19 1873, LDS Church Historian's Office Archives.

20. Flake, p. 34. Flake also writes of Navajos being baptized in 1950 as follows: "The old (age 82) Navajos were overjoyed to see the two missionaries and quickly called together several families nearby and asked for a meeting." Afterward, "the old man and woman asked to be baptized." They said that when they were only 18 years old many of their people had been baptized. Later, they were approached by other Churches, but "decided to wait until the Mormon missionaries returned," pp. 103-104. No mention is made of Hamblin in this reference, but given age of the Navajos, they or their parents and peers were almost surely influenced by Hamblin's work.

21. Ibid, pp. 32-36.

22. From Tenney's handwritten diaries. For best access to the correct diary for each time period, see Davis Bitton's *Guide to Mormon Diaries and Autobiographies*, p. 354, entry no. 2506. Bitton also gives a synopsis of Tenney's work among the Lamanites.

23. T. H. Haskell, p. 44.

24. For the entire account, see the *Journal of Mormon History*, Vol. 2, pp. 21-34.

25. *Mormon Country*, pp. 146-47

26. Research paper, Preface, LDS Church Historian's Office, SLC, Utah.

27. Ibid, p. 11.

28. "Indian-Settler Relations in the Early History of the Washington County Area," p. 33, 1975.

29. Kelly, p. 16 .

30. John A. Hamblin, *Heritage, a Personal History*, pp. 14-15.

31. Ibid, pp. 82-84.

32. Andrew Jensen, *LDS Biographical Encyclopedia*, p. 100.

33. Little, p. 94. The missionaries with Hamblin often went long periods without water in the hot desert sun. The incident was only one of several mentioned by Hamblin and Thales Haskell in their journals.

34. This reference is not meant to compare Hamblin with the four gospel writers; it is to point out how he depended on the Spirit as did they.

35. Powell, p. 321.

36. W. C. Sarrah, *Powell of the Colorado*, p. 154.

37. Robert S. McPherson, *The Northern Navajo Frontier*, p. 16. Another history, *Pioneer Days in Arizona*, pp. 308-11, calls Hamblin "strong, simple, devout, a man to whom fear is unknown, mild, kindly, just…so complete in his faith he went unharmed."

38. Preface, *Jacob Hamblin, Man of Devotion*, LDS Church Historian's Office.

39. "Jacob Hamblin, Apostle to the Lamanites," *Pacific Spectator*, Vol. 2, No. 3, Summer, p. 315.

40. Interviews at place of work, Kanab, 6-4-94, 11-18-94, 5-7-95.

41. Letter dated 4-13-93; interview at residence, Fredonia, Ariz., 5-14-94.

42. Interview at place of work, Kanab, 5-14-94.

43. Interview at place of work, Provo, Utah, 7-7-95.

44. Interview at place of work, Thatcher, Ariz., 2-17-95.

45. Interview at home, Provo, Utah, 5-6-95.

46. Interview at site of speech given by Echohawk, Provo, Utah, 4-22-95.

47. "And because iniquity shall abound, the love of many shall wax cold." Matt. 24:12.

48. Little, p. 147.

49. See Corbett, p. 267.

50. Little, p. 129.

51. Hunter, *Brigham Young the Colonizer*, p. 306.

52. Corbett, *Tribute*, p. 439.

APPENDIX A
Sources Cited—Primary

Note: Book titles are abbreviated here following first mention as well as in End Notes.

References written by Jacob Hamblin:

Hamblin's journal in original handwriting covering period from childhood to 1856) from great, great grandson, Mark Hamblin, Kanab, Utah.
From LDS Church Library Archives, Salt Lake City, Utah:
Autobiographical sketch and diary, 1819-54 .
Typescript copies of Jacob Hamblin diaries and journals
Hamblin Diary, 1854-57.
Hamblin Journal for years 1863, 1871-74, 1872-74, 1876-77.
Microfilm, Hamblin Journal.
Microfilm, Jacob Hamblin journal, 1854-57, LDS Church Library Archives (reaction to Mountain Meadows Massacre not found elsewhere)
From Brigham Young University Special Collections, Provo, Utah:
Two major forms: (1) "Journal and Letters of Jacob Hamblin." This journal is referred to frequently and is listed herein as "J & L." The title and page numbers are not Hamblin's; they are assigned by BYU. The J & L includes: autobiography and diary to 1850; diary, 1854-57; notebook, 1871; notebook, 1877; notes of trip with or in behalf of Major J. W. Powell; letter to Jacob Hamblin from Brigham Young; letter to J.H. from First Presidency. (2) "Journal Contents" (J-C) includes: entries from J.H. 1868 to 1870 plus missions to the Moqui [Hopi] Indians led by J.H.; important Hamblin documents, including letter from Wilford Woodruff as Church president and a patriarchal blessing upon the head of Hamblin; other miscellanous information about Hamblin, possibly written by him.

References written by Thales T. Haskell:

Journal provided by great, great grandson, Dr. Thales Smith, Provo, Utah (unpublished except as noted in text)

The 98-page journal "Thales Hastings Haskell" edited by
A. E. Smith, much written in third person, listed herein
as or "THH" (partially published)
The 42-page autiobiography of Haskell, the original
"Indian Mission" diary written in first person, focusing
on period 1859-60. Listed as "Haskell Diary" or HD.
The 22-page autobiography, 1834-86, with editor's notes.

A four-page journal relating the life of Haskell's second
wife, Margaret Johannah Edwards, written in first person with editor's notes. No title given.

Other primary references listed alphabetically:

Bible, Holy, King James Translation, New and Old Testament
Brind, letter to Bro. Lund-wall (first names unknown), from
U.S. Geologic Survey, Capt. Clarence S. Dutton, 1870-72
Bleak, *Book A, Annals of Southern Utah Mission*, 1854-1869
Bleak, *Book B, Annals of Southern Utah Mission*, 1869-1877
(The above books contain all letters attributed to Bleak in text.)
Dominguez-Escalante Journal, Brigham Young University
Press, Provo, Utah, 1976, pp. 79-115
Hamblin, John A., "Heritage, A Personal History," Embry
Originals, Mesa, Ariz., 1977
Higbee, John, "Diary," 17 pages, Utah Historical Society
Office, SLC (entries dealing with the Mountain
Meadows Massacre)
Hodge, Hiram, *Arizona as It Is*, Rio Grande Press, Chicago,
1877; later published as *Arizona as It Was*, 1965.
Fish, Joseph, Journal, 1876; LDS Church Historian's Library
Brown, Thomas, "Journal of Southern Utah Indian
Mission," March 18, 1855
LDS Church Publications: *Book of Mormon, Doctrine and
Covenants, Pearl of Great Price*.
Little, James E. (edited) *Jacob Hamblin, Autobiography*,
Deseret News Publishing, Salt Lake City, Utah, First
edition, 1888; Second edition, 1909. Note: page number-
ing and preface data differ in the two editions.
Lee, John D., *Confessions* ; originally *Mormonism Unveiled*
(edited by W. W. Bishop), Bryan Brand Co., St. Louis,
Mo., 1877.
Lee Transcript, on microfilm, two complete trials of John
D. Lee, LDS Church Library Archives, Salt Lake City,
Utah.
National Archives and Record Service, Wash. D.C., Aug.
30, 1966 (data on *Mountain Meadows Massacre*); also LDS
Church Library Archives
"Parowan Ward Files," LDS Church Library Archives

Riddle, Isaac, "Biography and Experiences of Isaac Riddle," film 920, No. 94, Special Collections, Lee Library, BYU, Provo, Utah

Sekaquaptewa, Helen, *Me and Mine*, University of Arizona Press, Tucson, Ariz., 1969,

Video, University of Arizona, "Native literature from the American Southwest," 1978

Smith, Joseph, *Documentary History of Church*, Vols. 3,4,6, Deseret Book, SLC, Utah, 1976 (revised editions)

Tenney, Ammon, diaries, LDS Church Library Archives

Tripp, Enoch Bartlett, "Diary," 1868, obtained from J. R. Johnston, Spanish Fork, Utah, 1994.

Wilford Woodruff Journal, compiled by M. F. Cowley, Deseret News Press, SLC, Utah, 1909

Personal Interviews (See End Notes, Ch. 17 for dates):

Alexander, Thomas G., Phd., History Dept., Brigham Young University, Provo, Utah

Clark, Stephen, researcher, John D. Lee and Jacob Hamblin

Hamblin, Mark, great great grandson of Jacob Hamblin, Kanab, Utah

Echohawk, Larry, former Attorney General, Idaho

Kimball, James, LDS Church Library, SLC, Utah. Also LDS Church Library Archives, Salt Lake City, Utah

Schipper, Rod, U.S. Burea of Land Management Office, Kanab, Utah

Schreiner, Jim, U.S. Forest Service, Fredonia, Ariz.

Sekaquaptewa, Ken, Hopi Indian

Marlene Taylor Mott, Thatcher, Ariz., librarian

Walker, Ron, Ph.d, Smith Institute for LDS Church History

Whitaker, David, Ph.d, BYU Library, Curator of the Mormon Experience

Vital Documents (copies):

Marriage certificate, Jacob Hamblin to Indian girl, Eliza, sealed in SLC (Latter-day Saint) temple on Feb. 14, 1863: Family Search, IGI, North America Dish 2, Lee Library, Computer Rooom, BYU, Provo, Utah; Book D, p. 543, S.L. Temple records: "Jacob Hamblin had sealed to him Eliza, born on the Shivwits Indian Reservation, date unknown, Feb. 14, 1863." See AFN 37CXQC.

Brochure, "Jacob Hamblin, Pioneer, Missionary, Peacemaker, 1819-1886"; Published by The Church of Jesus Christ of Latter-day Saints, with material provided by the Hamblin family.

Reprinted in entirety, Appendix B, from primary sources:
Letter from Brigham Young to Jacob Hamblin appointing him president of the Southwest Indian Mission. LDS Church Library Archives. (This original letter carries a line about Indians helping Mormons which was omitted from Little and other accounts)
Patriarchal blessing upon head of Jacob Hamblin by Bro. McBride (no first name given)
Letter from Wilford Woodruff appointing Jacob Hamblin a missionary at large in all parts of the United States and Mexico.
Letter from Brigham Young calling Jacob Hamblin to settle (and serve as a missionary) on the upper Little Colorado River of eastern Arizona.
See other documents in Appendix B

Sources Cited—Secondary

Publications and Research Papers:

Anderson, Nels, *Desert Saints*, U. of Chicago Press, Chicago, Ill., 1942

Backus, Anna Jean, *Mountain Meadows Witness, the Life and Times of Philip Klingensmith*, Arthur H. Clark Co., Spokane, Wash., 1995

Bailey, Paul, *Jacob Hamblin, Buckskin Apostle*, Westernlore Press, L.A. Calif., 1948.

Bancroft, Herbert H., *History of Utah*, History Publishing Co., San Francisco, 1890.

Barrett, William E., *The Restored Church*, Deseret Book, SLC, Utah 1958.

Bigler, Henry, edited journal

Birney, Hoffman, *Zealots of Zion*, Penn. Publ. Co, 1931,

Bishop, Brad, research paper, p. ll, Dixie College and LDS Church Library, 1974

Bitton, Davis, *Guide to Mormon Diaries and Autobiographies*, BYU Press, 1930, with specific reference to Ammon Tenney diaries, p. 354, entry 2506

Bradshaw, Hazel (editor), *Under Dixie Sun*, History of Washington County, 1850-1950, Washington County Chapter, Daughters of Utah Pioneers, St. George, Utah.

Brooks, Dudley Leavitt, *Pioneer to Southern Utah*, St. George, Utah, 1942, no publisher listed, pp. 43-44; *Mountain Meadows Massacre (MMM)*, U. of Oklahoma Press, Norman, Okla. and London, 1950; *John Doyle Lee: Zealot-Pioneer Builder-Scapegoat*, Glendale, Calif., 1962; *Jacob Hamblin, Mormon Apostle to the Indians*, Howe

Brothers, SLC, Utah, 1980 ;
A Mormon Chronicle, The Diaries of John D. Lee, 1848-1876.

Brown, Dee, *Bury my Heart at Wounded Knee*, Holt,
Rinehart and Winston, New York, N. Y., 1970

Carr, Stephen L., *Utah Ghost Towns*, Western Epics, SLC,
Utah, 1972

Carter, Kate, *Heart Throbs of the West*, Vol. 3, Salt Lake
City, Utah, 1919 p. 132,

Claridge, Eleanor, "Klondyke and the Aravaipa Canyon,"
p. 10, self- published, Safford, Ariz., 1989

Comeaux, Malcolm L., *Arizona, A Geography*, Westview
Press, Boulder Colo., 1981

Corbett, Pearson, *Jacob Hamblin the Peacemaker*, Deseret
Book Co., SLC, Utah, 1968

Creer, *Mormon Towns in the Region of the Colorado River, U.
of Utah Press*, SLC, Utah, 1958

Darrah, W. C., *Powell of the Colorado*, Princeton University
Press, Princeton, N.J., 1969.

Dellenbaugh, F. S., *A Canyon Voyage*, Yale University Press,
New Haven, Conn., 1926. pp. 154, 166-184, 342-343;
Breaking of the Wilderness, Knickerbrocker Press, New
York, 1905, pp. 324-325;
The Romance of the Colorado River, Knickerbrocker Press,
New York, 1906, pp. 93, 228-230;
"Diaries," pp. 149-59, New York Public Library.

Despain, Del, "Settler-Indian Relations in the Early
History of the Washington County Area," p. 33, 1975

Duff, Roberta, "Man of Devotion," Dixie College research
paper, St. George, Utah, 1975

Duchateau, Andre P., Missouri Colossus, doctoral thesis,
"The Mormon War," (Gen. A. Doniphan, comparison
to Jacob Hamblin) Ch. 5, pp. 44-67, 420- 430; U. of
Oklahoma Press, Stillwater, Okla., 1973

Encyclopedia of Mormonism, Edited by Dan Ludlow,
Macmillian Co., New York, 1992

Evans, John Henry, *Story of Utah*, Macmillian Co., New
York, 1933, pp. 125-136.

Everett, Arthur, *Calley*, Dell Publishing Co., New York,
N.Y., 1971

Faux, Jocelyn, *Our Mayflower Ancestors and their
Descendants*," Linrose Publishing Co., Fresno, Calif,
1992

Farrish, Edwin, *History of Arizona*, Vol. 3, pp. 252-53,
Filmer Bros., San Francisco, 1916.

Fish, Joseph, "History of the Eastern Arizona Stake of
Zion, LDS Church," Snowflake, Ariz., 1936.

Flake, David K., "A History of Mormon Missionary Work
with the Hopi, Navaho and Zuni Indians," master's
thesis, BYU, Provo, Utah, 1965

Godfrey, Kenneth, "The Mountain Meadows Massacre and its Historians: Separating Myth from Reality," research paper presented to the Utah Historical Society, St. George, Utah, 1992.

Women's Voices, p. 64, Deseret Book, SLC, Utah, 1982

Gowans, Fred and Campell, Eugene, *Fort Bridger*, pp. 59, 66, BYU Press, Provo, Utah, 1975

Hopkins, Virginia, *The Colorado River*, Chantwell Books, Secaucus, N. J., 1985

House, Dorothy, preface, *Under Vermillion Cliffs*, p. 26, LDS Church Historians Office, SLC, Utah,

Hunter, Milton R., *Brigham Young the Colonizer*, Deseret News Press, Salt Lake City, Utah, 1940, pp. 3010-314.

Utah In Her Western Setting, Deseret News Press, 1943, pp. 162-63, 283.

Jensen, Andrew, *LDS Biographical Encyclopedia*, Vol. 1, 111, Arrow Press and Publishers Press, SLC, Utah, 1920, 1930, pp. 100-101

Jesus Christ, The Life and Teachings of...and his Apostles, LDS Church Publishers, SLC, Utah, 1978

Kelly, Charles, *Outlaw Trail*, pp. 16-28, 145, Bonanza Books, New York, 1959

Larson, Gustive O., *Outline History of Utah and the Mormons*, BYU Press, Provo, Utah, 1958

Lavender, David, *Pipe Spring and the Arizona Strip*, Zion Natural History Assn., Springdale, Utah, 1984.

LDS Hymn Book, pp. 29-30, 336, LDS Church Publications, SLC

"Lee, The Trial, An Expose of the Mountain Meadows Massacre," SLC Daily Tribune Reporter, Tribune Printing Co., SLC, 1875

Lockwood, Frank, *Pioneer Portraits*, U. of Arizona Press, Tucson, Ariz., 1968.

Pioneer Days in Arizona, Macmillan Co., New York, N.Y., 1932

Lyford, C.P., *The Mormon Problem*, pp. 296-99, Phillips and Hunt, New York, 1886

McClintock, James H., *Mormon Settlement in Arizona*, U. of Arizona Press, Tucson, Ariz., 1985.

Mormons in Arizona, pp. 63-64

McPherson, Robert S., *The Northern Navajo Frontier*, 1860-1900, University of New Mexico Press, Albuquerque, N.M., 1947

Mencher, Melvin, *Basic Media Writing*, Brown and Benchmark, Columbia University, 1993.

Mullen, Robert, *The Latter-day Saints, the Mormons Yesterday and Today*, Doubleday and Co., Garden City, N.Y., 1966.

Murdock, John R., "Arizona Characters in Silhouette,"

self-published, 1939, reprints from the Arizona
Republic, 1933.

Nevins, Allan, Fremont, *Pathfinder of the West*, p. 418,
Longsman, Green and Co., New York, 1955

Nibley, Preston, *Brigham Young,the Man and his Work*,
Deseret Book, SLC, 1970

Penrose, Charles, *The Mountain Meadows Massacre*,
Juvenile Instructor Press, 1884.

Peterson, Levi, *Juanita Brooks*, Preface, pp. 175-180, 193, 196,
246, 274, 283, 384, U. of Utah Press, SLC, Utah, 1988.

Place Names in Arizona, Primer Publishing, Phoenix,
Arizona, 1954

Powell, John W., *The Exploration of the Colorado River and
its Canyons*, Dover Publications, New York, N.Y., 1961

Reber, Fay E., *The Trials of John D. Lee*, self-published, J.R.
Clark Law Library, BYU, Provo, Utah, 1978.

Reily, P. T., "*Roads Across Buckskin Mountain*," Self-published, The Journal of Arizona History, Tucson, Ariz.,
no date given.

Roberts, Brigham H., *A Comprehensive History of The
Church of Jesus Christ of Latter-Saints*, Vol. 4, Deseret
News, Salt Lake City, Utah,

Richardson, Gladwell, *Navajo Trader*, p. 88, U. of Arizona
Press, Tucson, Ariz., 1986

Sloan, Richard, and Adams, R., *History of Arizona*, Vol. 2,
Record Publishing, Phoenix, Ariz., 1930

Smart, William, *Old Utah Trails*, Utah Geographic, SLC,
Utah, 1988

Smith, Thomas W., "A Brief History of the Early Pahreah
Settlements; with excerpts from diary of James E.
Smith, companion to Jacob Hamblin."

Smith, Joseph Fielding, *Essentials in Church History*,
Deseret Book Publishing, SLC, Utah, 1979.

Stegner, Wallace, *Mormon Country*, Bonanza Books, New
York, 1942, pp. 145-46.

Stephens, Hal and Shoemaker, Eugene, *In the Footsteps of
J.W. Powell*, Johnson Books, Boulder, Colo., 1987

Sylvester, Rexann, Preface, Hamblin research paper, Dixie
College, and LDS Church Historian's Library, 1975.

Trailblazers, Time-Life Books, Alexandria,Va., 1973

Trumble, Marshall, Arizona, *A Cavalcade of History*,
Treasure Chest Publishing, Tucson, Ariz., 1989

Diamond in the Rough, a history of Arizona, Dunning Co.,
Norfolk, Va., 1988

Tufts, Lorraine, *Secrets in the Grand Canyon*, National
Photographic Collections, North Palm Beach, Fla., 1992.

Ullman, J. R., *Down the Colorado with Major Powell*, Houghton Mifflin Co., Riverside Press Cambridge, Boston, Mass., 1960

Van Cott, John W., *Utah Place Names*, U. of Utah Press, SLC, Utah, 1990

Wagoner, Jay, *Early Arizona*, pp. 321-322, University of Arizona Press, Tucson, Ariz., 1975

Whitney, Orson, *History of Utah*, George Q. Cannon and Sons Co., SLC, Utah, Vol 2, p. 710

Widstoe, John A., *Gospel Interpretations*, Bookcraft, SLC, 1947

World Book Encyclopedias (WBE), Field Enterprises, Chicago, Ill., 1968.

Work Project Administration, Writers Program, Utah, A Guide to the State, Hastings House, New York, several authors, 1941, p. 308

   Ibid, *A Guide to Arizona*, pp. 53, 283, 413

Young, Brigham, LDS Church Archives, SLC, History of, ms entries, See Aug. 17, 1858, pp. 929-937

Young, John R., "Journal of the Moqui Mission," 1869

Periodicals:

Anderson, Vernon, Associated Press article, letter from William Leany to John Steele involving J. Hamblin, Provo *Daily Herald*, 1994.

Arnold, Frank R., "Utah Piety on the North Rim of the Grand Canyon," Era, Vol. 29, p. 965.

Bigler, Henry, *Utah Historical Quarterly*, Vol. 5, No. 2, 1932.

Brooks, J., *Arizona Highways*, April 1943, "Jacob Hamblin, Apostle to the Lamanites;"

"Indian relations on the Mormon Frontier," Utah State Historical Society, Vol 7, Nos. 1-2, Jan.-April, 1944;

"Journal of T.H. Haskell" (1859, first journey to Moqui Indians, prepared for publication by J. Brooks), Utah State Historical Quarterly, SLC, Utah;

"Jacob Hamblin, Apostle to the Lamanites," Vol. 2, N. 3, Summer, Pacific Spectator, p. 315, Stanford University Press, 1948

"Cache Valley Newsletter," Newell Hart, editor, Preston, Ida., June 1979

Deseret News: Sept. 23, 1857; May, 1859; Sept. 4, 1886; Jan. 7, 1955

Kildare, Maurice, "Cowardly Saint in Buckskin," *True Frontier*, March, 1969, Vol. 1, No. 8, p 28

Los Angeles Star, October-November, 1857

Millenial Star, April 19, St. George, Utah, 1875

Miller, Henry W., *Deseret News*, Vol. XV1, No. 27, July 3, 1867

New York Times, June 14, 1858.

New York Tribune, June 12, 1858.

Mormon People in Arizona, no author listed, Arizona
Highways, April, 1943;

Paulson, J. R., "Arizona Strip is Area of Adventure and
Daring," *Daily Herald*, Provo, Utah, May 28, 1995.

Peterson, Charles, *Journal of Mormon History*, "Jacob
Hamblin, Apostle to the Lamanites and the Indian
Mission," Vol. 2, Provo, Utah, 1975

Richmond Conservator, Mo., Aug. 11, 1887

Smiley, W.W., (excerpts from diary of Ammon Tenney),
"The Journal of Arizona History," Vol. 13, No. 2,
Summer, Tucson,Ariz., 1972. (Smiley is a granddaughter of A. Tenney and "spent many years gathering
information about her grandfather.")

St. George magazine, "Tuacahn" (drama of southern Utah
and Jacob Hamblin), Jan-Feb., 1995, St George, Utah

Utah Lifestyle magazine, Spring, 1994

Valley Tan, The, Salt Lake City, Utah: May 10, 1859; Feb. 29, 1860;

Webb, Loren, story about letter from William Leany to
John Steele involving J. Hamblin, *St. George Daily
Spectrum*, Oct. 22, 1993

APPENDIX B

Letters and Documents

President's Office
Great Salt Lake City
August 4, 1857

Elder Jacob Hamblin,

You are hereby appointed to succed Elder R. C. Allen (whom I have released as President of the Santa Clara Indian Mission.) I wish you to enter upon the duties of your calling immediately.

Continue the conciliatory policy toward the Indians, which I have ever recommended, and seek by works of righteousness to obtain their love and confidence, for they must learn that they have either got to help us or the United States will kill us both. Omit promises where you are not sure you can fill them; and seek to unite the hearts of the brethren on that mission, and let all under your direction be knit together in the holy bonds of love and unity.

We have an abundance of "news." The Government have at last appointed an entire set of officials for the Territory. These Gentry are to have a body guard of 2500 of Uncle's Regulars. They were to start from Fort Leavenworth July 15th 400 mule teams brings their personal dunnage, & 700 ox teams 15 months provisions, 7000 head of beef cattle are to arrive here to supply them. General Harney it is supposed will command the expedition. Their errand is entirely peaceful. The current report is that they somewhat query whether they will hang me with or without trial. There are about 30 others whom they intend to deal with. They will then proclaim a general jubilee [and] afford means and protection to those who wish to go back to the States. We feel first rate about all this and think every circumstance but proves the hastening of Zion's redemption.

All is peace here and the Lord is eminently blessing our labors; Grain is abundant, and our cities are alive with the busy hum of industry.

Do not permit the brethren to part with their Guns or ammunition, but save them agains the hour of need.

Seek the Spirit of God to direct you, and that he may qualify you for every duty is the prayer of your.

Fellow Laborer in the Gospel of Salvation
(Signed) Brigham Young

The deposition of Brigham Young as entered in the court records, second trial of John D. Lee, is as follows:

TERRITORY OF UTAH   )SS
BEAVER COUNTY   )
IN THE SECOND JUDICIAL DISTRICT COURT   )
THE PEOPLE, ETC.   )INDICTMENT FOR MURDER
VS. SEPTEMBER 16, 1875

John D. Lee, Wm. H. Dame,
Isaac Haigh, et al.

Questions to be propounded to Brigham Young on his examination as a witness in the case of John D. Lee and others, on trial at Beaver city, this 30th day of July, 1875, and the answers of Brigham Young to the interrogatives here to appended, were reduced to writing, and were given after the said Brigham Young had been duly sworn to testify the truth in the above entitled cause, and are as follows:

First–   State your age, and the present condition of your health, and whether in its condition you could travel to attend in person, at Beaver, the court now sitting there?

Answer– To the first interrogatory, he saith: I am in my seventy-fifth year. It would be a great risk, both to my health and life, for me to travel to Beaver at this present time. I am, and have been for some time, an invalid.

Second– What office, either ecclesiastical, civil, or military, did you hold in the year 1857?

Answer– I was Governor of the Territory, and ex-officio Superintendent of Indian Affairs, and President of The Church of Jesus Christ of Latter-Day Saints, during the year 1857.

Third– State the condition of affairs between the Territory
        of Utah and the Federal Government, in the sum-
        mer and Fall of 1857.

Answer– In May or June, 1857, the United States mails for
        Utah were stopped by the Government, and all
        communication by mail was cut off, an army of the
        United States was enroute for Utah, with the
        ostensible design of destroying the Latter-Day
        Saints, according to the reports that reached us
        from the East.

Fourth– Were there any United States Judges here during
         the Summer and Fall of 1857?

Answer– To the best of my recollections there was no
        United States Judge here in the latter part of 1857.

Fifth– State what you know about trains of emigrants
        passing through the Territory to the West, and
        particularly about a company from Arkansas, en
        route for California, passing through this city in
        the Summer of Fall of 1857?

Answer– As usual, emigrants' trains were passing through
        our Territory for the west. I heard it rumored that
        a company from Arkansas, en route to California,
        had passed through the city.

Sixth– Was this Arkansas company of emigrants ordered
        away from Salt Lake City by yourself or any one in
        authority under you?

Answer– No, not that I know of. I never heard of any such
        thing, and certainly no such order was given by
        the acting Governor.

Seventh–Was any counsel or instructions given by any per-
        son to the citizens of Utah not to sell grain or
        trade with the emigrant trains passing through
        Utah at that time? If so, what were those instruc-
        tions and counsel?

Answer– Yes, counsel and advice were given to the citizens
        not to sell grain to the emigrants to feed their
        stock, but to let them have sufficient for them-

selves if they were out. The simple reason for this was that for several years our crops had been short, and the prospect was at that time that we might have trouble with the United States army, then enroute for this place, and we wanted to preserve the grain for food. The citizens of the Territory were counseled not to feed grain to their own stock. No person was ever punished or called in question for furnishing supplies to the emigrants, within my knowledge.

Eighth– When did you first hear of the attack and destruction of this Arkansas company at Mountain Meadows, in September 1857?

Answer– I did not learn anything of the attack or destruction until some time after it occurred–then only by floating rumor.

Ninth– Did John D. Lee report to you at any time after this massacre, and if so, what did you reply to him in reference thereto?

Answer– Within some two or three months after the massacre he called at my office and had much to say with regard to the Indians, their being stirred up to anger and threatening the settlements of the whites, and then commenced giving an account of the massacre. I told him to stop as from what I had already heard by rumor, I did not wish my feelings harrowed up with a recital of detail.

Tenth– Did Philip Klingensmith call at your office with John D. Lee at the time Lee made his report, and did you at that time order Smith to turn over the stock to Lee, and then order them not to talk about the massacre?

Answer– No. He did not call with John D. Lee, and I have no recollection of him ever speaking to me nor I to him concerning the massacre or anything pertaining to the property.

Eleventh–Did you ever give any directions concerning the property taken from the emigrants at the Mountain Meadows Massacre, or know anything of it disposition?

Answer– No, I never gave any directions concerning the property taken from the emigrants at the Mountain Meadows Massacre, nor did I know anything of that property, or its disposal, and I do not to this day, except from public rumor.

Twelfth– Why did you not, as governor, institute proceedings forthwith to investigate that massacre, and bring the guilty authors thereof to justice?

Answer– Because another Governor had been appointed by the President of the United States, and was then on the way to take my place, and I did not kow how soon he might arrive, and because the Univted States Judges were not in the Territory. Soon after Governor Cummings arrived, I asked him to take Judge Cradlebaugh, who belonged to the Southern District, with him, and I would accompany them with sufficient aid to investigate the matter and bring the offenders to justice.

Thirteenth– Did you, about the 10th of September, 1857, receive a communication from Isaac C. Haight, or any other person of Cedar City, concerning a company of emigrants called the Arkansas company?

Answer– I did receive a communication from Isaac C. Haight or John D. Lee, who was a farmer for the Indians.

Fourteenth–Have you that communication?

Answer–I have not. I have made diligent search for it, but cannot find it.

Fifteenth–Did you answer that communication?

Answer– I did, to Isaac C. Haight, who was then acting President at Cedar City.

Sixteenth–Will you state the substance of your letter to him?

Answer–Yes. It was to let this company of emigrants, and all companies of emigrants, pass through the country unmolested, and to allay the angry feeling of the Indians as much as possible.

(Signed) Brigham Young
Subscribed and sworn to before me this 30th day of July, A.D. 1875.
Wm. Clayton, Notary Public

Kanab, Kane Co., Ut.
Mr. McCarty:
March 10, 1874.

Dear Sir:

I deem it proper to open a communication with you concerning the unhappy occurrence of the killing of three and wounding one Navajo Indian at or near your place. I have traveled some eight or nine hundred miles and exerted myself to prevent, if possible, any more bloodshed and settle this unhappy affair.

I have just returned from the Navajo country, where the relatives of the persons killed lived. After the labors and pains I have taken this far, we have come to the conclusion that it would be just and prudent at least for you to forward to the father and the relatives of the Indians killed, the horses and other property they left behind them; or, if you will forward them to me, I will be responsible that the relatives get them. I herewith forward you an account of the before names property, as described by the Navajo...

I saw the wounded Indian a few days since. He is nearly well. The three who were killed had their tickets of leave from the agent at Fort Defiance and were of good character.

I think you would do well to comply with this request in returning the before mentioned property.

(Signed) Jacob Hamblin, Indian Agent

I fully endorse the above.
(Signed) Steward, Bishop of Kanab

P.S.

We want your earliest convenience for an answer. To Mr. McCarty, Stock Raiser at Circle or Grass Valley, on the Sevier River Post Master please forward.

(The following is a letter to Jacob Hamblin from the First Presidency.)

St. George
December 15th 1876
Jacob Hamblin

Dear Brother:

As you pass from this city to the Colorado South look out as good a track for a wagon road as you will have time to do without stopping to go to the right or the left. You are so well acquainted with the country that you can be of Some use to bro. Pierce who is building a ferry boat at the Colorado for crossing people; and make him acquainted with the initial points which will be beneficial to him for locating a wagon road. Then proceed South near Easterly to the west end of the San-francisco mountains to what is called the Beal road; thence easterly to what is called sun set crossing on the Little Colorado river. Make minutes as near as your judgment will admit, of distances between different points of water and feed in your travels. Draw a little map from day to day.

When you return home to Kanab we would like you to take your stock and such ones of your family and friends as you would like to have with you and locate, and take possession of a little place called "Surprise Valley," near near (sic) the Colorado river, and report to us your success.

We feel to caution you against those Mexican robbers that infest the country where you are going. Be always ready for them and keep your little Company together

We pray the Lord our father in heaven to bless you and give you success in your Mission and return you in Safety

(Signed) Brigham Young, Wilford Woodruff, Erastus Snow, Brigham Young Jn.

St. George, Utah
18 Sept. 1885
To the Twelve Apostles,
High Priests, Seventies,
Presidents of Stakes and
Bishops and their counselors,

And all whom it may concern:

This is to certify that Jacob Hamblin is here appointed a missionary to labor among the Lamanites in any part of the United States to preach the Gospel to them, and teach them the principles of self-sustaining industry, and peace toward all men, and as far as they receive his testimony of the Gospel of Christ, to baptize and confirm them as members of The Church of Jesus Christ of Latter-day Saints, and where no organization as members of the Church exists, to organized such as may be so baptized; doing so in the conformity with the revelations and the usages of the Church.

It is not expected that he will interfere with any organization of schools, or branches, which have already been organized ty the authorities of the Church; but, in connection with such organization he may render what assistance he can to further the work of God, as well as to open up new fields, as the spirit may direct.

It is desired that all Saints who have the opportunity, should assist Brother Hamblin as far as they can, to carry the Gospel to the Lamanites who are an important branch of the House of Israel.

(Signed) Wilford Woodruff
(Source: Journal and Letters, p. 17)

(Patriarchal blessing to Jacob Hamblin, in original language used. (No date given, but approximately 1885)

Jacob in the name of the Lord Jesus and buy the authority of the Holey Priesthood I seal upon the a Patrarchal Blessing and I conferm upon the all they former Blessings and all they former Blessings & ordinacions & I Say unto the though art of the Lineage of Joseph that was sold into Egypt and of the and of the royal blood of Ephram who is the first born of Israel holding the keys and blessings of the gospel and though hast ben caled to and chosen on many Mishions and I know that thou will be faithful because thou hast ben true to thy trust though art now caled to one of the greatist missions that hast ever ben given to Man in the dispensacion in which we now live to carry the gospel to from the Jentiles to the Jew House of Israel and in so doeing thou mayest expect some obsticles in thy way but the Lord will be with the and when thou are a lone thou shal not be a lone for the Angels of the Lord shal be with the and round about the and thou shalt be lead and directed by the Holy Spirit of Provisy to the Branch of the House of Israel and they Shal know the and Shal See the in visions and thou Shalt meet them and the power of the Holey ghost Shal fall upon them and Shall be with thee as it was with as it was with Peter when he cared the gospel from the Jews to he Jentils & thou Shalt exclaim within thy hart who Shal forbid water that these Shal not be baptized as well as we and thou Shal not hav not have not hav not have to leighbor as thou hast in time past hither to to don hither to of don for the lack of language to converse with them for the Lord will asist the and thou Shalt have the interpetacion of language and thy Mission will be to prepair the way for the establishment of the kingdome of god upon the Earth & of the government in to the Just & of restoreing peas to the Earth and it will be the entering wedge destroying all opsision oposition thrughout all the kingdome of the Earth though Shalt labor in the Temples of the Lord and they wives and they chidrin Shal help the and thou and though Shaalt goe no more out buy Day or buy night and mesengers Shal be with the and tell the what to doe and who for thou Shalt Save they fathers house many jeneracions back both for the living and the dedd for thare is a crown laid up for the of Eternal lives and though Shalt inherit all things and be blest abov above measure for unto this end was though born I Seal these words upon the in the name of Jesus Amen.

(Signed) Bro. McBride

Letter dated Aug. 12, 1858 "clearing" William H. Dame of "immediate responsibility" in the Mountain Meadows Massacre. The document was signed by 23 men, including Isaac Haight. (The letter is in possession of the Dame family, accordng to Juanita Brooks, MMM, p. 169)

"We have carefully and patiently investigated the complaints made against President William H. Dame, for four successive days, and are fully satisfied that his actions as a Saint, and administration as a President, have been characterized by the right spirit, and are highly creditable to his position in the priesthood and that the complaints presented before us are without foundation in truth."

(23 signatures)

APPENDIX C

Area Map

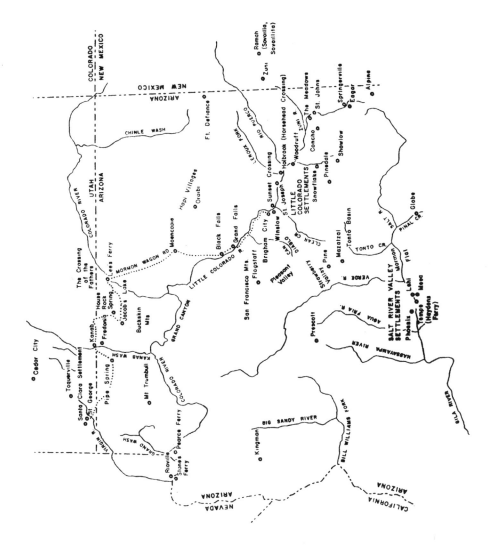

APPENDIX D

Photos

Photo 1: This portrait of Jacob Hamblin is found in the lobby of the Jacob Lake Lodge, leased from the Kaibab National Forest, Arizona. Artist: Willard Kirkpatrick.

Photo 2: Mark Hamblin, Kanab, examines the original journal of his great-great-grandfather Jacob Hamblin. It is the copy of a manuscript in Jacob's handwriting, found in an old saddlebag.

Photo 3: Santa Clara Cemetery contains grave markers of many of Hamblin's family and associates. This is the original marker for Jacob's wife Rachel.

393

Photo 4: original marker for Jacob's son, Duane

Photo 5: marker for missionary associate Sam Knight

Photo 6: marker for Hannah Maria, wife of Thales Haskell, close friend of Hamblin

Photo 7: These "Moqui" Indian ruins in the Grand Canyon resemble many Hamblin would have seen in his explorations of northern Arizona.

Photo 8: Sign north of Gunlock in southwestern Utah marks the Old Spanish Trail.

Photo 9: The author made several attempts to locate one of Hamblin's trails east of Johnson Wash in an area now known as Pioneer Gap. The heavily worn trail may have been one of those used by Jacob and his missionaries.

Photo 10: Dr. Rafael Del Vecchio points to the hurdles facing Jabob: flat, waterless stretches guarded by Buckskin Mountain in northern Arizona.

Photo 11: Signs found today warn visitors not to remove Indian artifacts which may be found in the Pioneer Gap area.

Photo 12: Jacob Hamblin's home in Santa Clara is now a visitor center operated by the Church of Jesus Christ of Latter-day Saints.

Photo 13: Pipe Springs in northern Arizona, now a national monument, was a frequent watering stop for Jacob and his entourage while enroute to Indian country across the Colorado River.

Photo 14: This authentic covered wagon, located near Pipe Springs, is a legacy to the days of old.